# The Correlates of War: I

# The Correlates of War: I

## Research Origins and Rationale

Edited by J. David Singer

THE FREE PRESS
*A Division of Macmillan Publishing Co., Inc.*
NEW YORK
Collier Macmillan Publishers
LONDON

To Karl Deutsch,
stern critic and
cherished colleague

The Free Press
A Division of Macmillan Publishing Co., Inc.
866 Third Avenue, New York, N.Y. 10022

Collier Macmillan Canada, Ltd.

Library of Congress Catalog Card Number: 77-18431

Printed in the United States of America

printing number

1   2   3   4   5   6   7   8   9   10

Library of Congress Cataloging in Publication Data

    Main entry under title:

    The correlates of war.

        Includes bibliographical references and index.
        CONTENTS:  v.  1.  Research origins and rationale.
        1.  War.  2.  International relations.
    1.  Singer, Joel David
    U21.2.C67      327'.11        77-18431
    ISBN 0-02-928960-2

# Copyright Acknowledgments

The editor gratefully acknowledges the cooperation of the following publishers in granting permission to reprint copyrighted material in this book:

# Contents

# Acknowledgments

My indebtedness to others is conveyed to some extent in the dedications of these volumes to Karl Deutsch and to Stuart Bremer. The former has been, to use one of his own phrases, "a tower of strength" for the Correlates of War project, and has been a source of inspiration to me for two decades. The latter, joining Melvin Small and myself as coinvestigator five years ago, has already left his distinctive mark on the project, as exemplified by many of the papers in Volume II.

Let me next mention those members of my favorite invisible college, including the authors and coauthors of these collected papers, who, as Michigan students or visiting scholars, have played so major a role in the project. Among the graduate students—from political science, history, and sociology—are: Craig Archibald, Sandra Baxter, Robert Bennett, Bruce Bueno de Mesquita, Cynthia Cannizzo, Ronald Cassell, Thomas Cusack, Richard Gill, Nils Petter Gleditsch, Charles Gochman, Lloyd Jensen, George Kraft, Alan Levy, Bernard Mennis, Stephen Meyer, Michael Mihalka, Warren Phillips, James Ray, Alan Sabrosky, Richard Stoll, John Stuckey, James Thompson, Michael Wallace, Hugh Wheeler, Yoshinobu Yamamoto, and Michael Champion. Over the years we have also had a fair number of scholars, largely from abroad, who have spent from one to three terms with us. Those visitors who have played a particularly vigorous role were: David Handley, Russell Leng, Urs Luterbacher, Harald von Riekhoff, and Kjell Skjelsbaek.

Critical, if not indispensable, behind the scenes were Dorothy LaBarr, project secretary when many of these papers were originally written; Sara Long and Linda Rhoades, who guided the book through its final stages; and Larry Arnold and Tim Pasich, computer freaks par excellence; James Miller, John Platt, and Gardner Quarton, under whose direction a research institute becomes an excellent place to work; and Robert Angell and Bruce Russett, two colleagues from whom I have been learning for many years. Finally, without the financial support of the Carnegie Corporation in the early years, and the National Science Foundation later on, much of this work would still be little more than a gleam in my eye.

J. David Singer

# Introduction

In the spring of 1963 the University of Michigan's Center for Research on Conflict Resolution received a modest grant from the Carnegie Corporation, of which some $15,000 was earmarked for a preliminary investigation into the conditions that have been historically correlated with international war in the past, or might be expected to be so in the future. Soon thereafter, with the guidance of colleagues from that department, I had hired three advanced graduate students of history, and the contemplated research project thus became an organizational reality. Although I appreciated the magnitude of the task, and was quite prepared to take on a commitment that could easily extend to the end of my career, only the general outlines of the Correlates of War project were manifest at the time.

I certainly had little idea that it would become as large, endure as long, and have the impact that it has had to date. Looking back on the direct and indirect results of the project so far, I am pleased and surprised, as well as slightly disappointed with our slow pace. But regardless of our progress so far and our pace in the future, the project has played its role in the dramatic changes in our discipline, and will, I trust, continue to make its effects felt in the world politics community for some time to come. Thus it now seems desirable to bring together a fair sample of our work, enabling students and colleagues outside of Michigan to obtain a more coherent view of the enterprise.

We do this via two separate volumes, each with a distinctive focus. This first volume is largely historical, and carries the reader back to the intellectual origins before any research plans were formulated, or even considered systematically. All of these articles, written alone or with colleagues between 1958 and 1974, have already been published elsewhere. In contrast, those in Volume II are much more recent; none of them has been published before, and all were prepared explicitly for that volume.

This first volume is divided into seven parts, reflecting to some extent the major phases in my effort to cope, politically and intellectually, with modern international war. But they may also reflect the several types of intellectual activity that now seem essential to success in that effort. First, there is the need to make explicit one's values and priorities as a scholar-activist, and to integrate those normative predispositions with one's theoretical orientation. What are the social objectives we pursue, and what are the major factors that must be understood—and then modified—in pursuit of those objectives? Parts I and II thus deal with the normative and theoretical assumptions with which one defines and clarifies, as well as pursues, those objectives.

In part III are three of the many papers I wrote during those years, dealing explicitly with policy questions. Some may wonder whether it is the same author who turned out papers of such a speculative sort who now writes highly detailed, quantitative articles. While the question may not always be so intended, I take it as a compliment. The division of labor among policy analyst, theorizer, and researcher is an unhealthy one, and the sooner we all try to become *complete* social scientists, the better. Although the earlier papers may reflect an interdisciplinary or scientific turn of mind, they are largely data-free, and little evidence is adduced in support of their premises, interpretations, and implied predictions. Their arguments may be compelling to some readers at some times and in some settings, but they certainly found few takers in the U.S. foreign policy establishment when they were originally published. Moreover, whether those arguments were largely correct then, or are today, is an open question, and will remain so until the basic researcher begins to examine the policy questions.

Turning to part IV, we focus on what might be called the critical nexus between policy and knowledge. It is no surprise that the emphasis is on the process and setting within which nations hammer out those compromises known as foreign and military policy, and on the type of information and knowledge that is, or might be, used in that process. Once that important set of assumptions is made clear, we move on in part V to one of my frequent papers addressed to problems of research strategy. Essentially, even as it reflects the basic theoretical orientation of the articles in part II, it raises and tries to answer questions concerning: (a) the sources to which we might turn for the knowledge we need; and (b) how best to extract that knowledge from those sources. Then in parts VI and VII are a few representative papers from the early phases of the project, ranging from those concerned with index construction and problems of data acquisition to the testing of some simple bivariate and multivariate models, and ending with one of the few papers in which we explicitly bring some of our findings to bear on contemporary policy issues.

Let me say a few words about some of the differences between Volumes I and II, and then turn to a brief discussion that might help put this first volume into a larger perspective. There is only the mildest hint of a collective research effort in Volume I; only four of the papers represent research conducted in the formal scientific mode, and all of these are, reasonably enough, collective efforts. In Volume II, all of the papers except for the gracious summary by Karl Deutsch represent scientific research reports, and even though most of them have a single author, they build on the prior and simultaneous work of others on the project and elsewhere. Whereas *my* thinking clearly dominates in Volume I, Volume II offers abundant evidence of vigorous interplay among bright, energetic, and highly competent young scholars, as well as my coinvestigators Melvin Small and Stuart Bremer and our monthly visitor over the past fifteen years, Karl Deutsch. Those who have participated in, or visited, the project's Friday seminars during these recent years can attest to both the liveliness of our dialogue and the central role of these three colleagues. They will appreciate, too, the appropriateness of my dedications of Volumes I and II to Deutsch and Bremer, while the frequency of Small's name at the top of many of our publications reflects *his* central role in the enterprise. From its inception in 1963, when he signed on as the project's first research assistant, Small has been not only our resident historian but a source of insight on everything from the big theoretical picture down to the intricacies of deciphering an ambiguous trace in the diplomatic archives.

Another distinction is that Volume I opens with a strong set of theoretical biases along with vigorous policy views, and reveals a growing agnosticism only toward the end, whereas Volume II is explicitly agnostic from beginning to end. This will be discussed further in Volume II, but I should remark in passing that there is nothing like the pursuit of systematic empirical research to cure one of theoretical certitude. The policy-oriented essays here in Volume I mark an early and naive hope that "right reason" (Hallowell 1950) might help to turn the U.S. and other nations away from strategies that had led to disaster in the past and seemed likely to do so again. But the essays that follow denote a rapid realization that more is needed than a mix of tight reasoning, compelling analogies, careful analyses, and human compassion. The inertia of collective beliefs and institutionalized folklore is a wondrous force indeed, and it soon became evident that some combination of an epistemological revolution and a cascade of hard evidence would be essential ingredients in the ultimate abolition of war and its related disasters.

The papers included here not only reflect and record that growing realization on my part, but also spell out in some detail the complex reasoning that lies behind the change. The brief headnote that precedes each paper should, in turn, serve to supplement the papers themselves by putting them into the context of time, place, and frame of mind. And given the extent to which Volume I reveals these shifts, those headnotes may also be of interest to social scientists outside the world politics field, and perhaps to specialists in intellectual history and the sociology of knowledge. The substantive problems that we all address may vary considerably, but the complex relationship between knowledge and practice is fundamentally the same, whether the concern is with urban sanitation, national economic development, or global peace.

In an earlier day some social scientists might have raised an eyebrow at a volume that focuses less on the results of one's work than on the reasoning that precedes the systematic research. They might have suggested that what matters to the scholarly community is the findings, and that the cerebral peregrinations and musings of the scholar are of more interest to himself and perhaps to intellectual historians than to those whose mission it is to advance our knowledge. Today, however, such naiveté is behind us, and if we are fortunate, permanently so.

While it may be presumptuous to compare the changes that have occurred in the social science community to the "lost innocence" of the nuclear physicists, the parallel is clearly there. Just as those whose research made atomic weapons possible had ultimately to face the question of "What have we done?," we in the social sciences have slowly begun to confront similar questions. When social science was in its infancy, we had a division of labor that all too many of us found all too comfortable. Some wrote, often agonizingly and at oppressive length, on the moral tragedies and intellectual paradoxes of the human condition; for reasons that still cast a pall over our discipline, they were called "theorists." A second group tended to the empirical gardens, trying to describe—and even to explain—specific events and conditions or classes of such events and conditions. While the "empiricists" and the "theorists" were equally preoperational, few in either group were indifferent to problems of contemporary policy. Thus the attentive publics and policy elites in the West have long had available from political scientists, sociologists, and economists a fair amount of analysis and advice on the major issues of the day. While the evidence in support of their suggestions and exhortations may have been meager, the policy-relevance question had hardly been ignored during the past century or so in Europe and America.

Thus as the macrosocial disciplines moved slowly out of the largely intuitive and impressionistic stage toward greater emphasis on operational procedures and reproducible evidence, those who led this effort tended to shy away from policy questions. Not only were others taking care of that responsibility, but many also felt that "science and politics do not mix." The democratic folklore had it that one citizen's judgment was as good as the next, and the scientific folklore had it that our research—or at least its credibility—would be contaminated if we advocated a particular set of policies or became visibly involved in a given public issue. Since the laymen's judgments on policy issues were deemed as good as the scholars', the latter *need* not engage in research (or offer opinions) on such issues. And since the scientist who became involved in such issues would be suspected of nonobjectivity, he *dared* not do so.

During the two decades following World War II, these views tended to dominate the social sciences in the West. While the problems facing humanity not only multiplied but became more visible, this division of labor was largely maintained. The more scientifically oriented scholars may have looked on with some concern as the media brought us face to face with racial strife, poverty, exploitation, and nuclear terror. But the connection between their scholarship and their citizenship remained obscure. Among other things, those of us who had invested heavily in the task of moving social analysis out of the armchair and off the soapbox were more than a bit nervous about sacrificing our modest and hard-earned respectability as "real" scientists. As I noted above, that stance has been considerably modified during the last several years—a testament to, *inter alia*, the slaughter in such places as Algeria and Indochina, racial confrontation in America, and a melange of grievances in universities around the world. It has become socially and intellectually too awkward for scholars to act as if they are somehow not "of this world" while enjoying its benefits. Nor could we, in good conscience, continue to accept the comfortable notion that the university's mission is to train people for positions in industry and government, but not to question, or encourage our students to question, the roles that they would play or the policies they could help carry out (Habermas 1970). While it is a source of embarrassment, I suspect that if the students had not begun to ask these questions, their professors would probably still consider them inconvenient and perhaps even in bad taste.

It should be noted, however, that not all of the more rigorous social scientists remained in the ivory tower. There were, for example, those who moved into the consulting business, under research grant or contract to governmental agencies or the many go-between organizations that were set up, particularly in the U.S., as the cold war became increasingly institutionalized. Thus did psychologists work on bomber-crew performance and anthropologists and political scientists on counterinsurgency programs, often while continuing to articulate the value-free, objective scholar doctrine. One apparent justification may have been the complacent belief that if one's own government—being both democratic and decent—followed a certain policy, it must be a decent policy and thus deserving of support. Some even saw such consulting as a citizen's duty, often in the context of the cold war struggle against communist imperialism.

Inevitably, the social science *consultant* role begins to blend into that of the social science *employee*, and in due course one found a slowly increasing number of "real" social scientists working fulltime in the U.S. and other Western governments. Of course, economists had been filling such roles for decades, and their example may well have been part of the problem. As I understand it, economists in the American and British administrations tended to work on the premise that the people's chosen representatives were responsible for deciding on objectives, and that the professional civil servant's role was that of helping to fulfill them (Laski 1930). To put it less gently, the politicians tell us *what* they want to achieve (ostensibly on behalf of the general citizenry), and we tell them *how*. Acceptance of such a role was dangerous enough when economists merely consulted or served to implement *economic* decisions. But because they could not only "do science," but could do so in a truly "professional" manner—like lawyers who can work for almost any client—it was not long before economists began to move into problem areas more remote from their expertise. Most disastrous, at least in the U.S., was the way that these "value-free" social scientists made themselves available to the military establishment. Either agreeing with, or acquiescing in—and, later on, helping to determine—the dominant policy line in the cold war and in Indochina, these economists helped considerably to legitimize that line, carry out its policy implications, and neutralize those who sought to challenge and question it.

My intention here, as will be evident, is not to criticize the social scientist who works for a national government either as a consultant or as a civil servant. Rather, it is to emphasize the narrow and ultimately destructive way in which many of us have tended to define those roles: essentially as professional specialists whose job it is to stay within some arbitrary sector bounding our expertise, and not to ask any of the big questions. To put it another way, my criticism is not directed toward the acceptance of policy roles, but to acquiescence in so limited a definition of those roles. Of course, not all of those described above merely acquiesced; as already intimated, quite a few fundamentally agreed with the dominant views on the larger political and strategic questions, and vigorously participated in the formulation as well as the execution of policy.

As the number of rigorous social scientists in the Western establishments grew, they were gradually "joined" by those professional colleagues whose normative and theoretical premises were of quite a different cast. Among them were the behavioral scientists who felt that the drift toward world war might be as much a consequence of ignorance as of other mental or moral shortcomings. Subsequently labeled "peace researchers," they began not only to take on basic research that might lead to a fuller understanding of the dynamics of international conflict, but to organize as well. Their efforts led to the establishment of research centers at about fifteen universities in the U.S., Western Europe, and Japan, to the creation of such journals as *Conflict Resolution*, *Peace Research*, and *Peace Science Society Papers*, and to a sharp increase in the volume of research that was directly or indirectly relevant to the war-peace question. I was, of course, an avid member of this group from its beginnings in the middle 1950s, and remain so today. In many ways this volume of the Correlates of War collection traces the intellectual history of the "peace research movement" as much as that of a single—if often deviant—member of that movement.

Let me shift from these questions—and they crop up often in both volumes—to the matter of the research objectives that arise out of these larger considerations. And since this subject also receives ample attention later in the two volumes, we can be brief here. The critical point is that the name of the Correlates of War project and the title of these volumes should not be misunderstood. It should not suggest that we seek only to uncover and catalog that range of events and conditions that has covaried with the incidence of war over the past century and a half. But the choice of words *is* intended to convey our understanding of what scientists can and cannot do. We should certainly *like* to discover the causes of war, and metaphorically our objective could be so described. *Causality* is, however, largely a metaphysical notion, and its presence or absence is not only not demonstrable; it is not even readily inferred by the scientific mind. *Explanation,* on the other hand, is at least meaningful in the psychological sense; scientists can usually agree that one explanation of a set of outcomes is better than the contending explanations, or that none of the available explanations is satisfactory. We devise explanatory models in order to represent or simulate those causal processes that we think obtain in the referent world, and then proceed to test them against our observations of referent world phenomena. As the observation, measurement, and data analyses go forward, gradually we accumulate a body of correlational knowledge that is increasingly large, increasingly integrated, and increasingly consonant with what we already know from related research. Of course, when we use the word "knowledge" it is understood to be tentative, and vulnerable to being overturned by new research or a new interpretation of existing research. Thus, to know is only to believe, along with other competent scientists, that a given proposition is true.

All of this is to suggest that our research objective is, in one sense, quite modest: to add what we can to the painfully small body of correlational knowledge on the incidence of war. As we do so, of course, the hope is that, through a complex array of research procedures, we shall be more and more able to fit these propositions together in an integrated fashion. As is partially evident in Volume I, and much more so in Volume II, we have begun with a small number of submodels, all emanating from, and quite consonant with, the classical balance of power framework. As these submodels are tested, refined, and arranged into a larger theoretical pattern, they should also begin to reinforce one another, moving us toward an increasingly coherent body of explanatory knowledge on the incidence of international war. And, as that body of knowledge grows, we continue to approach the essential synthesis of science, ethics, and praxis to which the responsible scholar must inevitably aspire.

# The Correlates of War: I

# I

# The Normative Orientation

One issue that should be dealt with at the outset, not so that it can be dismissed but so that it can be put into perspective, is what might be called the "law and order" issue. A number of critics have reproached those of us whose research focuses on war and peace as being too narrow—if not reactionary—in our outlook. It is said that we care only about "negative peace" but not about "positive peace," and that we care only about direct bodily violence but not about "structural violence." Put differently, the accusation is that much of what has been called "peace research" is addressed only to the conditions for establishing law and order in the global system, but is indifferent to matters of social injustice and human exploitation.

These charges of excessive preoccupation with law and order sting for two reasons. First, the critics seem willing to corrupt the communication channels by abusing the common and accepted meanings of important words. No one, for example, would confuse peace with such values as. justice, dignity, health, prosperity, or welfare. While some may believe that these values are a prerequisite of peace (a dubious but empirically testable proposition) and others may see peace as a prerequisite of *them* (a less dubious but equally testable proposition), they are not the same thing. Thus to speak of negative peace, meaning the absence of mass violence, in a condescending way because it does not embrace other values as well seems unnecessarily churlish.

1

Similarly, when peace researchers are condemned for indifference to "structural violence," we again seem to be in the presence of a conceptual confusion, unintended or otherwise. To put it bluntly, people who die slowly from malnutrition, incarceration, or environmental pollution are *not* victims of violence. They may be victims of outrageous injustice and oppression, but they do not, by and large, die violent deaths in any generally understood meaning of the word. They are ultimately as dead as if they had perished in battle or in a bombing raid, but their lives are not snuffed out in sudden, intended episodes. To call this violence is no more accurate than the right-wing use of the word to describe sit-ins or the burning of draft cards. I hope, then, that we have heard the last of such propagandistic or "consciousness-raising" phrases as "positive peace" and "structural violence."

Having rebuked this particular set of critics, let me now recognize that the charges also sting because—semantics aside—there *is* something to them. Students of conflict and violence in the global society do often take what could be called a "minimalist" position. Whether they approach the question from the viewpoint of international law, political science, or another discipline, they often convey the notion that: (a) direct, organized, armed violence is the *only* problem facing humanity; or (b) with the elimination of such violence, the other problems will tend somehow to wither away. As indicated above, I think that the second proposition, while overdrawn, is more accurate than its opposite, which would have us believe that most other problems can be solved despite the continued presence of armed violence and the preparation for it, and that with the elimination of these other problems, such violence will disappear. To repeat, this is an empirical question and, one notes with sadness, a question that has received virtually no scientific attention. My purpose here is partly to urge such research into the reciprocal relationships between the related, but distinct, phenomena of justice and peace, to contribute to a clarification of that relationship, and to put violence into context with other social pathologies.

# 1

# Individual Values, National Interests, and Political Development in the International System

*This paper should illustrate the extent to which we are (and should be) preoccupied not only with the elimination of mass violence, but also with other elements that are part of what we mean by political development at the global level.*

A widely shared notion among social historians is that almost every reformation or revolution is likely to be followed by a counterrevolution or counterreformation. Those who will examine the development of Western political science in the mid-twentieth century seem destined to have yet another case in support of that contention. Even as many scholars remain untouched by the behavioral revolution and several disciplines remain largely unmoved by its central themes, a counterrevolution of sorts is under way. Two dominant strands characterize this nascent counterrevolution. One is a renewed emphasis on normative and policy concerns, as opposed to the

---

Notes to this book appear in the section starting on p. 331.

alleged detachedness of the behavioral approach.[1] The other is a renewed interest in explanation, as opposed to the focus on "mere" description which allegedly characterized the behaviorist school.

At the risk of being identified with a doctrinaire behavioral position, and unsympathetic to any criticisms of that orientation, let me state my reservations vis-à-vis these two trends. Thus, while recognizing that some of the behavioral research looks suspiciously like mindless empiricism, I would nevertheless caution against the drive for premature explanation. Put bluntly, we cannot explain and account for phenomena until the regularities of such phenomena have been observed and described, and while admitting that a good many behaviorists have indeed embraced a "value-free" position, we would not only note that this point of view was with us in the social sciences long before the post-World War II developments, but that many of the behaviorists have explicitly rejected it all along.[2] In this paper, while working from the description-before-explanation viewpoint, our main concern will be that of the delicate and refractory relationship between science and the ethics of public policy.

As the title makes clear, however, we will limit ourselves to a single (but very broad) set of policy questions: how we might ascertain the level of political development in the international system and identify the instrumentalities which enhance or inhibit that development.[3] We begin from two assumptions: (a) the concept of political development is as applicable to this larger system as to any national social system; and (b) science is not only *compatible with* deep ethical concerns, but absolutely *essential to* serious involvement with those concerns. The paper will propose what seem to be some critical refinements in the concept of political development, and suggest and evaluate a number of indicators.

All of this, in turn, will be in the context of an explicit and self-conscious rejection of the doctrine (still widely held by economists) that the selection of ends is a purely political matter and that the scholar only enters the picture to recommend the means and policies designed to realize the assigned objectives. In addition to the fact that today's ends are tomorrow's means, and that means and ends impinge continuously on one another, I would argue that even the most fundamental ends can in principle be evaluated and compared by scientific criteria. Moreover, I urge that every man must be held accountable for the direct and indirect consequences of his public actions (and inactions), and that the extent to which he can *predict* those consequences will be a function of: (a) the state of social science knowledge, and (b) his grasp and application of that knowledge. Put another way, many of humanity's tragedies might have been avoided, had the social sciences been further along and had the relevant knowledge been available to (and credible to) those whose acts contributed to such tragedies.[4]

## Measuring Political Development

The concept of political development is as applicable to the global system or to a single urban region as it is to the national society. But regardless of the social-territorial unit to which it is applied, four important modifications would seem to be in order; two are essentially methodological, but the other two raise serious normative issues. The first is that the criteria must be converted from highly intuitive and subjective form into more operational language. To some extent, those who study national political development are beginning to recognize this need, and the issue need not be further belabored here. Second, development is meaningful only in a comparative context, and that comparison may be not only across *different* social systems at a single point in time, but also for the *same* social system across several points in time. By and large, most students of national political development are responsive to the need for comparison in the first sense of the word but remain relatively indifferent to the need for longitudinal comparisons.[5] These two modifications should require little discussion, and will be incorporated in the approach used here.

The next two modifications are, however, more fundamental and require some extended discussion. One concerns the need to differentiate between development in terms of the physical, structural, and cultural *attributes of the social system at hand,* and development in terms of the quality of life of those *human beings* who comprise the system. The other, intimately related, is the need to distinguish between indicators of development that are best thought of as *instrumental* and those that are more *intrinsic* in nature.

Most research on national political development remains ethically insensitive to the distinctions between *national* (or other group) interests and *individual* interests, and between indicators which reflect the growth or change in *instrumentalities* of development, and those which reflect the extent to which these instrumentalities have indeed led to the satisfaction or maximization of those *intrinsic* values by which the quality of life might be ascertained.

As to the first point, it hardly seems necessary to emphasize that what is "good" for a given social system, *qua* system, may not necessarily be "good" for most of the individuals who live within (or under?) that system. The literature of political philosophy and classical sociology fairly brims over with logical argument (and some empirical evidence) that the needs and interests of the rulers are not only different from, but often incompatible with, those of the ruled. Whether the focus be on order versus freedom, authority versus representation, coercion versus consent, stability versus change, or privilege versus equality, the picture is much the same: The preferences of elites and of masses can seldom be fully (or even adequately) reconciled. To put it another way, events and conditions which may be highly functional for a given system—or those who either exercise a high degree of control over it, or benefit most from its current state—are often considerably less functional (or even dysfunctional) for that much larger number whose influence and benefits are relatively low. In sum, one must be—as the expression goes—either a fool or a knave to equate the national interest with the individual interest.

Having taken this strong position, I do not mean to suggest that it is always a *very* few whose interests (psychic and material, short-run and long-run) are synonymous with that of the system, and that the overwhelming majority are necessarily the exploited and the betrayed. In many systems (and the United States during the past two decades may be a prime example), the short-run benefits of the status quo extend to an appreciable fraction and perhaps even half of the total population. And, as urged later on in the paper, the extent to which certain valued objects or conditions are equally distributed throughout any social system is indeed one important measure of political development.[6]

These comments lead to the other critical distinction suggested above. My view is that a valid measure of such development must not only differentiate between the systemic and the individual, but between the instrumental and the intrinsic. That is, Western students may believe that a high level of industrialization, a two-party political structure, or a complex communication network constitute evidence of political development, but I would contend that if there is no appreciable improvement in the quality of life of most of the system's members, it is invalid to speak of increased development. Put differently, it is essential to distinguish between development and such phenomena as modernization, mobilization, urbanization, and industrialization. As I define it, these latter are best viewed as potentially instrumental to the realization of certain intrinsically valuable conditions, but no more. To the extent that such changes *do* lead to improvements in the general quality of life, they may be treated as instrumental indicators of development, but rather than *assume* that they do, we must *demonstrate* that they do. At this writing, the evidence across time and across social systems is far from conclusive. With these considerations in mind, let us turn to the problem of intrinsic measures of political development, that we may later return to the association between them and those of an instrumental nature.

### Identifying the Intrinsic Values

So far, our references to the quality of life enjoyed by any population have been rather vague and general; the need now is to become more specific. But until we have identified the key dimensions, and defended that choice, operational measures would be premature. How, then, do we establish the criteria of the "good life"?

There are four basic routes. We can merely operationalize the revealed wisdom, as handed down by the tribal deities and their elite disciples. Second, we might conduct one version or another of an opinion survey, asking people what they desire in life. Or we can try to ascertain the particular or universal needs of people. Finally, we can select our own, reflecting the biases of Western, modern, liberal scholars. Let us consider each of these, briefly, in turn.

While sharing the view that the definitions of the good life handed down by the bureaucratic elites of church and state over the centuries have been essentially self-serving, the criteria they enunciated cannot all be dismissed out of hand. While some had only the effect of persuading people that servitude is righteousness, that pain is virtue, and that deprivation is the road to worldly or otherworldly salvation, others of these criteria may be worth preserving. This is especially true of those articulated (or rearticulated) by systematic philosophers who served no institutional masters; we will return to these shortly.

The alternative of asking people—the living and the dead, the rich and the poor, the educated and the ignorant—has the virtue of being democratic, but suffers from certain fatal inadequacies. First of all, neither the opinion survey nor the inference from historical traces (following, for example, the methods of McClelland's [1961] *Achieving Society*) gives us valid distinctions between the transitory and the persistent, or between the superficial and the fundamental.[7] Second, and more important, the preferences of too many humans in too many epochs have been artificially induced or "neurotically based" to use Bay's language (1965). Third, and perhaps most important, this approach requires an acceptance of the utilitarians' view that what people desire is indeed desirable, and what is desirable is therefore valuable. John Stuart Mill, for example, ended up defining virtuous behavior as that which leads to the "multiplication of happiness." Finally, how do we handle the distribution of incompatible preferences? Does a simple or special majority define the criteria for all who occupy a given time-space domain?[8] And, of course, how are the boundaries of those domains to be drawn?

The third option—that of trying to identify the basic and eternal *needs* of people—is ethically most attractive, since it requires little or no elite intervention. But it not only assumes that such needs can indeed be empirically ascertained, via the biological and psychological sciences, but it also assumes continuity in such needs across time and space. I suspect, despite the confidence of some biologists (for example, Gerard 1947) that such needs may turn out to be quite elusive, and that even if identifiable in a given empirical domain, they are just transitory enough to defy scientific generalization.

Does this suggest that the only defensible route is to recognize the inadequacies of the first three alternatives, and go ahead with an explicitly subjective delineation of the criteria by which the quality of men's life may be evaluated? Not quite. Rather, let me fall back on a synthesis in which each of the four components' contributions is admittedly quite uncertain.[9] The strategy is unsatisfactory, but given the number of philosopher-years which have been invested in the search for a solution so far—without success, in my judgment—one need not feel too sheepish about such an intellectual compromise. I argue, then, that there *are* certain basic needs typical of most humans across space and time and that these can be partly (and increasingly) inferred from behavior and verbal expression as well as from the sort of institutions men have built. Finally, I proceed from the assumption that, despite their basic inability to pin these needs down, the major Western philosophers have nevertheless given tentative expression to them.

## The Intrinsic Indicators Specified

Despite this somewhat unsatisfactory search for a legitimate basis, let me go on to a specification of the five intrinsic values by which we might measure the political development of the international, or any other, social system. Lest there appear to be any conceptual or definitional slippage in our argument, I repeat the basic theme here. Until we know the extent to which certain individual values have been realized in a given social system, one cannot evaluate its political development. Certain structural conditions or behavioral regularities may indeed be *conducive* to the realization of such values, but that is an empirical question; and even if these instrumental factors do turn out to enhance the intrinsic individual values in certain empirical domains, this is no basis for reifying them or treating them as eternal verities. Our ultimate task, then, is to: (a) develop valid and reliable indices of the intrinsic values; (b) ascertain the extent to which they have obtained over the past several centuries in the separate nations and in the world as a whole; and (c) identify the instrumentalities which best account for the presence and absence of these intrinsic conditions. Here, we can do no more than propose a set of criteria, discuss some possible measures, and present a few scattered observations. The value dimensions proposed are: (a) bodily survival, (b) material well-being, (c) liberty, (d) self-fulfillment, and (e) justice. The dominant preoccupations of Hobbes, Marx, Locke, Maslow, and Tawney, respectively, will be quite evident.

### Bodily Survival

Despite our sympathy with the view that there are things worse than death, and that there are indeed principles worth dying for, it is obvious that bodily survival is a precondition for enjoying any other values. Hence, any social system that is functional for its members is one that offers them a high probability of dying a natural death, and a low probability of dying violently and/or unexpectedly. In other words, in any particular social system with certain levels of medical care, public health measures, food, and shelter, there is a normal life expectancy. That expectancy figure may be pathetically low in contrast to other societies or more recent decades, but it is nevertheless a useful benchmark. However, not everyone lives that long, owing not only to the inevitable statistical distribution around the mean expectancy figure, but also to the less inevitable but ever-present incidence of violent and sudden death.

Among the philosophers who most concerned themselves with survival and physical security as a major purpose of political organization, Hobbes is perhaps best known. In Part Two of *Leviathan* he argued that the "final cause, end, or design of men who naturally love liberty and dominion over others, in the introduction of that restraint upon themselves in which we see them live in commonwealths, is the foresight of their own preservation. . . ."

The most valid and reliable measure of the ability of man's political institutions to assure him a "natural" death would be one that reflected its successes and failures in terms of deaths due to such events as war, revolution, massacre, execution, homicide, suicide, and occupational or transportation accidents. We choose, however, to eliminate two of these on validity grounds. Thus, even though there is a fair amount of data (however unreliable they may be) on the incidence of *suicide*, and that incidence is partially a function of societal inadequacies (and occasionally the only alternative to other forms of violent death), it is, in the end, a decision taken by the individual human being. Second, *accidents* of farm, factory, or road, in addition to being recorded for only the more recent years in many parts of the globe, are also to a large extent the result of the individual's own behavior. Like suicide, such deaths usually occur under specific societal conditions, but they fall outside our category of "violent death inflicted by others and unexpected at birth." In a later report, we will present some statistical estimates of the extent to which the political instrumentalities of the global system and its national subsystems have succeeded, failed, or actually produced death due to war, revolution, massacre, execution, and homicide.[10]

## Material Welfare

Once man's bodily survival is assured, it would seem that the next function of his political institutions is to permit him to live a life relatively free of disease, starvation, and punishment by the elements. To these ends, he may reasonably expect his institutions to provide, permit, or encourage an adequate amount of food, shelter, public health facilities, and medical care. This has indeed been a concern not only of men themselves, but of those who have theorized about the relationship of men and their social organization.

Traditionally, we think of the material needs of life as composed of food, clothing, and housing. The latter two may legitimately be combined under the rubric of shelter, not only on logical grounds, but also since there should be a high correlation between them in terms of both need (due to climate, etc.) and availability. One finds in the literature several possible measures of shelter, ranging from a crude dwelling unit per capita index to those reflecting number and quality of rooms per capita, and often including scales of modern plumbing, telephones, and so forth. Given the great variety of shelter requirements depending on climate, occupation, education, etc., the validity of any shelter availability index across regions, nations, or cities, as well as across so long a stretch of time is likely to be quite dubious, and an alternative approach is required. As to food, there are usually two basic indicators used; one is that of estimated caloric intake per capita per day (ranging from about 1,500 to 3,000) and the other is somewhat more refined in that it focuses on proteins only (with a range from about forty-five to ninety-five grams per day). These ranges tend to confirm the impression that food requirements, like those of shelter, vary too much to permit a compelling comparison of availabilities. That is, in both the shelter and food cases, one should first develop a baseline by which we can control for physical *need* before going on to comparing *availability*.

There may, however, be a fairly simple alternative by which we can get at the general variable of material well-being. If such well-being, in the form of food and shelter, as well as preventive and curative medicine, is important because of its contribution to the sort of physical environment within which humans can be born and then continue to thrive, it may well be that a very adequate indicator of the quality of that environment is the infant mortality rate. In other words, rather than try to get at this particular quality of life directly, the suggestion is that we look at those figures that seem most likely to reveal the *consequences* of material well-being. Some evidence that infant mortality rates do indeed offer a valid measure is the fact that we find a high (and of course, negative) correlation between these conditions on the one hand and such mortality on the other.[11]

## Liberty

Compared to bodily survival and material well-being, this third intrinsic indicator of political development is certainly more elusive, and quite subject to disagreement over the validity of almost any measure we might devise. One may think of liberty in individual or collective terms, and may differentiate among those several sectors of activity which characterize most social systems: political, economic, artistic, and so forth. We mean to embrace *all public and private sectors* of life, from the bedroom to the marketplace and from the artist's garret to the political forum, and to include not only those who conform to the norms of the moment but also those who do not. The idea may best be conveyed by the current expression "feel free," and has to do with freedom from constraint and the absence of anxiety over the political and economic consequences (but not that of mere social ridicule or disapproval) of one's thoughts, behavior, and associations.

Several possible ways of measuring this dimension come to mind, but none seem quite satisfactory. First, one *might* look at the statutory and administrative provisions which exist in the towns, provinces, and nations of the world, but this would be exactly the approach that is opposed here. That is, it would reflect the often unwarranted assumption that political rules almost always produce the consequences which are alleged to inhere in them, rather than treat the matter as one requiring empirical investigation. Closer to the intrinsic end of the continuum might be indicators that reflect—if the information for so many nations and years could be found—the frequency of political imprisonment, political trials, secret arrests, books banned or plays censored, correspondence intercepted, telephones tapped, houses searched, and so forth. Another approach might be to content-analyze representative samples of the literature, press, or correspondence, in order to estimate not only the extent of interference with expression and association, but to infer it even more indirectly on the basis of how much uniformity or diversity of views and styles is found.[12]

### Self-Fulfillment

Just as freedom and liberty represent the *absence* of constraints, the idea of self-actualization represents the presence of positive opportunities. While some may quarrel with its inclusion as a basic consideration by which to ascertain political development, it at least poses fewer measurement problems than that of liberty.

Dividing the dimension into its vocational and avocational sectors, the obvious measure for getting at the former (at least in its elementary sense) is that of employment. Using the standards of each period, we might first establish the extent to which all of the world's employable people are indeed so occupied; such a measure would have to take into account not only self-employment in agriculture, husbandry, retailing, and the crafts, but also the extent to which self- or other-employed people are underemployed due to seasonal or commercial conditions. But that is only part of the story. Equally critical—and here is where the values of the individuals concerned become most important—is the degree of satisfaction that is derived from such employment. It is difficult, at least for me, to imagine that Africans or Europeans or Americans who are often fully employed in the mines (for example) are really getting much satisfaction from such work, regardless of education, aspiration level, or cultural deprivation.

Then there is the matter of avocational opportunity. Even though it is only recently that social scientists in the industrial nations have begun to pay attention to the problem of leisure time, it is a phenomenon which anthropologists have noted regularly in their descriptions of preindustrial societies. Depending on the technological level of the society, one might be able to get at this factor by ascertaining the opportunity for, frequency of, and participation in, all sorts of ludic activity, ranging from dancing and lacrosse to concerts and cinema.

*Equality as Justice*

As broad and sweeping a concept as either liberty or self-fulfillment, the idea of justice is, in essence, a comparative one. That is, we tend to ask whether certain basic values are equally realized by all the people in a given social system or whether there is a discernible maldistribution in them. Alternately, instead of comparing one person's conditions with those of others, we might compare them to some desirable, but abstract, state of affairs. In this paper, we employ both approaches. The four intrinsic indicators are meant to reflect the extent to which those basic values have been fully realized by the people who constitute the international system; they reveal the discrepancy between some ideal condition and a given empirical reality. In this section, however, the first meaning is used: how equal is the distribution of the other four values, or in contemporary language, to what extent has *"distributive justice"* been achieved (Brandt 1959, chap. 16).

As most data-oriented scholars are well aware, almost all of the figures that are proposed here (along with many alternative indicators) are usually built around the nation as the unit of analysis. Thus, they not only offer little evidence as to the *intra*national distributions and inequalities thereof, but even less as to worldwide interpersonal inequalities. Quite clearly, any measures that do not reflect such inequalities at either the national or global levels can be quite misleading, and thus fail to offer valid indicators of political development.

In certain cases, however, there is an approximate solution. When the national data are broken down by region, social class, or ethnic groupings, for example, such frequency distributions permit us to go on to compute a measure of the intranational inequality. Furthermore, there will sometimes be Lorenz curves or numerical indices accompanying the data.[13] For those nations, years, and variables which meet either of these conditions, one strategy might be to calculate each nation's inequality score, multiply it by that nation's population, add up the total, and divide it by the number of people constituting the international system. This procedure has, however, a number of serious inadequacies. First, it assumes that intranational breakdowns will be fairly similar, permitting the calculation of comparable indices. Second, it assumes that most of the maldistributions will run in the same direction. And, third, because of these and other difficulties, it will tend to underestimate the irregularities when converted from the national to the international level. While any competent statistician could add to this catalog, we are not at all certain how they would propose to handle those cases in which there are no *within*-nation breakdowns.

Confronted with gross national data, or even national per capita data, there seem to be two possible strategies, neither of which is fully satisfactory. One is to try to estimate intranational inequalities by looking at a variable whose inequalities *are* known and which are likely to correlate highly with those of the variable under consideration (such as land ownership or education), and then proceed as above. The other is even more approximate and requires that we ignore intranational inequalities and go on to plot those of an *inter*national nature, weighting for each nation's population. Quite clearly, these are only stopgap solutions, and while the quality of some of the data available may not justify anything more refined, any improvement in the reliability and validity of the proposed indicators requires us to either "clean up" existing figures or search out better ones, and at the same time try to solve the problem of inequality indices.

So much, then, for the proposed intrinsic indicators of political development in the global system. Recognizing that they reflect an unspecified mix of traditional doctrine, classical concern, scientific generalization, and personal preference, they should nevertheless provide a point of departure and an interesting challenge to scholars of both an empirical and a normative bent, as well as those from a variety of disciplines. Let us turn now to the political development indicators of a more instrumental nature.

## Identifying the Effective Instrumentalities

In the opening section, we suggested that one must not only differentiate between intrinsic and instrumental indicators of the political development of any social system, but that those of the latter class which are generally used in comparative politics need to be examined with considerable skepticism. Even if the intrinsic indicators proposed here are largely normative in origin, the validity of the *instrumental* ones can only be evaluated on the basis of empirical evidence. What is needed, then, is a systematic search of the literature in comparative politics, political philosophy, political development, and international law and organization, as a first step toward identifying those structural, cultural, and behavioral conditions which allegedly contribute to the quality of life. Many of the potential indicators turned up in such a survey could, of course, be quickly dismissed on the grounds that they are obviously self-serving for the political elites, have since been shown to have no appreciable link, direct or otherwise, to the lives of the general publics, or have been shown to have an overall *negative* correlation with the intrinsic values.

Another problem that crops up often in this connection is the fact that few of the researchers from whom we might be borrowing make (or even recognize) a distinction between *indicators* of, and *predictors* of, political development. While some of the literature seems preoccupied with the matter of ascertaining how politically developed a given national social system *is*, some of it—often in the same work, but not explicitly differentiated—seems concerned with identifying those factors which lead that system to *become* developed. Rather than dwell on that particular sort of confusion each time it arises, let us note here that while our preoccupation is strictly with indicators and not with predictors, we will be considering a number of variables that their users might be using in either or both roles.[14]

## Types of Instrumental Indicators

There are, of course, many ways in which to categorize those aspects of a social system that affect (for better or worse) the quality of life of those who comprise the system. The taxonomy used here is that used in a number of earlier papers (Singer 1969a) and seems to be relatively straightforward and operational. Very simply, it differentiates among the attributes of any given system and the relationships, interactions, and behaviors that occur within it.

Every social system may be described, and compared to others, in terms of three sets of attributes: physical, structural, and cultural. The physical ones embrace geographic, demographic, and technological properties; the structural embrace organizational and institutional (but not necessarily static) phenomena; and the cultural (somewhat as in much of the recent literature on comparative politics) embrace the distribution of personalities, attitudes, and opinions found among those who comprise the particular social entity. Entities may not only be compared to one another at the same time and at the same level of analysis, but across different levels of analysis and with themselves at different points in time.

These entities behave and interact, and experience relationships with one another. Their relationships—or bonds or interdependencies—may well emerge out of prior interactions, but relationships should not be confused with interactions; the former tend to be stable and slow-changing, while the latter are more instantaneous. Furthermore, we may infer and describe the structural attributes of a system by observing the relationships among the people or subsystems which are its component units, describe its cultural attributes by observing the psychological attributes of the individuals who comprise it (Singer 1968b), and describe many of its physical attributes by observing the distribution of such attributes among its component units.

Needless to say, there is an intimate set of causal connections among these phenomena. Behavior (and therefore interaction) is certainly a function of the immediate social structure and culture within which it occurs, and to the extent that his personality, attitudes, and opinions affect each individual's behavior, there too we see the indirect influence of structure and culture on behavior. Moreover, any regularity of behavior manifested by some fraction of a population inevitably has some effect (reinforcing or modifying) on the structural and cultural attributes of the system. Finally, structure is often a consequence of the cultural patterns, and conversely, it is difficult to see how culture could fail to be at least partially shaped by the formal and informal structure of the system under examination.

We make the above digression not only to define certain key terms, but also to illuminate the ways in which the political phenomena of an instrumental nature which are associated with any social system can impinge on, positively or negatively, the intrinsic values outlined earlier. Let us now look at several possible instrumental indicators for the international system, via a brief glance at some of the representative ones which are found in the comparative national politics literature.[15]

### Some Indicators from National Politics

One of the most widely used paradigms of the politically developed social system comes to us from Weber, via Parsons, and embraces structural, cultural, and behavioral variables. Reference is to the bureaucratic society, manifesting the following general characteristics. First, there is a high degree of functional specialization and differentiation in the political structure, with a fairly large number of independent organizations and agencies, which are, in some versions, well coordinated through strong leadership. Second, associated with this structural condition are cultural norms that emphasize rationality over superstition in problem solving, achievement over ascription in the rise to power, and impersonal universality over a personalized particularism in the application of rules. Usually associated with these attributes are such cultural phenomena as loyalty to the regime, widely shared social values, a sense of collective identity and mutual trust, belief in the democratic process, a conviction of the importance of mass participation in the political process (Almond and Verba 1963), and often, an acceptance of broad political mobilization (Deutsch 1961).[16] Among the structural attributes generally connected with the idea of a politically developed society are interest aggregation and interest articulation (Almond and Coleman 1960), a high degree of pluralism in the sense of many crosscutting associations, and an accompanying degree of cross-pressure on many of the citizens.

This is but a sampling of the possible indicators that turn up most frequently in the comparative politics literature. It could be expanded not only by a more sustained perusal of that literature, but by converting many of these rather broad verbal concepts into more specific operational measures of an ordinal or interval nature.

## The Relevance of National Indicators
### for the International System

As the earlier discussion on inequalities in the distribution of intrinsic values suggested, there are some difficult empirical questions involved in the application of nationally based information to the larger system. But the conversion of our measures is only part of the problem; of equal importance and greater concern for the moment is the matter of theoretical applicability.

In recent years we have seen a number of excellent articles that try to formalize some of the critical similarities and differences between national and international politics (Alger 1963; Masters 1964; Parsons 1961). Needless to say, attention has been directed more to the differences than to the similarities, and even though our impression is that the differences tend to be overdrawn—partially because of the short time orientation of most political scientists— they are far from negligible.

In any event, if we use the traditional definition of government as it is understood in the national context, it is clear that many of the attributes of government by which we appraise political development just cannot be utilized at the global level. But if we think of it in a more literal sense, and note the great range in types and efficacy of those institutions by which men try to govern their public relationships, the comparisons become more feasible.[17] Following that orientation, let us look at the applicability and relevance of those indicators summarized in the prior subsection, especially those emerging from the bureaucratization outlook.

In a very rough way, we might be able to approximate a measure of functional differentiation and specialization by identifying the number of social groups that play a high, medium, or low (but some) direct role in international politics. Those organizations that interact across national boundaries, or which impinge directly (rather than in a mediated fashion) on national governments other than that of the territory in which they are located, could be classified as to their size or wealth, activity type, and intensity or frequency of such direct involvement. The point here is that this particular political development indicator would be very low when almost all international political activity is in the hands of national governments, but would rise as IGOs (international intergovernmental organizations), their specialized agencies, transnational corporations, professional associations, and the like, increased in number, size, and direct involvement. Likewise, as such functional differentiation rose, we might expect that the loyalties and interests of individuals and smaller groups would become more complex and multidirectional, leading to upward changes in any sort of pluralism index.[18]

But the other side of the coin also deserves attention. That is, to what extent would increases in the functional specialization and pluralism of the system be accompanied by the conditions that present the appearance of near anarchy? Thus, indices of effective centralized control as well as of shifts toward or away from a global loyalty would have to receive equal attention, as would the extent of shared norms regarding resource allocation, conflict resolution, and the like.[19] We might get at this by some such rough indicator as the ratio between expenditures of supranational political organizations and those of national governments (Neunreither 1967) or perhaps by staff size. But a more valid, if less reliable, index might emerge from some effort to identify the range of activities of the many overlapping and partially contending political aggregations in the system, and to measure the frequency with which each prevails in early bargaining or in a showdown.[20]

One of the ways in which social systems can often handle the sort of change outlined here, and the appearance of new and somewhat countervailing tendencies, is through interest articulation and aggregation. One would expect the former to correlate in a positive and fairly strong fashion with the growth in the number of direct actors, ranging from professional pressure groups to specialized IGOs. Interest aggregation would not, on the other hand, be an almost inevitable consequence of the growth in the number of direct actors. One might, more reasonably, expect a considerable time lag before the middle and upper elites of the world began to discern the erosion of power that national states and other territorially based entities were suffering as the more functionally specific entities moved into positions of influence. Once that trend was, however, both established and recognized, the formation of political parties could be expected to follow at a rapid rate. Based on a mix of considerations, including region, race, language, income, education, profession, personality, and so forth, as such parties grew in domain, scope, and power (Lasswell and Kaplan 1950), interest aggregation would appear as a political reality at the global level. But some scholars have pointed out that important variations in party organization, role, and strength can occur, and some of these might well suggest additional indicators. Cutright (1963), for example, uses the strength of minority party representation in legislative bodies, plus the degree of interparty competition in the selection of executive officials as measures of political development at the national level, and many would also look at the mere number of parties in the system (Lijphart 1968).

A closely associated structural condition in developed national societies is vertical social mobility, and this might well be measured in two ways when applied to the larger system. One would be the standard sociological way, in which we ascertain individual changes in social status, education, employment, income, etc. The other would take nations or other social entities as the unit of analysis, and try to ascertain *their* changing positions in hierarchies based on power (German 1960), diplomatic importance (Singer and Small 1966a), wealth, standard of living (Russett et al. 1964), and the like. Also of interest in this context is the structural notion of lateral mobility, in which we measure the rate at which nations or other entities move into or out of alliances (Singer and Small 1966b), trade networks, voting blocs (Alker and Russett 1965), diplomatic networks (Alger and Brams 1967), etc. Finally, one thinks of the idea of subsystem autonomy as an indicator (M. A. Kaplan 1957a), but we must then go on to ask which of the international system's subsystems are the ones whose autonomy might be more conducive to a maximization of the intrinsic values.

In addition to the above indicators, there are those less exotic ones that have enjoyed a traditional place in the literature of international politics and law, or which flow from the more recent literature on political integration and international organization (E. B. Haas 1964; Etzioni 1965; Sewell 1965). Even a straightforward count of the number of IGOs weighted by the number and importance of their memberships, as in Singer and Wallace (1970), could offer a useful guide. Beyond that, we might examine the content, scope, and applicability of the international and transnational law (Jessup 1956) of the past, as well as the yet unknown types of formalized norms that can be expected to spring up in the future. In this regard, a content analysis of elite and public attitudes toward such norms, combined with an analysis of the extent to which these norms are actually adhered to, would offer further and critical evidence as to the governance of the global system. Similarly, it would be a mistake to overlook the substance, depth, and reconcilability of divisions as revealed in debate, negotiation, and voting in many extranational and supranational organizations (Alker and Russett 1965; Hovet 1963; Riggs 1958).

One could, of course, go on cataloging the possible ways in which development of the international (or global) system might be measured, but this survey will have to suffice for the moment. In closing this section, it is necessary to emphasize that we have at hand a good many contenders among our alternative instrumental indicators, and that the measurement and data problems have barely been touched to date. For the international system, as for its national and other subsystems, we have yet to develop adequate descriptions by which each can be compared with itself over time and with others at the same point in time. As we urged in the introductory paragraphs, until we have described a set of phenomena, we can say very little about either the antecedents or the consequences of those phenomena, no less enter into ambitious explanatory enterprises.


## Conclusion

The social sciences in general and political science in particular are at a critical stage in their development. As the quality and quantity of the knowledge we acquire have shown a promising increase, too many of us have been remiss in designing our research and in teaching our students. While these sins are not nearly as extensive as the intellectuals of the New Left might have us believe, the charges are far from unfounded. The literature in comparative politics and its subfield of political development, as we see it, is particularly inadequate in the senses noted in our introduction, and particularly on matters ethical, neglecting as it does the crucial distinction between national or elite group interests on the one hand

and individual values on the other. Our purpose here is not only to make that distinction and apply it to the international system, but to prod those whose empirical focus remains at the national level of analysis.

As to any findings, it is perfectly clear that we have little evidence for believing that we know very much about the conditions or consequences of political development as defined here. First of all, it is difficult to know whether, on balance, we have made much progress toward improving the quality of life for most of the world's citizens. Second, whatever trends toward or away from the maximization of the intrinsic values have occurred, we have almost no data on the kinds of instrumentality that predict or account for such trends. Even if we shift our level of analysis from the system to the nations themselves, we find little in the way of longitudinal data that might permit us to say whether certain political structures, sets of social beliefs, or patterns of behavior are conducive to the realization of these values or not. At the international level, we have found, for example, that the establishment of structural arrangements such as IGOs shows almost no correlation with fluctuations and trends in the incidence of war (Singer and Wallace 1970), and that alliances, while helpful in this regard during the nineteenth century, have actually been associated with an increase in war during the current century (Singer and Small 1968). But even these modest investigations seem to have not yet been paralleled at the national level. Thus, let me conclude with a plea for considerable tentativeness in establishing and proposing instrumental indices of political development. Until we have not only agreed on the ends, but demonstrated which structural, cultural, and behavioral patterns are most conducive to the realization of these ends, it is premature to equate modernization or Westernization with political development in any place in the world.

Finally, my conviction is that we must, in one fashion or another, break away from the normative assumptions that seem to be implicit in so many of the formulations found in contemporary social science. Whether the orientation is toward national interests, social order, political stability, economic growth, or one or another of the many structural-functional paradigms, we seem to be in increasing danger of forgetting that the basic unit of any social system is the individual human being, and that any scientific formulation must take cognizance of that fact. In my judgment, no theory that ignores the single person is scientifically adequate or morally defensible. In sum, what is proposed here is that we begin some systematic research that can simultaneously "think big" and "think small," and which embraces in a rigorous synthesis both the lone individual and all of mankind. One of the more valuable by-products of such research might be the demise of the invidious distinction between empirical and normative theory in the social sciences.

# II

# The Theoretical
# Orientation

Having clarified my position on the scope of normative
concern, let me return to the issue of priorities alluded to in
that context. Since no researcher can work on too diverse a
set of problems efficiently or with much hope of success, he
or she must develop some set of priorities. These may flow
from normative assumptions or from pragmatic assumptions
or, more usefully, from some combination of the two. To use
a distinction that is elaborated later in this volume, a
thoughtful applied scientist will rest his or her priorities on a
complex mix of *preferences* about the future and *predictions*
about the future. The way in which preferences and predictions combine to shape the behavior of political elites—and
scholars—is explored later on, but one of the desirable consequences of high-quality research is the extent to which: (a)
the distinction can be sharpened; and (b) the reliance of
preferences upon predictions could be increased. In any
event, the opening essay in this volume should have made it
clear that my normative preferences go beyond the mere
reduction, or even the elimination, of war.

But, as already noted, one's research and policy priorities
must also rest on certain predictions as to the consequences
of certain events and conditions. These predictions, in turn,
must rest on *some* sort of theoretical schema, no matter how
primitive or incompletely defined. Given my stringent criteria
as to what qualifies as a scientific theory and the sort of
research that must precede the construction of a theory,

labels such as schema, model, orientation, or paradigm are more appropriate here. To put it another way, if theory is the body of knowledge that develops as the *consequence* of research rather than the set of assumptions and hunches with which that research *begins,* then our critics are correct in saying that the Correlates of War project is "without a theory." But that is not the same as saying that we proceed in a completely atheoretical fashion. Rather, as later papers in this and the subsequent volume make clear, we proceed in a multitheoretical manner.

But here I want to focus not on the extent to which one's theoretical framework and premises will affect the *specifics* of research design, but more on the extent to which they affect the larger research strategy, as well as the policy positions one takes along the way. The papers that are included in this section, then, are partially an answer to those who characterize this work as theory-free, but they should also be read as revealing the view of global politics that shaped (and continues to shape) my overall research strategy. More specifically, they should convey one man's notions as to how the global system works and how knowledge about consequences might modify the perceptions, predictions, *and preferences* of decision makers and those who study them.

# 2

# Threat-Perception and the Armament-Tension Dilemma

*The first article in this section on theoretical orientation was written about twenty years ago, when I was a postdoctoral fellow at Harvard's Department of Social Relations, and Herbert Kelman of that department invited me to submit a paper on the psychology of war and peace to the newly founded Journal of Conflict Resolution. The paper is included here not only to indicate that the Correlates of War project has theoretical origins of considerable age, but also to indicate something about a specific theoretical, or perhaps epistemological, bias. It should help to emphasize my strong conviction that we must eventually observe and measure the perceptions, preferences, and predictions of individuals if we are to come close to a scientific explanation of war. Because most of the data-based research of the project has been at the national, dyadic, and systemic levels, some may have concluded that we consider the individual level of little theoretical or policy importance. Nothing could, in my view, be wider of the mark. Not only are virtually all of my theoretical papers heavily focused on the individual level, but I have also gone out of my way in many of the more data-based ones to remind the reader that ultimately we must explain internation interactions in terms of the individual human being, or classes thereof.*

In his famous treatise on military affairs, Vegetius advised his emperor: "If you want peace, prepare for war." Theodosius followed this advice, yet within a few years was embroiled in a series of bloody conflicts. This crude doctrine of deterrence failed to preserve

27

the peace in the fourth century, did little better during the fifteen succeeding ones, and has thrice in this century failed to prevent mass bloodshed. Neither the evidence of history nor the application of logic would suggest that the *para bellum* doctrine holds out any peaceful prospects for the present; yet, as Madariaga (1929, p. 13) sadly concluded, "its vitality is incredible." Clinging to the dogma as if in a trance, the Soviet and Western blocs are today engaged in a hypertrophic race for superiority in weapons technique and production. Like the Hobbesian "Kings and Persons of Soveraigne Authority," they find themselves "in the state and posture of gladiators; having their weapons pointing and their eyes fixed on one another; that is, their Forts, Garrisons, and Guns upon the Frontiers of their Kingdomes, and continuall Spyes upon their neighbors; which is a posture of War" (Hobbes 1914, p. 65).

### The Perils of *Para Bellum*

The historical and logical inconsistencies implicit in this paradoxical doctrine of national security might be made more explicit by a brief examination of its application to the present bipolar "balance of terror." No political canon can survive the centuries without some kernel of truth, and that of *para bellum* is no exception. Thus, given the persistence of certain ideal and specified conditions, there might well be some modicum of security in the pursuit of weapons parity or superiority. At the very least, today's military stalemate does make highly unlikely any calculated initiation of large-scale hostilities by either the Soviet Union or the United States. The capacity of each to mount a massive and punishing counterblow does, in fact, provide a not insignificant deterrent. But any number of technological, diplomatic, or psychological developments could, with violent rapidity, reduce this precarious balance to a shambles. Several such possibilities will be alluded to here.

Perhaps the most dramatic illustration of the tenuousness of that balance is revealed in the recent Soviet protest over SAC flights in the Arctic. Despite the patently propagandistic intent, it is difficult completely to ignore the fears expressed by Ambassador Sobolev during the Security Council debate: "But what would happen if American military personnel observing their radar screens are not able in time to determine that a flying meteor is not a guided missile, and that a flight of geese is not a flight of bombers?" (*New York*

*Times*, April 22, 1958, p. 10). Both the Secretary of Defense and the Chairman of the Joint Chiefs of Staff have tried to assure the world that the "fail-safe" turnback system is foolproof (*New York Times*, April 20, 1958, p. 34), but "foolproof" military techniques have been known to fail before; a repetition of the combination of human and mechanical error which laid waste Pearl Harbor could be far more disastrous today. Furthermore, the two hours or more now available for the making of a responsible political decision will, when the Soviet ICBM becomes operational, be reduced to approximately fifteen minutes. And when the Western missile systems are in readiness, there will be no "fail-safe"; once launched, the ballistic missile cannot be recalled. In addition to the dangers inherent in an erroneous reading of the radarscopes or a failure in communication later on, the identical train of events could also be set in motion by the crash of a nuclear bomber or the accidental discharge of its cargo. Before the source of the detonation, if such occurred, could be identified, the retaliatory signal might have been given. Despite considerable precautions and frequent reassurances, these perils cannot be ignored.

A second development which might upset the delicate strategic balance is that of a major technological breakthrough, particularly if it were in the field of defensive weaponry. Were either power or bloc to come up with the means of preventing, or markedly reducing, an effective and devastating counterblow, it might certainly consider certain types of military adventurism and boldness which are now ruled out by the threat of massive retaliation.

Another possibility which might vitiate the stability of this precarious balance is the rise of "moral disarmament" in either of the camps. Certainty is the very essence of deterrence, and if at any time the willingness of either side to make good on its promise of retaliation is called into question, the other might well be tempted to take certain military risks. That such ambiguity already exists in the West is undeniable, and further evidence of loss of "nerve" can only serve to increase the danger. Finally, with the United States administration pressing the Congress for permission to make available the techniques and materials of nuclear weapon construction to its allies, the "fourth-power" problem takes on grisly significance. Nuclear bombs and advanced delivery systems in the hands of certain trigger-happy military leaders is far from a comforting thought.

This represents only a sample of those developments, any one of which could set in train a sequence of events culminating in total war. Faced with such risks, particularly when added to them are a multitude of domestic political pressures, economic limitations, and other policy considerations, those who shape policy in Washington, Moscow, or elsewhere are provided with a powerful incentive to search for other paths to national security. The purpose of this article is to explore several of those alternative paths, especially as they are affected by and might act upon the vicious circle of national armaments and international tensions.

## The Question of Cause or Effect

In examining the present pattern of bipolar hostility in search of a possible avenue of escape from its ominous paradox, one is insistently confronted with the armaments-tension phenomenon. That there is some sort of reciprocity between national military capabilities and international tensions would be difficult to refute, but the problem of illuminating this reciprocal relationship has proved consistently elusive. Positing the desirability of breaking out of this circle, the first question to arise is the old chestnut of "which comes first?"

One view is expressed by a former United States delegate to the United Nations, Benjamin V. Cohen; in addressing a meeting of the International Law Association, he stated that "if we knew of certainty that no nation was in a state of preparedness to undertake a war with any prospect of success . . . there would be a profound change in the climate of international relationships" (B. V. Cohen 1952, p. 3). In a more extreme form, this view is also expressed by some Quaker spokesmen, who are "convinced" that disarmament "in itself would so change the climate of world opinion that no power on earth could oppose it effectively" (American Friends 1955, p. 63).

At the opposite extreme is Sir Alfred Zimmern, who concludes that "armaments are not a cause of international tension; they are a symptom . . ." (Zimmern 1953, p. 81). Another Briton, Sir Alexander Cadogan, endorsed this stand when he told a meeting of the United Nations Commission for Conventional Armaments that "the reduction and regulation of armaments and armed forces depends primarily on the establishment of international confidence; the converse argument is misleading and dangerous" (U.N. 1947).

Rejecting both these polar and mutually exclusive positions would be found most of those who follow closely the pattern of world politics and who are not required to defend any specific governmental policy. For example, in his recent thoughtful study of international organization, I. L. Claude takes the position that "this is a circular problem, in which causes and effects, policies and the instruments of policy, revolve in a cycle of interaction and are blurred into indistinguishability" (Claude 1956, p. 298). The circularity view is also put succinctly by Governor Stassen's White House Disarmament Staff in an official publication: "World tensions and world armaments tend to reinforce one another. Each serves as a breeding ground for the other" (White House 1957, p. 7).[1] To summarize, it might safely be held that when students of international politics are in a position to observe dispassionately and are inclined to theorize, they will tend to describe the arms-tension relationship in predominantly reciprocal terms. Despite this, however, when pressed for an opinion, many will endorse either a tensions-first or arms-first approach, frequently to the exclusion of the other; concentrate on one, it is argued, and the other will take care of itself. Each of these broad approaches will be discussed presently, in light of the perceptual setting which is examined in the following section.

## Threat-Perception and the Decision Makers

Prior to an examination of the threat-perception concept, the writer feels obligated to articulate such of his assumptions on the nature of international politics as might influence his subsequent treatment of the central problem in this paper. And, while none of these assumptions will be likely to win universal endorsement, it is beyond the scope of this paper to enumerate all the arguments and adduce all the evidence upon which they rest.

First, it is posited that we are operating today in a rather well-defined or "tight" bipolar system, with the most crucial policy decisions being taken in Washington and Moscow.[2] Initiation, modification, encouragement, or obstruction may come from either set of allies, from the neutrals, or even from that sole and timid guardian of the *inter*national interest, the United Nations Secretariat; but, in the final analysis, it will be up to the Soviet Union and the United States either to perpetuate the present unstable equilibrium or to attempt to break out of it by a variety of means.

Second, it is assumed that the decision-making process in each of these powers is essentially a collective one. This is not to deny that the president or the first secretary will in effect have the final word in their respective governments or to suggest that there has not been a significant erosion of the collective leadership principle in the Kremlin in recent months. But it does posit the existence of a large and complex bureaucracy in each regime, responsible for collecting, interpreting, evaluating, and transmitting foreign-policy intelligence along the channels to the hierarchical apex. The implication here is that policy decisions are likely to be the result of consultation and compromise within each system rather than the whim or caprice of a single mind.[3]

The third, and perhaps most crucial, assumption is that the decision makers on both sides, despite the welter of conflicting pressures, demands, and interests, are more concerned with the preservation (and extension) of national power than with the fulfillment of abstract political dogmas. It is contended, therefore, that the final determinant is, and will continue to be for some time, the elite's conception of national security,[4] not the ideological utterances of Marx or Locke, Lenin or Jefferson, Manuilski or Wilson. The formulation and articulation of an ideological position have their very real applications and, as such, may condition or modify but will not *determine* Soviet or American foreign policy; national security is the categorical imperative.[5]

On the basis of these assumptions, attention may now be directed toward the central question confronting those who intend either to survive within or to escape from the armaments-tension dilemma. This question might well be examined by reference to what Thomas and Znaniecki (1947) have called the "definition of the situation"; this definition, as they see it, is the resultant of two sets of factors. First, there are the "objective conditions under which the individual or group has to act"; second, there are the "preexisting attitudes" which operate to select, combine, and interpret the objective conditions, thus producing a somewhat subjective definition of the situation. Of such preexisting attitudes, none is more central to world politics than that of ethnocentrism, a tendency which leads the citizen to "judge external phenomena in terms of his membership in a particular national group. The same item of behavior, objectively considered, has an entirely different meaning, depending on whether it is one's own or another nation which is responsible for it" (Klineberg 1954, p. 556). From this powerful predisposition to suspect and distrust the people and governments of all other nation-states, a combination of recent events, historical memory, and identifiable sociocultural differences provides the vehicle by which this vague out-group suspicion may be readily converted into concrete hostility toward a specific foreign power.

Now it may be argued that this tendency, while applicable to the masses, has little relevance to either the policy-making elite or the informed, attentive public. Admittedly, the phenomenon may be less apparent among the educated and urbane career officers of a foreign ministry, but the wielders of ultimate political power are seldom of that background and frequently exhibit a xenophobia even more virulent than that of their followers. In addition and despite the fact that role does tend to mediate attitude and personality, the policy maker is likely to manifest this hostility in its extreme form just because of the role which he *is* playing; he who is responsible for the protection of the nation from outside enemies is not likely to regard such potential sources of attack with either apathy or detachment. To the contrary, Soviet and American decision makers view each other today with cold, calculating, suspicious hostility.

Superimposed on this basic hostility is the additional exacerbation of mutually ominous military capabilities. Not only does each elite attribute to the other a desire to increase its power and national security at the expense of the other, but each recognizes that the other has at its disposal an array of weapons and delivery systems which might be put to direct use when and if the potential gains appeared to justify the risks of retaliation. Aware of the possibility that the other may initiate either a limited or a total attack or politically exploit any strategic imbalance, each continues to drive harder for military superiority. (Parity will not suffice; there is the ever-present danger of underestimation or major technological breakthrough.) And within this sort of perceptual framework, built of hostility plus capability, the inevitable consequence is that each elite will interpret the other's military capability as evidence of military intent. Failure to equate such capability with intent or unwillingness to infer design from physical capacity might produce disastrous national consequences; all error must be on the side of cynicism. In such a situation, proposals will be viewed as propaganda, criticisms as intimidation, and concessions as duplicity. The circularity and self-generating nature of the arms-tension pattern is manifest, and threat-perception is its prime ingredient. Thus is the "Richardson process" (Richardson 1950) perpetuated and the feverish arms race nourished.

To summarize, it is contended here that threat-perception arises out of a situation of armed hostility, in which each body of policy makers assumes that the other entertains aggressive designs; further, each assumes that such designs will be pursued by physical and direct means if estimated gains seem to outweigh estimated losses. Each perceives the other as a threat to its national security, and such perception is a function of both estimated capability and estimated intent. To state the relationship in quasi-mathematical form: Threat-Perception = Estimated Capability × Estimated Intent. The reasoning implicit in this capability-intent relationship is best illustrated by reference to two current military-psychological patterns. The British today maintain a relatively formidable military establishment, capable of rendering extensive damage to both the U.S.S.R. and the United States. While there is little threat-perception in Washington when these capabilities are assayed (almost no estimation of intent), the Kremlin regards that same potential with considerable alarm (high level of estimated intent). Conversely, the extreme hostility of the Egyptian government, because it is not coupled with significant military capability, has not produced any important level of threat-perception in Washington. In other words, as either capability or intent appears to approach the zero level, threat-perception tends to diminish. The major premise of this paper is that any attempt to break out of the arms-tension circle must successfully reduce threat-perception by addressing itself to the reduction of both military capability and estimated military intent.


## An Examination of Some Alternatives

There are some students and practitioners of diplomacy today who would suggest that any discussion of the disarmament question,[6] directly or indirectly, now or in the near future, would be at best fruitless and at worst suicidal to those giving it such consideration. In this category would be those who accept one or more of the following premises: (a) war is inevitable, and thus emphasis should be upon winning it, not preventing it; (b) armaments are a necessary and permanent aspect of man's existence in this imperfect world; (c) one or the other of the superpowers will give up its imperialistic designs and reform, thus making arms unnecessary; and (d) the very terrors implicit in modern weapons make war today unthinkable.

However, there are those who take a somewhat less fatalistic view than these extreme pessimists (a, b) and optimists (c, d). Without doing violence to any of the approaches to disarmament, it is proposed to deal with each in turn, depending upon the point of departure which is emphasized: (*a*) the tensions-first approach; (*b*) the political-settlement approach; and (*c*) the armaments-first approach. Having discussed the risks implicit in the perpetuation of the arms race, identified the decision makers, and explored the perceptual setting within which the latter must operate, we may proceed to an examination of each of these approaches, particularly as they relate to the phenomenon of threat-perception.

## The Tensions-First Approach

The recent Soviet-American cultural-exchange agreement was hailed in its communiqué as "a significant first step in the improvement of mutual understanding between the peoples of the United States and the U.S.S.R."; the text then expressed the hope that the agreement would be carried out "in such a way as to contribute substantially to the betterment of relations between the two countries, thereby also contributing to a lessening of international tensions" (*New York Times*, January 28, 1958, p. 8). To many, this sort of program illustrates the most fruitful approach to the arms-tension dilemma; cultural exchanges, educational and literacy programs increased travel, and expanded trade are all viewed as the way to reduce or eliminate peoples' "ignorance of each other's ways and lives . . . through which their differences have all too often broken into war" (U.S. 1946, p. 13). The reasoning upon which this so-called "UNESCO approach" is based, though not always made explicit, is quite clear: Provide the people of the quarreling powers with an opportunity to meet with and learn about one another; this will lead to increased mutual tolerance, understanding, and respect, and a consequent reduction in tensions between them. This new set of attitudes will, in turn, influence governmental relations, and, once such intergovernmental tensions have commenced their downward swing, it is contended, the national elites will no longer see any need for the maintenance of expensive and dangerous arsenals. With this realization will come a willingness to disarm or at least a more tractable approach to multilateral disarmament negotiations. Until such a diminution of international tensions has occurred, national armaments will remain as their fearsome manifestation.

Without attempting any thorough diagnosis of the "UNESCO approach,"[7] two closely related questions raised by that point of departure will be examined here. First, if the approach is aimed primarily at the *people* of the separate states, what is the connection between popular attitudes and the readiness of policy makers to engage in bellicose behavior? Second, what are the really effective forces at work in the shaping of those popular attitudes? Regarding the first question, the connection would seem to be unmistakably clear in this "century of total war." Whether it be limited or global, war today requires the fullest mobilization of a nation's resources—military, industrial, governmental, and psychological (Aron 1954; Knorr 1956). Moreover, such mobilization must be undertaken long before the appearance of armed conflict; without preparedness, there can be little deterrence and, without deterrence, no security. The citizenry must therefore, in the name of national security, send its men into uniform, finance the ravenous military machine, adapt to new and dangerous levels of radioactivity, and acquiesce in the inevitable transfer of individual liberties to the agents of the evolving garrison state. That popular attitudes are an essential element of national preparedness would be most difficult to deny.

Less obvious is the answer to the second question; yet it is in the reasoning of the first that we find the answer to the second. If, as has been stated, the public's attitudes are so crucial to national preparedness, can it be reasonably expected that governmental elites will encourage, or even permit, more than token opportunities for the public to develop an image of the potential enemy in other than hostile and menacing terms?

Classically, public opinion is seen as a resultant of two general sets of factors. One of these is the sociocultural framework or national ideology; vague and amorphous, yet internalized and powerful, the national ideology provides the cognitive and affective setting within which specific attitudes on particular problems are formed. The myths and symbols associated with the ideology need only be tapped and manipulated by those who control the second set of factors: the presentation and interpretation of recent and immediate experiences. By the adept use of the appropriate cues, the elite can readily generate a menacing and hostile image of the potential enemy; given the high concentration of ethnocentrism in most national ideologies, the opinion maker need merely single out and label the appropriate foreign target. Just as there are techniques for inducing pacifistic attitudes (Eysenck 1950), there are those which are equally effective in creating an atmosphere of tension and bellicosity.

Thus there are three main conditions which come into play. First, there is the dominant preoccupation of the elite with national security. Next there is the urgent necessity for public support of any preparedness program. And, third, there is the relative ease with which this support may be induced. The implications of this three-way interaction are evident. The public's support is contingent upon its perception of a genuine threat to the nation's way of life and political independence; and, since the potential threat may rapidly become an immediate one, some marginal surplus of popular threat-perception must be maintained. Therefore, while tension-reducing programs are exercising some impact upon a selected few intellectuals, artists, farmers, or workers, little permanent headway is made. A visiting group returns from the other country, perhaps with considerably modified views (though this is by no means guaranteed), and disperses among its own citizenry. As the returnee attempts to recount his experiences and demonstrate the peacefulness (or other virtues) of his Russian or American counterpart, he runs headlong into the inevitable reaction from those who have not shared his experience. "Surely," it will be said, "many of those people are indeed peace-loving, but after all, they are not the ones who make policy. Our enemies are the fanatic Communists [or the war-mongering imperialists]. It is their aggressive leaders who drive them to war against us." Within this simplification there is the usual germ of truth. The attitudes of the masses may influence the policy makers, but the setting within which the people form these attitudes is something less than objective reality. Their simplified and exaggerated definition of the situation is formulated for them to a considerable degree by those responsible for national security.

The logic of the process is inexorable. Each elite perceives the other's military capabilities in terms of aggressive intent. They transmit this perception to their people, and the tension between the governments makes impossible any reduction of tension between the people. As long as each nation retains the capacity to wage aggressive war, mutually perceived threat will continue to flourish, and tensions will be perpetuated and exacerbated, not eliminated. Disarmament based upon a prior elimination of tensions will be a long time in coming.

## The Political-Settlement Approach

As might be anticipated, not all adherents of the tensions-first school are convinced of the fruitfulness of any direct assault upon the "minds of men." Rather, while accepting the chronological precedence of tensions vis-à-vis armaments, some of them seek to back up a step and look for the indirect source of such tensions. In his *Politics among Nations*, Morgenthau traces them to the "unformulated conflicts of power" (1956, p. 404), while Kennan discovers them as arising out of "substantive political differences and rivalries" (*New York Times*, November 18, 1957, p. 10). Arguing that any direct search for disarmament would be placing the "cart before the horse," such observers stress that the "reduction of armaments must await the political settlement" and that disarmament is "impossible as long as there exist unsolved political issues which the participating nations regard as vital to themselves" (U.S. 1956, pp. 1015, 1092).

Proceeding from these premises, the political-settlement approach suggests that the first step is therefore to identify the areas of political conflict, define the interests of the protagonists, and then attempt the negotiation of a realistic settlement. As Kennan describes it, this process requires "taking the awkward conflicts of national interest and dealing with them on their merits with a view to finding the solutions least unsettling to the stability of international life" (1952, p. 94). In order to achieve success in this diplomatic pursuit, national decision makers are advised to: (*a*) arm themselves with "an attitude of detachment and soberness and readiness to reserve judgment"; (*b*) rid themselves of "arrogance or hostility toward other people"; and (*c*) exercise "the modesty to admit that our [their] own national interest is all that we [they] are really capable of knowing and understanding." So prepared psychologically, the professional diplomatists may then actively engage in the pursuit of the national interest," an activity which "can never fail to be conducive to a better world" (Kennan 1952, p. 100). Of course, in this reasonable pursuit of the national interest, each nation shall rely upon "physical strength, armaments, determination, and solidarity" and meet the other with "unalterable counterforce at every point where they show signs of encroaching upon" the former's conception of a peaceful and stable world. Within the context of this particular approach to world peace, both sides will pursue their respective national interests by the intelligent application of national power; this will eventuate in a series of negotiated political settlements, leading to a relaxation of international tensions; and, from such a tension-reduction, disarmament may legitimately proceed. It is little wonder that Professor Kennan refers to disarmament as a "utopian enthusiasm" (1952, pp. 143–44; 1954, p. 21).

In addition to the inability of the political-settlement approach to get to the heart of the threat-perception problem by ignoring the role of weapons in that perception, it suffers from a further logical contradiction. In their writing and lecturing, Morgenthau and Kennan (with their colleagues of the "realistic" school) assume a sharp and identifiable distinction between political settlements and armament reduction; this distinction is made explicit in their demand that the one must precede the other. Yet this distinction is far from self-evident. In pursuing the national interest, an elite's primary instrument is national power, much of it in the form of military hardware; its other elements might be bases for the stationing of forces and the deployment of the weapons, accessibility to raw materials and industrial products, the strength and viability of the economies and political systems of one's allies, and perhaps the attitudes of the elites and masses in the uncommitted areas. The realist might argue that national power is a vast, complex, and all-inclusive phenomenon and that one cannot separate a single element, such as armaments, and deal with it individually. Yet Kennan has only recently stirred intellectual Europe by proposing a modified disengagement. Apparently the granting of significant politico-strategic concessions differs in some way from scrapping of military hardware. The reduction of bomb and missile stockpiles is "disarmament," but the surrender of the bases from which they might be deployed is merely "political settlement."

## The Armaments-First Approach

Believing that no direct attack upon tensions themselves will be successful and that any political settlement which disregards the primary instruments of national power is doomed to failure, some students of international politics have begun to give serious consideration to the problems inherent in the disarm-by-disarming approach. Within this school there is a wide and complex range of alternatives, which, for the sake of clarity in analysis, will be divided into four general categories: (I) unilateral and complete; (II) unilateral but partial; (III) multilateral but partial; and (IV) multilateral and complete.

Alternative I is that espoused by the pacifist movement and is embodied in the proposals of such groups as the Fellowship of Reconciliation and the American Friends Service Committee; their position is based upon two primary and well-articulated assumptions. First, there is no genuine national security in adherence to the doctrine of *para bellum,* and, second, if one major power or bloc were to take the decision for unilateral and total disarmament, "it is entirely probable that other heavily armed powers would follow the lead" (U.S. 1956, p. 728).[8]

The first assumption has already been discussed here, but it should be emphasized that it is accepted not only by the critics of preparedness but by many of those responsible for the formulation and execution of that very policy. In testimony before the Disarmament Subcommittee, Secretary Dulles himself referred to the "constant menace of destruction," and Commissioner Murray observed that "it is by no means clear that a balance of terror furnishes an assurance that aggression . . . will not be undertaken. . . . A balance of terror is too easily upset" (U.S. 1956, pp. 48, 336). Similar reservations have been expressed, not only by those out of power such as Gaitskill and Ollenhauer, but by those currently responsible for their nation's security, such as Eisenhower, Khrushchev, Macmillan, and Nehru; there is today an almost universal recognition of the tenuousness of a peace or a security based upon either parity or superiority in military capability.

As to the second assumption, there is greater room for doubt. While it is true that spokesmen for both blocs continually protest that they arm only for self-defense and imply that their opposites need only demonstrate their peaceful intent by scrapping their weapons and they will immediately follow suit, several obstacles arise. Since it is, by definition, the *other* power which arms for aggression, *they* obviously must disarm first; who will take the first step? Even if one power agrees to begin disarmament unilaterally, how do the others know that the process has in fact been started? And, in addition, some powers will raise the question of "fulfillment of international obligations" (usually the United Nations Charter is invoked here) without military forces available. In the absence of an effective ethical or legal code assuring high correlation between promise and performance, it is difficult to expect a government elite to commence disarmament on the *hope* that its opposite numbers will do likewise. The responsibility for and preoccupation with the national security assures that such an act of faith will appear far too risky to even the most sanguine policy maker.

Alternative II, however, is a somewhat different proposition, despite apparent similarities; whereas alternative I calls for disarmament which is both unilateral and complete, down to the last weapon of mass destruction, this requires only a partial reduction and, as a result, has many more adherents. It proceeds from the same first premise as I—the inability of weapons to assure any lasting national security—but it relies to a considerably lesser extent upon the likelihood of one power or bloc following the other in stripping itself of aggressive military capability. Rather, it views such an eventuality as possible, rather than probable, and therefore seeks a modification which might minimize the risks inherent in the unilateral and total scheme.

In fuller terms, the partial unilateral approach takes a less simplistic perspective of the arms-tension dilemma than does alternative I. Recognizing the grip which threat-perception has upon the minds of the decision makers, the opinion makers, and the general public, it proceeds to address itself to a relaxation of that grip. It appreciates that protestation and promise will not materially diminish reciprocally perceived threat and that concrete deed is essential to break the spell. For example, the Committee for a Sane Nuclear Policy, in a series of newspaper advertisements, has proposed that missiles and nuclear weapons be considered separately from other weapons and that all nations immediately suspend their testing and development. While the committee does specifically refer to the need for United Nations monitoring and control, it is nevertheless willing to see the United States take the first step unilaterally and unconditionally, prior to the establishment of any international control system (*New York Times*, November 15, 1957, p. 15; April 11, 1958, p. 15). In this same category are the British Campaign for Nuclear Disarmament and the West German Fight against Atomic Death. Each of these seeks a bilateral or multilateral inspectable agreement prohibiting both the further testing of nuclear weapons and the stationing of delivery systems within their territories; but each is willing to engage in immediate and unconditional unilateral nuclear disarmament in the Western bloc. The assumption of all three movements is that, despite the genuine military risks inherent in such unilateral action, nothing less will suffice to demonstrate Western sincerity and diminish the degree of threat which the Kremlin infers from the NATO military posture.[9]

While it may be reasonable to expect that such deeds *might* reduce the sense of insecurity in the Soviet camp, it does not necessarily follow that diminution of threat-perception will lead the Soviets quickly to reduce their own arsenals. Their policy makers may hail the action as "a welcome step toward the strengthening of peace," yet interpret it as: (*a*) a reflection of domestic economic, popular, or partisan pressures; (*b*) a propaganda device; (*c*) a shift in military or technological strategy; or (*d*) a ruse to generate complacency. Concern for national security requires that each place the most cynical interpretation upon such a gesture. An excellent example of this array of reactions to a unilateral cutback is found in the American response to Soviet announcements of a troop reduction of 1,200,000 men in May, 1956. A *New York Times* article by Harry Schwartz carried the caption "Domestic Economic Pressure and Desire to Embarrass West Believed Involved," while another by Elie Abel was headed "Russian Arms Cut Laid to Emphasis on Nuclear Power" (*New York Times*, May 15, 17, 1956, p. 1). Any suggestion of a new Soviet peacefulness was quickly scotched.[10] The almost inevitable reaction to such a "tension-reducing" step is found in Prime Minister Eden's letter to Premier Bulganin: "My own feeling is that unilateral reductions of this kind are helpful. I do not think, however, that they are of themselves sufficient if international confidence and security are to develop as we wish" (*New York Times*, July 10, 1956, p. 12). Unless unilateral cuts are followed up quickly on both sides by further reductions, any diminution of threat-perception will be of only the briefest duration. They might make preparedness somewhat less expensive, but they would not make it any less necessary. It might even be argued that if a unilateral reduction on one side were not promptly succeeded by a similar move on the part of the other, the originators might experience a sharp increase in threat-perception and return to the arms race with renewed vigor; thus the long-range effect of unilateral action might be to heighten, rather than reduce, international tensions.

Turning now to alternatives III and IV, we come across an element which was lacking in I and II—that of reciprocity. In the bilateral and multilateral approach, each side makes its arms reductions contingent upon a similar reduction by the other. Such a reduction might flow from a negotiated treaty, agreement, or convention, or possibly (and not to be excluded) a process of "tacit bargaining" proceeding out of a public exchange of conditional statements and communications (Schelling 1957). Whether such disarmament is partial or total, it is clearly contingent and reciprocal.

Alternative III (multilateral but partial) is that which has been most frequently pursued in the twentieth century. For a variety of reasons, the governments of the major powers might seek to enter into (but not necessarily conclude) negotiations on some measure of weaponry limitation or reduction.[11] Generally, such negotiations would deal with a specific category or type of weapon; during the interwar period of the 1920s and 1930s great importance was attached to the distinction between offensive and defensive arma-

ments; Lord Davies' "principle of differentiation" was based on pre-
and post-1914 hardware (D. Davies 1931), and today's dichotomy
tends to separate conventional from thermonuclear and chemical
devices. In addition, implied is some measure of verifiability, either
through reciprocal or third-party inspection of territory, bases, or
such official records as budgets, which would reflect levels of military preparedness.[12] Such has been the nature of almost all disarmament proposals and negotiations since World War II.

The benchmark against which this type of arms reduction must
be measured is the same as that applied to the unilateral alternatives:
How effectively does it break into the arms-tension circle? Today
there is under consideration a range of possibilities which includes
the cessation of nuclear or missile tests, cutbacks in mobilized
manpower, or withdrawal of all foreign forces from certain specified
areas of central Europe. Let us suppose that one or more of these has
been successfully negotiated, an adequate inspection system
installed, and that both sides have commenced the required action in
accordance with a mutually acceptable schedule.

Such reciprocal and verifiable adherence to the arms-reduction
agreement would certainly tend, despite the inevitably cynical interpretations, to produce a more relaxed atmosphere for some measurable period of time. The policy makers on each side would have
rather clear evidence that the other had actually diminished its
capacity for armed attack, albeit to a limited extent; each could
logically infer that such a diminution of the other's aggressive military capabilities reflected a corresponding diminution of aggressive
intent. Furthermore, each would have concrete evidence that, under
certain clearly defined conditions, the other would adhere to its
commitments. Though such affirmative interpretations and results
are by no means assured, the experience of the early interwar period
suggests that they may reasonably be anticipated. Similar limitations
and reductions were negotiated in 1922, 1930, 1936, and 1937 (this
latter between Germany and Britain), and to some extent they
resulted in a temporary reduction of mutually perceived threat and
consequently of international tensions.

However, if such a first step were limited to inspected partial
reduction (or merely aerial inspection to prevent surprise attack), the
impact of the agreement would tend to decrease as time went on and
no further reductions in striking capacity were negotiated—or undertaken unilaterally. The agreed and verified decrease in capability
would be less and less interpreted as an indicator of peaceful intent

and more and more in those cynical terms outlined earlier. Such was the final interpretation placed upon those agreements negotiated in the pre–World War II era, and such is the interpretation already being put upon the several disarmament proposals now being bruited back and forth across the Iron Curtain. Inability or unwillingness to go beyond some limited, partial agreement implies unwillingness to accept total disarmament, and when one side sees the other insisting on the retention of some military capability, it may reasonably assume that such weapons as are retained may be for other than purely defensive purposes. Referring to the reductions and limitations negotiated during the 1920s, Madariaga observed that "so-called disarmament discussions are in fact *armament* discussions, and that whatever the label, the commodity bought and sold in the market is power" (1929, p. 63). Bilateral or multilateral partial disarmament may temporarily mitigate the mutual perception of threat, but to expect any lasting diminution of this ingredient of war is to overlook the transcending preoccupation of the decision maker with the security of his nation-state.

Finally, we turn to alternative IV (multilateral and total) of the various arms-first approaches. Is there anything in this alternative which permits it to overcome the liabilities inherent in the tensions-first, political-settlement, and previous armaments-first approaches? It will be recalled that the crucial element in the latter's inability to break out of the circle was the failure to maintain, over any durable period of time, the temporarily decreased levels of threat-perception. Each time that a halt in the reduction of military capability was reached, the natural tendency was for a sense of national insecurity to reappear, with a commensurate reestablishment of the original levels of mutual threat-perception. The problem, therefore, would seem to be one of *continuing and perpetuating*, once commenced, the gradual diminution of military capability.

This, however, is precisely the core of the problem; two factors arise which might well paralyze this total reduction process even before it had begun. First, even with the establishment of a thorough inspection system, there would always be some possibility of evasion or the development of a new and unexpected weapon or delivery system which would make invalid the assumptions upon which any schedule had been negotiated.[13] Given the preexisting condition of mutual hostility and fear, each side must and would operate on the premise that such an evasion or development was quite possible, if not probable. Second, some power not covered by the agreement might secure enough military might to become an aggressor-by-proxy for one of the signatories.

While this latter danger might be avoided, in theory at least, by insistence upon universality, the first menace would be much less readily mitigated. Whereas in any partial disarmament scheme the risks of an evasion are significant but not tragic, in a complete and total disarmament program the hazard is almost intolerable. In the former, the nation has not denuded itself completely; its defensive or retaliatory power may be diminished, but it is not eliminated. In any complete disarmament schedule, there comes a time when each government is virtually incapable of self-defense and when, if another has successfully concealed any significant offensive weapons, it may be faced with the choice between surrender and annihilation.

It may safely be said that it is the awareness of this haunting possibility which will, in the final analysis, deter any national elite from agreeing to any total disarmament schedule of the nature described above, no matter how effective the inspection provisions may seem. They may perceive the continuation of the spiraling weapons race as a major gamble, pregnant with dangers, but the other alternative may well be discerned as an invitation to national suicide. Given the choice between the two sets of risks, national policy makers will probably continue in the path, at least familiar, of their predecessors. It would appear, then, that, whereas unilateral or partial multilateral disarmament could not, if attempted, produce the necessary effect upon threat-perception, complete disarmament implies hazards so great as to preclude even its attempt. Thus, by themselves, none of these approaches would appear to offer a road out of the arms-tension dilemma. Each fails the acid test of national security; each seems incapable of meeting the rigid requirements of those responsible for national self-preservation.

## Conclusion

Having analyzed the tensions-first, political-settlement, and armaments-first approaches, and finding them separately incapable of escaping the inexorable logic of the arms-tension dilemma, one might conclude that there is, in fact, no escape. Such a conclusion has already been reached by a staggering number of statesmen and students of international affairs, and much of the evidence, historical and logical, would seem to substantiate this gloomy judgment. Yet this writer cannot acquiesce in such a conclusion. Be it tender-minded optimism or ordinary human obstinacy, he is convinced that there exist, within the mind of man, the ingenuity and the persistence to discover a workable solution. Such a conviction leads him, despite the limitations of space and intellect, to hazard a few brief paragraphs suggesting those modifications and combinations of the separate alternatives which might possibly hold the promise of reprieve.

It will be recalled that each approach, considered separately, was ruled out by its inability to cope in any lasting way with the problem of perceived threat to national security. For example, the tensions-first and three of the arms-first approaches failed to provide anything more than a temporary mitigation of threat-perception, while the political-settlement approach, by attempting to ignore weapons entirely at the outset, failed even to initiate a trend in that direction; none seemed to produce a situation out of which might develop an increasingly permanent sense of national security. And the total multilateral approach, probably the most promising of the traditional alternatives, appeared to be doomed at the start because of the risks involved later.

Let us suppose, however, that a radical change in the concept of disarmament were introduced. In place of the traditional reliance upon the scrapping of weapons or their conversion to peaceful purposes, let us assume that certain specified national weapons were instead transferred—slowly, cautiously, but regularly and in accordance with a prearranged schedule—to previously designated United Nations depots, where trained members of an international gendarmerie were prepared to receive, account for, maintain, and man such weapons. Further, let us assume that this gendarmerie had been assigned certain clearly defined and limited, yet very real, legal and political responsibilities for their operation and deployment, such responsibilities extending to the protection of the signatory nations as their military capabilities approached inadequacy while those of the United Nations agency were gradually increasing.[14] Might such a procedure not ultimately remove the greatest psychostrategic barrier to the policy makers' willingness to engage in any long-range and total arms reduction program? If it is true that the gamble of finding one's nation militarily denuded, while the potential enemy has managed secretly to preserve a part of his striking power, is in fact the single most paralyzing factor in the path of global disarmament, perhaps the substitution of an international agency, armed with the requisite legal, political, and military powers, might serve to eliminate the dread with which that gamble is contemplated.

This brief suggestion probably raises more questions than it answers, but the implication should be clear. No national statesman, Western, Soviet, or neutral, has yet proposed a disarmament plan that has any chance of lasting success, and it is unlikely that any will until the basic, crucial issue is faced squarely. In order to protect the people of a nation which has willingly surrendered its weapons, the United Nations will require a range of powers and a delegation of authority considerably greater than that now entrusted to it. To deal effectively with the arms-tension dilemma, the organization will need certain of the powers which have come to be associated with those of a federal government. But that would imply an abrogation of traditional state sovereignty, and, as long as such transfer of sovereignty is perceived as a greater threat than thermonuclear obliteration, disarmament negotiations will remain as before—on top of dead center.

*"Threat-Perception and the Armament-Tension Dilemma," by J. David Singer, is reprinted from the* Journal of Conflict Resolution, *vol. 2, no. 1 (March 1958), pp. 90–105, by permission of the Publisher, Sage Publications, Inc.*

# 3

# Internation Influence:
# A Formal Model

*Remaining at the psychological level, and further emphasizing the reductionist element as crucial to our understanding of international violence and war, this paper outlines a scheme for examining the ways in which national governments try to modify or reinforce the behavior of one another.[1] Written originally in 1961 for the U.S. Arms Control and Disarmament Agency as part of their effort to integrate a great deal of speculative work on strategic deterrence (as a form of influence attempt) and arms control (efforts to change the environment within which influence attempts are undertaken), the paper has two objectives. First, it takes the amorphous and ill-defined concept of influence (and, indirectly, power and capabilities) and decomposes it into a systematic set of situations in which influence attempts occur. Second, it articulates a set of hypotheses as to which strategies are most likely to be successful in each of eight influence-attempt settings. Needless to say, our understanding of how conflicts escalate into war will rest heavily on the extent to which we understand the internation influence process.*

Students of international politics often state that power is to us what money is to the economist: the medium via which transactions are observed and measured. Further, there seems to be a solid consensus that power is a useful concept only in its relative sense;

such objective measures as military manpower, technological level, and gross national product are viewed as helpful, but incomplete, indices. The concept does not come to life except as it is observed in action, and that action can be found only when national power is brought into play by nations engaged in the process of influencing one another. Until that occurs, we have no operational indices of power, defined here as the *capacity to influence*. In this paper, then, my purpose is to seek a clarification of the concept of power by the presentation of a formal, analytic model of bilateral internation influence.

Two caveats, however. First, I am using the word "model" in its most modest sense; I mean somewhat more than a conceptual framework, but considerably less than a theory. If, by theory, we refer to a body of internally consistent empirical generalizations of descriptive, predictive, and explanatory power, it is much less than a theory. And since it is not a theory, there is no need to label it "normative" or "descriptive"; it is merely analytical, with normative or prescriptive implications.

Second, it represents in no sense the result of a systematic search of the historical past from which we might draw empirical generalizations. Nor is it a systematic survey of those other analogous worlds from which such generalizations might be drawn: the experimental or empirical literature of psychology, sociology, or anthropology.[2] Recourse to all of these worlds would be valuable, but would go beyond the task I have set myself here. Moreover, such empirical investigations are best not undertaken until we have a clear picture of the sorts of data we seek. To do so in the absence of such a picture might produce some interesting anecdotes, and an occasionally valuable insight, but it would open no direct path toward a body of empirically "verified" and logically consistent propositions of such explanatory power or predictive reliability as to be useful for either theory building or policy purposes. Until these prior model-building steps have been taken, any comprehensive search of the historical literature would be little more than a fishing expedition, or a ransacking of the past in search of support for *a priori* convictions.

In attempting this preliminary examination of internation influence, I will begin with a search for clarification of the central concepts and variables; then suggest a systematic linking of them; follow this with a search for some general rules about the role of reward and punishment and promise and threat; and conclude with a discussion of the particular limits and uses of threat.

Some General Properties of Influence

In trying to clarify what we mean by influence, and to articulate its dominant properties, the first point to be noted is that all influence attempts are *future-oriented*. The past and present behavior of the potential influenc*ee* (whom we will label B) may be of interest to A (the influenc*er*) and will certainly affect A's predictions of B's future behavior, but there is nothing A can do about controlling such actions. He[3] may *interpret* the past and present behavior of B in a variety of ways, but obviously he can no longer *influence* it.

The second general observation is that influence may or may not imply a modification of B's behavior. While the tendency (there are exceptions) in both political science and social psychology is to define an influence attempt as one in which A seeks to *modify* the behavior of B, or to identify A's influence over B in terms of "the extent to which he can get B to do something that B would not otherwise do," there are several objections to this restricted meaning.[4] One is that it excludes that very common form of influence which we might call perpetuation or "reinforcement."[5] That is, it overlooks the many cases of interpersonal and intergroup influence in which B is behaving, or is predicted to behave, in essentially the manner desired by A, but in which A nevertheless attempts to insure the continuation of such behavior, or the fulfillment of the prediction, by various influence techniques.

The second (and more elusive) objection is that it implies no difficulty in A's prediction of what B will do in the absence of the influence attempt. If A could, with a very high degree of confidence, predict how B will act if *no* attempt to modify or reinforce is made, then reinforcement measures would be unnecessary and influence would only be attempted when changes (from predicted to preferred) are sought. For a multitude of reasons, ranging from the complexity of the international system to the theoretical poverty of the disciplines which study that system, such predictability is a long way off. Consequently, A will tend to seek insurance against the possibility of an error in his prediction as long as he is modest in evaluating his predictive abilities.

This leads in turn to a third difficulty, if not objection, which is the probabilistic nature of all predictions. Even if the "state of the art" in international relations were well advanced, there would still be no *certainty* (probability = 1.0) on the part of A that B will behave in the predicted fashion. Consequently, there will always be some incentive to attempt to influence.

Having made the case for both the modification and the reinforcement types as legitimately belonging in the influence attempt category, however, it would be misleading to suggest that they are of equal significance in internation relations. The fact is that if A's decision makers are *reasonably confident* that nation B either *will* behave in a fashion *desirable* to A or *not* behave in an *un*desirable fashion, the incentive to attempt to influence B will diminish, and A may conserve its limited skills and resources for application elsewhere. As the forces at work in A's foreign policy processes move A's decision makers in a pessimistic direction, there will be an increasing application of A's available resources to the influencing of B, until the point is reached where A predicts that *no* influence attempt would be successful.

A third preliminary observation is that internation influence is far from a one-way affair. In the first place, while A is planning or attempting to influence B, B is itself exercising some impact on A's behavior. The very classification of B by A as a potential influencee immediately leads to some degree of influence by B upon A, even when B makes no conscious influence attempt. And in the second place, the international system is neither a dyad (duopoly) nor a multitude of dyads. For analytical purposes, it is often convenient to scrutinize only two nations at a time, but we cannot forget that all are influencing all, directly or indirectly, merely by sharing the same spatial, temporal, and sociopolitical environment. Thus, the system is characterized not only by reciprocity but by multiple reciprocity. For the sake of simplicity, however, we will restrict the analysis which follows to direct bilateral relationships between nations of more or less equal power, in which influence or influence attempts are a conscious effort of the national decision makers.[6]

Finally, we might distinguish between an influence *attempt* and the *outcome* of such an attempt. Not only are they not the same phenomena, but they are described and measured in terms of different variables. An influence attempt is described primarily in terms of: (a) A's *prediction* as to how B will behave in a given situation in the absence of the influence attempt; (b) A's *preference* regarding B's behavior; and (c) the techniques and resources A utilizes to make (a) and (b) coincide as nearly as possible. The outcome of such an attempt will be a function not only of (c) above, but also (d) the accuracy of A's prior prediction; (e) B's own value, utility, or preference system; (f) B's estimate of the probabilities of various contemplated outcomes; (g) B's resistance (or counterinfluence) techniques and resources; and (h) the effects of the international environment.

## The International System as an Influence Environment

Before turning to more refined characteristics of influence, let us place its general properties, as noted above, in their larger setting within the international system.

The fact that nations invest a great deal of their energies in attempts to influence one another is perfectly obvious, but *why* this should be so is somewhat less apparent. One of the most frequently recurring themes among the peacemakers is that all would be well if nations would only "live and let live." The naivete of this prescription becomes evident, however, when we recall that such a doctrine can only be effective if one of the following conditions is present: (a) each nation is so completely isolated from all the others that the activities of one have almost no impact on the others; or (b) each is so completely self-sufficient that it has no dependence upon the goals or behavior of the others in order to meet its own "real" and perceived needs. Neither of these conditions characterizes the international system, and it is doubtful whether they ever did. Not only do nations rely heavily upon one another for the commodities (tangible and otherwise) which are sought after, but it is extremely difficult for any nation to trade with or steal from another without this interaction having some impact on some third party.

But this is only part of the story, and it is the part which is equally applicable to relations among many other forms of social organization. The international system has another characteristic which distinguishes it from other social systems: Each actor has the legal, traditional, and physical capacity to severely damage or destroy many of the others with a considerable degree of impunity. In interpersonal, interfamily, or other intergroup relations, regardless of the culture, normative restraints and superior third-party governors are sufficient to make murder, plunder, and mayhem the exception rather than the rule. But in internation relations the gross inadequacy of both the ethical and the political restraints make violence not only accepted but anticipated. As a consequence, the scarcest commodity in the international system is security—the freedom to pursue those activities which are deemed essential to national welfare and to survival itself.

To be more specific then, we might assert that under the survival rubric the highest priority is given to autonomy—nations are constantly behaving in a fashion intended to maximize their present and future freedom of action and to minimize any present or future restraints upon that freedom. In such a system, no single nation can afford to "live and let live" as long as the well-established and widely recognized anarchic norms are adhered to, acted upon, and anticipated by most of the others. Any social system must contain some inevitable competition and conflict, but in the international system they are handled in a more primitive fashion. Moreover, there seems to be only the barest correlation between the way a nation pursues its interests and the nature of its leadership or its sociopolitical institutions. To suggest otherwise would be, to quote an excellent analysis of the problem, to commit the "second-image fallacy."[7] Rather, we might more accurately conclude that the international system itself is the key element in explaining why and how nations attempt to influence the behavior of one another.

### Perceived Behavior as a Determinant in Influence Attempts

Though the international system is definitely one in which influence and counterinfluence attempts are a dominant characteristic, our interest is in analyzing the factors which tend to produce any given such attempt. The first prerequisite for an influence attempt is the perception on the part of A's decision makers that A and B are, or will be, in a relationship of significant interdependence, and that B's future behavior consequently could well be such as to exercise either a harmful or beneficial impact on A.

Not too long ago, most nations were in such a relationship with only a handful of other nations. Even in today's highly interdependent world, one still finds, for example, little interaction between Paraguay and Burma or Egypt and Iceland. Moreover, no nation has the resources to engage in serious efforts to influence a great many of the others at any given time; we select our influence targets because of the perceived importance of our relationship to, and dependence upon, them. In addition, there is a particular tendency to concentrate such efforts upon those nations with which we are already in a highly competitive and conflictful relationship, devoting far fewer resources to those with whom our relations are either friendly or negligible.

Not only do our perceptions of interdependence and conflict-cooperation strongly determine whom we will attempt to influence, but, as subsequent sections will suggest, they affect the types of influence attempt we will make and the likelihood of success or failure in that attempt.

### Predicted Behavior as a Determinant in Influence Attempts

The second determinant is that of the *predictions* which A's decision makers reach regarding the nature of B's future behavior: What is B likely to do, in the absence of any conscious influence attempt by A? This expectation may be of two rather distinct types. One deals with the affirmative *commission* of an act, and the other deals with the more passive *noncommission* or *omission* of an act. In the first case, illustrations range from the American expectation that, in the absence of any conscious influence attempt by ourselves, India might endorse a troika arrangement for arms control supervision, to the fear that the Soviet Union might employ military force in an effort to drive us out of Berlin. In the second case, we think of such examples of noncommission or failure to act as Germany *not* meeting its ground force commitment to NATO, or mainland China *not* participating in a disarmament conference to which it had been invited. Though one can often describe expected acts of omission as ones of commission (*i.e.*, Germany *refusing* to draft more soldiers or China *rejecting* the conference bid), and with somewhat greater conceptual straining even describe acts of commission in the semantics of omission (India *not rejecting* the troika, or Soviet *not refraining from* force), one or the other of these two emphases is almost always more obvious and salient to the influencer, as discussed in the next section.

### Preferred Behavior as a Determinant in Influence Attempts

Finally, and perhaps most important, there is A's *preference* regarding B's future behavior. Without preferences, the perception of B's present behavior and predictions regarding his future behavior have only limited importance to A and would exercise only a minor impact on A's tendency to invest in an influence attempt. Here we might illustrate by reference to the contingent predictions suggested above. The United States prefers that India *not* accept the troika plan, and that the Soviets *not* use force in Berlin; we care much less what administrative arrangements New Delhi *does* accept, or what other techniques the Kremlin *does* apply iñ Berlin. Our main concern is that they *not* do the specified, but partially likely, act from among a number of possible acts. For us, removing or reducing the likelihood of what they *might* do is much more salient than which one of a host of alternative acts they select in its place. Conversely, the concern of our decision makers (as the potential influencers) over what the Germans do *not* do with their limited manpower, or what the Chinese do *not* do regarding a disarmament conference, is much less than our concern that they *do* engage in the act which we prefer. The salience of what they *do* do is higher for us than the salience of what they do *not* do, because of the nature of our preferences.

To illustrate this crucial distinction further, let us suppose that A predicts that B is about to supply weapons to an insurgent group opposing the government of an ally of A's; A's concern is not so much what else B does with these weapons as with seeing that B does *not* supply them as predicted. B might, at this juncture, scrap them, sell them to a neutral nation outside the immediate conflict area, or give them to an ally, and A would have a much less intense concern over which of these alternatives B selected. In another—and very real—case, A might want desperately to prevent its major adversary B from supplying nuclear weapons to an ally of B with whom A has had a number of disastrous military encounters in the past. Whether B gives these nuclear weapons to another ally, converts them for peaceful uses, or retains them in its own arsenal is of much less moment than that they *not* be supplied to the feared recipient. In both these cases, avoiding or preventing a specific outcome is of considerably greater salience to the influencer than is the remaining range of alternatives open to B.

Perception, Prediction, and Preference:
Their Composite Effect

So far, we have discussed individually the way in which A's perceptions, predictions, and preferences will tend to move him toward an influence attempt *vis-à-vis* B. What are the implications of combining these three sets of variables? More particularly, what are the possible combinations, and what is the effect of each upon: (a) the motivation of A to undertake an influence attempt; (b) the relative amount of effort required for success; and (c) the techniques and instruments A will employ?

As table 1 will indicate, there are eight possible combinations of influence situations, four dealing with cases in which A prefers that B *do* a certain act ($X$) and four in which A prefers that B *not* do a particular act, but do almost anything else (non-$X$ or $O$) instead. The first four might be called *persuasion* cases, and the latter four *dissuasion*. Since each of these eight cases would seem to pose a different type of influence problem for A and call for varying combinations of techniques, let us list and label them as in table 1.

Table 1. Types of Influence Situations

|  | Persuasion Situations: A Prefers X | | | | Dissuasion Situations: A Prefers O | | | |
|---|---|---|---|---|---|---|---|---|
|  | *1* | *2* | *3* | *4* | *5* | *6* | *7* | *8* |
| Preferred future behavior | $X$ | $X$ | $X$ | $X$ | $O$ | $O$ | $O$ | $O$ |
| Predicted future behavior | $X$ | $X$ | $O$ | $O$ | $O$ | $O$ | $X$ | $X$ |
| Perceived present behavior | $X$ | $O$ | $X$ | $O$ | $O$ | $X$ | $O$ | $X$ |

In cases 1 through 4, A prefers that B do act $X$, and in cases 5 through 8, A prefers that B *not* do act $X$, but do $O$ (anything else but act $X$). Cases 1 and 5 are relatively simple and normally would call for no impressive influence attempt: B not only is already acting or not acting as A prefers, but the prediction is that such behavior will continue into the relevant future. Cases 2 and 6 are, however, slightly more interesting: Again B's predicted behavior is seen as congruent to that which A prefers in the future, but A observes that for the moment B's behavior is different from the preferred or predicted. And in cases 3 and 7, B's present behavior *is* what A prefers, but the prediction is that it will *not* remain so without any effort on A's part. Finally, in cases 4 and 8 we have the most difficult situation for A: he perceives B not only as not behaving as preferred, but as unlikely to do so in the future, without some effort on the part of A. These, then, are the eight typical situations confronting a potential influencer, ranged more or less in order of increasing difficulty.

The Influencee's Decisional Calculus

Having examined the varieties of influence situations, we should notice one other consideration prior to evaluating the range of techniques available to the influencer in these situations. This is the influencee's decisional calculus: the abstract dimensions upon which he (*i.e.*, those individuals who, alone or together, act on behalf of the target nation) weighs a range of conceivable outcomes in any influence situation. For every outcome which any decision maker can conceive of as possible, there are at least two such dimensions. The degree to which he likes or dislikes the prospect is called the *utility* or *disutility*, and the likelihood which he assigns to its ever occurring is called the *probability*. Both of these are, of course, subjective variables: preferences and predictions of the influencee (B).

In the abstract, the combined judgments which the influencee makes along both of these dimensions will determine his contingent expectations and thus his response to the influence attempt. Before combining them, let us examine each in somewhat more detail. As to the subjective utility dimension, we proceed from the assumption that an individual or a group does—implicitly or explicitly—have a set of benchmarks by which it is able to arrange conceivable outcomes (be they threatening, rewarding, or more typically, both) in some order of preference. These benchmarks usually derive from value systems and goal structures and, though they are by no means uniform from nation to nation, those relevant to foreign policy behavior tend to have a great deal in common. For example, outcomes that appear to restrict short-range freedom of action will almost invariably be placed very low in any such utility scale; they will be assigned a high *dis*utility score. Conversely, those which seem likely to minimize the power of some other competing nation (A, C, or D), and hence reduce that competitor's capacity to restrict one's own (B's) freedom, are normally rated high on utility. If we go much beyond these basic drives of .nations, however, we get into the peculiar webs of their secondary goals and their varying formal and informal ideologies.

We may pause, though, to point out that national preferences are by no means fixed and permanent. Not only do successive parties and factions in a particular nation bring differing preference structures into office, but even the same subgroup or individuals undergo value changes while in power. Consequently, we must not overlook the usefulness to A of seeking to induce attitudinal (especially value and preference) changes in B's elites as an alternative means of influencing B's existing preferences, or of seeking to change them now in order to make it easier to appeal to them later.

Nations do not, however, commit themselves to actions merely because one possible outcome of such actions seems to be extremely attractive or because it may avoid an extremely *unattractive* outcome. No nation has the unlimited resources and skills which such behavior would require. They must compare these possible outcomes not only in terms of a *preference* ordering, but also in terms of their estimated *likelihood*. And just as there are important differences between nations in the matter of assigning utilities and disutilities, there are equally important (but more subtle) differences when it comes to assigning probabilities to future events. Some are more willing than others to play the "long shot," and pursue an objective whose probability of attainment may be quite low. On the other hand, there do seem to be strong similarities here, as in preference ordering. A perusal of recent diplomatic history strongly suggests that most nations are remarkably conservative in foreign policy; *i.e.*, they seldom commit resources and prestige to the pursuit of an outcome which seems improbable—no matter how attractive that outcome may be. Individuals, on the other hand, reveal far greater ranges of risk-taking propensities, with many getting a large measure of psychological satisfaction from the low-probability-of-success decision (see Edwards 1962).

The point which concerns us here, however, is that—despite idosyncrasies on one or the other dimension—nations *combine* both sets of considerations in responding to an influence attempt or in any other choice situation. In graphic terms, we might depict this combining process as in figure 1.

Suppose that A is attempting to influence B by the use of threatened punishment in order to deter B from pursuing a certain goal (*i.e.*, A is trying to induce *O*). If B attaches a high utility to the outcome which he is pursuing while the threat which A makes would—if carried out—constitute a loss whose disutility is of approximately the same magnitude, these two considerations will tend to cancel out and the important dimension becomes the probability of each outcome actually eventuating. If B estimates that the probability of A carrying out the threatened punishment is quite low (let us say .25) and that he therefore has a .75 probability of pursuing his goal *without* A executing the threat (perhaps its cost to A is seen as quite high), the resultant product would tend to make B adhere to

**Figure 1.**   Influencee's Decisional Calculus.

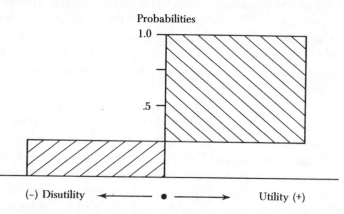

his original intention. Though he realizes that there is *some* chance that A will act to punish him, the combined probability and disutility is so much less than the combined probability and utility of A's *not* acting that B decides to take the gamble.

This is, of course, a rather abstract model, and it not only deviates from the kinds of articulate, as well as implicit, calculation which policy makers employ, but it oversimplifies the choice situation with which nations are ordinarily confronted. For example, B must normally weigh his utility-times-probability product against not only the disutility-times-probability of A's *threatened* punishment but against a range of greater or lesser punishments which A is capable of inflicting and against the probability of each of these occurring.[8] Furthermore, this model assumes that choice situations and influence attempts, as well as their possible outcomes, occur at discrete and identifiable moments in time. The assumption is extremely useful for analytical purposes, but it pays insufficient attention to the overlapping and highly unpredictable time scale along which such situations and alternate outcomes may occur. Finally, it ignores three important quantitative considerations. One of these is the relative weight which a given set of decision makers might assign to each of the two dimensions; in their implicit fashion, nations do differ in the degree to which they emphasize either the probability or the preference element in their appraisal of an outcome. Moreover, these two dimensions are by no means psychologically independent; the more highly valued an outcome is, the greater the tendency to exaggerate the probability that it can be achieved (the wish is father to the thought), and conversely, when a probabil-

ity looks very low, the tendency will be to downgrade the attractiveness of the associated outcome. Thirdly, there is the tendency toward polarity: As subjective probabilities move up or down from .5 they will be exaggerated in the direction of either the certainty (1.0) or the impossibility (0.0) end of the scale. Recognizing these limitations does not, however, invalidate this influencee's decisional model. It merely reminds us that it cannot be employed for either descriptive or predictive purposes in a purely mechanical way. But used in a careful, self-conscious fashion it can be helpful to both the study and the execution of the decision process. For the scholar, much of the confusion and mystery of that process could be clarified, and for the policy maker, regardless of the weights and values he attaches, it could identify the range of alternatives and indicate the implications of each. It might even lead to consideration of a larger number of alternatives and hence mitigate one of the greatest causes of diplomatic disaster—the prematurely restricted repertoire.

### Influence Techniques

Up to this juncture, we have delineated some of the general characteristics of internation influence, identified its three major dimensions alone and together, and articulated a submodel of the influencee's decisional considerations. Now let us turn to the two broad classes of technique available to the influencer: threat and promise. Each may be used either to modify or to reinforce, although, as we shall see later, not with equal efficacy. Each has an appropriate role, but careful choice must be made in determining which is best suited to the various classes of influence situation.

By *threat* we mean the communication to the influencee (B) by the influencer (A) that if a certain preferred act ($X$) is not taken, or nonact ($O$) is not avoided by B, there is a given probability that A will act to punish B in a particular fashion. That punishment may take the form either of withholding a reward, denying a preference, or positively damaging that which B values.[9]

By *promise* we mean the communication to B that if he complies with A's preference, A will, with some given probability, act to reward B. Again, that reward may range from withholding a contemplated punishment to the enhancement of one or more of B's values and preferences.

Threat and punishment and promise and reward go together, but the distinction must be constantly kept in mind. Threat and promise refer to nothing but contingent, probable future events, while punishment and reward are concrete acts that already have taken, or are in the process of taking, place. Thus punishments and rewards may be threatened or promised respectively, and they may be contemplated by both A and B, but they have none of the empirical concreteness in a future situation that they have in past or present situations.

In internation influence, reward and punishment for past or ongoing behavior may be said to serve primarily as a link between B's experiential present and his anticipated future. The outcomes which accompany particular actions in B's past and present serve as predictors of such associations in the future. Therefore, the use of rewards and punishments by A should be devoted, among other aims, to increasing the *credibility* of the promises and threats which he transmits to B. This is not to suggest that credibility-building is the only relevant use for reward and punishment in attempting to influence an opponent of approximately equal power. Present-oriented techniques might also serve the supplementary purposes of (a) hastening an influencee's *shift* from nonpreferred to preferred behavior; or (b) reinforcing current preferred behavior if there is some indication that it might not continue.

Be that as it may, we have little evidence at this point to justify any confident generalizations regarding the applicability of the four types of influence technique to the eight classes of influence situation. Let me therefore pause briefly in order to hypothesize, before going on to suggest what next needs to be done to develop a coherent theory of internation influence. Given the speculativeness of these hypotheses and the limitations of space, let me present them in the form of a chart which is merely an extension of table 1.

In table 2, we have added five rows to the original three. Row 4 emphasizes that cases 1, 3, 5, and 7 are reinforcement or behavior stabilization situations, in which A, regardless of his predictions, prefers that B's future behavior remain as it is in the present. Conversely, cases 2, 4, 6, and 8 are modification or behavior change situations, again disregarding A's prediction of B's future behavior.

Then in rows 5 and 6 we ask whether punishment and reward (our present-oriented techniques) are relevant to each of these, while in 7 and 8 the question is whether the future-oriented techniques of threat and promise have any applicability. In situations 2 and 6 and 1

## Table 2. Hypothesized Relevance of Influence Techniques

| | Persuasion Situations: A Prefers X | | | | Dissuasion Situations: A Prefers O | | | |
|---|---|---|---|---|---|---|---|---|
| | *1* | *2* | *3* | *4* | *5* | *6* | *7* | *8* |
| Preferred future behavior | X | X | X | X | O | O | O | O |
| Predicted future behavior | X | X | O | O | O | O | X | X |
| Perceived present behavior | X | O | X | O | O | X | O | X |
| Reinforce or modify | R | M | R | M | R | M | R | M |
| Punish? | No | P | No | Yes | No | P | No | Yes |
| Reward? | Yes | No | Yes | No | Yes | No | Yes | No |
| Threaten? | P | Yes | Yes | Yes | P | Yes | Yes | Yes |
| Promise? | Yes | Yes | Yes | Yes | Yes | Yes | Yes | Yes |

and 5, the ambiguous entry (P for "perhaps") is meant to suggest that A's confidence in his prediction regarding B's future behavior will be controlling. If, in the two ambiguous modification situations (2 and 6) A's subjective probability that B will change without any influence attempt is not satisfactorily high, A might consider punishment as an appropriate technique. Likewise, in the two ambiguous reinforcement situations, A's lack of confidence in the prediction that B will continue his present behavior might well impel him to utilize threat as a form of insurance.

### Some Experimental Possibilities

Can the hypotheses in table 2 be confirmed or disconfirmed? Clearly, the preferable long-run method of proof would lie in direct testing within the international system, and though the bona fide experiment is hardly a routine matter in this area, some modified form of it seems possible. I refer to the so-called *ex-post-facto* experiment, in which we determine some reasonable and fixed limits in time and space, and then devise the criteria by which our population of influence situations is selected. From that population we then sample in such a manner as to get a sufficient number of each of our eight classes of influence situation. Of course, the difficulty here is in setting up and refining the operational rules by which we identify each of these situations in the ongoing welter of diplomatic history so as to permit reliable classification by two or more independent coders. Once the experimental cases are selected, we then go on (again with operationally articulated criteria) to determine which influence techniques were used in each. Following that, we measure—with either a simple yes-no dichotomy or (at later stages in the study) a graduated scale—B's compliance with A's preference. By correlating our predicted influence attempt outcomes with those observed in the "experiment" we get a test of the hypotheses generated by the model.

If this particular project worked out satisfactorily, a more nearly "natural" experiment, involving *pre*diction rather than *post*diction, could be attempted. In this case, we would want to ascertain the applicability of our historical findings to the real world of the present, by classifying some sample of influence situations as they unfold, and then actually predicting the attempt outcomes before they are known.[10] The central problem in either of these "real world" types of study is that of developing, pretesting, and applying measures or indices of an operational and unambiguous nature. Until we have devised a means for recognizing and recording perceived, predicted, preferred, and actual outcomes, such experimental research is impossible.

While the development of measures for the key variables in internation relations goes forward—and it is doing so at much too slow a pace—another possibility remains. Systematic data gathering with relatively operational classification and measurement criteria has been going on in sociology and social psychology for several decades. As a consequence, these disciplines have accumulated a respectable body of empirical generalizations regarding intergroup and interpersonal influence. These generalizations, moreover, have two possible linkages to a theory of internation influence in particular and internation relations in general. The more useful one is that of empirical inputs into the interpersonal and intergroup interactions which occur in the foreign policy decision process. There is no reason to expect that the findings in industrial, academic, community, or other social settings should be too disparate for application to the interpersonal and intergroup influence processes which obtain in governmental policy processes. Enough inference is called for, however, to preclude any automatic assumption that the results will be identical in, for example, business firms and foreign ministries.

Requiring a somewhat longer inferential leap would be the effort to analogize directly from our interpersonal and intergroup results to internation influence situations. Though this sort of extrapolation is often more legitimate than the naive critic would have us believe, one must first demonstrate a high degree of isomorphism between the setting which produced our data and that to which the generalizations are to be applied. But whether one employs the indirect or direct application of these psychological and sociological findings, it should be clear that they cannot suffice for confirmation or disconfirmation of our hypotheses. The final test must be made with data from the real world of internation relations.

## The Limits and Uses of Threat

Despite these caveats, it might nevertheless be useful to examine some of the propositions that emerge from the interpersonal and small group literature, in order to suggest their possible relevance. For these illustrative purposes, let me summarize and speculate upon some of the empirical findings regarding one of the four major influence techniques: threat. First, what do these interpersonal experiments suggest regarding the dysfunctional effects of this future-oriented influence technique?

The most obvious undesirable side effect of threat is that it may often do no more than "modify the form of anti-social behavior which is chosen" (Comfort 1950, p. 74). In other words, by making one path of behavior which is undesirable to A seem unattractive to B, A may merely drive B into other behavior which, while more attractive to B than the action which has been associated with impending punishment, is equally undesirable to A. And for A to threaten B for so wide a range of anticipated acts could either exceed A's capabilities or create such a dilemma for B that he has no choice but to carry out the action and accept (or retaliate for) the consequences.

As to the effect of threat on B's capacity to respond rationally, a number of disturbing findings appear. First of all, threat often exercises a negative influence on B's capacity to recognize signals and communications accurately. Not only might B become less able to identify and respond to neutral messages, but he may also lose some of his ability to recognize subsequent threats. Thus, threats might well make it difficult or impossible for A to convey the very messages upon which his capacity to influence B must rest (Smock 1956). An equally dysfunctional result is that of "cognitive rigidity": the inability of B to respond efficiently and adequately to changing stimuli, and a consequent breakdown in B's problem-solving capacity (Pally 1955). This experiment also suggests that the ultimatum is a particularly dangerous form of threat, inasmuch as the subjects dropped markedly in their capacity to respond appropriately when the experimenter reduced the time allowed for making that response.

Similar results were found when subjects were threatened with a physical shock. The threat of this highly undesirable possibility produced a high level of stress and markedly hampered their problem-solving capacity (R. E. Murphy 1959). The stress induced by threat has also been reported as not only degrading an actor's predictability but his own confidence in that predictability as well (Landfield 1955).

On the other hand, there is a tendency among some observers of international relations to exaggerate the dysfunctional effects of threat and to ignore the very real role it does and must play in the contemporary international system. These critics forget that most of the influence and social control situations from which they analogize take place in an ordered, hierarchical environment in which influence is normally based on legitimate authority, recognized roles, and accepted norms. To illustrate, one of the more thorough analyses of social power lists five major bases of such power: reward power, coercive power, legitimate power, referent power, and expert power (French and Raven 1959). Of these five, reward often requires more resources than are found in a highly competitive influence relationship between equals, legitimate power can only be exercised through the frail channels of international law or organization, referent power is generally absent between rivals, and expert power is seldom recognized by national decision makers. Coercion via threat is, by process of elimination, one influence technique upon which we must continue to rely until we have markedly modified the international system.

A point worth noting in this connection has been demonstrated in a number of experiments on group performance under varying degrees of stress. The results "indicated that the performance of the group was best under mild stress" (Lanzetta 1955). If threat produces stress (as we assume), the absence of threat may often be as detrimental to successful influence attempts as too heavy a dose of it. The lesson seems to be to use enough threat to generate stress, but not so much as to produce high anxiety. If the upper threshold is crossed (and it varies from nation to nation and situation to situation) we are likely to generate the sort of undesirable effects which reduce B's rationality. The less rational B is, the less likely he is to consider the entire range of alternative actions open to him, and the less likely he is to analyze adequately the implications of each such alternative. Anxiety induced by excessive threat may be said to contract B's repertoire of possible responses as well as his ability to predict the payoffs associated with each.

In the same vein, we have some experimental results which indicate the impact of threat upon group cohesiveness. While it is generally true that external threat exercises a unifying effect, there are some important exceptions, and when cohesiveness in B is reduced, some serious problems arise (e.g., Pepitone and Kleiner 1957). Admittedly, internal divisions may lead to a diminution in B's power *vis-à-vis* A, thus enhancing the credibility of threat even further. But on the other hand, a drop in B's relative power is not necessarily a precursor to compliance. Moreover—and this is a frequently overlooked consideration—the creation of divisions within B may make an intelligent response to A's influence attempt almost impossible. When B's top elites are in firm control of their nations, they are more capable of: (a) making rational choices; and (b) making the concessions necessary to A's successful influence attempt. Conversely, when they are preoccupied with critics, conspirators, and powerful "inevitable war" factions at home, they must resist influence attempts in order to stabilize their shaky power base.

Another point that seems to emerge in regard to the role of threat (and, to a lesser extent, promise) is that B must be provided with two categories of information. One is the precise nature of the action which A prefers to see B take ($X$) or avoid ($O$); without this information B is unable to respond in a mutually advantageous fashion. The other is the availability of alternatives, and this is particularly relevant in the dissuasion situation.[11] For A to try to dissuade B from a given action (to induce $O$) when B must clearly do $X$ or something similar to $X$, without helping B to ascertain which $O$ acts are available to B and acceptable to A, is to call for a probable showdown. If B is completely thwarted, he has little choice but to resist.

Also worth considering, in terms of the limitations of threat, is the fact that A may well be able to modify B's decisional calculus in the appropriate fashion and still fail in his influence attempt. Even though, in the time period implied by the effort to modify or reinforce, B might find A's preferences the most attractive alternative behavior for himself, he may nevertheless refuse to comply. The explanation lies primarily in the context of longer-range considerations on B's part: precedent. B (or A, when in the B role) may be concerned that his compliance under threat will set a precedent. Each time that B does the rational thing and complies with the preferences of A, he increases A's propensity to believe in the efficacy of threat, and to utilize it again and again. As a result, B has an additional reason to do the thing which is, in the specific and discrete influence situation, irrational. Moreover, B must combine his refusal to comply with a more-or-less immediate counterinfluence effort, in order to compel A to reallocate those resources which might otherwise be used to carry out his threat. In a simplified way, this is what an armaments race boils down to: threat and counter-threat, coupled with the drive toward ever-increasing military capabilities with which to resist these threats.

Conclusion

Without laboring the need for an empirically based theory of internation influence, it should not be amiss to note that its lack is both a cause of intellectual embarrassment to political science and a menace to the human race. For the policy maker to select intelligently from among a wide range of alternative decisions, he must be able to predict their outcomes with *some* degree of reliability. Such prediction requires far more than the "hunches" by which we operate today; having no sound criteria for behavior choices, the policy maker will tend, as he has in the past, to adopt those policies which have the most powerful or persuasive advocates, regardless of the accuracy (or even the existence) of the "theory" upon which those policies are allegedly based. And as long as the nations continue to base their policies on so flimsy a foundation, our understanding will be incomplete, our predictions unreliable, and our policies deficient. I would not want to exaggerate the reliability of any theory we might build, nor minimize the difficulties of injecting it into the policy process, but neither we nor our adversaries of the moment can afford these present deficiencies. The probabilities of error are already much too high, and the disutilities could be disastrous.

# 4

# Escalation and Control
# in International Conflict:
# A Simple Feedback Model

*The final paper in this section represents the most explicit formulation of my theoretical orientation vis-à-vis conflict and war among nations.[1] To reiterate a point made earlier, it is not a theory, but merely a systematic statement of one observer's understanding of the escalation process, combined with some suggestions as to how we might weaken the self-aggravating elements in the escalation process, and strengthen some of the self-correcting ones. One finds here, as in many of my papers, both an explicit effort to bring the concepts and findings of our own and other disciplines to bear on the problems of war and peace, and a willingness to lay out specific short- and middle-run policy suggestions. That most of the latter have not been accepted reflects, I suspect, less on the supposed naivete of the proposals than on the failure of social scientists to help reshape the psychocultural context within which the policy process unfolds in most nations. This theme receives considerable attention in later papers here and in Volume II.*

As social conflict in the modern world becomes increasingly menacing, our incentive to control it likewise increases. But conflict control requires not only the will but the knowledge, and our knowledge remains painfully inadequate. In no sector is the need greater and the knowledge base more flimsy than in international politics. As I see it, this scientific inadequacy stems from several general conditions.

First, the amount of scientific research, in which we test our ideas against the benchmarks of evidence, has been close to negligible. This is partly a function of the reluctance to treat international politics in general, and international conflict in particular, as legitimate objects of scientific inquiry. First of all, there is the still widespread belief that all social phenomena are so unique and discontinuous that the search for general laws is a waste of time. In addition, the conventional definitions of loyalty usually require a predisposition to believe in the righteousness of your own nation's cause, making rigorous analysis of foreign policy problems quite unnecessary; and scholars have been no more immune to this definition than have their fellow citizens.

Another factor, one which is by no means independent of the others, may well be the nature of the models we use. While a good model is no guarantee of success, a poor one virtually assures that we will, at the least, ask the wrong questions. While the others also deserve further examination, it is to the problem of a model of international conflict that this paper is addressed. Before suggesting a particular one, however, a few preliminary comments are in order.

## Some Criteria of a Useful Model

What do we mean by a "good" model in the social sciences? There are several epistemological requirements, as well as some substantive ones, to which we will turn in a moment. First, it should reflect whatever we think we know at the time and should be neither ignorant of, nor incompatible with, such knowledge. Second, it should be built around propositions and conceptual relationships that can be put to the test. Third, it should be adaptable to relevant new knowledge and not need a drastic overhaul with each discovery, as long as that discovery is logically and empirically compatible with the model. A fourth and related requirement is that, in accord with the general systems outlook, the model should be able to exploit relevant knowledge from other disciplines and other levels of social organization. Fifth, it should provide an accurate—if simplified— representation of the referent world. Finally, it should be built around as few variables as are necessary to eventually account for the phenomenon to which it is addressed.

These criteria (as well as the definition of model which they imply) are, of course, not beyond dispute, and the social sciences today are alive with epistemological and methodological controversy. But given the nature and generality of our concern in this paper, they seem to offer one set of appropriate benchmarks.

Shifting now from the affirmative to the negative, what are the inadequacies of the models generally in use for the analysis of international conflict? In addition to their failure to often satisfy the above methodological requirements, most of the typologies and models now found in the literature suffer from a number of more substantive inadequacies. Among these, two would seem to be critical. One major flaw is that most extant models are not explicitly longitudinal, and I mean this in two senses. One, there is little systematic effort to compare a large number of international conflicts over time, in order to ascertain recurrent regularities or secular trends. Two, there is little explicit concern with the extent to which the configuration of any given conflict may be both a consequence of those which preceded it, and a predictor of those which follow it. That is, international conflicts are seldom treated as either comparable (in the operational, systematic sense of the word) or sequentially interdependent.

The second, and perhaps fatal, flaw lies in the general tendency to focus on only one level of analysis, rather than treat the interactions that occur across the several relevant levels. That is, the model often puts most of the explanatory burden on: (a) human nature; (b) certain "vested interests" or economic classes, as in the Marxian mode; (c) specific types of "aggressive" nations; or (d) the structure and culture of the international system. Despite the rhetorical attractiveness of many such single-level models, and the virtue of parsimony, I suspect that they will lead us nowhere.

As I see it, a model that might carry us to a fuller grasp of the dynamics of international conflict must not only satisfy the epistemological criteria outlined above, but must also be both *longitudinal and multilevel* in its focus. The present paper represents a modest effort to approximate such a model, to explore its contemporary policy implications, and to suggest some possible ways in which the ominous consequences of its dynamics might be mitigated, if not eliminated. Lest there be any misunderstanding, however, there is no suggestion that it satisfies all of the key requirements of a scientific model; it is, at the least, preoperational.

## Interlocking Political Systems:
## National and International

In any examination of global politics, there are at least five levels of analysis available to the observer. First, there are the three which are most frequently utilized in the disciplines as mentioned above: the individual, the national state, and the international (or global) system. For the period from approximately the Treaty of Utrecht (1713) up to perhaps World War II, these three system levels turn out to be more or less sufficient, but for a longer historical view, into the future as well as into the past, two additional levels of analysis seem essential. Let me refer to them in general terms as the subnational and the extranational. With the individual, plus these four classes of social system, one can put together a fairly complete description— cross-sectional or longitudinal—of global politics for any epoch (Singer 1969a). In this section and the next, I will focus primarily on the national and global levels and will reintroduce the subnational and extranational levels later in my argument.

One of the more important but less obvious characteristics of modern international politics is the fact that the same sets of individuals play the dominant role in both national and international politics. These are of course the national political elites—those individuals who comprise what is variously called the government, the regime, the administration, or less frequently, the court. *Within* the national state there may well be other elites with a fair degree of autonomy who dominate provincial or local politics, but who are normally subordinate to those who comprise the national regime. On the other hand, however, there does not yet exist any legitimate authority *above* the hundred-odd national regimes. Given the extraordinary durability of the doctrine of national sovereignty, most influence in international politics is exerted in a horizontal direction—nation vis-à-vis nation—and almost none in the downward vertical direction. There are of course many international organizations and even some supranational ones, but they remain largely the creatures of their nation members; hence we speak of the global system as "subsystem dominant" (M. A. Kaplan 1957b).

One consequence of this state of affairs is that national elites constitute the major actors in both national and international politics. Moreover (and of central concern to us here), the demands of these two systems are often quite incompatible. Behavior which leads to success in one environment may often lead to disaster in the other, and vice versa. The balance of this paper will be addressed to:

(a) the nature of the conflicting incentives, temptations, and constraints which are generated by both sets of systems; (b) the resulting inadequacy of their homeostatic mechanisms in terms of their impact on both the escalation and control of the conflict process; and (c) some possible short-run modifications of a self-correcting nature that might reduce the magnitude of these conflicts which are so inevitable a part of international politics.

What makes a certain level of such conflict almost inevitable? In the global system, given the absence of legitimate supranational authority, national elites have relied on the ultimate threat of military power as a means of defending "national interests" against possible interference by other nations (Singer 1965d). This traditional reliance on force as the final arbiter has, in turn, inhibited the growth of an alternative basis for internation harmony: a widely accepted normative code which provides for peaceful settlement of the inescapable conflicts and clashes of interest. In the absence of both coercive authority and normative consensus, and in the presence of many material and psychic scarcities, the only remaining basis for cooperative behavior is a utilitarian one—a payoff matrix which rewards short-run restraint and accommodative strategies.

And there is the rub. If two nations become involved in a conflict, the general options are two. The most natural, and probably the most frequent, response is to stand firm on the original conflict-inducing position, or perhaps to even increase the original demands. Within most well-integrated national societies, this response tends to be applauded, and the limited opinion survey data suggest that it generally enhances the popularity of the regime. Moreover, this behavioral response tends to reinforce the existing norms of world politics ("this is the way things are done") and hence the probability that other nations will handle subsequent conflicts in the same general manner.[2] But this is a fairly standard and stylized opening-round routine, and not particularly pregnant with danger. The critical question is whether the protagonists now succeed in "backing off" sufficiently so that routine diplomatic procedures can be brought into play, or whether one or both parties continue to press their claims in the original and more vigorous fashion.

The other general option is to recognize the opening moves for what they are and to then initiate and reciprocate moves of a more conciliatory nature. But the probabilities are all too high that the competence, courage, or patriotism of one or both sets of elites will then be challenged by a "hard-line" domestic opposition, be it a legitimate political party in a democratic system or a less institution-alized faction in a more autocratic system.[3] Moreover, the efficacy of that challenge from the "outs" will generally be high, due largely to the prior actions of the "ins." That is, political elites cannot man an army and finance a military machine without some sort of psychological mobilization (Deutsch 1953). In persuading an appre-ciable sector of their society that preparedness is necessary, they inevitably create a climate which must be relatively responsive to jingoistic appeals from the opposition. As a matter of fact, had some minimum psychic and material preparedness not existed prior to the conflict, there might well have been no conflict; had the nation been militarily weak or psychologically unprepared, the competitor would probably have had its way *without* any diplomatic conflict.[4]

Having suggested the general linkages between the national and the international systems, creating largely incompatible sets of demands on the national elites, let me now describe the feedback processes in greater detail. My purpose here is to indicate more precisely where the self-aggravating tendencies are greatest, and then to suggest some possible feedback mechanisms whose effects might tend more in the self-correcting, and less in the self-aggravating, direction.

## Some Self-Aggravating Links in the Feedback Process

Given the limitations of space here, the most feasible procedure is to bypass any *thorough* description of the structural, cultural, and physical setting within which foreign policy decisions are made and executed, and concentrate rather on those few variables which are critical to the scheme outlined here. As I suggested earlier, one of the reasons for our failure to understand and more fully control interna-tion conflict is the tendency to treat such conflicts as discrete and separable events. By viewing them rather as part of an oft-recurring feedback process, we might better appreciate that the way in which any single conflict is handled is both a consequence of prior such experiences and a predictor of the way subsequent ones will be handled. The position taken here is that intranational and interna-tional events all impinge on one another in a cyclical and ongoing process within which the self-aggravating propensities frequently exceed the self-correcting ones by an unacceptably large amount (Deutsch 1963; Milsum 1968). As I see it, there are four points at which the self-aggravating effects of positive feedback are particularly critical during the internation conflict. Let us discuss them, one at a time, noting how the traditional Western notion of confrontation between a government and its citizenry is viewed here as a highly symbiotic relationship.

## Regime and Opposition[5]

The first point is found at the apex of the foreign policy hierarchy within the nations themselves. The political elites, often unwittingly, "paint themselves into a corner" in order to accomplish two short-run objectives when engaged in diplomatic conflict. One objective is to demonstrate to the foreign adversary that they have both the intent and the capability to stand firm; the other is to head off any potential domestic attack based on the inadequacy of that intent and capability. In order to satisfy both these objectives, however, the elites will ordinarily resort to the kind of rhetoric which does little more than "raise the ante" all around. The intended message to the adversary may be merely one of firm determination, but since it will be heard at home as well, it cannot be too conciliatory; as a matter of fact, by making a commitment audible to the domestic audience, the decision makers may hope to make their foreign policy threats more credible, given the domestic costs, real or apparent, of capitulation.

Assuming for the moment that the early verbal behavior has demonstrated the appropriate degree of firmness abroad and at home, what are the likely consequences? The adversary's regime, of course, "will not be intimidated," and so responds in public messages to the several relevant audiences. At this point in the scenario, if we are fortunate, the interactions shift toward quiet diplomacy, both domestic oppositions turn their attention to other matters, and the publics forget the episode in short order. Suppose, however, that the prior episodes had been so handled by the regime, the opposition, and the media that there was sufficient public hostility toward this particular adversary, and, further, that the opposition prefers not to let the issue drop out of sight. Quite clearly, the regime takes a fairly serious domestic risk if it ignores the cries for justice, revenge, national honor, and so forth; but it takes a different (and also far from negligible) risk of escalating the conflict if it tries to satisfy the domestic critics.

## Military and Psychological Mobilization

In order to examine the second point at which positive feedback can get us into serious trouble, we can focus on another set of factors. Let us assume, reasonably enough, that both nations in the conflict are moderately well-armed by contemporary (but nonnuclear) standards, but that one enjoys a discernible superiority over the other in the relevant military categories, and that neither can turn to close allies for diplomatic or military support. The regime of the disadvantaged protagonist, having permitted the conflict to pick up some momentum, now has the choice of: (1) bluffing; (2) retreating; or (3) delaying while improving its military position. The first can lead to a sharpening of the conflict and a more humiliating retreat later (or even a stumbling into war); the second makes it vulnerable to political attack at home. Thus there is always some temptation to try to close the manpower and weapons gap in order to bargain from a position of parity or even of greater strength. If this route is taken, the regime will first need to launch a program of psychological mobilization, without which neither the volunteers and conscripts nor the funds for weapon acquisitions might be forthcoming.[6] In the process of mobilizing public and subelite support for these preparedness activities, however, two new conditions are generally created. First, the adversary is not likely to sit idly by, watching its superiority disappear; its regime therefore embarks on a similar set of programs. Second, both publics must become more persuaded of the need to resist the menace to their nation's security, and as a consequence, offer a more fertile ground for any militant domestic opposition. Given the almost irresistible temptation to exploit this state of affairs, the net effect is to raise hostility levels in both nations, and therefore to raise the expectations as to what would constitute a satisfactory settlement, negotiated or otherwise. Since these rising expectations tend to be fairly symmetrical, neither regime is in as good a position to compromise as it was during the first round of the conflict. The probability of further escalation, diplomatic rupture, or war itself is now appreciably greater.

*Amplification via the Media*

Let me now turn to a third source of danger in the cyclical conflict processes that seem to characterize so much of international politics. To this point, the role of the media has had little attention, yet mass communications would seem to play a particularly central role in helping along the self-aggravating process. Again, the differences between a highly autocratic and a relatively democratic nation are seldom as profound as contemporary elites—communist, anticommunist, and other—profess to believe.[7] At almost any point along the autocratic-democratic continuum, the political elites need the media, and the media need the political elites, be they regime or opposition. The regime relies on the media to help mobilize the population, to bargain with and ridicule the domestic opposition, and even to communicate with other nations.

While "managing the news" may be simpler to arrange when the party in power exercises *formal* control over its media, any effective and stable regime has little difficulty in doing so. First of all, the words and actions of the elite are, by definition, newsworthy, and therefore widely transmitted. Secondly, members of the regime have information available which can be of great help to the reporter or commentator to whom it is made available. Thus, by judicious release or righteous restraint, government officials can all too readily help or hinder the careers of many media employees. Thirdly, as regimes become more conscious of the need—and possibilities—of domestic propaganda, they begin to recruit media people into their very ranks as "public information" officers. Many newsmen are thereby involved in competition for these often attractive bureaucratic positions, and one way to stay in the running is to describe the appropriate agency's activities in a generally favorable fashion. While access to, and control over, the media may not be quite as simple for the "outs" as for the "ins," factions or parties in legal opposition are not without the sorts of media amplifier they need to berate the regime for being "soft on . . . ," devoid of courage, or incapable of defending the nation's honor. In some nations, each political party has its own newspaper, magazine, or radio station; in others, the possibility of the opposition coming to power can make the media somewhat more responsive than might be expected.

I am not, in this section, arraigning the media of most nations on charges of "selling out," although the charge would be far from groundless. Rather, despite the existence of a vigorous and independent sector in the media services of many nations, the general impression is that the incentives work to make these institutions a major factor in amplifying internation conflicts and contributing to the positive feedback, escalation, process.[8]

## The Redistribution of Domestic Power

The fourth and final factor to be considered in this analysis is the effect which a nation's participation in an escalating conflict can have upon the distribution of social, economic, and political power within the society. Without accepting those conspiratorial models that see generals and "munitions makers" actively fomenting rivalry, conflict, and war, one must be extraordinarily naive to expect no systematic biases in the foreign policy preferences of those who comprise the military-industrial-labor-academic complex.[9] Even more than with newsmen, questions of ambiguity will regularly tend to be resolved in the hard-line direction by many military officers, corporate executives, labor leaders, government bureaucrats, defense intellectuals, and technical consultants, as well as by the standard phalanx of patriotic organizations. Given the state of our knowledge about international politics, most foreign policy problems are indeed matters of opinion, rather than of knowledge or fact; and *in* matters of opinion, the point of view which gets the benefit of the doubt can be expected to win out most of the time.

The problem here of course is that in most nations the major positions of power—as well as the public plaudits—go to those who are in the ideological mainstream; this seems to hold even if the mainstream of the moment is allegedly pragmatic and nonideological, as in the United States of today and (probably) the Soviet Union of tomorrow. Having acquired power, prestige, and credibility by advocating, or acquiescing in, the modal foreign policy positions, these middle elites are seldom likely to shift too far in their views. And they are particularly reluctant to shift toward a position which could be interpreted (or misinterpreted) as giving aid and comfort to the enemy, whoever the enemy of the moment may be.[10]

Furthermore, as the intensity of the internation conflict increases, the higher becomes the value of the professional and extracurricular services of these middle elites. On top of this, as their individual influence and status increases, the *size* of their sector also increases. When the armed forces expand, officer promotions accelerate, and when more weaponry is being designed and produced, more engineers and technicians are promoted and recruited; even academics in the social and physical sciences find that foreign policy conflicts lead to increased opportunities for money, status, and influence in the modern world. The high-energy physicist or the professor of biology has his role to play in the preparedness program, just as the political scientist or anthropologist finds himself consulting on log-rolling tactics in international organizations, military strategy, or counterinsurgency. If for no other purpose than to give intellectual legitimacy to the conventional wisdom, academics are almost as likely to be co-opted into the foreign policy mainstream as are the more obvious members of the military-industrial complex.

My point here is that it does not take a so-called totalitarian regime to mobilize key sectors of the society. The basic properties of the sovereign national state in the industrial age are such that this mobilization occurs with little effort. No secret police, no dictatorial government, not even any veiled threats are required to generate the joint "conspiracies" of silent acquiescence and noisy affirmation, once a nation becomes embroiled in a conflict of any intensity, or a preparedness program of any magnitude. For the past century or so, the self-correcting mechanisms have gradually withered, despite the assumptions of economic liberalism and classical democratic theory. In the absence of vigorous countervailing forces within the nations or in the larger global community, the self-correcting mechanisms of international politics are feeble indeed, with the consequence that all too many of the inevitable conflicts among nations are free to grow into costly rivalries and, occasionally, into tragic wars. In the next two sections of this paper, I will try to suggest certain limited procedures whereby these four basic self-aggravating mechanisms might be partially weakened or controlled.

## Self-Initiated Self-Correcting Mechanisms

Is the interaction between and among nations in global politics as dismal as I have painted it here? Is the relative potency of our self-correcting mechanisms this much less than that of the self-aggravating ones? Considering the paucity of scientific, data-based research on global politics, and the absence of much evidence at either the micro- or macro-level, it is a bold man indeed who will take so dim a view and embrace so pessimistic a formulation. The picture may, admittedly, be overdrawn for the sake of emphasis, and it may even be that, as a science of global politics develops, this characterization of the nation-state system will turn out to have been seriously incomplete or inaccurate. Be that as it may, responsible scholars must act on the basis of the little that *is* known, even while working to enlarge that knowledge base, and the interpretation offered here will therefore have to suffice for the moment. The word "act" is used quite literally, since I intend in this section to shift from the descriptive mode to that of prescription. Having described how these aspects of the global system look to me, I suggest now a set of modifications that might conceivably reduce the probability of any given conflict erupting into war, and of any given war converting great parts of humanity into a nuclear rubble. With so much at stake, it is embarrassing to propose so little, but the approach offered here may possibly generate some self-amplifying processes of its own.

Assuming that this formulation is essentially correct, and reiterating that a great deal more rigorous research is called for, I would single out the communication and norm-setting modes in the national societies as one of the more high-priority points of intervention. Until decision makers become aware of the many ways in which their own behavior exacerbates conflicts, and converts the possibility of win-win outcomes into zero-sum ones, the chances are they will continue to act in the traditional manner, and often find themselves, unexpectedly, in situations from which extrication is costly or impossible.[11] Journalists and commentators, for example, could pay more attention to the effects of such moves on the internation conflict itself, and less to the effects on the regime's popularity vis-à-vis its domestic opponents. The various private or semiindependent groups that exist to influence foreign policy, or the public's attitudes toward it, could devote as much of their attention to the regime's conflict management techniques—and the opposition's acquiescence in, or exploitation of, such techniques—as they do to pursuing their own particular and narrow goals or applauding "our side" in world politics.

Perhaps more critical, but demanding much more in the way of short-run self-sacrifice, is the need for the political "outs" to play a less opportunistic game. Support for a "vigorous defense of the national interest" may win the opposition a word of thanks from the regime, and criticism of "a policy of appeasement" may win it some support from a large sector of the public, but neither of these tactics is likely to make the regime's diplomacy any more successful.

Nor will they have led to any improvement in the future. This is an utterly critical phenomenon in all social processes, yet it is very rarely acted upon, or even appreciated, and may deserve more than this passing allusion. Consider for a moment the relationship between two classes of phenomena in any social system: beliefs (embracing preferences, predictions, and perceptions) and behavior (including verbal, decisional, and physical). Every public action, especially if taken by a highly visible reference figure, exercises some impact, however minor and however indirect, on the beliefs and attitudes of those who observe or hear about the act. It may lead to the strengthening and reinforcement of some attitudes among some people, and to the weakening or modification of some attitudes among others. Given this dynamic interdependence, it behooves us to pay attention to the possible consequences of every foreign policy action that occurs. Each act of the opposition—no matter how weak its power or how cynical the public—helps shape those attitudes which will, in turn, shape the behavior of many of the participants in the foreign policy process. If, for example, the "ins" and the "outs" are seen to agree on the rights and wrongs of a foreign policy conflict, many citizens will conclude that there *is* no other reasonable position. And if they disagree to the extent that the regime is accused of appeasement, the regime will either modify its policy in a more militant direction, or try to *appear* as if the policy were indeed at least as militant as that advocated by the opposition "outs." Either way, citizen attitudes will be strengthened in a more nationalistic and short-ranged direction.[12] Unfortunately, many of those so influenced will be reference figures who themselves are "opinion influentials."

The importance of these positive feedback mechanisms is relevant not only *during* conflicts and crises, but before and after. If a conflict is finally resolved in a more or less satisfactory fashion, the contending regimes are likely to emphasize the diplomatic "victory" they have achieved by their firmness in the face of the adversary. Once again, this may enhance their prestige for a few weeks or months, but the main effect is to increase the popular expectation that all subsequent conflicts will end in victory-through-firmness. If it ends unsatisfactorily for one side, the norm is a refusal to acquiesce in the "unjust" outcome, and a pledge to redress the nation's grievances at the earliest opportunity. In either case, the prognosis for peaceful resolution of future conflicts is not favorable. Likewise, there is a great and naive myth in many more or less democratic societies that elections have one purpose and one purpose alone: to decide which party or faction shall be in power. Thus the campaign strategists first try to ascertain the dominant views of the various voting blocs and then proceed to pander to these views. With few exceptions, then, election campaigns—because they receive fairly wide and sustained publicity—tend to serve as a powerful reinforcement for existing views on many domestic and some occasional foreign policy issues. And, as I have already mentioned with some frequency, these are not views which make it easy for decision makers to pursue peace abroad and honor at home.

For the information channels to play a useful part in reducing the dominance of positive over negative feedback mechanisms in international conflict, several groups will have to contribute. Scholars need to identify which points are most critical in different classes of conflict and which behavioral patterns account for most of the self-aggravating and self-correcting tendencies. Journalists and other media people need to take a more detached and critical view, accepting the important difference between their professional roles and those of politicians.[13] Politicians need to appreciate the trade-off between short-run tactical gains vis-à-vis the domestic opponent and the middle-run liabilities that accrue when, in negotiating with foreign elites, they find little room for maneuver.

At first blush, these look as if they might indeed be steps which individuals and groups in each nation could take on a unilateral basis (C. E. Osgood 1962). If they could be taken unilaterally, one might feel somewhat more optimistic, but the fact is that too much progress along these lines in any single nation could put that nation at a modest (some would say disastrous) disadvantage vis-à-vis other nations in the global system. After all, each of these steps implies, almost by definition, some reduction not only in the level of political and psychological mobilization within the affected nation, but also a longer-range trend toward public resistance to the standard mobilization appeals. When the attentive public in a nation becomes more sophisticated, farsighted, and tolerant of compromise with foreign powers, its regime must enter diplomatic bargaining at a disadvantage. As a matter of fact, a favorite ploy in such bargaining is to inform the adversary that one's own public (or legislature, or press, etc.) just would not accept a particular settlement, and certain concessions must therefore (and regrettably) be requested in order to get an agreement which could be "sold" at home. If this is indeed an accurate portrayal, the only way to start the trend toward more realistic diplomacy is for the initiative to be taken by those nations which are clearly in the strongest bargaining position in any such negotiations. On the other hand, a generally accepted dictum in diplomacy is that the stronger power *need* not negotiate and the weaker one *dare* not, and this has all too often been the rule applied.

## Some Negotiable Mechanisms

Let me shift now from some of the reforms which might be taken—albeit with some risks—within individual nations, to some which might conceivably be negotiated between and among nations, the better to mitigate the oft-disastrous consequences of positive feedback in international conflict. These suggestions will strike many as utopian and unrealistic, and if realism be defined as conventional, they clearly are vulnerable to this charge. But, as many observers, from E. H. Carr (1945) onward have pointed out, nineteenth-century diplomacy is pregnant with disaster in the environment of twentieth-century technology and ideology. If these interim measures of a palliative nature (or measures of a comparable sort) are not instituted, those who think and act in national state terms will find their system shattered even sooner than some predict. In my judgment, the national state is already beginning to falter in its ability to solve a variety of problems (domestic and international) and is beginning to lose the support and loyalty of its citizens. New forms of social organization are already in the wind, and though their precise form remains far from discernible at the moment, my guess is that one or another of these alternative forms will in time supersede the nations as major bases of human organization.[14] The major question probably is whether these transformations will come about in a relatively nonviolent fashion, or as a consequence of a major military catastrophe.

### Moderating the Media

Be that as it may, let me outline in the barest detail some possible arrangements which might be negotiated in either an overt or tacit fashion between and among certain members of the international system. Focusing first on the role of information and/or propaganda, it was noted earlier that much of the self-aggravating tendency in international conflicts may be attributed to the attitudes and expectations that are generated and reinforced within important sectors of most societies. Suppose for the moment that we could readily devise a measure whereby, via content analysis, it could be ascertained how many bits of self-correcting and self-aggravating information are being directed at the public in a given nation (Singer 1963b). Given the rather rapid advances in computerized content analysis (Stone et al. 1966; Holsti 1969) and the respectable fund of experimental data which social psychologists have accumulated, there is no reason to believe that we could not design a system which produces a weekly or biweekly index of the ratio between exacerbating and ameliorating information addressed to each population from within. Presented in matrix form and published widely and frequently, the domestic output within each nation regarding all other nations could show: (a) which other nations are receiving most of the attention in each nation's media; and (b) how much of that attention is of a hostile, neutral, or friendly nature.

When the attention level reaches a certain threshold, the international agency in charge of the enterprise could begin to make and publish more frequent analyses, and if the ratio of self-aggravating to self-correcting output approached some previously agreed magnitude, the offending government and their media would be sent a prompt warning. If the ratio is exceeded, certain penalties of an appropriate nature might be imposed, although their precise characteristics need not be discussed here. More important than any sanctions, however, is the mere fact that national governments would themselves be alerted regarding the extent to which they may be losing their freedom of action and painting themselves into that diplomatic-political corner alluded to earlier.

Now, some will argue that such a system requires some degree of government manipulation and management of the news, and I can only agree. This might be a serious liability if the news were not now managed and manipulated in most societies, but, persuaded as I am that the virtue of most mass circulation newspapers and other media was lost at a very early age, I cannot work up much concern over threats to the innocence of a "free press." The relationship between media and regime is sufficiently symbiotic in most nations that this innovation need hardly cause a ripple.

*Inhibiting Mobilization Rates*

World War I is often cited as the classic example of a disaster which might have been avoided had not the contending regimes been in such haste to mobilize their armies. But military mobilization was merely the last phase in a feedback cycle which had begun years before, and many historians marvel at the fact that the war's onset was delayed as long as it was. Almost from the close of the Franco-Prussian War in 1871, the major powers began to build not only their alliances but their war machines. While new war plans were being drawn up, slow but steady mobilization of human and material resources got under way. Between 1907 and 1914, for example, the annual defense budgets for the Triple Entente rose from 152 to 239 million pounds sterling, and those for the Triple Alliance rose from 84 to 151 (Richardson 1960a, p. 87).

All of this of course provided little more than the volatile setting for the six weeks embracing Ferdinand's assassination (June 28), the Austrian ultimatum (July 23), the Serbian and Austrian mobilization of active and reserve forces (July 25), Russian mobilization (July 29 and 30), and the catastrophic events of July 31, which saw the German ultimatum to Russia and the French and German general mobilization. Had there been some regulatory mechanism at work during the arms race period and during the 1914 crisis period, the war might well have been avoided. That is, whether the pace of escalation is slow and steady (as in most arms races and other conflicts which require long lead-times) or rapid and erratic (as in most crises), there is a very high probability that the positive feedback tendencies will gradually increase in their potency, while the negative and self-correcting ones will diminish in their effectiveness. Left unchecked, such processes must culminate in war.

Suppose, however, that the leading nations were to negotiate an agreement according to which every increase in military capability were accompanied by an increase in certain socially desirable nonmilitary capabilities. For example, every expenditure for weapon development or production might be matched by an equal expenditure for agriculture or housing, and every training program for military personnel might be matched by a comparable program for social science training, and so forth. While military preparedness in today's world is often enhanced by a wide range of activities, with farming improvements freeing more manpower for the army, and education in social or physical science tending to have militarily useful by-products, this is not the major problem. Of course, the stipulated activities and allocations should be of maximum *con*structive usefulness and minimum *de*structive usefulness, but even when they are not, the regulatory mechanism will have a self-correcting effect due to the bounds imposed by every society's resources. Human resources are strictly limited, and fiscal-material resources can only be increased at modest rates; thus, whatever is allocated to essentially peaceful activities is to some extent not available to military activities. Moreover, in order to make the inhibitions against rapid preparedness even stronger, the signatory regimes could agree on a steeply graduated scale of matching allocations; modest expenditures might be matched on a one-for-one basis, but above a certain threshold the compensatory allocation might be set at the square or the cube of the military allocation. In the same vein, per capita preparedness expenditures could provide the basis for contributions to the United Nations and its specialized agencies, also on a steeply progressive scale.

Considering the two kinds of mobilization—psychological and material—which need to be retarded and inhibited if international conflicts are to terminate in war less frequently, several regulatory mechanisms have been suggested. Others come to mind, but discussion of them will have to wait. It will surely be suggested by some readers that, if the sorts of agreements of unilateral initiative outlined here could be undertaken, we probably would not need them in the first place. This argument overlooks a fundamental concept in social science, which, when put in the common vernacular, is known as "timing." If we recognize that the relationship between any two social entities tends to fluctuate widely between friendship and hostility over any length of time, the virtue of the approach suggested here becomes more evident. During periods of low tension, for example, nations can negotiate agreements whose contemplation at another time would be labeled as treason. If we can take advantage of such opportunities, national regimes can establish—before conflict develops—procedures which will give them or their successors considerably greater flexibility and more options *during* a conflict.

A closely related virtue is the fact that few arrangements of this type could be expected to function unless an extranational or supranational agency of appreciable authority were responsible for the bookkeeping. The information which such an agency puts out must be highly credible, and such credibility depends on accurate data inputs, the development of valid indicators, and rigorous data analysis. This proposal is, then, very similar to that which Quincy Wright

(1957) made in the inaugural issue of the *Journal of Conflict Resolution*. Recognizing the need for and the feasibility of "a quantification of political and psychological conditions and trends" over a decade ago, he recommended the establishment of a privately endowed, nongovernmental World Intelligence Center which would publish periodic reports on the "climate of international relations."[15] As important as the information itself might be, a useful by-product might be some modest increase in the skepticism with which attentive citizens greet much of the information disseminated by their own governments and national media.

*Negotiation by Proxy*

In a paper several years ago, I tried to outline another procedure whereby the conflict resolution responsibilities of foreign policy elites might be partially depoliticized (Singer 1965d). Let me recapitulate here in a few paragraphs. One way in which to reduce the positive feedback effects might be to recapture some of the *virtues* of eighteenth- and nineteenth-century diplomacy and put this delicate activity back in the hands of relatively anonymous professionals. As a number of labor unions and industrial firms do, so might national governments hire law firms whose staff would actually conduct most of the negotiations.

The "mercenary negotiators" would, first of all, be thoroughly briefed on the background of the conflict and would also engage in independent research in order to have a balanced and accurate understanding of the issues. They would then be informed as to the range of outcomes that are envisaged, from most satisfactory to least satisfactory, with the quid pro quo associated with each such outcome. Having been so briefed, they would then negotiate with their sponsors a contingent fee schedule such that the most satisfactory outcome within a fixed period of time would produce a maximum fee, whereas no agreement at all would bring little more than compensation for their basic costs. In addition to providing some insulation from domestic politics, such an arrangement would require the contracting regime to specify exactly what it was after and exactly what concessions it was willing to make in pursuit of those goals. This, of course, is not always done under present conditions.

The negotiators could, but need not be, nationals of the government they represent, and need not necessarily be lawyers. Quite possibly a United Nations diplomatic academy (or an agency such as UNITAR) could take on the responsibility of training and perhaps accrediting people from a variety of professional and national backgrounds. While this approach may have something in common with traditional practices of conciliation and mediation, it remains clearly a matter of domestic jurisdiction. It is not proposed here that negotiation be compulsory or that any third party intervene in any fashion. All that need be agreed is that, for a given conflict, both parties will resort to mercenary negotiators, the better to remove the conflict from the temptations of domestic maneuvering and global posturing.

A mechanism such as this admittedly raises a number of new problems, ranging from the danger of collusion between the lawyers representing the governments involved, to resistance to a secrecy which violates the basic tenets of democratic practice in some nations. Other difficulties also come to mind, but in my judgment it is an innovation which deserves further investigation and perhaps limited experimentation between and among those nations whose conflicts are mild and whose populations have little distrust of one another. If it were to prove successful, the practice might spread, and even though it represents a move away from the direction in which global politics seem to be headed, it might help us to survive the dangerous transitions that lie ahead.[16]

To sum up this section, three possible mechanisms for the more successful resolution of international conflict have been outlined. While the assumption is that preconflict agreement on such hopefully self-correcting arrangements could be reached, it should be noted that any of the three *could* be, in principle, undertaken unilaterally, with the hope that others might, in turn, also adopt them.

## Conclusion: Homeostatis and System Transformation

In this paper I have tried to describe those relationships and behavioral propensities which account for a great deal of the positive feedback in the international system, and therefore help to convert many minor disputes into major conflicts. Now, some will urge that the mechanisms which I propose in order to strengthen some of the negative feedback tendencies are little more than short-run palliatives, and that the system is basically inadequate in its present design. The charge is probably a fair one, but it is also somewhat beside the point; this is the nature of the system as it now stands, and our immediate concern is to devise those homeostatic mechanisms which will keep the fluctuations in conflict within the safe range. Moreover, there may well be some "natural" tendencies toward more self-correcting behavior even in the absence of such innovations. For example, war has by and large not been a particularly effective conflict-resolving technique in this century, and the nature of the cost-benefit ratio is increasingly appreciated (Singer and Small 1972). Certainly, nuclear weapons and missile delivery vehicles can do nothing but increase that ratio—even if they do contribute somewhat to the tendency toward preemptive attack. Likewise, the drive for overseas possessions, once a major source of international conflict, has become less and less attractive. Colonialism, at least in its older form, just did not pay (Clark 1936). A third element of built-in stability is the trend I noted earlier: an increasing disenchantment with national states and nationalism, even in the "third world"; many of earth's inhabitants are beginning to look for alternative and more efficient forms of human organization. If this alleged trend continues, many regimes will find it increasingly difficult to mobilize support for traditional foreign policies.

Despite these favorable possibilities, the need for supplementary control mechanisms nevertheless remains. We must of course explicitly differentiate between mechanisms which are designed to perform a largely homeostatic function, such as those outlined here, and those designed to initiate a self-reinforcing feedback process which might lead to fairly radical system transformation. Even though we have alluded to some potential tendencies in this direction, we cannot go beyond them here. My major concern, then, has been to formulate a model of international politics which highlights, however crudely, those factors that are most relevant to the escalation and control of the conflict process, and to suggest some short-run adjustments that might keep such conflict within tolerable bounds. The next step—even as the present scheme is being refined and put to the test—is to focus on those elements which might actually initiate and/or accelerate the system transformation process. If such a more complete (and epistemologically satisfactory) model can be developed, it may not only help us to keep the inherent self-aggravating tendencies within safe limits, but also give us what may be a final opportunity to design a global system which is fit for human habitation.

# III

# Policy Analyses
# and Proposals

Having outlined the normative outlook that informs our work on the problem of war and peace, as well as having articulated my theoretical orientation to the understanding and amelioration of that problem, we can now take a closer look at the policy issues involved. While these papers reflect a preoccupation with the Soviet-American conflict of the post-World War II period, there are implicit, and occasionally explicit, reminders that this struggle is by no means unique to that given time and place. Rather, I suspect that the phrase "modern international war" can be applied to a large fraction of the armed conflicts that have, or have nearly, occurred any place in the world over the period since the Napoleonic Wars.

# 5

# The Strategic Dilemma:
# Probability Versus Disutility

*In putting together part III, there were many papers from which to select, including about a dozen written for the less academic readership of journals such as* The Nation, *beginning in the late 1950s. We begin with a paper that focuses on the "hottest" issue of the early 1960s: the relative merits of what was then called a "credible first-strike capability." Some might expect a book review (of Herman Kahn,* On Thermonuclear War *[1960]) written in 1961 to be dated, but I doubt whether that concern is justified here. First, the strategic and psychological principles probably apply to a broad swath of international history. Second, and more ominously, as this anthology is being assembled, the same issue is being debated anew in the capitals of the Northern Hemisphere, even as "détente" remains a guiding principle of Western and Eastern diplomacy. Fortunately, in my judgment, a combination of technological and budgetary constraints in the West plus a rapid Soviet buildup precluded the creation of any but the most temporary credible first-strike capability in the early 1960s. But since we know little more now than we did then about the conditions that increase or decrease the likelihood of war, the arguments of those who see some national, parochial, or personal advantage in yet another acceleration of military expenditures are not easily refuted.*

Perhaps one of the most fruitful ways of examining individual or group decisions is by using a probability-utility model (Snyder et al. 1954; Thrall et al. 1954). In such a model, one is able—for analytical

91

purposes at least—to divide the considerations which went into the decision into two distinct sets of variables. One set deals with the decision-making unit's estimate of the probability of a wide range of outcomes; the more "rational" that decision maker (individual or group) is, the closer he will come to considering, and assigning a subjective probability to, all possible outcomes. The other set of variables concerns the positive or negative value which he assigns to each of these postulated outcomes; in contemporary parlance, these are known as utilities and disutilities.

Such a model has two virtues. For those making the decisions, it compels them not only to delineate the whole range of conceivable (to them) alternative outcomes, but to articulate their value preferences by ranking possible outcomes in order of such preference. It leads to a conversion of implicit values into explicit ones which may be discussed and debated when a choice point is confronted. The second virtue is that it permits the observer to discover the value system of the decision maker or policy proposer, even if that individual or group did not itself make these considerations explicit. Thus, the student of politics is able to translate a welter of subjective decisional criteria into a manageable set of variables, even while recognizing that both are completely subjective to the decisional unit (Snyder et al. 1954).[1]

In Herman Kahn's *On Thermonuclear War* (1960), the author has provided us with an opportunity to employ this probability-utility model in examining a number of proposed policy decisions. He closes his preface by indicating that the book was written in the "hope of decreasing the probability of catastrophe [thermonuclear war] and alleviating the consequences" if it comes. Thus, Mr. Kahn begins with at least an implicit concern for the probability and the disutility of an outcome which concerns us all. What shall concern us in this review is the relative priority he gives to a variety of probabilities and utilities/disutilities in reaching his own decisions and those he would press upon an anxious nation. To put the issue another way, is the author more interested in lowering the probability of nuclear war, or in lowering its destructive effects? Is he more interested in lowering the probability of direct attack or in lowering the probability of diplomatic blackmail? The burden of my analysis will be that, in matters of strategy, interests of this kind are always to a great extent incompatible, and that one is always compelled to assign greater value to one or the other of them. Let us examine, in turn, some of the major policy recommendations which emerge from this long- and eagerly awaited tome.

## The Probabilities of Success

Let us look first at the type of decisions Kahn would have the United States make in order to deter the Soviet Union from various forms of aggressive behavior. That is, what kinds of strategies and capabilities does he predict will produce what kinds of probable outcomes?

Though not completely comparable, the three types of deterrence which concern our author are, for the most part, distinguishable and significant.[2] What he calls Type I deterrence is that intended to prevent a direct strategic assault on continental North America. Type II deterrence is designed to prevent or inhibit extreme provocations—political or military—other than direct assault on the United States. Type III deterrence—which seems to overlap considerably with type II—is intended to restrain the adversary from going beyond certain territorial or weaponry bounds in a limited military conflict. Let us examine the doctrines and capabilities which Kahn considers appropriate to these types of deterrent.

The deterrence of direct military assault on the United States (or Canada) seems to be the one to which he assigns primacy, and he starts out by flogging several very dead horses. First, he implies that his is a voice in the wilderness (if I may mix my metaphors) in urging that the crucial figures are not preattack inventories on both sides, but "estimates of the damage the retaliatory forces can inflict after they have been hit and hit hard" (p. 128). Similarly, he is hardly alone in emphasizing the naiveté of assuming that the victim's[3] retaliatory force will have been launched *prior to the impact* of any opening first strike. The literature, the press, and the halls of the Pentagon are full of talk about hardening, dispersal, concealment, etc., as techniques of achieving "invulnerability"; i.e., preserving enough of one's strike-back missiles and bombers from an attack in order to permit a punitive retaliatory blow.[4]

He then goes on to inveigh against the "finite" or "minimum" schools as being inadequate for the demands of a type I deterrent, noting (metaphorically) that it will have to work in the darkness of a winter night as well as in the sunshine of a bright summer day. This inadequacy, he contends, arises from the erroneous assumption that nuclear war is tantamount to mutual annihilation. As a matter of fact, his entire approach to strategy is based on the assumption that, while it would be an "unprecedented catastrophe" (p. 10), it would not be a limitless one; this will be brought out below in discussing passive defense. By their postulation of automatic mutual annihilation, Kahn contends that the finite deterrers not only overlook the limits of destruction which a damaged strike-back force can inflict, but those limits imposed by an active and passive defense system instituted by the attacker and alerted well in advance of the reprisal. Further, he disputes the notion that a temptation to get in that all-important first strike will be negated merely by the possible loss of a number of population and industrial centers. Next, he ridicules the finite deterrers for neglecting the role of accident, miscalculation, or irrationality in initiating a nuclear-missile exchange. And finally, he assails this school on the ground that it would eschew any emphasis on active or passive defense. Here the straw man becomes too obvious, and it is only by accepting Kahn's definition of the finite deterrence doctrine that we can accept his criticisms as valid.[5] As far as I know, those of us in the finite deterrence school are not opposed to *active* defense (ground-to-air interceptors, etc.) and only some of us are dubious about *passive* (civil) defense. Moreover, none of us would deny the value of pursuing invulnerability and certain types of alert and early warning; nor is there any lack of concern for the probability of accident or miscalculation.

Having slain a rather feeble and fictitious dragon, Kahn then goes on to the problem of the type II deterrent, and here he is more interesting and more accurate. The question now is not so much the obvious one of deterring attack by threat of "certain" reprisal, but of utilizing a military capability for the other and more subtle purposes of diplomacy in an anarchic international system. The goal here has two facets: One is to *prevent the Soviets* from threatening nuclear war in order to make political gains, and the other is to *permit the United States* to threaten nuclear war in order to make its own political gains.

According to Kahn, both of these are only likely to be realized if the United States creates a credible first-strike capability.[6] Thus, one can threaten to use this capability if the adversary does not back down from a threatening position, or if he refuses to accede to a demand of your own. His major illustration here is a Soviet attack (nuclear or conventional) on Western Europe, following which the White House would face an awesome dilemma. The threat to retaliate *could* be carried out, but since it would be based upon little or no counterforce (i.e., able to destroy Soviet launch sites, etc.) capability, and no active or passive defense of consequence, it would not only mean that the United States had *started* the war, but that it would then have to absorb a devastating retaliatory blow. Therefore,

Kahn argues, a finite strategy leaves the West in a terrible quandary, whose resolution can only be achieved by acquiring a counterforce capability and by instituting active and passive defense measures at home. This is essentially what he means by a credible first-strike capability, and though space precludes a fuller inquiry into some of the more fascinating speculations he introduces, this is the essence of his approach.

To the initiated, these seem to be the same arguments made by the advocates of a limited war (conventional and/or nuclear) capability (Kissinger 1957; Morgenstern 1959; R. Osgood 1957; Schelling 1960a; M. Taylor 1959) and though Kahn does favor the development of such a capability in order to cope with these less clear-cut situations, he considers it less than adequate. Furthermore, he would contend that a type II deterrent also requires a preattack mobilization base so that, in times of tension, that base can be visibly mobilized in order to enhance the credibility of one's first-strike threats and impose an additional inhibition against potential aggression or "outrageous provocation."[7]

Summarizing Kahn's proposals for minimizing the probability of nuclear war, we find that he insists on going well beyond the finite doctrine associated with an invulnerable countercity capability to be fired only for retaliatory purposes. He would have the United States develop: a counterforce and hence credible first-strike capability, a doctrine which does not exclude the preemptive or preventive strike, and a preattack mobilization base, including a massive evacuation and shelter program. Without this combination of doctrine and capability, he would argue, one cannot expect to deter the wide range of behavior with which the adversary might be inclined to confront the West. Let us now turn to what is perhaps the most distinct contribution of *On Thermonuclear War*—what if deterrence fails?

## The Disutilities of Failure

As I have already indicated, Kahn considers the institution of passive, civil defense measures to be a major element in reducing the probability of nuclear war.[8] However, he also urges such a program in order to reduce the disutility of such war if the overall deterrent turns out to be unsuccessful. Based on studies which he directed earlier at Rand (Kahn 1957; 1958), his discussion of civil defense centers on the proposition that nuclear war is *not* equivalent to mutual annihilation, and that with appropriate measures, a nation's damage may be materially diminished.

He therefore proposes a one- to two-year program involving an expenditure of 500 to 600 million dollars (more than ten percent of the current annual United States defense expenditures) for: radiation meters (100 million), modifying existing buildings (150 million), research and development in shelter building (75 million), and other programs.[9] His justification is based on the following predictions. If the Soviets were to get in a first strike aimed at SAC bases and the fifty largest urban areas, the casualty level could be reduced from about 90 million to somewhere between 5 and 25 million Americans, were a minimum fallout and evacuation program instituted. A later attack directed at SAC and 157 urban areas could likewise (according to Kahn's calculations) produce casualties ranging from 3 to 160 million depending on the degree of protection in which we have invested (p. 113).

Another argument he makes concerns the recuperative process for the people and equipment remaining after a nuclear attack.[10] He does this by dividing the nation into two "countries": A country contains fifty to one hundred of the largest cities, and B the remaining smaller cities, towns, and rural areas (p. 77). In pointing out that only a small portion of A country's activity is contributed to B country, and that A needs B while B does not need A, he concludes that the resources and skills of B country could rebuild A in about ten years, depending on destruction absorbed. For example, he calculates that with only 2 million casualties, the United States could recuperate economically in one year, while 10 million would take 5 years, 80 million 50 years, and 160 million 100 years. At the end of this chart (p. 34) he asks the rhetorical question: "Will the survivors envy the dead?" He is not sure.

Another crucial element in his case for civil defense and for discounting the destructive effects of nuclear war is his analysis of the genetic hazard, especially in terms of dosages of radioactivity that can be absorbed safely and the degree of illness or malformation we experience even in peacetime. This is an extremely complicated business, which I do not claim to comprehend, and as Kahn points out frequently, it is a highly charged emotional one as well. Thus, rather than discuss his extensive findings and predictions, let me urge the reader to evaluate this material himself. Some have charged Kahn with callousness and a complete contempt for human life because of his statistical approach to casualty and survival figures, but I doubt whether the arraignment is fair.

My own criticism is that the context employed contributes to what might be called the "rising threshold of acceptable destruction," but if one is willing to discuss nuclear war at all one must also discuss the degree of human catastrophe which might be involved. Moreover, it would be irresponsible of the author to have proposed policies which could lead to these consequences without admitting their nature and extent. And since Kahn is one of the few who is not entranced and bewitched by the deceptively optimistic speculations of the deterrent doctrines, it is to his credit that he also gives serious thought to the disutilities which must accompany any low probability of successful deterrence.

## Provocation and Reconciling the Incompatible

Having discussed the author's efforts to minimize both the probability and disutility of failure, let us turn now to the problem of reconciling these two concerns. I have already indicated the impressiveness of Kahn's deterrent proposals, especially those designed for type II deterrence, and it is clear that his case for civil (as well as active, antimissile, etc.) defense is equally compelling. The real question, however, is whether one can advocate a type II deterrent, relying heavily as it does upon counterforce and civil defense measures, without seriously jeopardizing one's type I (direct attack) deterrent. I will argue that this is extremely improbable, and that by adhering to the type II deterrent strategy he recommends we must seriously jeopardize the success of our deterrent of type I. Why should this be so?

Basically, what Kahn is proposing is a highly asymmetrical set of operational codes. He wants us to engage in the sort of behavior which is supposed to deter the USSR, but which, if employed by them, would almost certainly compel us to opt for a preemptive strike. For example, in a crisis situation, he would have the United States engage in one or more of the following acts (pp. 211-15):

1. Put bombers and missiles on maximum alert.[11]
2. Evacuate civilian population.
3. Jam and spoof the other's warning nets.

Without going into a detailed "scenario" (a wonderful word used by strategists in describing their speculative fantasies), it would seem perfectly evident that any one of these acts would produce an extremely high probability of the other's deciding to preempt.

More important, both the counterforce capability and the civil defense system convey an overwhelming impression of first-strike, rather than retaliatory, *intentions*. If one's strategy is purely one of deterrence, and the deterrent is supposed to be a function of certain retribution and punishment, why shoot for inanimate missile pads or air bases, especially if they will have done their job before being hit? Moreover, of what use is a large-scale evacuation or shelter program if you are resigned to accepting the first blow? A counterforce capability is very handy for a preventive or preemptive strike, but almost useless for a retaliatory one. Likewise, civil defense is fine if you have time to evacuate and shelter your population while *your* strike is on the way and if the retaliatory blow may not come for several hours. In other words, to acquire these two capabilities is to generate in the minds of Soviet strategists a high degree of fear, coupled with a rising expectation of surprise attack (Schelling 1960a; Singer 1962a). The record of folly that is man's political history is replete with illustrations of the results of such perceptions, as is the literature of psychological research. Does an adversary of approximate parity back down and surrender in face of such ominous threats, or does he decide on getting in the first of what has come to look like an inevitable exchange of strikes? Unhappily, we can only analogize and speculate on this, as any empirical evidence would be a bit too dramatic, but I would argue strongly for the likelihood of preemption.

Instead of going for counterforce and civil defense, I would suggest that we do exactly the opposite. Since Kahn himself recognizes the destabilizing characteristics of his credible first-strike posture, would he not attribute equal perspicacity to the White House and the Kremlin? Why not press the Soviets for an agreement—easily inspectable—banning the institution of any civil defense construction? He intimates that the Soviets already have begun a large-scale program of training and construction, but produces not a shred of evidence. And despite the asymmetry of present target intelligence, and the greater technical difficulties, why not propose a ban on the further acquisition of counterforce-type target information? Despite the impending functioning of Samos, Midas, and other surveillance satellites, there may still be time to seek a ban on their use for ground target (launch site) acquisition. These devices might rather be assigned to the United Nations and so instrumented as to be useful for surprise attack warning only, but not for target location. Furthermore, there still seems to be plenty of time to institute a ban on tracking missile-firing submarines, though the technology of this may be even more elusive. I hope that Kahn and his Rand colleagues—if these notions make sense—will address themselves to the problems inherent in such an approach.[12]

Of course, my criticism of counterforce and civil defense as constituting a first-strike image is exactly where our disagreement arises. The author considers such visible capabilities as advantageous, and I consider them disadvantageous. The problem is that we employ different criteria of advantage. If we use a minimize-the-probability-of-nuclear-war criterion, both of us agree that such a capability is destabilizing and provocative. And if we use a don't-let-the-enemy-bluff-us criterion, we again agree that it would be useful. But it strikes me as utterly absurd to employ the latter criterion if—as both of us concur—it clashes with a prevent-the-war criterion.[13]

The point is that we cannot have the best of both possible worlds, and must decide which disutilities are most awful to contemplate and therefore which probabilities we want to minimize. Apparently Mr. Kahn dislikes the possibility of an occasional Soviet diplomatic victory more than he dislikes the possibility of nuclear war, while I would—given these two alternatives—opt for the other; the beauty of our probability-utility model is that it makes these preferences painfully clear. However, these are not our only two choices, and it seems perfectly possible that we can negotiate and deal and bargain successfully with the adversary without keeping one finger constantly on the mutual mayhem button.

## Conclusions

Reviewing this book has been a most frustrating experience. Granted, the subject matter is extraordinarily complicated and demands a great deal of speculation. But the author has made it even more complicated than it need be, by arranging the book in an unbelievably whimsical and capricious fashion. And the "tables," normally used to *clarify* an author's ideas, require considerable ingenuity and clairvoyance before becoming coherent; they do, however, because there are so many, serve as a rough substitute for an index, whose lack is particularly noticeable in a book of such discursiveness and chaos.[14] But these are peripheral objections.

My major criticism concerns the substance of Mr. Kahn's recommendations. He calls for an invulnerable strike-back capability to deter direct aggression, but then says that "firing it would result in self-destruction" (p. 526). He demands a counterforce capability to demonstrate our ability to fight as well as deter war, but concludes that this is insufficient. Next he insists on a credible first-strike capability to cope with crises, but admits that it may "destablize type I deterrence" (p. 527). He urges an active air defense capability, but acknowledges that "defense against attack was hard even before the missile age" (p. 100). He presses for passive defense only to recognize that its deterrent effect is so small "that it seems proper to ignore it" (p. 115), and that it may do no more than keep casualties well below 160 million (p. 113). He finds arms control increasingly essential, as an alternative to an "uncontrolled situation [which] . . . involves greater risks" (p. 537), but would "enforce" it by retaining "a credible capability to initiate thermonuclear war" (p. 241). And finally, he recognizes that "even a poor world government might be preferable to an uncontrolled arms race" (p. 7) but implies that its advocates go in for "hysteria . . . excessive accommodation, or unilateral disarmament" (p. 527).

In short, despite many brilliant insights and delightfully sophisticated analyses, the study is laden with inconsistency and is lacking in strategic coherence. Perhaps this must be true of all solutions which are essentially military in nature. It may well be that we and the Soviets are enmeshed in that fabled "prisoner's dilemma," in which the "rational" strategy of each produces a cataclysm fatal to both. Moreover, it is certain that we will not escape the dilemma if we build our strategies on self-fulfilling prophecies.

If Kahn is serious about deterring nuclear war, let him accept a higher disutility if it comes. If he is serious about arms control (and he discusses it often and incisively), let him eschew the postures that will inhibit it. And if he is serious about disarmament, let him begin to study *its* problems. Now that this valuable analysis is completed, I hope that he and his Rand colleagues (and ORO, IDA, and the rest) will get down to an even more difficult, but far more promising, research undertaking: that of converting the international system from one of armed instability to one of disarmed order, where nations can settle their quarrels like tough-minded businessmen rather than ruthless hoodlums. It won't be a Utopia, but neither will it be an Inferno.

*"The Strategic Dilemma: Probability Versus Disutility," by J. David Singer, is reprinted from the* Journal of Conflict Resolution, *vol. 5, no. 2 (June 1961), pp. 197–205, by permission of the Publisher, Sage Publications, Inc.*

# 6

# The Return to
# Multilateral Diplomacy

*Shortly after completing the preceding review and a number of related papers on the military aspects of the cold war, I began a paper that was intended to make more explicit the connection between a nation's military posture and its diplomacy. The Indochinese war was still largely an internal and localized affair and, as suggested above, technology was working against either side's likelihood of acquiring an effective first-strike nuclear force. Further, there was already some evidence in 1961 (when this article was written) that neither superpower could control its allies as it had in the 1945–1960 period. Unhappily, a number of distinguished journal editors were reading the international system differently, and the paper made the rounds among them for a year and a half before being accepted by a journal that was well outside the U.S. foreign policy establishment. Although some thought my argument naive and even dangerous fifteen years ago, it reads much like today's conventional wisdom. Also worth noting is the continuing emphasis on symmetry and reciprocity between conflicting nations—a recurrent fact of international life that has recently been rediscovered by our revisionist historians in the West.*

Though the details are still far from clear, the main outlines of a radical change in world politics are now beginning to emerge. The striking element of this change is, of course, the growing disintegration of the two major coalitions. Incompatibilities of interest and clashes of style, partially hidden during the first fifteen years of the cold war, are now coming to the surface. As the centrifugal forces in the Soviet coalition become more apparent, those latent in the American-led bloc are increasingly free to seek expression, and vice versa. Even though the trend is by no means irreversible, and fluctuations in it are inevitable, the reciprocity of the bloc-breaking process is increasingly evident, with each side responding to anticipated or actual movements toward both tightening and loosening of the other's alliance ties.

This emerging new pattern in international politics brings with it both danger and opportunity. One source of danger lies in the possibility that either of the superpowers may exaggerate the schisms and weaknesses of the adversary's coalition, and assume that a more aggressive diplomacy would encounter little resistance—that exploiting the other's weaknesses and divisions will produce external gain and internal solidarity. As in the past, a miscalculation of the opponent's strength—and more important, his will—could easily lead to a showdown stemming from overconfidence and overcommitment. General war—nuclear or conventional—might readily follow.

Conversely, the perception of *declining* relative power and unity could also generate more bellicose behavior on either side. This phenomenon may normally be expected when one party sees itself in a position of approximate parity, but anticipates a relative deterioration in that power position. Fearing that the adversary will exploit this emerging imbalance in the future, the declining party is under powerful temptation to strike now in order to forestall defeat—diplomatic or military—later.

In other words, as the solidarity of the two coalitions becomes more dubious, accurate appraisal of the power balance becomes more difficult and predictions of each other's behavior more unreliable. The modest stability of the present stalemate shades off into even greater disequilibrium. But this shift away from the familiar bipolarity of the postwar era also offers the United States and the USSR some interesting opportunities. These opportunities are of two kinds: a short-run opportunity to maximize the "national interest" at the adversary's expense in an environment of continuing international anarchy, and a longer-run, more sophisticated opportunity to modify the international system itself. The central problem, of course, is to concentrate exclusively on neither, but to seek the mixture of the two that is appropriate to surviving the present while shaping the future.

Though the two opportunities are intimately connected, let us look at them separately for the moment. In the first place, this is certainly not the time to act as if the Soviet-American struggle is a thing of the past. Not only do serious incompatibilities of our respective legitimate security interests remain, but we have as yet little evidence that the USSR is willing to settle for these legitimate and limited security interests. There certainly is little doubt that the Kremlin's foreign policy code is vigorous and opportunistic. The Russians do not act like a nation which is satisfied with the present distribution of power, influence, or control, and any opening for a cheap gain is most likely to be exploited. Our immediate and continuing task, therefore, is to offer few, if any, such openings in the areas of confrontation.

Thus, our military deterrent must be maintained at a convincing level of readiness. In whatever areas we believe a military deterrent to be relevant and wherever we have both the desire and the capability to stand off any incursion, there should be no doubt as to both that desire and capability. And in the gray areas, while practicing deterrence by ambiguity, we must be prepared for limited and contingent military action, carrying with it the possibility of either gain or loss. In strategic deterrence, regarding both Western Europe and North America, we must likewise demonstrate the capability and credibility of our threat to respond. Moreover, these multiple deterrents must be coupled with vigorous diplomacy in the traditional sense, as well as with the newer strategies of economic assistance and cultural cooperation.

Having recognized these requirements, however, several caveats are distinctly in order. Most important, we must scrap what the game theorists would call the zero-sum, or fixed-sum, outlook. This outlook is one which views every American gain as a Soviet loss, and every Soviet gain as an American loss. It denies the possibility of what we might call win-win or loss-loss outcomes, and sees all outcomes as win-loss or loss-win. Such a model of international politics is not only objectively inaccurate, but strategically debilitating. Not only is it obvious that nuclear war would constitute a loss-loss outcome, but it should also be clear that an effective curb on the arms race could constitute a win-win outcome, in both the foreign policy and domestic requirements realm. For example, the German and Chinese acquisition of a bona fide nuclear capability would most likely be a loss-loss outcome, while stability in the Eastern Mediterranean would tend strongly in the win-win direction.

The point is that we—and the Soviets—must recognize that we have some genuine compatibilities, as well as incompatibilities, of strategic interest.

Two such compatible or common interests deserve particular notice. First, there is the matter of neutralism and nonalignment. In the earlier postwar period, each of us acted as if there were no such thing as marginal utility in picking up allies. Assuming that the signing up of nation N meant an automatic increase in one's own power array and an automatic decrease in the adversary's, we went at alliance building like fraternity men during rush week. Conservatives and isolationists asked whether these allies were "worth" the investment, but they were seldom heeded; in the holy war it was almost sacrilegious to question the wisdom of adding to our phalanx.

Apparently, the Soviets tired of this strategy before we did, and by the close of the Korean War, they were actively encouraging nonalignment in South Asia, the Middle East, Latin America, and Africa. While we suffered the material and political losses associated with the Baghdad and Manila pacts, for example, they were acquiring a reputation as defenders of national independence and self-determination among the underdeveloped and/or uncommitted nations. Though the Cuban and other possible Central American adventures may represent a renewed interest in collecting satellites, the general aim seems to be to deny allies to the United States rather than to add them to the Soviets. But it was not until the recent emergence of the new African nations that we made our own partial shift, and decided that, as long as the USSR was denied them as its allies, there was no point in our paying the costs of making them ours.

Though this represents a sensible approach from the point of view of the national interest of both the USSR and the United States, it fails to appreciate a more important long-run advantage and hence remains something less than a fixed and durable policy. I refer to the potential role of nonalignment in the overall stability of the international system. Almost all students of international politics agree that the closer the system comes to bipolarity, the greater the probability of major war. If most of the nations of the world were in either of the two coalitions, with all lines drawn and little room for maneuver, war would be highly probable. But as we move away from bipolarity to a three-bloc, four-bloc, or multibloc arrangement, the balance of power is given a greater opportunity to operate. With a multiplicity of pluralistic pressures and forces at work, the "invisible hand" of the separate national interests offers a large number of possibilities for bargaining, trade-off, and compromise. Historically, this principle seems to have obtained, and though the international environment—technologically and ideologically—is markedly changed from the 1815–1914 period, for example, the basic diplomatic forces seem to be remarkably similar. If the pluralism of multipolarity is, in fact, likely to be a stabilizing factor, it behooves both superpowers to encourage its growth. Certainly, there will be occasions when to do so may run counter to a short-run objective, but as we outgrow the fixed-sum, win-loss frame of mind, the temptation to engage in shortsighted tactical ploys will diminish.

In other words, we (and, it is to be hoped, though it does not necessarily follow, the adversary) can and should actively encourage nonalignment and pluralism in world politics to a far greater extent than we have encouraged it in the past. And this strategy must apply not only to Asia, Africa, and the Middle East, but to Latin America and to Western Europe as well. For the first time since the creation of NATO and the Warsaw Pact, Europe (West and East) has an opportunity to deviate from, and mediate in, the Soviet-American confrontation there. Those nations need no longer act primarily as pawns in the struggle between the titans, fearful lest a chink in the armor of diplomatic uniformity appear. Their interests are not always necessarily those of either America or the USSR, and the fiction that they are has been perpetuated long enough. Furthermore, the often preposterous demands of intrabloc unity will play a less paralyzing role in the diplomacy of Washington and Moscow. To a large extent, the Soviets could be freed of the inhibitions generated in Warsaw, Prague, and Pankow, and we of the paralysis stemming from Bonn, Paris, and Brussels. Just as Gomulka and Ulbricht have blackmailed Khrushchev, so Adenauer and De Gaulle have deprived the diplomacy of Eisenhower and Kennedy of much of its vigor and flexibility. Bipolarity has converted bargaining into sellout and negotiation into perfidy, with the consequence that both sides have traded skillful maneuver for a straitjacket.

For the West, a trend toward multipolarity need overcome only inertia, shortsightedness, and parochialism, but for the Communist side, such a shift must contend with another and more painful problem as well. I refer to the mythology of the "socialist camp" and the illusion of an ideological monolith. Thus, even as the Kremlin has accepted or encouraged nonalignment outside the Eurasian land mass, it has clung passionately to the monolithic model at and around its geographical center. Perhaps the experience with Belgrade, Budapest, Posnan, and East Berlin in the earlier days, and more recently with Peking and Tirana, will persuade the Kremlin to bend to the inevitable, but it will be, at best, a difficult pill for Khrushchev to swallow. Not only will it weaken (but not destroy) their control over the East European satellites, but it *could* be interpreted as a victory for Mao Tse-tung in the emergent struggle between the two Communist contenders. But that interpretation could, with skillful footwork in the Kremlin and an assist from us, be easily scotched.

Finally, whatever successes the USSR has enjoyed in creating pro-Soviet regimes or opposition parties in the Southern Hemisphere are, to some appreciable extent, attributable to the "wave of the future" notion, which has Moscow as the ideological, technological, and cultural center of an ever-expanding Socialist camp. If the Eurasian section of this camp turns out to be only a loosely cooperating cluster of sovereign states, a sphere of influence rather than a tightly ordered combine, its monolithic attractiveness must be expected to diminish. However, the Kremlin must also appreciate that one of the greatest liabilities of its friends in the newly independent nations is the charge that they are tools of Moscow rather than genuine nationalists; Khrushchev or his successor(s) will have to choose between the two lines.

More to the point, however, is the degree to which we and the Western Europeans will determine whether or not the USSR will permit socialist polycentrism to develop. As I suggested earlier, the rigidity of the alliances is very much a reciprocal affair. As we permit our divergent interests—economic as well as political—to find their expression in foreign policy, the members of the Soviet bloc will find decreasing justification for, and need of, perpetuating their own rigid phalanx.

Of perhaps even greater importance will be the way in which we enter into the Sino-Soviet schism, as enter into it we must. If, as seems evident now, the central issue is which of two strategies will gain most for the nations in the Soviet orbit, we have a most powerful lever at hand. By giving the Kremlin some of the things it wants via tough-minded negotiation, and denying the Chinese any of their objectives which we control, we could seriously tip the balance away from the "hard-liners" in Peking. We can make it profitable for the USSR to be reasonable and we can make it costly for the Peoples' Republic to be bellicose. One possibility of the former is a recognition of Polish claims to the Eastern territories (which, under our present relationship with Germany, is nearly impossible). Conversely, the Chinese and others might draw "the correct conclusions" from our stolid intractability regarding Formosa, Quemoy, and Matsu, or from our active support of India and other nations threatened by Chinese expansionism.

If we and the Soviets can, indeed, accelerate the processes by which the two alliances might be loosened, two other mutually advantageous developments might be set in motion. One, which I shall mention only briefly, concerns the growth of the United Nations system. If the General Assembly and the Secretariat are ever to play a useful stabilizing role in world politics, the lockstep behavior of the Soviet-dominated and (to a lesser extent) Western-led blocs must be modified. What makes any parliamentary or representative machinery operate effectively is the opportunity for log rolling and side payments. This kind of honest bargaining is impossible as long as both sides insist on retaining instructed delegations of nine or twenty-odd votes respectively. As long as "crossing the aisle" is equated with treason, all issues—whether they bear directly on Soviet-American relations or not, and many do not—will be debated and decided in the sterile rhetoric of the cold war. By our permitting defection, the Assembly will reflect much more realistically the central and pluralistic issues of world politics. Likewise, the inevitable and not necessarily disadvantageous politicization of the Secretariat need not be nearly as threatening as it now appears. With every bureau and office a miniature troika or worse, the injection of politics into the international civil service could destroy the Secretariat, but if the nationals on the staff felt less like instructed cold warriors and more like independent experts with the natural biases of their own nationalities, a healthy realism could be developed in this increasingly important vehicle of the international interest.

The second, and more important, development concerns the matter of military relations, and it is on this subject that long-run and short-run considerations most need to be joined. It will avail us little if, as the world returns to some sort of multipolar balance, we follow the atavistic path toward a fortress America. Such a stance will not only deny us diplomatic opportunity, but could readily catapult us from a single crisis to global holocaust. As I suggested earlier, we have no choice but to meet military probes with military power, ranging from marines with carbines to missiles with megaton warheads. But, to counter any present or potential military threat we require more than an impressive range of capabilities and a willingness to apply them in remote places. We need a strategic doctrine appropriate to the shifting international environment. It must be one which not only discourages aggression but encourages competitive coexistence, one which enables us to survive in the present international system while shaping the system of the future. Unfortunately, our post–World War II doctrines, while more or less adequate on the first count, almost guaranteed the perpetuation of that unstable present into the indefinite future.

More specifically, we almost always acted as if *all* the bellicosity originated East of the Iron Curtain and that *none* of it was justified. Without knowing a single detail of postwar events, one would still have to recognize the moral presumptuousness of such an assumption. And even a hasty scrutiny of the cold war era suggests that: (a) the Soviet Union was occasionally doing little more than pursuing its legitimate security interests; and (b) a fair amount of American or American-supported policy could only be interpreted as threatening to those interests. Our military policy has, all too often, reflected our "good versus evil" model of the world and carried the implication of a holy war against the infidel.

Perhaps the most dramatic index of such a posture is found in the short-lived and ill-starred "credible first-strike" doctrine which had emerged rather clearly by the time of the fiscal 1963 defense budget and which evaporated by the time the 1964 figures were presented. Just as weapons technology had advanced to the point where a successful first strike could be almost ruled out, with a consequent increase in the stability of the standoff, we succumbed to the eternal temptation of nuclear blackmail. Hardening, dispersal, and mobility were making it impossible for either side seriously to contemplate an attack without the prospect of a highly destructive retaliatory blow, when we sought—via accelerated missile production, retention of soft-site IRBM's in Europe, and an ambitious civil defense program—to persuade the Kremlin that an opening strike was *not* out of the question.

Not only did this temporary retreat into strategic simplicity fail to cow the USSR and produce a more compliant adversary, but it may well have had the converse effect. Conceivably, it was the very provocativeness of our hardware, deployment, and articulations which impelled the Soviets first into their abrogation of the nuclear testing moratorium, and second into their Caribbean adventure. More to the point, however, the cries of protest at home—from the universities, the military research organizations, and even some governmental agencies—finally began to strike home. Thus, the defense secretary's famous Ann Arbor speech of June 1962 aroused such concern among those who could never be accused of pacifist tendencies that even the most ardent disciples of the "we-might-go-first" school began to reconsider.

If the fiscal 1963 strategy has not been specifically renounced, it has at least been quietly—but markedly—modified in the past several months. The dismantling of provocative Thor and Jupiter installations in Southern Europe has begun. Missile procurement has almost totally shifted from the highly vulnerable, liquid-fueled Atlas and Titan to the solid-fueled, strike-back Polaris and Minuteman. Civil defense proposals are much more modest. Administration speeches seldom sound like those we were hearing in the spring and summer of 1962. And some might interpret the cancellation of Skybolt and the refusal to go into RS-70 production as further indication of a trend away from the more destabilizing weapons and toward those which need not "go" first.

Most telling of all, however, is the defense secretary's presentation before the House Armed Services Committee on January 30 of this year. First, he noted that "it is even more important today than it was last year that we concentrate our efforts on the kind of strategic offensive forces which will be able to ride out an all-out attack, by nuclear-armed ICBM's or submarine-launched missiles, in sufficient strength to strike back decisively." Second, Mr. McNamara noted that Soviet hardening and mobility make it "increasingly difficult, regardless of the form of the attack, to destroy a sufficiently large proportion of the Soviet's strategic nuclear forces to preclude major damage to the United States, regardless of how large or what kind of strategic forces we build. Even if we were to double and triple our forces we would not be able to destroy quickly all or almost all of the hardened ICBM sites. And even if we could do that, we know no way to destroy the enemy's missile-launching submarines. . . ." Third, he noted that a minimally acceptable retaliatory blow could be assured only by "an extensive missile defense system and a much more elaborate civil defense program than has thus far been contemplated. Even then we could not preclude casualties counted in the tens of millions." He then summarized this series of arguments by specifying that "what we are proposing is a capability to strike back after absorbing the first blow. This means we have to build and maintain a second-strike force."

All of this is a far cry from the McNamara and Gilpatric statements of last year, and a large part of the explanation may be found in the simple arithmetical equation which we use to calculate the survivability of a missile force under different types of offensive and defensive conditions. Very briefly, the calculation widely used up until late 1962 was that (given the numbers the Soviet could build in the mid-1960s) a superiority of three- or four-to-one could permit us to get in a first strike of such magnitude that the remaining enemy force would be capable of mounting a retaliatory blow of so feeble a nature that, with a decent civil defense program, we could "live" with it. The Kremlin's awareness of these "facts" was supposed to produce a more meek and conciliatory diplomacy. But some crucial changes in that survivability equation, plus the hue and cry mentioned earlier, led to some pronounced reappraisals. The effect of the new calculations—which increase the exchange ratio from three- or four- to nine- or ten-to-one—is found in the statement quoted above to the effect that a successful first strike could not be mounted, or threatened, "even if we were to double and triple our forces."

Thus, it is safe to assume that we have backed sharply away from the earlier doctrine, and the probability of preemption—on either side—is consequently reduced. However, some confusion still needs to be cleared up if we are to persuade our adversaries, our allies, the neutrals, and our own informed observers that we have renounced any intention of being the first to use nuclear weapons. This confusion also has to do with the exchange ratio and survivability calculations. Simply stated, if the victim of a first strike could still retaliate with a blow of unacceptable proportions even if hit by a force almost ten times its size (given present and projected hardening, dispersal, mobility, warhead yields, and guidance accuracy), the question is: Why build a force three or four times greater than the Soviets'? Such a ratio is far *less* than we need to get in a decisive first strike, but it is also far *more* than we need to present an effective retaliatory threat. Though the explanation may lie partly in procurement policies, production momentum, and domestic politics, it will not reassure the rest of the world.

Moreover—and this is the central problem now—this American superiority will make it almost impossible to exploit the emerging new shape of world politics with some serious negotiation in either arms control or arms reduction. I have recently completed a content analysis study comparing Soviet and American operational codes, and one of its findings strongly supports the widely accepted thesis that neither power in a conflictful relation will negotiate seriously from a position of significant inferiority. Under present American plans, the Soviets will remain in that position of strategic inferiority at least until 1968. To some, this looks like a sure way of preventing any negotiated inhibition of the arms race.

This consideration leads, then, to the most important opportunity presented by the emerging thaw in alliance rigidity. That opportunity is to discover and build a structure of international politics within which we and the USSR can play out our inevitable conflicts without plunging all the world into nuclear war. To put it another way, we need to find a way to make the world "safe for conflict." Our tacit renunciation of first-strike *intentions* via renunciation of first-strike *capabilities* is—or could be—a significant opening move. But it is important that we convey this intention to the Kremlin and make it clear that, with some reciprocity, a measure of arms control is attainable. On the other hand, they have gone to great pains to persuade us that controlling or stabilizing the arms race is of little interest to them, and that arms *elimination* is the only worthwhile goal. Thus, an indication of our sincerity must be found in our linking together of arms control and disarmament; we have to persuade them that arms control is, for us, not the ultimate goal but an opening step—a bridge to enforceable multilateral disarmament down to very modest internal security levels.

If the Soviets are serious in their disdain for arms control per se, one way to arouse their interest would be for us to demonstrate its intimate link to disarmament. But that requires that we demonstrate our own interest in equitable disarmament, and that we accept some approximation of strategic parity not only during the *disarmament* process, but—and this is the key problem now—during the *negotiation* process as well. In other words, even if we were to meet all the Russians' disarmament treaty demands (which would be a serious error), they would still back away from a treaty. This is not, of course, to suggest that moving toward some sort of tacit parity assures progress toward disarmament; it does not, but *failure* to do so not only hastens the proliferation of increasing arsenals elsewhere, but virtually assures that we and the USSR, our limited nuclear test-ban agreement notwithstanding, will continue down the road to mutual disaster. If we can show the way to strategic parity, our short-run security will be in no greater jeopardy than it is with our present insufficient but tension-generating superiority, and it may bring the adversary to understand that we have grasped the degree of mutual interest which binds us.

In summary, the loosening of the alliance ties, East and West, need not cause us to panic. These tendencies do constitute a danger, but they constitute to an even greater extent an *opportunity* for creative diplomacy. The degree to which this administration has already shown a willingness to recognize that we and our European friends will not always have identical interests is a promising omen. Though it is difficult to ascertain in any nation's news media, it takes two to quarrel, even if they are allies; the fact is that we have resisted the demands of our friends as often as they have resisted ours. This is as it should be, and reflects the escape, in both the Soviet and Western coalitions, from a myth which says that official ideological conformity precludes serious clashes of interest. If we can learn both to tolerate and to encourage nonalignment, in our own spheres of influence as well as in the "socialist camp" and in the already nonaligned areas, the separate national interests may well permit a return to diplomatic normalcy.

And if, at the same time, we can develop a coherent military policy—embracing both deterrence and disarmament—there is the possibility that both our interests and our survival can be assured. The chances of our making these two reorientations are admittedly remote, given the administration's willingness to cater to, but not seek to modify, the dominant foreign policy views in America; but if the administration gave more attention to educating the public and mobilizing the nation's sense, and less to pandering to the jingoists of both parties (in and out of government) we might be able to accelerate the return to diplomacy. And if we do, there is a fair chance that others will come to recognize the relevance of an old dictum: that alliances are affairs of convenience, rather than marriages of passion.

# 7

# Inspection and Protection in Arms Reduction

*Whereas the preceding article seeks to embrace the problem of diplomatic-military conflict in rather general and sweeping terms, this one takes a more restricted and technical approach.[1] The basic theoretical orientation is the same, but here we get down to a more specific obstacle to the resolution of international conflict. Moreover, not only do we examine the familiar armament-tension dilemma in the context of possible arms reduction, but we spell out a fairly specific strategy by which that dilemma might be ameliorated. As with the other papers in Part III, very little empirical evidence is adduced in support of the generalizations presented. This reflects, of course, not so much a disdain for evidence as it does the very absence of evidence.*

Almost every serious effort to understand and explain the failure of post-World War II disarmament or arms control negotiations concludes that the major stumbling block has been that of inspection (Barnet 1960; Bechhoefer 1961; Nogee 1961). The consensus, simply stated, is that the Western powers would not (and will not) accept any strategically significant restrictions upon or reductions of weapons testing, production, or deployment without Soviet acceptance of an "adequate" degree of inspection, and that the Soviets refuse to permit the kind of inspection deemed adequate by the West.

Although this is an oversimplification, there is no denying that the inspection issue has been one of the stumbling blocks on the road from armed anarchy to international order. As one astute observer put it, "the hope for disarmament in a context of acute distrust between powerful nations lies in solutions to the problems of inspection" (Wiesner 1961, p. 140). Given the centrality of the issue and the degree of technical expertise which is now being brought to bear on the question, this may well be an appropriate occasion for a reexamination of the problem in its broader political and strategic context.

This paper, then, represents an effort to sort out and order some of the key variables which must be considered in the design, negotiation, and operation of a disarmament inspection system, with particular emphasis on the dual role of an international control organization in such a system. It does not, however, deal with the structure or composition of that organization, nor in any detail with its relationship to the United Nations.

## Some Basic Requirements

Perhaps it might be useful to move in on the inspection problem by starting with the more general question, not of whether the major powers *want* the reciprocal reduction and ultimate elimination of strategic weapons, but whether they want such disarmament enough to pay the necessary prices and take the necessary risks. There is little doubt that most of the national decision makers and populations believe that a world of effectively disarmed nations would be *relatively* advantageous to almost all concerned parties.[2] However, they (especially the decision makers) also realize that: (1) the transition to such a condition is full of risks; (2) such a transition will require considerable restraints in areas where nations have been traditionally unfettered; (3) a disarmed nation in a world of disarmed nations may well be disadvantaged by the nonmilitary strengths of other, competing nations; and (4) certain friendly regimes might be subverted or toppled once they have lost the tools of coercion.

Moreover, making predictions about the processes or outcome of a disarmament scheme is extremely difficult, given the unfamiliar nature of the factors involved. Thus, even if those who make strategic policies were utterly convinced that the probability-utility product[3] of disarmament is greater than that of continuing the arms race, they might well choose to continue in the more familiar path. The various utilities and disutilities are rather easily calculated, but the probability (prediction) dimension is the one in which decision makers reveal a serious, and justified, lack of self-confidence. Put more simply, they do not find it particularly difficult to describe an outcome *if* such-and-such an action is taken by the adversary or the control organ, for example, but they do find it difficult to say how *likely* it is that such an action will be taken. Therefore, there is little point in discussing a disarmament inspection system if we are virtually certain that governments are unwilling to give serious consideration to the disarmament[4] which the system is designed to inspect.

On the other hand, it may well be that one of the major inhibitions to such serious consideration lies in the fears and uncertainties which decision makers attach to that very inspection problem. Consequently, the a priori clarification of the costs and gains of various inspection alternatives may produce greater certainty about such risks, and hence alleviate some of the concerns which now constrict and inhibit the consideration of disarmament policies.

Perhaps a fruitful way of introducing these possible costs and gains would be by posing this question: What is the central requirement of any multilateral disarmament program to which the major powers are likely to agree and adhere? A general response would be that it must not jeopardize the security of the participating nations, during, or at the completion of, the process. That is, those who act for their nations must be convinced, not only that continuing reliance on national military deterrents is highly dangerous and unlikely to work over any long period of time, but that a reciprocal program of arms reduction and elimination would be considerably less dangerous and more likely to succeed.[5] But to be more specific, we would have to say that the program must profoundly minimize the likelihood that the "other side" might gain any relative military advantage during or after the process.

How can such a terrifying probability be reduced appreciably? *First,* by doing so effective a job of detection and surveillance that the probability of clandestine testing, production, stockpiling, or deployment is extremely low; *second,* by offering a degree of protection (via some redress of any imbalance) to the complying nation, in the event that any attempted evasion does go undetected.[6] In other words, the arrangement must be able to: (1) minimize the probability of successful evasion; and (2) minimize the disutilities if such evasion does occur. Some indications of the type of arrangement which might be able to meet both the inspection and the protection requirements can be had by examining the two functions which must be exercised by an inspection and control agency. One of these is the information-gathering and transmitting activity, and the other is the reacting-to-information activity; they may be thought of as the generating of stimuli and the providing of response. Let us examine each of these major types of activity in turn, bearing in mind that they are separated primarily for the sake of clarity and that the relationship between them is extremely intimate.

## The Information-as-Stimulus Activity

Turning first to the information-gathering, evaluating, and transmitting activity, we note that information can be of two distinct types: assuring information and warning information.[7] But having made this distinction, we must immediately recognize that the line between the two is by no means clear and unambiguous. Rather, the sum total of information being acquired and generated by the control agency may vary along an arc which extends from high assurance through low assurance to low warning through high warning. In visual terms, this information range would look something like figure 1.

This information will, of course, come from a number of sources, describe a multitude of activities, and be processed and transmitted through a variety of channels and nets. In order to identify the sources of such information, we may try to indicate the types of activity that are covered by the disarmament arrangement, and

**Figure 1.** Types of Information Acquired and Generated.

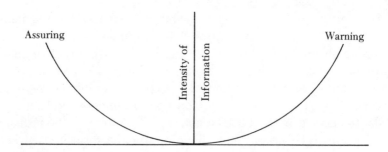

classify them in terms of this three-pronged question: What kinds of *limitations* are to be applied to what *phases* in the development and use of what *classes of weapons? Limitations* may include prohibition, quantitative limits, and registration or reporting. Among the relevant *phases* are: basic research, construction of experimental models, testing of experimental models, producing operational weapons, stockpiling them, deploying them, transferring them to other nations, and using them. As to *classes* of weapons, the range of alternatives and criteria is almost unlimited, but we will use the simple but adequate conventional-nuclear dichotomy;[8] delivery systems will be classified according to the payload with which they are normally paired. In this paper, our concern will be with the whole range of limitations (prohibition, limitation, registration) on all but the basic research phase, in the development and use of both conventional and nuclear weapons; basic research is explicitly not included on the grounds that a limitation on that phase would be neither desirable nor feasible.

To be a bit more concrete, then, the information-gathering activity could eventually be concerned with such prohibitions as the *testing* of nuclear warheads, rockets and missiles, and BCR weapons; the *production* of all the above plus naval vessels, military aircraft, artillery, and tanks; and the *deployment, transfer, and use* of all of the above plus such other light armaments as are vulnerable to inspection. Note that, as we move down the list of prohibitions, we find that only a few classes of weapon are vulnerable to inspection for prohibition on tests; that somewhat more are vulnerable to inspection at the production stage; and that a still larger number are so vulnerable at the deployment, transfer, and use stages. Though there may well be some deviations from this principle,[9] it seems to hold true in most cases, and to apply, not only to prohibitions of such activities, but to quantitative limitations and registration restraints as well.

Several other tentative generalizations regarding the inspectability of weapons also seem to emerge from the burgeoning quantity of studies in this field.[10] The first is that, as the number of weapon classes to be inspected increases, the inspection requirements for any single class diminish. This is due to the fact that almost every detection device is likely to be useful in (and applied to) the search for evasions in other weapon classes so that we can expect effectiveness to rise and unit cost to diminish as we move toward overlapping surveillance. Second, the more of a given activity that we want to prohibit or limit, the more intensive and costly (in monetary and political terms) must be the surveillance, until we begin to approach the 100 percent objective, at which point detection becomes easier again. Third, if we raise the degree of certainty demanded of the inspection, we likewise get a rising curve of cost and difficulty, but without the drop as we approach 100 percent. And fourth, the longer the inspection system has been in operation, the greater the coverage and certainty we can get for any given level of surveillance effort.[11]  Each of these propositions seems plausible, but further calculation and experimentation is definitely called for.[12]

So much for the objects of inspection and the sources of information regarding those objects. The next question is one of how information regarding these inspected objects and activities is obtained.[13]  The most obvious means is to station control agency personnel at the physical locations where the prohibited or limited activity is likely to occur. An alternative measure, sometimes cheaper and often more reliable, is to substitute machines for men, or combine them. Or perhaps, the surveillance may more efficiently take place, not where the proscribed activity might occur, but at those points through which goods, people, records, or messages must move in the flow from design to deployment and from mine to mill. These may be physical points in space or conceptual points on paper, with records and accounts rather than men and material as the objects of surveillance.[14]  Finally, one may engage in "knowledge detection," a technique which is just beginning to get serious and comprehensive attention. In other words, it may well be more convenient, inexpensive, and reliable to inspect people's information and attitudes rather than the physical objects they have seen and handled. But the inadequacies of such techniques, when not used in conjunction with others, are quite apparent (see Milburn *et al.* 1961; Pool 1961; Gerard 1961. A further refinement is explored in Singer 1963b).

The third aspect of the information-gathering activity of the control agency concerns the matter of what is done with the plethora of garnered data. Very briefly, we may say that such information must be pooled and combined, evaluated, classified, recorded, and then transmitted. The recipients of such transmission would normally be regional and central offices of the control agency, related international organs, and frequently, appropriate agencies of the governments concerned. Obviously, the dissemination of this information will depend heavily upon: (1) where it falls on the assurance-warning curve; (2) its estimated reliability; (3) its strategic significance; and (4) the needs and demands of its ultimate recipients, as embodied in treaty, administrative regulations, and practice.

### The Response-to-Information Activity

The gathering and dissemination of information by the control agency can eventually become a highly routinized activity with well-established and clearly understood procedures, and the more this is so, the more effectively can the agency carry out its most crucial activities—those of response to information. What kinds of information ought to stimulate what forms of response on the part of the control agency?

#### Investigation as Response

The first point to bear in mind is that information providing clear evidence of violation will be extremely rare. Rather, the more likely result will be an endless flow of small pieces of ambiguous information, producing a fairly constant, but hopefully low, "noise" level. This noise will eventuate from an ongoing multitude of routine checks and inspections plus a relatively steady number of special investigations generated by events and occurrences which deviate enough from the normal to qualify for further inspection.

What the criteria of "enough" are is difficult to say, and the correct choice between precision and ambiguity is elusive. Perhaps the optimum solution here is to set up specific classifications of events which can be expected to occur (and be observed) at each limited or proscribed activity, and arrange these event classifications along the assurance–warning curve described earlier. The inspection personnel or the readers of mechanical devices would be supplied with fairly detailed instructions as to how specific observations made at specific types of installations are to be classified along that curve, and as to what classifications of observation are to be transmitted to whom and by what means. Obviously, most classifications need only be fed into the control agency's communication net on a steady and regular basis for transmission to headquarters and hence to the governments concerned. To maximize the assurance-generating effect and to obtain the most rapid warning when necessary, it might be advantageous to give the appropriate agencies of all member governments continuing access to the entire net. In this way, they will be able to compare the results of their own intelligence monitoring with the stream of information arriving from the control agency at a somewhat later time. [15]

Another aspect of the response-to-information activity of the control agency is to supplement and follow up any information gathering which exceeds certain designated thresholds.[16] In a sense, this is the minimum form of sanction which nations must suffer if and when these thresholds are crossed. Again, most such supplementary investigations (such as the on-site investigation of certain types of seismic events connected with the proposed ban on underground nuclear tests) should normally produce a reclassification in the assurance direction, but if the suspected event is not disconfirmed, more careful surveillance is called for.[17]

*Limited Sanctions as Response*

Though we may prefer to assume that most information which crosses the zero point and ends up on the "low warning" side of the curve will tend to be replaced with an "assuring" classification as the result of increased inspection activity, it is essential to consider the response to warning-confirmation types of information. As suggested earlier, the most appropriate response is additional investigation of a more thorough and detailed nature, until fairly certain classification is possible. What if such certainty is achieved in the middle or high ranges on the warning side of the curve?

First of all, it is possible (especially during the early stages) that an activity is in violation without its operators being aware that they are violating; such unintentional violation can usually be corrected in a routine fashion by the filing of an informal complaint and promised acquiescence. At a second level of difficulty is the violation which the operators either deny to be a violation (a matter of law) or deny to exist (a matter of empirical and circumstantial evidence). In either case, the control personnel will have to file a formal complaint and arrange an administrative hearing whose objective would be a finding in law or in fact.[18]

If the finding does confirm the existence of a violation, appeal to a higher quasi-judicial tribunal must certainly be available, but in the meantime the control agency must be free to seek some form of injunction against continuation of the subject activity. If no appeal is made, or it is denied, or the charges are confirmed, the whole arms-reduction process is threatened. At this junction, we have a direct and unambiguous confrontation between the agency and the member government, and the nature of appropriate sanctions at this point is absolutely crucial.

One possible solution, and probably the most desirable, is that hearings and charges be directed, not against the national governments or the specific department or bureau or ministry, but against the responsible individuals. But for this to occur, national governments will have to recognize, by treaty, that individuals are, in the disarmament and arms control case, legitimate objects of international law.[19] If this extension and formalization of a well-established principle is taken, a major hurdle in the sanction problem is cleared. Likewise, the further extension of the principle to such "legal persons" as corporations would be extremely helpful. But until these formal steps are taken, the control agency's only recourse is to take sanctions against national *governments*.

Among those are, first, the increase in the degree and extent of inspection to which nations would be required to submit; a refinement might be for the suspected government to bear the cost of such extra surveillance and investigation. A second technique might be a graduated scale of monetary fines, periodically renegotiated by the signatories, with the scales appropriately publicized. Third on the list might well be an increase in the rate at which the offending nation would have to reduce weapon stocks, cut back weapon production, or dismantle testing and fabricating facilities. Beyond this, whether penalties are set by tribunal or articulated in the treaty, the control agency cannot go without resort to force; it might even be argued that the threat or use of force might well be required to go beyond the routine and regular inspection procedures.

In recognizing this enforcement dilemma, those responsible for designing a disarmament program will be compelled to make some painful decisions. At the moment, most Western students tend toward free abrogation and withdrawal as the ultimate (or even the only) sanction, arguing that anything else is unrealistic. The case for abrogation as sanction rests on the premise that "no arms control plan will remain effective and dependable unless it continues to serve the national interests of each of the parties . . ." (Bowie 1961). But this approach neglects the iron law of international politics that at any given moment in time, as between two nations in a competitive or conflictful relationship, the situation is more to the advantage of one than to the other. The international system is such that one nation's short-run advantage is almost invariably the adversary's short-run *dis*advantage. Thus, events may often *pass through* the point of mutual advantage, but they seldom linger there; most of the time, one or another signatory to a disarmament treaty will be under some pressure and temptation to withdraw. This must be made as difficult, awkward, and time-consuming as is acceptable; the doctrine of "self-help" may have provided a faithful mirror of the international society, but it has certainly never helped to stabilize it.

In addition to the likelihood that this response to detected evasion would mean a very short-lived disarmament system, abrogation and withdrawal must also be criticized as basically unjust solutions. That is, the party which adheres conscientiously to its contract, on discovering that the other has not, has no means of redressing the wrong and restoring the balance. On the contrary, it is the victim who must bear the onus of abrogation.

A modification of the abrogation and withdrawal approach is the "restorative action" approach, in which the aggrieved party not only withdraws from the program, but resumes military preparations at the original or, perhaps, a stepped-up rate.[20] One wonders whether, under this procedure, there is any profound difference between withdrawal from the agreement and a "declaration" of war. A disarmament system relying solely on unilateral measures would seem to have a very high probability of both a short life and a violent death.

## Protection and Arms Transfer

It will be recalled that earlier we raised the question of how a control agency might provide some modicum of protection to the victim of a *successful* evasion attempt. Now we have raised the question of sanctions if the attempt, by virtue of detection, is *un*successful. Is there any means by which we can build some adequacy on both of these counts into a disarmament system? Or, to put it another way, how can we successfully combine the straight inspection-as-stimulus function with these two essential response functions?

An answer is to be found, I would suggest, in the concept of *weapons transfer.* Heretofore in this paper, as in most others on the subject, the assumption has been that disarmament implies the scrapping, dismantling, and conversion of weapons.[21] What is proposed here is that we modify our standard notion of disarmament to the extent that we think of it as *disarmament of the individual nations in combination with the armament of the control agency.* Thus, the disarmament schedule, as (and if) negotiated, would provide not only for the gradual cutback in the production and testing of future weapons and in the stockpiles of existing weapons, but for the physical transfer of these latter weapons to control agency depots.

These depots might be of two kinds. The first would be for the gradual receipt and storing of nuclear warheads (tactical and strategic) and their delivery systems, including IRBM, ICBM, and long-range jet bombers, i.e., the major instruments of either a possibly decisive surprise attack or a deterrent retaliatory capability. These *strategic* weapon depots would be widely dispersed either within or near the nation from which the weapons have come, so that in the event of a breakdown in the program or successful evasion by the other side, the transferring nation is in a position to regain these weapons quickly. Moreover, each would be entitled to station some of its own nationals at these depots in order to assure that the warheads and delivery vehicles are properly maintained and that they are not illegally removed.[22]

On the other hand, repossession of these weapons would be simple, but it could never be clandestine. The depots must be so located, guarded, and integrated into the control agency communications net that the first move toward repossession would be immediately detected and broadcast. Thus might one aspect of the security-while-disarming process be partly managed.

The second type of depot would have to be more numerous and more distant from the major powers' territory. To these depots would come a gradual but steady flow of most classes of *conventional* weapons. But these would not be held in waiting for repossession by their former owners at some future moment of crisis. Rather, they would be accompanied by a handful of military or civilian technicians, whose task it would be to train the control agency's personnel in the maintenance, repair, and use of these classes of hardware. These would, in time, become the weapons of the control agency; the tools by which it might gradually assume a credible role

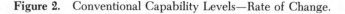

**Figure 2.**   Conventional Capability Levels—Rate of Change.

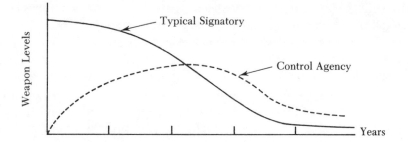

of response in the event of evasion, be it detected or otherwise. Figure 2 suggests the rate at which such transfers of military capability might occur. The idea is to have the diminution of national capabilities commence at a fairly slow pace, permitting the development of confidence on the part of the nations and of skills on the part of the control agency, prior to a more rapid arms-reduction process. On the other hand, it will be necessary to build up the conventional forces of the control agency fairly rapidly at the outset, and then taper off this growth after two years or so. Eventually, the conventional forces of the control agency would exceed those of any single nation, and both levels could then begin to remain fairly constant. Somewhere near that point, the control agency might begin to turn over some of the nuclear warheads for reutilization of the fissionable and fusionable materials in peaceful activities.

Such a transfer arrangement offers certain promising advantages. First, it permits rapid repossession of strategic weapons in the event of major breakdown. Second, it provides for the gradual establishment of some sort of conventionally armed international police force during the period of diminishing national capabilities in the nuclear and conventional fields. Third, and of particular interest at this juncture, it markedly simplifies the basic inspection problem and offers more reliable information of both the warning and assurance types. Why should this be so?

It will be recalled that a disarmament schedule calls for, *inter alia*, the phased reduction of existing weapons, and that these would be spread over many points in the territory of the owner as well as in overseas bases. In order to ascertain whether the required number of each class of weapon had been destroyed or dismantled by the signatory governments (and whether remaining inventories were within agreed maxima), the control agency would have to set up a surveillance force of awesome size, scope, and intrusiveness. Inspecting for mines, refineries, fabrication plants, and test facilities located at fixed and readily detected (if not identified) sites is a relatively manageable operation. But to do so for millions of pieces of mobile military hardware would require the establishment of a large and elaborately equipped inspection system, empowered to periodically seal off the world into many zones, out of which no hardware would be permitted to move, during a lengthy inspection period once or twice per year.[23] At present levels of surveillance technology, we would need as many "seekers" as "hiders." When we compare the complexity of that type of operation to one that lets the *weapons come to the inspectors*, the transfer-to-depots approach looks extremely attractive.

The key weakness, however, is that this type of arrangement offers fewer opportunities to confirm and authenticate the very crucial prereduction inventory figures claimed (or admitted) by the signatories.[24] In other words, an inspectorate which is not looking particularly for *existing* weapon stockpiles, but rather for *testing* and *producing* facilities and activities, is less likely to gather the types of information needed for this stockpile authentication purpose. On the other hand, the critical nature of this inventory figure may be partially mitigated by using it only for the first few periods of the disarmament process. By this time, the control agency will have gathered enough other information to permit fairly reliable periodic reappraisals of the predisarmament inventory figures submitted, as well as the more important *existing* levels. In the early stages, high accuracy on this item is not too crucial, but as inventories diminish, small quantitative discrepancies become increasingly decisive. Fortunately, they also become less likely.

Having explored the major outlines of our proposed inspection-protection system, let us turn now to the most critical aspect of all: the degree to which such a system might be expected to inhibit any attempt to violate or circumvent it.

## Deterrence of Violations

It is axiomatic in politics that the more carefully and thoroughly designed a policing or enforcement procedure is, the less likely it is to be used. Likewise, an indication of the effectiveness of our

Figure 3.   Potential Evader's Outcome Calculus.

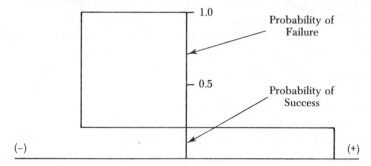

inspection and protection system may be found in the infrequency with which its capabilities are put to the actual test. That is, how successfully can the control system proposed here do the job of deterring a would-be violator? The problem is not unlike that of strategic deterrence, except that the deterrer here is not one of the protagonists but a more detached independent actor, and while the retaliation may be painful, it need not be destructive.

A measure of the system's deterrent capacity is the degree to which the decision makers who might be inclined to consider an evasion attempt are persuaded that the combined probability-utility of evasion and success is quantitatively lower than the probability-disutility of detection and failure. In graphic terms, their estimated outcome calculus should look something like figure 3, with the attractiveness of the alternative choices varying with the product of the two dimensions.

What this figure indicates is that the potential evader, in order to be deterred from such an attempt, must estimate that when he combines the low probability of successful evasion with the moderate value (utility) of such success, it must appear smaller than the combined probability of detection (quite high) and the disutility (not necessarily very high) of such detection.

Putting it in such terms, we can see that deterrence depends, not only upon the technical effectiveness of the systems, but on: (1) the degree to which the potential evader perceives it as effective; (2) the kinds of gain he thinks might accrue if his evasion attempt is successful; and (3) the kinds of loss he would expect to sustain if the attempt is unsuccessful.[25] Thus, a "foolproof" inspection system, in addition to being almost impossible to achieve and extraordinarily expensive in fiscal and political terms, is completely unnecessary. On the other hand, the probability of detection must certainly be fairly high and at least better than 0.5. But equally important is the question of gains, if successful, and losses, if not.

Looking at the gains-if-successful dimension, it is evident that the whole strategic environment will be a key variable. That is, the scale and timing of arms reductions will markedly affect this consideration; hence the strong emphasis on a schedule which does not upset the approximate military parity of the major signatories at any stage in the reduction process. By retaining such parity, the nation which does not evade is always in a position to inflict some degree of retaliatory punishment on the nation which does, should the evader either use or threaten to use the secret weapons.[26] As both sides move closer, however, to the minimum capability levels that had been negotiated, this retaliatory power becomes less and less significant, and that of the control agency nonnuclear force becomes increasingly relevant. Hence the emphasis on both the preservation of an "accessible" retaliatory force available to the individual governments and the gradual buildup in the conventional military capability of the control agency. As national deterrent capabilities diminish, they must be augmented, and eventually replaced, by supranational ones. The institution of such arrangements, then, should be expected to diminish the gains-if-successful attractions.

Regarding the losses-if-detected dimension, the system must clearly be so designed as to impose fairly painful losses on the detected evader. As suggested above, one of the more promising penalties for attempted evasion (or more operationally, actions which generate warning signals) will be more intensive and vigorous inspection. Just as the taxpayer is careful to produce an assurance-generating return in order to avoid the painful scrutiny of an inquiry or investigation, most responsible national decision makers should be deterred by this possible consequence alone. If a part (or all) of the cost of any special investigation is charged to the suspected evader, the deterrent effect could be further increased, and any pecuniary considerations which might inhibit the control agency's eagerness to conduct such inquiries would be alleviated. But again, it must be emphasized that we cannot afford to have any simple "yes-no" or "complying-evading" classification. The punishment must fit the "crime," and graduated responses to graduated warning levels are essential, if the system is to deter rather than provoke the signatories.

As to the major intentional violations initiated by middle-ranking managers or civil servants, the expectation is that these would be deterred by the sort of response which could be anticipated from both the other signatories and the control agency. The possibility of apprehension, trial, fining, or incarceration of the individuals concerned will have a deterrent effect varying markedly with the degree to which the individual's government is committed to the disarmament arrangement and the degree to which that commitment is conveyed to its public.[27]

But if the top decision makers decide to violate and are able to line up nearly unanimous support for the attempt throughout the inspected activities, a much more difficult and dangerous situation is reached. The problem is to design the disarmament system in such a fashion that the incentive to evade is constantly diminishing. Thus, as weapons transfers begin to assume significant proportions, the efficacy of the inspection and protection activities must increase sharply, and the peaceful settlement and adjudication capabilities of the United Nations will need to improve appreciably. In other words, as the nations' abilities to practice self-help diminish, the international organization will have to provide an increasing measure of protection for their legitimate and vital interests. The degree to which the organization's physical, legal, and psychological power is improved will determine whether or not the major, intentional, government-approved violation will be deterred. Needless to say, the multiple deterrents which embrace both threat and promise are at least as likely to deter a would-be disarmament evader as is the single, simple, threat-of-punishment deterrent upon which the major powers now pin their hopes of survival.[28]

## Political Acceptability

Whether this means of providing for the protection of the nations during and after a disarmament program will be acceptable to the governments concerned (assuming that it has no other serious defects) is by no means certain. Though the Soviet and Western positions on the role of an international force are vague, imprecise, and often contradictory, the picture is by no means totally black.

On the Soviet side, there has been considerable ambivalence. In October, 1959, Khrushchev spoke to the Supreme Soviet as follows:

> The discussions on disarmament have hardly begun, and the skeptics have raised the question of what international forces should be created in place of the national forces. . . . When all countries disarm and all armies have no arms, then nobody will be able to start a war. The question arises: For what

purpose, then, are supranational armed forces necessary? [*Pravda*, November 1, 1959, p. 3 (Document 386 in U.S. 1960)]

But a year later his tune (and audience) had changed slightly:

It has been said that, after agreement on disarmament has been reached, international armed forces should be formed. We are, in principle, in agreement with this.

In this context, however, he ridiculed the idea that such forces could be under the command of the secretary-general.

There can be no disarmament, there can be no international armed forces, in the absence of guarantees for all three groups [capitalist, communist, and neutral] against the misuse of these armed forces.

The following week, the Soviet delegation tabled a draft disarmament resolution calling for

States to make available to the Security Council, where necessary, units from the contingents of police (militia) retained by States for maintaining internal order. . . .[29]

If verbal articulations are any guide, then, the present Soviet position would be somewhat as follows. There may well be the need for such a force, but it should: (1) be subject to the veto and not be supranational; (2) not be directed by the secretary-general; (3) be composed of earmarked national contingents only; and (4) be representative of the three major international groupings.

On the Western side, the picture is quite similar. Though Secretary of State Herter called, in his February, 1960, speech to the National Press Club, for the linking of disarmament with "effective means of enforcement . . . , that is, by international armed force . . . ," the United States also has opposed a *supra*national force. Thus, in the Western proposal of June, 1960, reference was made to national "contingents" in such a force, and in the April, 1962, draft treaty the focus is on Article 43 of the Charter, with similar provisions.[30]

The point is that both major powers are committed to some sort of international force, but that almost no attention has been given to the question of when such a force would be instituted. The West tends to prefer that it be "progressively established" beginning in stage II, and the Soviet has implied an even greater vagueness in speaking of a control organization "to carry out control over, and inspection of disarmament. . . ."[31] Thus, neither superpower has come close to embracing the view of a protection force suggested here, and it may be partially explained by the traditional tendency to preserve and maximize "national sovereignty." But a more convincing explanation is that neither has given any serious and detailed study to a disarmament plan which has much likelihood of acceptance by the other. When (and if) such study does take place, the possibility is that this transfer technique for linking inspection and protection may turn out to be a distasteful, but necessary, approach.


## Summary

What has been suggested here is that a combination of technological innovation and political upheaval has made the existing international order profoundly inadequate as an environment in which nations and people can survive and prosper. That order must be markedly transformed, and the disarmament of the nations is a major element in that transformation. Disarmament, however, cannot occur if we adhere to the plans which were considered and rejected in the relatively safer environment of the 1930s and which are still mustering only the barest sort of support today. The major powers must—if we are ever to get a negotiated disarmament treaty—not only be persuaded that all the others are adhering to their obligations under a disarmament program, and be warned if such is not the case, but they must be protected during and after that program.

A control agency assigned the dual role of inspection and protection could, under a system of weapon transfer, fulfill both roles. But such a transfer of weapons requires a parallel transfer of legal and political power as well, and many will balk at so drastic a change in the international system. In the introduction to his notes on the American Constitutional Convention, James Madison explained the disunity of the states in terms of, *inter alia,*

> the natural repugnance of the parties to a relinquishment of power . . . a natural jealousy of its abuse in other hands than their own . . . [and] the selection and definition of the powers, at once necessary to the federal head, and safe to the several members [E. H. Scott 1893, pp. 32–33].

Their hesitations, in times much less critical, were remarkably similar to our own. Let us hope that we can do as well.

# IV

# The Possible Role of Scientific Knowledge

The midstage of this anthology is more than a convenient line of demarcation between my prescientific policy efforts and the more rigorous research that was to follow. Rather, this part contains the papers that "make the case" for me and, I would hope, for others. Here one finds expressions not only of the policy disenchantment to which I alluded in the Introduction, but of a heightened appreciation of the need for—and potential applicability of—knowledge. It is a sad commentary on the history of the social sciences, as well as on the graduate (and undergraduate) education that was available to my generation, that this was a relatively new idea. Scholars and perhaps even practitioners have probably sensed for some time that there might be a connection between the findings of basic research and the responsibilities of the decision makers. Often, I suspect, those who appreciated this possible connection best were also those who would most resist seeing the connection consummated. Much better, they may have reasoned, to continue that symbiotic relationship in which the academics enjoyed a sense of intimacy with the seats of power, and the bureaucrats basked in the polysyllabic benedictions written for them. Reference, of course, is to the long tradition of co-optation by which officeholders have traded with such intellectuals as professors, journalists, and publicists access to information and apparent influence in exchange for the standard encomia.

Regardless of the inordinate delay in our recognition of the relevance of scientific knowledge to the conduct of national policies—and the explanation would have to go beyond the conspiratorial element alluded to above—the case must be made. Consequently, the purpose of the three papers presented in part IV is to summarize and illustrate that case from the point of view of a dovish analyst and consultant who gradually came to realize that more would be needed than the types of analyses provided in the first half of this volume.

# 8

# The Scientific Study of Politics: An Approach to Foreign Policy Analysis

*This paper summarizes the elements that seem to go into the decision process and urges that a larger dose of knowledge might help, but the reader should be alerted to the limits as well as the opportunities of this approach. The points raised in the conclusion of the paper should thus be kept in mind. For example, I do not mean to suggest here or anywhere in this volume that the acquisition and application of scientific knowledge will be sufficient. A myriad of other difficulties—ranging from the personal morality of the decision maker to the historically determined constraints of the global system—can get in the way. Nor do I suggest that, even if we were to experience a hundredfold increase in high-quality research, we would necessarily know which are the "right" policies in both the normative and the pragmatic sense. Scientific knowledge, then, cannot eliminate the large questions of right and wrong, but, as these papers urge, it can help us to answer them in a more concise and thoughtful manner. It can help us to predict the consequences of our acts, and if morality lies to some extent in selecting acts that do the most good and the least harm, improved predictability must be viewed as desirable. Human history is strewn with the victims of those who "didn't know it was loaded."*

The Policy Setting

When a national government makes those daily, weekly, and yearly decisions that constitute the policy-making process, a great many elements impinge upon and shape those decisions. Exactly which elements are most important in different types of nations and in certain classes of problems we do not know; the necessary research has just not yet been done. But we *do* know that decision making is essentially an *information-processing* operation; the relevant bureaucrats, legislators, and staff personnel must gather, evaluate, integrate, and interpret information about their environment and the other actors in that environment. To the extent that it is accurate, such information may be thought of as *knowledge.*

We can divide such information or knowledge into three basic types, and while we shall define them more fully in the next section, a brief summary might be useful here. The first type is *existential* knowledge, and it can range from a few isolated *facts* (such as those gathered by a government's intelligence agency) up through a comprehensive and integrated set of *data.* An example of the former might be the fact that a given army had a 40 percent turnover in personnel during the past five years; the latter might show the size of the NATO and Warsaw pact forces every year since 1955. The second is *correlational* knowledge: the extent to which two or more conditions are usually associated. An example might be the general principle that there is a high and positive correlation between a nation's GNP per capita and the size of its contribution to the regular UN budget. The third is *causal* or *explanatory* knowledge: the extent to which a given class of outcomes or events was "caused" by a given sequence of prior conditions and events. A purely hypothetical example (since we don't really know) might be that the level of bellicosity in the foreign policy of industrial nations is "caused" by the rate and direction of their unemployment index plus the rate and direction of their neighbors' armaments levels.

All three types of knowledge are used to make predictions, and making predictions is the name of the game in the public policy decision process. That is, conscientious decision makers *want* to be able to predict what outcomes will flow from the policies they decide upon. This means that they *should* be able to predict how other governments, or units within their own governments, or political parties in other societies, and so on, will respond to the actions they—or other units acting on their advice—take. Factual or existential knowledge is, of course, central to successful prediction. Unless one has most of the relevant facts, or fairly accurate estimates, one's predictions become too dependent either on luck or on all sorts of nonrational or irrational considerations.

But unless one also knows which sets of facts usually go together, having only *one* set will not be much help; we also need to know the generalization or principle that associates them. For example, knowing that a potential enemy enjoys a numerical edge in offensive weaponry is of little use unless the decision maker also knows whether nations of that particular type, under a given set of conditions, tend to behave in a more conciliatory manner or a more bellicose manner when they are militarily superior. The answer, despite the assertions we find in the literature, is far from obvious. But factual and correlational knowledge—even of very high accuracy—can also carry the decision makers only so far. The more *explanatory* knowledge that is available—especially in the form of well-tested models and theories—the better one can predict in complex or unfamiliar situations. That is, in the absence of good correlational knowledge, one may nevertheless deduce such principles from a good theory, and use them as the basis for prediction.

If these three types of knowledge are important to the success of the policy-making process, what happens when they are in short supply? First of all, it is very difficult to draw the line between knowledge and *belief*. To the extent that decision makers are misinformed, but *believe* they know a given set of facts or a given correlational principle, they may act with confidence, yet end up in disaster. To put it another way, even though "wishing [or believing] can make it so," certain objective realities respond very slowly, and often not at all, to inaccurate perceptions or predictions. Second, to the extent that decision makers appreciate how much or little knowledge they have, they tend to respond to those nonrational or irrational inputs mentioned earlier. That is, if there is insufficient knowledge to predict which of two contending moves is more likely to result in the preferred outcome, the strength of one protagonist's personality may well carry the argument. Similarly, if the proponents of strategy A have more political "clout" than the proponents of strategy B, the undecided people may—in the absence of credible predictions in either direction—side with the advocates of strategy A. Continuing in the same vein, a relatively uncertain bureaucrat, unable to see much difference between the virtues of two or more strategies, often selects the one that seems more likely to advance his career or make the fewest waves. Finally, bureaucrats show an almost universal tendency to postpone or "waffle" their recommendations (and the predictions on which they are based), and the less knowledge available, the more likely they are to follow this dangerous practice.

A major assumption in this module is that the policy makers do not know nearly enough about the political systems in which they operate. In my view, their factual knowledge is grossly incomplete, their correlational knowledge ranges from partial to wrong, and their explanatory knowledge is often no better than that of Neanderthal man trying to understand the weather. Further, I'd argue that this is almost as true of a nation as "developed" as Britain as it is of Afghanistan. But the inadequacy of the knowledge of policy makers is only part of the problem. The "textbook" model often has it that policy is made by: (a) intelligent and rational men; (b) pursuing well-defined collective goals; (c) on behalf of the entire nation; (d) utilizing all the necessary knowledge; (e) according to rational problem-solving strategies. This may not be a bad model of how public policy *should* be made, but no careful observer of human history can believe that it reflects what actually *does* happen. Were it otherwise, how could mankind have experienced so much poverty, indignity, and violence? Some might attribute the failures of collective decision making to stupidity, but that simple genetic explanation just won't suffice. Too many collective decisions *are* successful, in the social as well as the physical realm. Perhaps it's not so much stupidity as irrationality. There *is* evidence that those who rise to positions of political influence are different from those who do not, but no evidence that they are less rational and less capable of processing information than the man in the street, on the farm, and so on (J. Davies 1963).

Could it be, as some philosophers and political activists suggest, a matter of selfishness, in which case the political elites act on behalf of their own class and are indifferent or even hostile to the needs and aspirations of the general public? This brings us a bit closer to the mark, and whether one "buys" a class-exploitation model of the world or not, there is little doubt that individual, bureaucratic, partisan, or class interests *do* influence the policy-making process. Or, in terms of the checklist above, the goals they pursue will often be ill defined, will almost always (and inevitably) be *in addition to* those of the nation as a whole, and will occasionally be clearly *inconsistent with* the goals of the nation as a whole. Finally, skipping over the matter of knowledge already discussed above, there is the problem-solving strategy they employ. Here, too, deviation from the ideal is all too frequent. Time pressure may be too great to permit full discussion of all the options and the predicted consequences of each, and personality clashes and ego needs can lead key officials to ignore certain critical bits of knowledge. Further, bureaucratic or partisan conflict may actually lead to withholding or distorting relevant knowledge held by one of the constituent groups in the process.

With so many places at which the decision process may go astray, little wonder that the results leave a great deal to be desired during the period in which men have organized their lives and conducted their affairs largely through the vehicle of national states. That is, we can hardly count as successful a problem-solving mode that has led to—or at least permitted—hundreds of wars, millions of battle deaths, mountains of destructive weaponry, recurrent depressions, continuing poverty and starvation, and rather modest progress toward human freedom, social justice, and individual dignity.

## Realism Versus Idealism?

Given this mix of elements that enter into, and shape the outcome of, foreign policy decisions, what sorts of response are morally and intellectually appropriate? One possible response—closely identified with the "realist" school—is to resign ourselves to the Hobbesian nature of international politics, the intellectual intractability of its complexities, and the moral imperfections of those who act on behalf of the nations, and hope that we may somehow muddle through. The "idealist" school, on the other hand, finds such an orientation quite unattractive. Its proponents tend to believe that we can get at least somewhat closer to one or another ideal state of international politics. Whether the idealist advocates stronger international organization, greater popular involvement in foreign affairs, or moral reform of those who act on behalf of the nations, he clearly finds the realist's resignation an unsatisfactory response.

But as any who has ever thought seriously about any social problem realizes, there are always more than two basic responses to any situation. This is certainly true in regard to the awesome problems of international politics; more accurately, it has become increasingly true as the implications have become more ominous and apparent. At the risk of continued simplification, we can say that this third response—which we identify with the "scientific" school—reflects an ambivalence toward the other two orientations. On the one hand, it largely accepts the realist's view that the international system is highly conflictful, its dynamics very complex, and its practitioners somewhat less than saints. But it rejects the conclusion that we cannot hope really to understand international politics or do much about the policies of the nations whose behavior constitutes its essence.

And though sharing these particular views with the idealists, the scientific school takes a dim view of the reforms usually called for. Whereas most of these reform proposals imply that we know pretty well how the international system works, the scientist tends to agree with the realist that we really do not. The important point, however, is that whereas the realist asserts that this will *always* be so, the social scientist denies that, and believes we can indeed discover some of the laws that govern the workings of the system.

To put it another way, and returning to our original formulation, the scientific school recognizes that there *are* all sorts of irrational and nonrational inputs into the foreign policy decision process, and believes that its intellectual style can, to some extent, cope with them or reduce their impact. A good many wars and other diplomatic disasters have been stumbled into because of the inadequacies in our knowledge, and whereas the realist may accept such a state of affairs, and the idealist may deplore it, the scientist thinks it can be reduced, and perhaps even eliminated. What is this scientific school, and what makes its devotees believe they can make foreign policies more rational and the quality of international life less grim and dangerous? The balance of this module is one man's attempt to answer that question.

## Transition or Revolution?

The changes that have been taking place in the study—and to some extent the practice—of foreign policy over the past decade or so are often referred to as a "revolution." But I suspect that this is too strong a word. First, much of the new type of research in foreign policy and international politics was forecast in the 1920s, and in some cases even earlier. Second, what it involves is not revolutionary at all, but merely an extension of two well-established patterns.

Looking at this latter point first, we note that scientific method (which I shall define in a moment) has been utilized for centuries in the solution of all sorts of physical and biological problems. From Archimedes to Newton and from Pasteur to Pauling, these fields have seen the utilization of scientific method in the acquisition and application of knowledge for a very long time, and with fairly impressive results. But for a variety of reasons ranging from religious taboos and superstition to the allegedly greater complexity of social phenomena, men have shied away from (if not vigorously resisted) its application to the study of social problems. That orientation has, however, been gradually eroded, partly through the work of courageous and creative scholars and partly because of the increasingly obvious need to replace folklore with knowledge.

In addition to the fact that social science is merely an extension of a given intellectual style already well established in the study of physical and biological phenomena, it is also quite nonrevolutionary in that it is little more than an extension of certain problem-solving processes we have always used. While it *is* clearly an extension, the fact is that man has used a combination of logic and sensory observation for centuries in coping with social problems. In trying to understand what people did under certain conditions, and why they did it, philosophers, kings, merchants, and soldiers have often employed a rudimentary form of scientific method. That is, they tried to: (*a*) identify and classify a variety of social events and conditions; (*b*) ascertain the extent to which they occurred together or in sequence; and (*c*) remember those observed co-occurrences.

But since they seldom used explicit criteria when they were classifying, they often placed highly dissimilar events and conditions in the same category; and since they seldom used constant criteria, they often forgot which criteria they had used for earlier classifications, with the same garbled results. Moreover, because one couldn't put social events on a scale, or measure the length and breadth of a social condition, their basic belief that social phenomena were not tangible, and therefore not measurable, was reinforced. This failure to measure and scale further reinforced the philosophic notion that whereas physical (and later on, biological) phenomena were inherently *quant*itative, those of a social nature were inherently *qual*itative. Given this widespread belief, there was of course little effort to develop either the instruments of observation or the tools of measurement.

For centuries, then, men could study social phenomena in a no more reliable or accurate fashion than if they had studied physical ones without yardsticks, balance scales, or telescopes. To put it another way, they used the primitive essentials of scientific method, but ignored the critical refinements. Instead of aiding and enhancing their natural capacities to observe, remember, and reason, they made a virtue of these very frailties and inadequacies by arguing that the incomprehensibility of social phenomena was inherent in the events and conditions themselves, rather than in the grossly inadequate methods they used in that effort to comprehend. Modern social science, then, is nothing more than an application of methods already found useful in the other sciences and an extension and refinement of the basic methods we have always used. To repeat the familiar cliché, we have been "speaking prose" all along, but prose of a rather poor quality.

Returning to my first argument as to why a science of international politics is not particularly revolutionary, let me document my assertion that its precursors have been with us for several decades already. While some would assert that it is centuries rather than decades, and point to scholars such as Thucydides, Vegetius, Plato, and Polybius, or more recently Hobbes, Grotius, Hume, Machiavelli, and Ibn Khaldun, my view is that these were all prescientific in their work. As a matter of fact, given the absence of scientific refinements, their intellectual accomplishments are all the more impressive. The same would hold true, in my judgment, for such nineteenth- and twentieth-century scholars as Clausewitz, Marx, Jomini, Proudhon, Madariaga, and Shotwell.

As I see it, the first explicitly scientific treatise on international politics was Bloch's (1899) six-volume *The Future of War*, published in Russia in 1898. In that opus Bloch introduced a large body of data (as opposed to facts and impressions) and subjected these data to some simple types of statistical analyses. His main conclusion—that economic costs and military technology would render war impractical and thus obsolete—was unfortunately wide of the mark, reminding us that scientific method, even if very sophisticated (which his was not), is no guarantee of arriving at the truth.

Other forerunners of the scientific movement in foreign policy analysis were Quincy Wright, Pitirim Sorokin, and Lewis Richardson. All three of these scholars began major projects in the 1920s, and perhaps not accidentally, all concentrated on the causes of war. In addition, the major works of all three are both historical and quantitative. In his two-volume *Study of War* (1942), Wright gathered much historical data on the incidence of war since the fifteenth century and the many conditions and events that might possibly have accounted for it across a broad spatial and temporal domain. The work is characterized by diligence in gathering and generating data, ingenuity in constructing measures, and a thorough discussion of the possible interpretations of the historical facts and systematic data, but it is almost devoid of any statistical analyses. Sorokin, whose *War and Revolution* is the third volume of *Social and Cultural Dynamics* (1937), goes even further back in time, beginning with the Greeks and Romans, but he gathers little data on the possible causes of the war fluctuations he documents. His concern is, however, not so much to *account* for war as to demonstrate that it rises and falls in long cycles along with many other social phenomena.

The British physicist, Richardson, even though covering a briefer time span than Wright or Sorokin, and less attentive to the quality of his data, must be counted the most scientific of these four pioneers in quantitative international history. In *Arms and Insecurity* and *Statistics of Deadly Quarrels* (both published posthumously in 1960), he produces the first major effort to apply mathematical models and rigorous statistical inference techniques to the study of international politics. Having made earlier contributions of importance to meteorology, physics, and statistics, Richardson provides a dramatic illustration of my earlier point regarding the extension and transfer of scientific methods from physical and biological to social research.

*     *     *

## Conclusion

Since an earlier draft of this module has been reviewed by several scholars and practitioners, I have some idea of the kinds of reaction it may provoke among its readers. Let me exploit that advantage by trying to summarize my line of argument while responding to some of the more relevant criticisms.

First, some will not recognize my brief characterization of the foreign policy decision process and will think it an unfair caricature of the way modern governments formulate and execute that policy. Space limitations preclude my going into chapter and verse, and I've therefore said more by *im*plication than by *ex*plication, but there is little question in my mind as to the basically chaotic nature of that process. As the quantity and quality of research in the comparative foreign policy field increases, I expect that this "dim view" will be vindicated and that the standard textbook and public information descriptions will be seen as naive, if not worse. And I have in mind the autocratic as well as the democratic societies, the industrial as well as the developing, those in Asia and Africa as well as those in Europe and the Americas, and those of the nineteenth as well as those of the twentieth century.

We will, I suspect, also discover that the idea of the national interest has been a chimera, perpetuated by relatively ignorant men trying to solve extremely difficult problems with the most primitive types of idea, information, and organization. Further, we will probably discover that the concept is as ethically indefensible as it is pragmatically misleading, and that the acts of savagery and cupidity committed in its name should have been occasions for shame rather than pride.

Second, despite the affirmative (some might say dogmatic) tone, I do not argue that all we have to do is embrace the scientific mode and all our foreign policy problems will be solved. I merely claim that it can accelerate the growth of knowledge about international politics. Nor do I assert that those of us who style ourselves as scientific have already made great strides. By and large, all we have done so far is generate a number of valuable data sets, discover a few interesting relationships, and articulate a handful of fairly rigorous and suggestive models; the limited progress we have made in the past decade or so is reflected in such journals as *Conflict Resolution*, *Peace Research*, and *Peace Research Society Papers*, and in the recent anthologies edited by Kriesberg (1969), Mueller (1969), Rosenau (1969a), and Singer (1968c).

Nor am I claiming that knowledge alone will make that great a difference in the behavior of national governments vis-à-vis one another. First, there are such difficulties as we have already noted: the conditional nature of social science predictions, the uniqueness of future cases, and the probabilistic element in social systems; then there are the eternal problems discussed at the outset. These are the conflicting interests of the disparate groups that dominate a nation's foreign policy process, plus the psychic and intellectual inadequacies of the individuals who must try to resist these parochial interests, or reconcile them with the putative national interest, not to mention their own personal ones. In sum, all I am saying is that an increase in the amount of factual, correlational, and explanatory knowledge about international politics can not only reduce the incidence of erroneous predictions, but also diminish the potency of the nonrational and the irrational elements in the selection of goals and strategies. The magnitude of that impact remains, of course, an empirical question.

A third concern might be that my discussion of the relation between social science and foreign policy treats too lightly the questions of altruism and ethics. Like that of rationality, this is a murky issue, and again I take a somewhat unconventional view, suggesting that the ancient debate over "facts versus values" is often beside the point. A good many debates (not to mention duels, assassinations, executions, and wars) that allegedly revolve around questions of good and evil turn out, on closer examination, to be matters of *prediction* rather than *preference*.

Let me illustrate, using U.S. involvement in the current Indochinese war. Most of the war's supporters in the West are no more indifferent to the losses of life involved than are its opponents. But many of them justify the slaughter on the grounds that a "Communist" victory now will lead to even greater bloodshed later. Or they assert that such a victory will lead to enduring dictatorial control over the region and its people. Leaving aside those romantics who believe that the North Vietnamese and Vietcong are the agents of liberation and human dignity, many opponents of the war reject both of those predictions. They (myself included) predict that the withdrawal of U.S. forces will not lead to violence anywhere near as vicious and extensive as the war itself has brought; moreover, they predict that the Communists will not be able to govern effectively for any length of time without important concessions to both the neutrals and the present pro-Saigon factions.

Of course, this argument merely pushes the ethical issue back a few notches, and does not displace it entirely. That is, given the lack of hard knowledge on which we can base these differing predictions, the burden of proof should be on those who did and do support U.S. policy. To put it bluntly, it is morally indefensible to engage in such sustained and vicious violence when the predictions that justify it are so far from persuasive. An important corollary, however, is that it is also indefensible to deny that differing predictive models are at issue in dilemmas of this type, and to suggest that better knowledge would be of no relevance. As a matter of fact, some of the most vigorous supporters of this and other wars are the first to admit that their governments stumbled into them out of ignorance and incompetence. Or, to put it in the language of the introductory paragraphs, the knowledge base was so flimsy and the predictions so difficult to evaluate that the irrational and nonrational inputs often carried the day. This, for me, is the indisputable message that emerges from the recently released "Pentagon Papers."

A number of other criticisms can also be expected, but they will probably turn on differences of opinion regarding the nature of scientific method: interpretation of correlation coefficients, prediction to the future from observation of the past, the validity of certain types of measurement, and so forth. Without being cavalier, I can only say that there is indeed room for a variety of positions on questions of method and epistemology; some of the positions taken here could indeed turn out to be foolish, but they may also turn out to be fully justified by the research developments of the next few years.

In sum, I have tried here to introduce some of the more important ideas associated with the social science outlook as it bears on the study and conduct of national policies, foreign and domestic. A lot of it may be strange—or even threatening—to some students, and for others it may be largely "old hat." But in either case, my hope is that the line of reasoning is clear, the examples relevant, and the jargon minimal. Failure to satisfy these criteria is all too frequent in the social science literature, and may be why so many students think of science as a rather esoteric activity. As I suggested in the first part, there is nothing particularly revolutionary in either scientific method or its application to human affairs. They represent logical extensions of man's basic problem-solving skills, and if used intelligently and creatively, they may yet change the odds that now seem to point toward a third—and perhaps final—world war.

# 9

## The Outcome of Arms Races:
## A Policy Problem and
## a Research Approach

*In the two papers that follow, I go beyond some general observations regarding the utility of knowledge and examine a number of more specific problems from the applied knowledge point of view. The first of these lays out a general scheme by which we might approach a more specific policy problem. It was prepared for the 1969 conference of the International Peace Research Association, held in Karlovy Vary, and I recall the events all too well. Set in this charming resort town in northwest Czechoslovakia, only a year after the Soviet occupation of Prague, one heard a surprising amount of pro-Soviet (as well as pro-Chinese) propaganda from young Western European scholars who thought of themselves as peace researchers. As the other American paper giver, Kenneth Boulding, put it, "They have a fancy for what might be called academic guerilla theater . . . and seem singularly insensitive to the virtues of political freedom or to the possible defects in the totalitarian societies." To carry this criticism a step further, many of the revolutionary peace researchers seemed to be remarkably soft on violence as well as on attentiveness. My paper is brief and concise, suggesting that we might be able to discover the differences between those arms races that do end in war and those that do not. Yet one of my discussants rose to demand why I thought that all arms races necessarily ended in war! For a long-time peace researcher, this was a very depressing conference, particularly since our West European colleagues continue, by and large, to spend more time reciting the vices of American imperialism than they do trying to discover the causes of war and the conditions of peace.*

One aspect of international conflict which has long intrigued historians, practitioners, and social scientists is that of the "arms race." But until the seminal studies of Lewis Richardson (1939; 1960a; 1960b), most of that interest found expression only in abstract speculation about the phenomenon in general, or detailed chronologies of single cases.[1] Since Richardson's *Arms and Insecurity* appeared posthumously, however, there has been a small but growing amount of more rigorous work, (Abelson 1963; Boulding 1962; Burns 1959; Cady 1966; Caspary 1967; Chase 1968a; 1968b; Gleditsch 1967; Intriligator 1964; McGuire 1965; Saaty 1968; Smoker 1964; 1965; 1967; Wolfson 1968). But even these more recent efforts, while clearly informed by the scientific outlook, leave us very far from the sort of knowledge we seek. While the models are more formal now than in the pre-Richardson days, they all seem to be variants of his basic approach (Rapoport 1957), and if they introduce any evidence at all, it usually embraces no more than one or two historical cases.[2] Given the implications for policy, as well as for science, in a fuller understanding of arms interactions in international conflict, it would seem timely to mount a more ambitious assault on the uncertainties and ambiguities of this process which is so frequently a precursor of war. Hence the following comments on one possible research strategy.

## From Policy Problem to Research Questions

One very good reason for wanting to study arms races is that the resulting knowledge might possibly be helpful in understanding—and perhaps extricating ourselves from—the one which has engaged the Soviet Union and the United States for the past two decades, at great material and psychic cost and attended by some considerable risk of nuclear war. The policy problem might be posed as follows: Under what conditions, if any, can the Soviet-American arms race be slowed down or terminated, or at least made less costly and less dangerous? Since arms races are unlikely to occur in the absence of a protracted conflict, and are usually an integral component of such conflicts, and since a good many internation conflicts have terminated without war in the past, it is not too naive to believe that some arms races—including the one at hand—may find a nonwar resolution.[3]

An answer to this question rests, in turn, on successful predictions about the future. Under what environmental and behavioral conditions may we expect this arms race to continue, to taper off, to terminate, to escalate further, or to explode into war? Are there any changes in the behavior of the contending governments, in the structure, culture, and capabilities of their respective societies, or in the attributes of the global system, that might lead to any of the above types of outcome in the contemporary arms race? To what extent are these changes already inherent in the process and to what extent would conscious modification be required?

### Alternative Bases for Prediction

In order to make such predictions about international political phenomena, we have several alternative bases. The most frequently used one is, of course, the pooling of collective hunches. Relying on the shared recollections and common folklore of these concerned, government agencies find this sort of speculation quite appropriate to their needs (including severe time pressure) and capabilities (such as personnel, organization, and knowledge base). Even though predictions of this sort are more often right than wrong (and if wrong, frequently remediable), we need not overlook the fact that a fair number of such predictions have not only turned out to be wrong, but catastrophically wrong. In the Correlates of War project at the University of Michigan, for example, we find 50 "severe" interstate wars occurring between the Congress of Vienna and 1965, and though we have not yet coded and scaled them on this variable, my estimate is that (despite Abel 1941) fewer than a half dozen will turn out to have been intended or expected by the decision makers until after the process had become almost irreversible.

Are there any alternative and more satisfactory bases for prediction of the sorts of interstate interaction which concern us here? The most obvious alternative is, of course, the recent (or not-so-recent) diplomatic and military *history* of the states at hand, or perhaps of those states which are sufficiently comparable to them. Since this requires us to examine events and conditions found in an empirical domain which is not identical to that of the U.S. and the USSR of the next few decades, however, we may be justified in going even farther afield. Thus, we might try to "game" or *simulate* these alternative futures in order to predict the most likely consequences of certain changes—or continuities—in the behavior of one or both of the states at hand. Or, wanting a more rigorously generated knowledge base, we might make a systematic examination of the *experimental literature* in the field of intergroup or interpersonal relations. Finally, we could delude ourselves into believing that a sufficiently solid theoretical foundation already exists, and that we need merely *deduce* from that theory those propositions most relevant to the problem at hand.

Before advocating any one of these four research strategies, we must note that, in addition to the fact that any predictions arising out of any of them will be based on phenomena which are not identical to (but merely similar to) those which concern us here, there is another difficulty. I refer to the fact that most social and political phenomena tend to be less deterministic and more probabilistic than those found in physical or biological domains. Thus, even when a very consistent regularity *is* discovered within N cases in any social system, there still remains the possibility that, in the N + 1th case, the pattern may not hold. Despite these dangers, however, evidence-based predictions nevertheless remain preferable to those of a more conjectural nature.

These briefly outlined considerations lead me to propose that the first three of the above strategies be followed, but that highest priority be assigned for the moment to the *historical* project. A systematic search of the experimental literature could profitably begin at the same time, but the simulation should not be undertaken until an appreciable fraction of the historical data has been gathered, on the grounds that an all-machine simulation (as opposed to a man-machine or all-man simulation) could be useful, but only if it is built around data inputs from the referent ("real") world; and these can only be generated by the sort of historical study outlined here.

## The Empirical Domain

Having described the policy problem in very general language, and indicated three scientifically relevant paths to the acquisition of the applicable knowledge, let me now break the question down into more specific and researchable questions. Before doing so, however, I propose that the search for answers to these questions be confined to sustained arms interaction sequences involving at least one major power, and for the period 1865–1965; thus the conflict and associated arms moves preceding the Franco-Prussian War would constitute our first case, and the several arms interaction processes involving the current major powers would be our final cases.

The population of cases would include, at the minimum, the arms race elements of those conflicts which preceded the following major power wars:

| | |
|---|---|
| Russo-Turkish (1877–78) | Sino-Japanese (1931–33 & 1937–41) |
| Sino-Japanese (1894–95) | Russo-Finnish (1939–40) |
| Spanish-American (1898) | World War II (1939–1945) |
| Russo-Japanese (1904–05) | Palestine (1948) |
| Italo-Turkish (1911–12) | Korean (1950–53) |
| World War I (1914–18) | Sino-Indian (1962) |

### Defining the Behavioral Variables

But since our major concern is to ascertain wherein those arms races which terminate in war differ from those which do *not*, we must next identify all cases which fall into this latter category. This leads, of course, to a key question which has so far been avoided: What constitutes an "arms race?" Is there a discernible threshold of intensity or duration in weapons interaction which *clearly* demarcates the bona fide arms race from those many other internation rivalries in which weapons acquisition and development play a relatively minor role? We believe so, and suggest that the following procedures might lead to a delineation of those cases which would constitute our population.

The first step would be to examine each major power's diplomatic and military history in order to identify each of the sustained conflicts in which it was engaged during the last century. Conflict is defined here as an interaction process which is short of war, but more than routine competition, isolated dispute, or sustained but low-level rivalry. The criteria would be in terms of allocation of attention, elite expression of hostility, and frequency and intensity of disputes. If our prior experiences in this sort of research are any guide, one would expect a fair amount of agreement (as to what constitutes conflict) between the relevant historians' evaluation of these processes and such operational indicators as might be generated by content analysis of public and private communications, the coding and scaling of detailed chronologies, and the examination of national budgets, manning tables, and so forth. The assumption here is that we are unlikely to find any arms interaction sequence that could be classed as an arms race except in the context of a conflict. With the number of major powers in the system ranging between five and ten at any one time over these one hundred years, the number of conflicts might turn out to be about forty, depending on whether we decompose multilateral ones into their bilateral subsets, or treat them as if they were N-party conflicts of a bilateral nature, with coalitions of nations serving as the separate protagonists. After examining these conflict sequences in some detail, it should be a relatively simple matter to ascertain a valid threshold which would differentiate those which involved arms races and those which did not.

At this juncture, any operational definition of arms race would probably be premature. But it would certainly revolve around the following classes of events:

a. Weapons *acquisition* decisions, ranging from first signs of governmental interest, through R & D, field testing, the various stages of budget authorization and appropriation, and the letting of contracts, up to delivery of finished products.
b. Weapon *deployment* moves, ranging from early small-group decisions, through various stages of the decision process, up to actual emplacement and distribution.
c. Weapon *use* moves, ranging from early planning and verbalization, through development and enunciation of doctrine and field maneuvers, up through actual use in combat.

For each of these three classes of move, we must also be able to differentiate, classify, and measure in terms of weapon types (including efficacy) and numbers thereof. As to the ultimate definition, it must certainly be based on indicators of the sort just noted, but must also be sensitive to the *interdependence* of events between the nations (and blocs) on opposing sides.

## The Questions and a Framework

Having posed the major question, tentatively identified the class of cases within which one might seek an historical, data-based answer to it, and identified the major types of move, we may now go on to a specification of the more detailed questions that must be answered, followed by an outline of the research strategy which might be followed. The questions are of two general types: (a) those which deal with *each* state's arms moves during an arms race; and (b) those which deal with the *interactions* between the states in each arms race and the relationship between the protagonists' moves.

More specifically, we would want to ascertain whether or not there is any general pattern or statistical regularity in the separate state's sequence of moves. Thus, can a given state's moves at $t_n$ be predicted from the frequency of different types of moves between the onset of the arms race and $t_{n-1}$? Is the pattern a purely incremental one, or are there discernible fluctuations? If the former, is it characterized by an arithmetic or geometric rate of increase? Is it linear or curvilinear? Is it asymptotic? Do the early moves largely determine the pattern of later ones? Is there any connection between acquisition moves and deployment moves? For example, does one type serve as a functional substitute for the other? In a different vein, do acquisition moves have to reach a certain threshold before any serious deployment moves begin? What is the chronological overlap, if any? Or do they tend to reinforce one another from an early point in the sequence? And so on.

In any event, it seems imperative that we begin by examining each protagonist's moves in isolation from the others, since it is quite possible that each move or set of moves is, by and large, self-induced. That is, once an arms race gets under way, a large fraction of a state's behavior may be in response to purely domestic events and conditions, with the adversary's mere *presence* being sufficient. That is, the adversary's moves may have little or no impact on the first state's behavior once the process has begun.[4] But unless each is examined separately, we may never discover how independent the moves are, and conversely, may be misled into seeing a strong interaction pattern when in reality there is nothing more than a pair of fairly simultaneous, but causally independent, series of behaviors on each side.

Whether we do or do not find, in some or many of the cases, certain regularities when the protagonists are examined in isolation, we must nevertheless then go on to an analysis of the interactions between them. That is, we may discover on the one hand that no pattern is discernible *until* the two adversaries' moves are examined together. On the other hand, it may be that the separate patterns fit one set of equations when considered independently and quite another when both sides' moves are treated together. Our suspicion is that this latter will indeed often be the case, suggesting that most arms races receive their impetus from a combination of domestic and foreign stimuli. Alternatively, it might well be that those which end up in war are of this combined type, whereas those which find a nonwar resolution are characterized by a high degree of self-stimulation. Further, we need not be surprised to discover that either set of patterns will be associated with those races which lead to war, and that the nonwar races are much more random and erratic in nature.

Another way to look at the sequences of moves is to drop the search for symmetry and look for two rather distinctive patterns. That is, it could be (as is often claimed by the participants) that one state's moves clearly identify it as holding or taking the initiative in round after round, with the other's moves turning out to be largely responsive in nature. One indication of this might be the difference in time lags, such that the initiator's moves come at relatively long (and perhaps even random) intervals, while the reactor's moves consistently follow close on the heels of the former's actions. And if the reactor shifts back and forth from acquisition to deployment in the same sequence as does the initiator, this could provide further evidence that it is indeed adhering to a largely responsive and countermove sort of strategy.[5]

In sum, once we have the typology (and coding rules) by which we can ascertain which governments have made which moves regarding which of their own weapons, we can begin to describe all the actions taken by each of the individual states involved in each arms interaction process. It is, of course, imperative that each state's sequence of moves be classified and scaled by independent coders who have no appreciable knowledge of either the adversary state's moves or the alternative hypotheses under examination.

## The Intervening Variables: Psychological and Domestic

A key problem in this type of research—in addition to identifying the data sources and developing the coding and scaling rules—is the formulation of the model or models to be tested. Enough has been said to indicate the sort of framework we have in mind, and it would be premature to go into their formalization here. One important problem does, however, still remain. It is one thing to find a close fit between a formal model of behavior or interstate interaction and one's data, but quite another to *account* for it, in the explanatory sense. That is, a model which fails to embrace the perceptions, preferences, and predictions of the relevant decision makers—no matter how elegant or persuasive—still falls short of providing an adequate theory of arms races (Singer 1958). Thus, once the macro-level data have been generated, and tested for goodness of fit to the competing models, the next step is to get at the data which would permit us to describe the causal chains and feedback loops which characterize any patterned interaction sequences between governments that are uncovered. In that manner, we can go beyond a mere *inference* as to what psychological processes accounted for the observed behavior, and actually *identify* some fraction of them.

One may also want to get at—in the name of a more complete model—those key domestic factors which serve as intervening variables: distribution of political power, degree of industrialization, state of the economy, national mood, and the like.

On the other hand, our immediate concern is not with the development and verification of a full-blown theory of arms races; that may be highly *desirable* from both a scientific and a policy point of view, but it may not be essential in the short run. That is, if we can ascertain (and demonstrate) that certain behavioral patterns on the part of one or both sides in an arms race are highly correlated with the incidence of war, whereas other patterns usually characterize those arms races which do not end up in war, that in itself could be quite valuable. Even if the decision makers know only what types of move to *avoid* in the current arms race—and each side knows that the other knows—the chances of breaking out of it will be improved. And at this juncture we hardly even know what arms moves are self-aggravating in their effects and which are self-correcting.

## Conclusion

The present arms race is obviously a costly one, and it appears to be dangerous as well. But *how* dangerous it is, we can only surmise, largely because we really do not know what type it is. A major need, then, is to systematically observe and classify a number of major power arms races which have already unfolded in order to ascertain:

(a) which class of race we are now in; (b) whether that class has most frequently ended up in war, or found some other termination (via fatigue, negotiated or unilateral arms reductions, or some form of capitulation); (c) what sequences of moves might most probably lead to the various outcomes.

There could be, in addition to the obvious payoffs, a more subtle but equally valuable result. It is often averred that nations get into conflicts and wars because, *inter alia*, they do not have a common and shared model of reality. Their reconstruction of the past and their models of the future can be so different that many moves are misinterpreted; a move *intended* to reassure may often have the opposite effect, and vice versa. With an operational and data-based history of arms races in front of them, Soviet and American decision makers could have a reconstruction of the past which is sufficiently credible to help reduce the probability of disastrous misperceptions and misreadings. To the extent that each side's elites find the reconstruction credible, and believe that their opposite numbers also do, faulty evaluations and inappropriate responses can be appreciably avoided.

This leads to an important corollary. If it turns out that negotiated arms reduction becomes a major objective of the present protagonists, such a study could markedly facilitate those negotiations. That is, to the extent that predictions about the future can be based on events in the past, it would increase each side's confidence in their own predictions as well as in the other's threats and promises. And the more confident one is that the adversary will indeed respond in a certain way to a particular stimulus, the more willing one is to provide that stimulus; this would seem to apply to both the negotiating phases and the arms reduction phases.

In conclusion, let me reiterate that our knowledge regarding arms races is meager indeed. With so much at stake, it borders on the irresponsible to try to make policy decisions on the basis of hypothetical models and anecdotal evidence. There is probably a great deal of relevant knowledge buried in the arms races of the past, and the above discussion suggests at least one way to go about uncovering it.

# 10

# The Peace Researcher and
# Foreign Policy Prediction

*When we speak of the applicability of peace research findings, another question concerns the identity and orientation of those who will make such applications. This is not merely a pragmatic matter of whether national decision makers will recognize, appreciate, and know how to interpret and apply the knowledge that scholars generate. On top of that very real problem is the possibility that some decision makers will use such knowledge effectively, but not necessarily for humanitarian purposes. As emphasized in Chapter 1, all "national interests" can be expected to clash with the values and interests of some individuals within the nation, not to mention those who reside elsewhere. To use the familiar cliché, scientific knowledge is not morally neutral, and some findings could indeed be used toward destructive or exploitative ends.*

*The appropriate rejoinder is that the destructive capacity of social science knowledge usually rests on its limited availability and diffusion. If only a handful of people have access to certain techniques for social manipulation, and their potential victims (at home or abroad) do not, then the knowledge can be far from morally neutral. Hence the need to create, in due course, an epistemological revolution that makes every member of the human race reasonably knowledgeable about social science. The idea is not to provide the equivalent of a graduate degree in the social sciences to every man, woman, and child, but to destroy the mysticism and taboos that keep us in thralldom. At the outset, if most of us were merely able to reason in a manner that approximates the scientific mode, even if we had little of the knowledge that has been generated, we would be better equipped to question foreign policy assertions in a fairly effective fashion. Hence peace researchers must worry not only about bringing their results to the attention of the practitioners, but to the opposition—loyal or otherwise—and to the public as well. This paper, originally serving as my presidential address to the 1972 meeting of the Peace Science Society, comes to grips with issues of this sort, looking well beyond the relevance of scientific work for the decision process alone.*

With all of the foolishness that has characterized the "futures" game over the past decade or so, it is clearly time to put this question on the agenda of a group which is committed to an *applied social science.* No matter how I turn it over in my mind, the number one task for peace research always turns out to be that of prediction: the ability to forecast, with increasing reliability, the outcomes which are most likely to emerge out of a given set of background conditions and behavioral events. And it seems to me that this holds whether our concern is to aid, augment, bypass, or subvert those who now decide questions of war and peace.

One important distinction should, however, be made at the outset, and that is the distinction between contingent and noncontingent predictions. In the *contingent* prediction, we explicitly recognize—no matter how strong the historical momentum may be—that conscious human intervention can deflect the march of history. That is, one *may* look into the future and spell out the expected conditions with no mention of those events which could effectively intervene between the prediction and the outcome. This deterministic sort of forecasting has been the dominant mode throughout history, and is still very frequently used, but it strikes me as grossly inadequate.

Even though it may be academically stylish and "realistic," as well as psychically and morally comfortable, the noncontingent prediction appears to me as empirically and ethically unsound. From the purely scientific point of view, we know that some of the variance in any set of social (or even technological) outcomes is accounted for by events which occur shortly before the observed outcomes. How much of that variance is, of course, an important empirical question (Cantril 1938; Goodman 1952; Grundberg and Modigliani 1954). And from the ethical point of view, the responsible social scientist *must* care about that nondetermined variance, try to measure it, and then go on to explore the ways in which it can be exploited by and for humanity.

My point, then, is that if we peace researchers are to nudge human history onto a slightly different course—and we can strive for nothing less—we must radically revise the style and method of social forecasting as we know it today. Let me devote my remarks tonight toward that end.

## Some Current Methods of Prediction

Leaving aside such dubious methods as the contemplation of one's navel, the distributions of tea leaves and chicken entrails, the patterning of palm lines, and the positions of the stars, one may discern four major orientations.

First, there is simple projection or extrapolation, in which we assume that past trends will continue in direction and rate of change through the present and into the future. One of the more interesting, but risky, examples is that of Fucks's effort (1965) to predict the distribution of national capabilities around the turn of the next century. Even riskier, and more ominous, was the Pentagon projection of Soviet and U.S. production rates in the late 1950s, leading to the prediction of a "missile gap" which never developed. In the absence of any other information, this basis of forecasting is better than nothing, but it contains six serious flaws. One, of course, is that it is completely fatalistic, in that it ignores the possibility of any future modification in the human behavior which produced the prior pattern of events. Second, it ignores the very frequent occurrence of upper and lower limits, and tends to assume that growth and decline curves do not flatten out at some upper or lower threshold. Third, it ignores the real possibility that the causal relationships among the variables that are affecting the trend line might themselves undergo change.

Fourth, simple projection ignores the possibility of self-correcting or self-amplifying mechanisms in that the very growth or decline in the variable itself could exercise an effect on one of the variables affecting it, and thus indirectly influence its own rate and direction of change. This holds for such ecological phenomena as found in the lynx-rabbit (Lotka 1932) and the fuel consumption-pollution relationships (Meadows et al. 1972), or in the more micro-level phenomena associated with the "self-fulfilling prophecy" (Merton 1957; Simon 1957). Fifth, it is often based on so brief a time span, or so few observations, that we might be extrapolating from a short-run perturbation rather than a long-run trend. Finally, when observations are insufficiently frequent, there is the possibility that what appears to be following a secular trend is really a cyclical phenomenon. Despite these and other dangers, extrapolation continues to be widely used for predictive purposes in social systems.

A second major method of forecasting is the "seat of the pants" scenario, made famous by some of our more enterprising military and political analysts (Kahn and Wiener 1967; De Jouvenel 1967). Essentially, this is little more than combining imagination with the conventional wisdom, and while it offers greater flexibility than straight extrapolation, the method rests—as Jensen's results suggest—on an even more flimsy foundation (1972). Closely related to this is the Delphi method (Helmer et al. 1966), in which a number of separate—if not independent—specialists send their predictions to a central agent who tabulates the results and sends the collated figures back to the original forecasters. In light of that distribution, they are asked to revise (or stand with) their original predictions. While this is merely a paper and pencil formalization of what often happens in foreign ministries, it does have the virtue of revealing how "other-directed" the respondents are. Thus, it may serve as an excellent replication of the Asch (1952) and the Sherif and Hovland (1961) experiments, but it is hardly a basis from which confident forecasts can be made.

A third major method is the game or man-machine simulation (Bloomfield and Padelford 1959; Guetzkow et al. 1963). In this case, rather than have one or two specialists "brainstorm" their way to a scenario, we assign roles to professional students or practitioners and instruct them to play out a scenario from some given point of departure. This basis not only depends on the accuracy of the conventional wisdom, but also—depending on how carefully programmed it is—lacks the reproducibility which we can at least get from the written reasoning behind the armchair scenario.

A fourth method is the computer simulation. And even when it proceeds from hypothetical "data" and naive untested models, it offers a more solid basis of forecasting than the first three methods. This is because it requires us to make explicit the variables we employ, our guesses as to their magnitude, and the processes which allegedly lead to the simulated outcomes. But if the data inputs are imaginary and the model is merely a formalization of the shared hunches of the analysts, a policy maker would have to be most imprudent to take the results seriously. I will return to this particular and rather promising method in due course.

There are many variations on these four basic themes, and volumes could be written to summarize and evaluate the procedures and results to date. But our concern this evening is not so much to belabor the more familiar methods but to lay out some of the problems and possibilities associated with a more rigorous strategy.

## Preferred Methods of Prediction

Having spoken critically of some of the more familiar methods of foreign policy forecasting, it is incumbent on me to suggest some preferred alternatives. As I see it, there are two, with one being essentially an extension of the other. The first might be called the postdict-predict method, and the other—and much to be preferred— might be called the theory-based method. Let me try to illuminate the difference while describing each.

### From Postdiction to Prediction

By this caption, I mean nothing more than a method by which we first ascertain the direction and strength of association among one or more predictors and an outcome variable in the past, and then project that historically observed correlation into the future. This method is likely to be the most feasible one in the short run, but it has some of the earmarks of simple projection. There are, at the same time, some important distinctions.

In simple extrapolation, one merely estimates or measures the value (magnitude) of a given variable at several points in the remote and recent past, plots them on a time axis, fits a straight, curved, or sinuous line to those points, and then continues that line out into the future. Thus, if a nation's military expenditures have been rising an average of 5 percent per year for the past decade, one plots the rising curve into the future with each successive year showing a 5 percent increase over the prior one. The same would hold true for such easily measurable variables as contributions to an intergovernmental organization, or for such elusive ones as the similarity of two nations' alliance membership profiles, or the concentration of capabilities among the major powers.

In the method proposed here, however, we extend or project the observed prior *relationship* between or among two or more variables. That is, if we have discovered that underdeveloped nations of a certain class become less conciliatory in dealing with one another as their Gross National Products move upward to $280 per capita, and more conciliatory after they exceed that threshold, we can (with certain caveats) use that observed historical relationship as one possible basis for predicting into the future. Or, if our postdictive analyses show that bilateral conflicts marked by threat-to-promise ratios of less than .4 result in war significantly less often than those above that threshold, we can use that observed relationship as a possible basis for predicting the outcome of future conflicts.

To return to an earlier issue, note that these are contingent predictions rather than fatalistic ones. That is, they tell us that *if* certain nations exceed the GNP per capita threshold, their foreign policy behavior patterns are likely to change, and that *if* the threat-promise ratio is kept low, wars will be less frequent. Thus, we articulate our model, operationalize the predictor and outcome variables, and then test the bivariate or multivariate relationships implied by the model for some relevant time-space domain in the past. To the extent that our postulated relationships are borne out by the historical facts, we can say that our simple models have postdictive power. Further—and this is the important caveat—to the extent that we are willing to assume a continuation of those observed relationships from the past into the future, we may use them for purposes of prediction. And, as Rapoport reminded us in last year's presidential address (1972), this can be a risky assumption.

A second caveat is that these predictions are, at best, probabilistic ones (Meehl 1954). Even in the event that we discover a perfect set of correlations between our predictor and outcome variables—and this is extraordinarily rare in international politics—we would do well to discount the strength of the contingent relationship. And if—as is more likely—we find partial or multiple coefficients in the .5–.8 range, we should assume that the predicted association is unlikely to be any stronger in the future.

A third and obvious caveat is that, no matter how strong and consistent the postdicted correlation may be, the *ceteris paribus* assumption just may not hold into the future. Any simple predictive model, partly because it ignores the effects of several (or many) unobserved and unmeasured intervening variables, may just not apply to subsequent cases (W. Moore 1964; Russett 1965). To illustrate, the correlation between the threat-promise ratio and war may be based on a fairly long period in which the larger international system had a rather low bipolarity index. But if new alliance formations were to produce a sharp increase in bipolarity in the period just ahead, third and fourth parties may encourage their allies to stand firm at the critical moment in a diplomatic conflict, even while their early verbal exchanges remained below the critical threshold. And so on.

To sum up, observed historical associations will almost certainly increase the accuracy of our contingent predictions, especially if combined with creative (but disciplined) scenario construction (Bloomfield and Beattie 1971; Singer 1970). And while this is a considerable improvement over what we can do *without* such correlational knowledge and postdictive models, it still offers a weak reed in a tense or unstable environment. If the peace researcher is to appreciably enhance the survivability of mankind, he or she must do better.

## Theory-Based Prediction

Two points emerge from the preceding discussion: (a) correlational knowledge is not the same thing as explanatory knowledge; and (b) the closer we come to the latter, the more accurate our predictions are likely to be. But what constitutes explanatory knowledge is very much a function of one's point of view or scientific purpose. For example, some operations researchers will claim to have an "explanation" for some outcome pattern as soon as they've found the equation that produces a predicted distribution close to that which is actually observed. At the other extreme, some social scientists might insist on establishing the connection from predictor to outcome variables via the intrapsychic (or even the biochemical) processes of those whose decisions and behavior allegedly link up those two sets of variables. In between these extremes are many other views as to what constitutes an adequate explanation, and to which level of analysis one must descend (or ascend) in order to produce a satisfactory descriptive sequence of events and conditions. For our purposes here, let us settle for a statement of the sequential events and conditions which link together several predictor variables and an outcome variable in a sufficiently self-evident, compelling, and plausible fashion to gain the assent of most competent observers.

Note that competence is left undefined, that compelling and plausible carry a strong intersubjective connotation, and that those links which are "self-evident" need not be articulated, observed, or demonstrated. Note also that the word "causal" is not used. While we can speak with some confidence about "causal" processes of a very primitive sort (such as pressure on this lever causes this gate to open, or an injection of adrenalin causes the membranes to relax), the social scientist would be wise to forget about (or, at least, sidestep) causality. Almost any social process of interest can occur via so many different and unobservable routes that we would have to make inferential leaps of heroic proportions in order to specify causality.

Returning, then, to the need for a theory in order to make really solid contingent predictions, I would define a reproducible and compelling explanation of a given class of events as a theory. Conversely, the term "theory" should not be applied to a hunch, a vague suspicion, a widely accepted scenario, an untested mathematical model, or even a clearly demonstrated bivariate or multivariate correlational pattern. Given this view of an explanatory theory (to be redundant), what can it do for predictive purposes that observed correlations cannot do?

The key difference lies in the weakness of prediction based solely on observed correlations out of the past. That is, correlations only tell us the general strength of association between our predictor and outcome variables, and tell us little about the exceptions (Rothstein 1972, pp. 163-64). More specifically, they give us only the crudest hints as to when, and why, the general pattern does *not* hold. To put it another way, they reveal little about the timing, direction, and magnitude of changes in the often interdependent relationships among our predictor variables. Nor do they offer much guidance in helping us explain those almost inevitable system dynamics which act continuously on the ways in which the predictors impinge on the outcomes. In the absence of such knowledge, it is almost as dangerous to project an historically observed *correlation* into the future as it is to project a single variable's magnitude into the future. In sum, correlational knowledge can carry us part way, but until we have built and empirically tested a theory which offers a compelling explanation of the changing as well as the constant associations in the past, we make predictions of less than desirable solidity. As Comte reminded us (and I paraphrase), *on doit savoir pour prevoir.*

## Routes to Policy Relevant Theory

It is, of course, one thing to agree that solid explanatory theories offer the most reliable basis for making foreign policy predictions, and quite another to agree on the most promising routes to the construction of such theories. While I cannot go here into any thorough discussion of alternative theory-building strategies, a few subjective comments might be in order. Restricting ourselves to theory in the scientific sense used here, let me outline and comment upon five general orientations.

One strategy is the heavily *in*ductive one, in which we articulate and test a number of simple hypotheses against the relevant historical past. As we test, discard, modify, test again, and confirm these hypotheses (or, for the purists, disconfirm their null versions), we can begin to assemble them into an increasingly integrated and internally consistent body of predictive and explanatory knowledge. While this is not the route to theory that the philosophers of science and the textbooks usually advocate, it often turns out to be the most effective. But that effectiveness also depends on the researcher's theoretical sophistication, epistemological subtlety, and "feeling" for the data.

At the other end of the spectrum is the heavily *de*ductive strategy, in which one constructs a theory out of the whole cloth, as it were. That is, we think of alternative possible explanations for the outcome phenomena which concern us, select the one which seems most plausible, most internally consistent, is most compatible with our general theoretical orientation, and (less often) most consistent with the findings of others. We then articulate the putative explanatory model in mathematical, diagrammatic, or verbal form. Some of us would then claim to have produced a theory, but most would agree that the formalized model must be refined further into operational language, and then subjected to a series of systematic empirical tests against the relevant past.

As a matter of fact, most successful scientists work with a mix of these two strategies, moving back and forth between the building of models and their systematic testing. Pure inductivism is ineffective because it offers little guidance for selecting and then synthesizing the tested propositions into a coherent and internally consistent whole. And pure deductivism is ineffective because our discipline has virtually no larger body of theory worthy of the name from which to begin, and because the resulting explanation may—despite its elegance and plausibility—be quite inconsistent with the historical facts. Further, until a fair amount of correlational knowledge has been generated by the inductive strategy, we have little basis for taking seriously one or another of the many plausible models we can construct from our armchairs.

A third strategy is that of analogizing, in which we build models on the basis of assumed similarities between the world of international politics and that of small groups, industrial organizations, urban communities, and so forth. While it is highly desirable for all the social sciences to borrow and compare across disciplinary boundaries, it is quite risky to assume that nations behave analogously to individuals, sales divisions, or metropolitan agencies in comparable situations (Singer and Ray 1966). Such analogizing does, of course, offer a rich source of ideas for foreign policy relevant models, but, as before, there is no substitute for the empirical test vis-à-vis the hard facts of history.

Fourth is the all-man or man-machine simulation, in which individuals or small teams are assigned roles as nations, given a description of the "state of the world," and told to go ahead and play out the scenario. When this activity is highly structured and controlled, it can help alert us to the less obvious implications of our models, but when run in the more informal "gaming" mode—as suggested earlier—it is a waste of time, if not downright dangerous. The danger, of course, lies in the fact that the players bring one or another version of the conventional wisdom to their roles, play according to some mix of it and their own psychic needs, and are then led to understand that they have simulated some aspect of international politics (Singer 1965a).

A fifth strategy, and in my judgment, the one toward which we should move with all deliberate speed, is that of the computerized simulation (Alker and Brunner 1969; Gorden 1968; Bremer 1970). As I see it, this approach to theory building offers us the major virtues of the other four strategies, with only one serious liability: that of cost. The number of minutes needed to run a half-century scenario, for example, plus the disk and cell storage space, plus the many weeks of a programmer's services, could easily amount to several thousand dollars.

But the advantages are (in principle, at least) very impressive. If we build our computerized models in the form of component subroutines, we can experiment with a large number of contending explanations. If we begin with a reasonably extensive and accurate data base, we can experiment with differing magnitudes of our key variables. And if we are willing to move back into the referent historical world when we run into dead ends in the simulation, we can achieve a valuable interplay between our deductive and inductive emphases. These and other virtues add up to a method in which we can ultimately—by a systematic trial-and-error procedure— "reproduce" diplomatic history. We begin with the most plausible and parsimonious model by which we hope to explain the fluctuating occurrence of crises, war, alliance formation, the establishment of international organizations, etc., and then examine how closely that model fits the historical patterns which have been observed and recorded earlier in the project, or by others. The chances of getting a good fit for more than a few of our historical cases are not very good, so we continue to modify the subroutines to reflect changes in the relationships among the key variables. If a series of such experiments leads eventually to a fairly good fit, we are fortunate. More often, at this stage in our discipline's development, we will conclude that some important variable has been omitted, and we then must either gather the time series data reflecting the historical values of the variable, or make some reasonable estimates of those values, to see whether its inclusion improves the postdictive-predictive power of the model.

One serious problem, however, is that—if the early findings from the Correlates of War project are accurate—the relationships among key variables are not constant over long periods of time (Singer 1972a). That is, we not only find that most of the more interesting variables show appreciable variation from month to month and year to year, but that the *correlations among them* also change, albeit less obviously. The 1890s, for example, produce a change in the direction of the relationships between alliance patterns and war, and between capability concentration and war; some systemic conditions which predicted *to* war in one century predicted *away* from war in the other, and vice versa (Singer and Small 1968; Singer, Bremer, and Stuckey 1972). These inconvenient but apparently genuine shifts can be a source of frustration, but they can also be a source of inspiration, helping to identify important watersheds which historians may (or may not) have noted and interpreted accurately.

For purposes of policy prediction, the computer simulation strategy does more than this. First, it offers the most feasible way of ascertaining when, and in what fashion, the theoretical dynamics of the international system change. Second, it helps us to identify the factors that most strongly account for those changing relationships among our variables. Third, and most important for predictive purposes, the well-designed and carefully tested simulation has built into it the mechanisms which account for and produce such systemic dynamics. Thus, we can move from runs of the past to runs of the future, and be much less likely to commit the sin of mechanical extrapolation from past into future. In sum, a high-quality computer simulation is a representation of that sector of world politics which interests us, and a manifestation of that solid theory which is essential to accurate foreign policy prediction.

## Epistemology, Education, and Prediction

So far, I have outlined several methods by which to make foreign policy predictions and discussed some of the ways in which we might build toward the more promising of those methods. But the construction of sound explanatory and predictive theories is only part of the game. What doth it serve us if our potential clients are incapable of distinguishing between shoddy merchandise and that which more closely approximates the "real thing"? It is, of course, no coincidence that most of the producers of foreign policy analyses and predictions come out of the same intellectual subculture as the consumers. While few single-nation, and to my knowledge, no cross-national studies have been conducted, the very clear impression is that defense ministry and foreign office personnel the world over are largely products of either a liberal arts or a law school education (Harr 1965, pp. 14-16). Outside of that unfortunate aberration exemplified by the U.S. Defense Department's "whiz kids," we find very few scientifically oriented people staffing these agencies around the world. And the same would seem to hold for most of those who serve as their advisers and consultants.

Rather than look for some conspiratorial explanation, we would do well to look at ourselves and the several roles that we do or should take on. While most peace researchers are in their twenties and thirties and thus hardly responsible for the epistemological innocence and theoretical clumsiness of today's foreign policy elites, we are not doing nearly enough to change that state of affairs. The implication, then, is that we have to be more than creative and careful researchers; we have to assume a variety of educational roles as well.

Perhaps the most important educational role is, paradoxically enough, in our research. By and large, macro-social scientists do a poor job of explicating their models or writing up their findings. Insufficiently attentive to the canons of scientific reproducibility, the untidy organization and semantic imprecision (not to mention the virtual absence of grace or wit) of our books and articles can do a great deal of harm. First off, we lose many of our prescientific readers, in and out of government, early in the opening paragraphs. Thus, the specific piece of work seldom gets read, not to mention understood, in policy-making circles. Secondly, and more harmful, our writings help to reinforce the prejudices and make more credible the general skepticism with which a graduate of the Fletcher School, Ecole Pratique, or Oxbridge approaches this "behavioral science stuff." Given their educational preparation, it is little wonder that even our elite clientele is often left confused or bored. Let me plead with all of you, then—and especially those of you who edit or referee for the various peace research journals—to give considerably greater attention to the quality of our written work. From the choice of title and statement of the problem, through the description of data-making and data-analysis procedures, to the interpretation of results, there is enormous room for improved literary craftmanship and semantic clarity.

Second is the educational role we might play in our public lives. As consultants to governmental and intergovernmental agencies, for example, it is essential that we make more clear the reasoning behind our recommendations, the epistemological criteria we hope to satisfy, and the very real limitations on our ability to give much guidance. We have discovered precious little about war, peace, and social conflict to date, and it is incumbent on us to give as much emphasis to our ignorance as we do to our expertise. There has already been, at least in the U.S. and Western Europe, a fair amount of overselling by consultants, contract seekers, and grant applicants; too often, peace researchers can be as careless on this score as their less rigorous (or more hawkish) colleagues.

Closely related are the missed opportunities to call public and elite attention to dubious analytical arguments, primitive procedures, and ignorance of the available evidence. Since fewer than perhaps 5 percent of all media executives, reporters, and commentators have had any formal or informal training in scientific method, the opportunities should be legion. And even when the media people are substantively and methodologically competent in reporting and interpreting foreign policy material, we can be fairly sure that those governmental officials who dish out "the news" will not be.

The third educational role is, of course, in the classroom. An overwhelming majority of peace researchers are employed by schools and colleges to perform a pedagogical role. And while we seem to be doing better at this than at our less institutionalized teaching tasks, a few constructive criticisms seem to be in order. My particular concern is with undergraduate courses in the social sciences and our tendency to underestimate our students' intelligence and motivation. Thus, we work hard to instruct our graduate students in the basic rules and fine points of scientific method, and then turn up in undergraduate classes sounding all too similar to our most prescientific colleagues from departments of speech or history. Even though this practice also seems to hold for colleagues who are not part of the peace research community (thus making it more difficult to break into the vicious circle), the task need not overwhelm us. Without necessarily getting into the finer points of statistics, or too deeply into mathematical notation, we can surely convey the basic sense and style of social science. My own experience is that students do better if we introduce new methods within a substantive context, rather than in isolation; one such effort is reflected in a recent "learning module" on the scientific study of politics (Singer 1972b). In sum, the undergraduate education sector may well be the most important one to which we address ourselves. Most of the world's foreign policy elites are college educated, as are those who serve in the mass media; and increasingly, the rest of the world's "ordinary citizens" will follow the lead of the Western nations in receiving some sort of higher education. If we can help to equip these people with an appreciation of the difference between authoritative assertion and reproducible evidence, their political leaders will find it much more difficult to sell them one absurd bill of goods after another.

To conclude this argument, then, there seems to be a strong connection between the research we undertake and the educational roles we assume. No matter how solid the base from which we make policy predictions, it could easily be for naught. The policy elites must understand the difference between and among the various methods of prediction, and not be impressed with anything less than the most rigorous and careful, no matter how familiar the accents in which delivered, or the "stature" of the source. The media must begin to examine foreign policy pronouncements and predictions with considerably greater competence, no matter how symbiotic (or antagonistic) their relationships with the political elites. And the attentive public must experience a marked improvement in its ability to discriminate, and in its willingness to press both the government and the media when the usual foreign policy propaganda begins to flow. Each sector can reinforce the more wholesome tendencies in the other, thus creating a system of national states in which foreign policy is more intelligently—if not more humanely—formulated. It is not too strong to say that the world needs an epistemological revolution, and peace researchers can play a central role in that revolution.

## Conclusion

You will notice that I did not use this occasion to deal explicitly with some of the important schisms that have divided the peace research movement during the past eight years or so (Burton 1964; Schmid 1968; Galtung 1969; Schwartz 1969; Rapoport 1970a; Kent 1971; Krippendorf 1971; Carroll 1972). It was, indeed, my first instinct to do so, but I then thought better of it. Why? First, my views on most of these issues are already well known, and I hope that—for example—no one doubts the strength of either my opposition to *all* injustice, including physical violence, or my commitment to the pursuit and diffusion of knowledge as a major weapon in the struggle against injustice (Singer 1971b).

Second, there is so much of real importance to be done that we ought not spend valuable time recapitulating the arguments of the revisionists in our ranks. The world cannot wait for us to wrap up yet another round in the interminable debate as to why mortal man cannot scientifically study his own problems. Nor can it wait for us to resolve the alleged dilemma posed by the fact that each observer is partially shaped by his or her place in society and is incapable of objectivity. The same holds for endless verbal gymnastics regarding positive peace and negative peace, or structural violence and manifest violence, to mention one of the more durable semantic quarrels. In the same vein, it seems retrogressive and defeatist for us to now enter into lengthy debate over the need for a new paradigm (Alker 1976). While there is considerable room for improvement in the dominant paradigm, it seems to me that the flaws are not that fundamental.

Finally, my hunch is that many of these problems can be better clarified and resolved in the context of serious ongoing research. Naturally, if such research is of the mindless empiricism, armchair speculation, or demagogic denunciation varieties, the problems will *not* be clarified and resolved. But I have in mind something which is not only more rigorous, but also more self-consciously critical.

Let me conclude, then, by putting the prediction question into a somewhat broader context. As I see it, war—and other large-scale dramatic events—may be seen as a consequence of three kinds of factor. These are: (a) deterministic; (b) probabilistic; and (c) voluntaristic. Needless to say, they are neither independent of each other nor easily disentangled.

By the deterministic factors, I mean those events and conditions over which it is too late to exercise any control, and whose impact markedly limits our options as we seek to ameliorate (or, for some, amplify) a conflict before it spills over into overt mass violence. This is not to imply that they fully determine or guarantee that the conflict will or will not erupt into violence, but only that—because they are beyond our temporal control—they set some of the constraints within which we operate.

Then there are the probabilistic factors, reflecting both the inadequacies in our models and measures, and the stochastic element that is probably inherent in all social phenomena. While a goodly share of what appears to inhere in the latter will, in due course, turn out to be really a function of the former, we nevertheless must reckon with those unpredictables (including human capriciousness) that are *not* the fault of an inadequate knowledge base. Further, some would include here that self-negating element which leads people to behave in ways contradictory to the predicted ways, once they know what they are "supposed" to do.

But this latter element—cited by cynics as well as romantics as the reason why we can never build a science of peace—may be our salvation as well as our frustration. I refer, then, to the third kind of factor, the voluntaristic one. This element may be crucial in two ways. First, precisely because humans *are* different from lemmings, we need not act as certain scientific models predict we will act. With reasonably solid and credible knowledge as to the consequences of repeating the behavior of similar groups in similar situations in the past, we need not march, lockstep, over the cliff.

Second, the better our knowledge about the processes by which groups move from incompatible interests to conflict to mass violence, the more readily we can distinguish between those factors which *are* beyond our control, and those which we had best try to modify. If, near the brink, it is too late to change certain structural, cultural, or material properties of the system, but still possible to change others, the knowledge which permits us to make that distinction is of no mean consequence. Moreover, the more accurately we can predict which actions at $t_0$ will lead to conditions which are both dangerous and largely unalterable at $t_5$, the better the chance to head off those actions.

In sum, there seems to be a reasonably clear line from theoretical knowledge to contingent prediction to adaptive behavior. First, of course, our existential, correlational, and explanatory knowledge must expand. Second, that knowledge must be integrated into coherent theoretical form. Third, it must be evaluated critically and understood by the leaders and the led. And, fourth, it must be used to generate contingent predictions which are credible as well as careful. If we peace researchers can contribute to all of these objectives, we will have earned our keep.

# V

# The Acquisition
# of Knowledge

Much has been said so far regarding the costs we incur and risks we run because of the meagerness of our knowledge regarding international conflict. Similarly, I have urged at some length how such knowledge, were it available, could make an appreciable difference in the way that foreign and military policies are designed and implemented. It is, therefore, time to shift from the matter of "what if" to that of "how to."

Those who are familiar with my work know that this has been a heavy (but not favorite) preoccupation of mine, that is, writing on questions of epistemology and research strategy. Despite the temptation to include here a large sample of these writings, a sense of proportion leads me to hold back. The basic arguments as to the *feasibility* of a science of world politics are by now all too familiar, and those concerning the *desirability* of such a science have been summarized adequately in the preceding selections. Moreover, the highly detailed questions of index construction, data analysis, statistical inference, and so on, are better dealt with in the context of specific empirical investigations, many of which are reported in the second volume of this series.

# 11

## The Historical Experiment as a Research Strategy in the Study of World Politics

*Here we look at only one paper on research strategy.[1] It concerns the dual question of where we look for evidence regarding world politics and the way we look for that evidence.*

As one looks back on the important developments in political science over the past two decades, there is much to be applauded. While it may be premature to say that we have come "of age" as a scientific discipline, the field is clearly in better shape today than it was in the early 1950s. One indicator is the ratio between mere speculation and observed empirical regularities reported in our journal articles. Another is the decline in the percentage (if not in absolute numbers) of our colleagues who insist that political phenomena are just not amenable to scientific examination. A third might be the dramatic increase in the number of political scientists who have been exposed to training in the techniques and rationale of data making and data analysis. The list could be extended, but we need not do so here.

On the other hand, a stance of comfortable complacency would be very premature. Not only have we fared badly in coming to grips with the knowledge-action relationship in the abstract, but we have by and large done a poor job of shaping the policies of our respective national, provincial, and local governments. Since others as well as myself (Singer 1970) have dealt with these issues before—if not definitively—let me eschew further discussion of the knowledge *application* question for the moment, and go on to matters of basic research. Of the more serious flaws to date, two stand out particularly. One is the lack of balance between a concern for cumulativeness on the one hand and the need for innovation on the other. My impression is that students of *national* politics (at least those who work in the vineyard of empirical regularities) have been more than conscientious in staying with one set of problems, such as the relationship between political attitudes and voting behavior. But students of *inter*national politics have, conversely, tended to move all too quickly from one problem to another, long before cumulative evidence has been generated and before our findings are integrated into coherent wholes.

A second weakness, as I see it, is our general failure to appreciate the full relevance of the experimental mode to our research strategies. This observation is meant in two senses. First, when we do longitudinal studies, we often fail to conceive of them in experimental terms. Second, and perhaps more important, macro-social scientists tend to focus heavily upon contemporary phenomena, and thus overlook the great scientific potential of longitudinal analyses conducted in the experimental mode. This *should* be a matter of some surprise, when we consider the extent to which our data analysis techniques rest upon, and flow out of, the experimental metaphor. From the pioneering work of Pearson (1957) and Fisher (1925; 1935) up through Stouffer (1962), Blalock (1961), and Campbell and Stanley (1966), a strong preoccupation of our best methodologists has been with experimental (or quasi-experimental) design in one version or another. Yet, with few exceptions (Eldersveld 1956; Simon and Stern 1955; and Eulau 1971, for example), we have tended to view experimentation in rather narrow terms, and to think of it as a research activity that should be confined to the laboratory.[2]

In the pages that follow, I should like to offer a somewhat broader view of the experimental mode, and suggest that we have barely begun to exploit its possibilities in the investigation of political phenomena. And although my illustrations will draw heavily from the study of international politics in general, and the war-peace question in particular, my hope is that the possibilities that are illuminated here will find relevance in other sectors of the discipline as well.[3]

## Three Types of Experiment

When the concept of experiment comes up, most of us—scientists as well as laymen—tend to think of laboratories. In them, we expect to find all sorts of instruments by which one observes and measures the phenomena associated with the predictor or outcome variables. These might include, for example, a bubble chamber or spectroscope for the physical scientist, a microscope or centrifuge for the biological scientist, and a moving picture camera or GSR console for the social scientist.

The laboratory is, of course, associated with scientific research because it facilitates the conduct of "controlled" experiments, in which one can: (a) manipulate many of the factors that might affect the outcome; (b) isolate the effects of one factor at a time; and (c) run the same experiment over and over to ascertain the consistency of a given set of results (Rapoport 1969). As I hope to demonstrate in a later section, there are serious obstacles to a clean experiment even in the laboratory. But let us first take note of the fact that two *other* types of experiment can also be envisaged.

The second type occurs, not in the laboratory, but out in the "field," or in "nature." Here, the investigator need not—and often cannot—generate all the events and conditions of interest. Rather, he or she first observes and records the normal sequence or concatenation of events, and then either waits for or instigates some intervening event in order to ascertain its effect on the previously observed pattern of outcomes.[4] The astronomer, for example, waits for a number of planets to arrange themselves in a given configuration, and then tries to measure the effect of that configuration on the orbit of an Nth planet. Or the medical researcher divides a number of patients into two groups whose members are more or less identical on the relevant background characteristics. He or she then subjects each group to a different treatment (or perhaps a placebo "treatment") and waits to see whether one treatment "produced" more cures or ameliorations than the other.

Similarly, the sociologist might identify twelve cities that are closely matched along the most relevant dimensions and then anticipate (or arrange) that the appropriate agencies will divide them into three groups, using a new job referral policy A in four of them, another policy B in another four, and retaining the old policy in the others. A year later, the unemployment scores can be compared to ascertain which of the three policies "leads to" the lowest unemployment figure. While such field experiments do not offer the same opportunities for control as do those conducted in the laboratory, we can appreciate that a modicum of control is nevertheless achieved. Equally important, in the field, one often makes up in realism what one loses in control, or to put it in more formal language, the threats to the experiment's *in*ternal validity may be more than compensated for by the improvement in its *ex*ternal validity (Campbell and Stanley, 1966).

So far, then, we have considered the well-known laboratory experiment and the by-no-means-unknown field experiment. Let us turn now to the third type, or *historical* experiment. Some will object to the pairing of these two words, and this is quite understandable. Treating events or conditions which have already transpired, in which no intervention—obtrusive or otherwise (Webb et al. 1966)—is possible, does not seem consonant with our traditional ideas of experimentation, or perhaps even with "quasi experimentation," to use Campbell's term.

To sum up this section, one might prefer the conventional definition of experiment, but as Laponce (1972, pp. 4-5) reminds us, the more restricted interpretation is "fraught with dangers," and could lead us to focus "too exclusively on the laboratory." The more narrow definition, he adds, "is ill-adjusted to the variety of data and conditions to which the social scientist can apply experimental techniques." The balance of this paper should, however, not only indicate that the historical experiment is a perfectly legitimate mode of research, but that it actually offers certain advantages vis-à-vis those experiments that are carried out in the laboratory or in the field.

## Key Problems in Scientific Experimentation

Having committed myself to demonstrating the proposition that the experimental mode is as applicable to history as to the laboratory or the field, the question remains as to how best make that demonstration. One promising point of departure is to identify some of the major preoccupations and key problems of the scientific experimentalist, and then compare the opportunities and constraints offered by each of the three experimental settings. Let me, thus, attempt that in a rather general sense in this section, and then go on to *the* central issue—that of control—in the subsequent section.

## Observation and Measurement

While systematic observation is highly interdependent with data analysis and inference, one can separate out these activities for the sake of expositional clarity. Once one's model or hypothesis is reasonably well formulated, the next major step is the acquisition or generation of one's data. And unless another researcher or some problem-oriented "consumer" has generated the necessary data, one must set about the establishment of procedures for systematic observation and measurement.

In the laboratory, this task *can* be as simple as defining a "known material" and then weighing out the specified amount of it or measuring its spatial dimensions. But, with increasing frequency, the physical or biological experimenter must wrestle with more complex procedures. For example, without the elaborate device known as a bubble chamber, the high-energy physicist would be unable to observe and photograph the path of ionizing particles. Similarly, without the diffusion of a silver nitrate solution that blackens on contact with organic matter, the medical researcher would be unable to trace those proteins whose presence may indicate the symptoms of certain forms of schizophrenia.

For the social scientist working in the laboratory, the range of observational techniques can likewise range from the simple to the complex, and from the direct to the indirect. A simple and direct technique would be the identification of each experimental subject by sex, height, weight, and hair color, but if one required indicators of less tangible phenomena, the technique would be less direct. In experimental games, we can classify the subjects' response to a variety of electoral ballots (Laponce 1966) or to a combined stimulus of payoff matrix and opponent's moves via a simple behavioral coding scheme (Rapoport and Guyer 1969). More elusive, but fairly operational, might be the use of trained observer-coders who infer the motivation behind a wide variety of acts emitted by the subjects

(Bales 1950; Leary 1957) and whose performance can be checked in part by tests of intercoder reliability.

Shifting now from laboratory to field, the experimentalists' problems again have a great deal in common, regardless of discipline. The astronomer can now ascertain the size or infer the orbital pattern of a given planet with high-powered telescopes. And the meteorologist's observation techniques can range from the simple reading of barometric pressure to the complex interpretation of radar traces left by a passing storm. Similarly, the medical scientist will work with such easily measured factors as vital lung capacity or blood pressure, and such elusive ones as level of anxiety or family medical history. And, once more, the social scientist can conduct field experiments in which the observation and measurement problems may range from the highly operational to the ambiguous, and from the obvious to the improbable. For example, we can code and scale children's behavior (Hutt and Hutt 1970) or scale the differential campaign appeals directed to different members of the electorate (Eldersveld 1956), or measure the degree of centralization in the decisional process of two different government agencies as part of an inquiry into problem-solving efficiency.

Even at the international level, a field experiment might require the measurement of, let us say, the voting consensus of a given United Nations bloc before an expected crisis or series of weapons tests, in order to ascertain the "effect" of those events on the subsequent voting pattern. To take another example, one might scale the threat-perception levels in one nation's diplomatic articulations prior to, and then following, a major election in an adversary nation. To go a step further in emphasizing the extent to which one can satisfy the requirements of reliability and validity in the measurement of historical phenomena that are germane to comparative and international politics, let me note that many events and conditions do indeed leave traces and records. And, with a modicum of ingenuity, political scientists have already observed and measured—long years after the fact—many critical types of event and condition. Among these are alliance configurations, diplomatic rankings, polarization and fractionalization of various systems, the frequency and magnitude of wars and insurrections, the shifting capabilities of nations, and so forth.[5] And as some of these labels suggest, one need not be restricted to simple and direct measures such as a nation's territorial size, population, or even the reconstruction of its national income. One may also get at more complex, derived measures whose reliability and validity will turn out to be every bit as high as those generated in the laboratory or field.[6] The point, then, is that the observation and measurement problems and opportunities are essentially the same for all the sciences, and regardless of the setting within which the experiment is carried out.

### Ascertaining Covariation

Although it is now a truism to note that correlation is not equivalent to causation, few scientists would object to the proposition that the establishment of covariation—while not *sufficient*—is indeed *necessary* to the search for causation. Given the central role of covariation, then, it behooves us to examine the ways in which it may be ascertained in the three different research settings—laboratory, field, and historical—and the three—physical, biological, and social—sciences.

This discussion can be briefer than that concerning observation and measurement, since the similarities are even more evident as we move from one setting to the next. That is, once we have satisfied certain minimal conditions of reliability and validity in our indicators, and have gone on to generate the data sets for predictor and outcome variables, the statistical problems begin to look very much alike.

For example, there is the universal problem of adopting the analytic technique that is appropriate to the fineness of our measurement scales. If our data are measured on a nominal scale only, we have little choice but to analyze them via contingency tables, using such coefficients of association as the chi-square, Yule's Q, tau-beta, phi, and so forth. If we can do better than mere nominal classification of our data, and rank the observations on some sort of ordinal scale, we may then utilize such rank-order coefficients as Spearman's rho, the Kolmogorov-Smirnov and Mann-Whitney tests, or one of Kendall's several measures of rank covariation between (or across) ordinally scaled data sets. And as we improve the precision of our indicators and utilize data that are measured on interval or ratio scales, we can go to more refined coefficients of association and covariation. One of the most widely used is Pearson's product moment correlation ($r$), and beyond that is a panoply of statistical regression techniques, most of which permit a modicum of prudently inferred causality (Kort 1973).

The measures of covariation that we use will depend more on the quality of the data with which we work, and on where we stand on the road from exploration to discovery to confirmation of associations, than upon the milieu within which the investigation takes place. One can, for example, think of no good reason for avoiding the path analysis technique when involved in an historical experiment, or a simple contingency table analysis when in the biological laboratory.

### Inferring Causality

As we move from the data-making and data-analysis phases of a scientific investigation to the problem of interpreting the results, the apparent differences among laboratory, field, and historical experiments take on greater magnitude. Thus, even if the arguments of the preceding two subsections seem quite reasonable, some will urge that in *this* subsection we find the inescapable gulf between "real" science and social science, especially that version of the latter that does not occur in the controlled environment of the laboratory.

In the methodological literature, one increasingly encounters the concepts of internal and external *validity* when examining a research design (Campbell and Stanley 1966). Essentially, the validity issue can be translated into the question: To what extent does the research design permit us to infer "causality" or some approximation thereof? To be more precise, the issue is not one of the validity of the *design* (or of the experiment), but of the *inferences* we seek to draw from the results of the investigation.

The labels are slightly unfortunate in another sense as well, since *inter*nal validity is seen as germane to the study itself, whereas *exter*nal validity refers to the generalizability of the study's findings to some larger population of unobserved cases. While agreeing that: (a) the design must reflect both concerns; and (b) they are interdependent and one must therefore often accept trade-offs between the two, I would nevertheless prefer a sharper semantic and conceptual distinction. In any event, let us attend mainly to the first of these considerations at this juncture.

In *any* research setting, the central issue is that of experimental *control*: the arrangement of the investigation such that any inferences we draw will not turn out to be ill founded or spurious. Or to put it another way, adequate controls permit us to conclude that the specified predictor (independent) variables were indeed the ones that produced the variation in the outcome variable, and that such variation cannot be attributed to other events or conditions. The virtues of the laboratory, versus the field or history, in the social sciences may be summarized briefly. One is the ease with which we control the environment within which our subjects are observed. *In principle*, only those external incentives and constraints which we want are present in the laboratory, whereas such control is very difficult to achieve in the natural or historical setting. Second, we can (again, in principle) control and manipulate the specific social stimuli to which our subjects are exposed. Whether those stimuli are generated by the experimenter, a stooge, or other subjects, our control over them is thought to be quite effective. Third, we can control the information which reaches our subject to a degree not found in the field. Fourth, and in some social scientists' eyes the most important, is the reproducibility of the experimental setting. The operations may be repeated as often as necessary—and with successive groups of subjects—at modest cost in time or effort. Conversely, one must wait days, months, or years and still not find the "same" set of conditions again in the natural world.

On the other hand, *all* the problems of experimental control are not easily solved by using the social science laboratory setting. One of the more serious is that of a behavioral baseline. That is, if we want to ascertain the effects of certain experimental stimuli on the behavior of individuals or groups, there is little value in using some artificial baseline to represent the "before" regularities. Yet it is well known that we often get rather different behavior patterns in the laboratory than those that really occur in nature or in the field. Sometimes we try to get around this artifact by relying on the subjects' self-reports as to their actual, prestimulus, behavior patterns. But this is often just as unreliable as the laboratory-generated behavior, and the experimenter is thus left uncertain as to what the actual prestimulus patterns might have been.

Other disadvantages of the laboratory experiment also come to mind as possible threats to effective control, and these range across all eight items listed by Campbell and Stanley (1966, p. 5) in their treatment of experiments and quasiexperiments, which I take to mean field experiments.[7] Rather than go into further detail on the disadvantages of the laboratory or field setting, however, let me move now to the ways in which one might solve some of the control problems in conducting historical experiments, noting similarities and differences vis-à-vis the other two settings as the discussion unfolds. Before doing so, however, a modest epistemological digression is in order. So far, we have acquiesced in the implicit assumption that "causality" exists in the physical, biological, and social worlds, and that in due course we will identify the causes of all those phenomena that interest us. As I see it, this view contains two possible flaws.

First, a great many phenomena occur as the "result" of several alternative processes; thus a given outcome pattern could arise out of two or more causal sequences. In some cases, we will find that a single variable, if present in sufficient strength, will largely determine the outcome. In others, the specified outcome may require the presence of two or three variables, whose additive strength exceeds the critical threshold. In more complex cases, the outcome is dependent, not upon the total *sum* of the magnitudes of our necessary and sufficient conditions, but upon their *interactions*. That is, the potency of certain variables—no matter how great their magnitude— will be negligible until combined with some catalytic variable.

To illustrate, some European nations might have all of the attributes necessary to fight a successful war of colonization in the Middle East, but if all the potential colonies have already been seized by other European powers, the former will not get into a colonial war. Their capabilities are *necessary* for them to wage such a war, but *not sufficient*; an available target area is also necessary. In contrast to this *interactive* model, consider the following *additive* one. Here, the would-be colonizers may be weak in terms of naval power, but because they have access to the target area by land and their land forces are large, well organized, and well equipped, there is a substitutability of predictive factors. Thus, their entry into colonial wars can be accounted for by a minimum total of capabilities, no one of which is itself necessary.

Second, "causality" usually implies a deterministic process, in which the outcome is *not* a result of random or stochastic elements. This may be true of such trivial outcomes as the descent of a cannon ball in a perfect vacuum, but not of the more interesting and humanly important outcomes that occur in the referent world. All social events may be thought of as the outcome of a concatenation of some deterministic, stochastic, and voluntaristic elements; and, of course, the so-called voluntaristic elements are themselves the consequence of both deterministic and stochastic elements. In that vein, even though we recognize that our "unexplained variance," error terms, or residuals, are indeed partly a function of our limited knowledge, we also recognize that there will always be *some* fraction of the observed variance that cannot be attributed to a specific causal element.

Thus, in place of the notion of "causality," my preference is for the related notion of "explanation." In using that concept, we explicitly come to terms with the fact that knowledge results from the interactions between the observer and the referent phenomena. Further, it recognizes that the adequacy of an explanation, in the final analysis, rests on the intersubjective agreement of the relevant specialists in that research sector. In sum, we design our investigations and go about observation, analysis, and interpretation in such a way that we not only satisfy the more or less objective canons of scientific method, but satisfy the skepticism of our more competent and critical colleagues. In the balance of this paper, then, our focus will be more on the devices by which we can enhance the explanatory power of our models, and less upon the search for that chimera known as "causality."[8]

## Establishing Controls in the Historical Experiment

Shifting now from the concept of experimental controls in the abstract, let us examine some of the specific devices by which such controls may be established in the macro-social sciences. These are of three basic types. The first is the comparative case study, in which we actually find in the referent world two or more situations which appear to be similar in certain of their key variables, and whose *dis*similarity in other variables is the object of investigation.[9] The second device is that of post hoc statistical manipulation, whereby we systematically isolate the effects of one variable or group of variables at a time. The third is simulation of either the all-human, all-machine, or mixed human-machine combination, in which we seek to replay or recreate the historical processes under investigation. Let us examine these devices, comparing their assets and liabilities for the historical experiment as well as vis-à-vis the other two experimental modes.

*The Comparative Case Study*

The moment that one goes beyond the telling of a single narrative or the interpretation of a single case, one is into the "nomothetic" mode, and thus laying the groundwork for cumulative knowledge. Although most historians remain within the "ideographic" mode, and seldom attend—in any explicit fashion—to matters of comparison and accumulation, social scientists do invade their empirical domain, using a rather different intellectual style.[10]

One element in that style is the self-conscious search for two or more historical cases, on the basis of which a systematic comparative analysis might be constructed. There are four basic options in making that search. First, one might try to identify *all* the cases that satisfy the inclusion criteria and that fall within the specified spatial-temporal domain. Second, one might identify that population (or universe) of cases, but only examine a sample drawn from the population. Third, one might bypass the very costly and frustrating task of identifying the population, and merely draw a "sample" whose relationship to the population remains unspecified. And fourth, one may search out a finite number of cases (two or more) whose characteristics are such that they permit the sort of comparison desired. In this section, let us focus on the fourth option, as it is the simplest device for approximating (if not establishing) certain minimal controls.[11]

Here, we explicitly look for those few cases that are identical or similar in *some* specified characteristics, and different in others. If, for example, we wanted to test the proposition that communist regimes make for longer life expectancy than capitalist ones, we would look for two or more nations whose *other* cultural and structural characteristics are fairly similar, but whose political regimes are of the two crude types mentioned above. Then, if satisfied that the relevant genetic, environmental, and social conditions were reasonably similar, any difference between the two sets of (allegedly reliable) life expectancy figures *could* be attributed to the regime differences. This would be a primitive, but by no means useless, device for establishing a degree of experimental control. That is, it permits a crude isolation of certain variables so that they can be held constant while the "experimental" variable is, in effect, manipulated to ascertain its effect upon the outcome variable.

To take another illustration, suppose that we seek to differentiate between those few international conflicts that ended in war during a given time period, and those many that did *not* end in war. We might well begin the inquiry by measuring the relative military-industrial capabilities of the protagonists, and then isolating all those cases in which the difference between their scores is 10 percent or less. This rests on the reasonable assumption that if a greater discrepancy in their relative strengths obtains, the weaker party will tend to make sufficient concessions to avoid a military confrontation; the weaker lack the *strength* to fight, and the stronger lack the *incentive* to fight. Having now divided our cases into those of "approximate parity" and "clear disparity," the next step is to further subdivide the former cases according to their *dis*similarity on one or more other variables.

One reasonable candidate might be the polarization of the inter-state system at the onset of the crisis. Then, we ask whether—controlling for relative capabilities as the parameter variable—those crises that occur in periods of high polarization show a significantly higher frequency of ending up in war than those that occur in periods of medium or low polarization. (The relevant assumption here is that nations will have fewer cross-pressures working on them when the system is polarized, with most of the other nations readily identifiable as friend or foe.)[12] Even though all of the events and conditions have unfolded prior to the analysis, and even though we know the outcome of each crisis, we do *not* know what the statistical distribution will be until the analysis has been conducted. In several senses, then, we have conducted a controlled experiment, albeit a rather simple one, and it seems appropriate to answer a partial "yes" to Beer's rhetorical question (1968, p. 19) as to whether the comparative case study might be regarded as "the social scientists' equivalent of the natural scientists' laboratory."

## Statistical Manipulation and Sequential Analyses

In one of the more suggestive papers to come out of the comparative politics literature, Lijphart (1971, p. 684) asserts that "the statistical method can be regarded, therefore, as an approximation of the experimental method." He then goes on to quote Nagel (1961, p. 452) to the effect that "every branch of inquiry aiming at reliable general laws concerning empirical subject matter must employ a procedure that, if it is not strictly controlled experimentation, has the essential logical functions of experiment in inquiry." This is

Table 1. Predictor Variables of War

| Amount of War | Stratification | Polarity | Concentration |
|---|---|---|---|
| 5 | 14 | 1 | 10 |
| 98 | 3 | 87 | 3 |
| 76 | 90 | 5 | 19 |
| 14 | 4 | 20 | 4 |
| 29 | 11 | 3 | 7 |
| 87 | 13 | 7 | 88 |
| 93 | 22 | 89 | 11 |
| 64 | 81 | 4 | 2 |
| 85 | 19 | 1 | 90 |
| 2 | 2 | 3 | 9 |
| 7 | 7 | 12 | 3 |
| 95 | 5 | 92 | 12 |
| 81 | 86 | 14 | 2 |
| 86 | 13 | 2 | 97 |
| 91 | 10 | 88 | 1 |
| 94 | 87 | 26 | 5 |
| 1 | 28 | 47 | 16 |
| 40 | 7 | 13 | 10 |
| 16 | 42 | 18 | 27 |
| 90 | 23 | 4 | 79 |
| *min*   1 | 2 | 1 | 1 |
| *max*   98 | 90 | 92 | 97 |
| *mean*   57.7 | 28.4 | 26.8 | 24.8 |
| *s.d.*   38.05 | 31.10 | 33.70 | 33.44 |

essentially the point of view I hope to reflect here, in examining a second type of device for achieving or approximating the controls essential to an historical, post hoc, experiment.

While the comparative case study (with a low N) usually rests upon nominal or ordinal differentiations and can be analyzed via contingency table analyses, we now rely upon interval or ratio scales, and on concomitantly more elaborate data-analysis techniques, but the difference goes beyond matters of measurement and analysis.

Here, we usually turn to the construction of abstract models that reflect our theoretical hunches and/or prior research findings, and then go on to test them for "goodness of fit" vis-à-vis the observed referent world. Those models may, in turn, reflect a variety of methodological orientations as well as substantive foci. At one extreme, one might use product-moment correlations in order to ascertain which of several alternative predictors are most strongly associated with the variations in our outcome variable. At the other, we might postulate a complex model in path analysis form and then use the relative strengths of the path coefficients to ascertain which

Table 2.  Product-Moment Correlation Matrix of Predictor Variables of War

|  | War | Stratification | Polarity | Concentration |
|---|---|---|---|---|
| *War* | 1.00 | | | |
| *Stratification* | .25 | 1.00 | | |
| *Polarity* | .39 | − .24 | 1.00 | |
| *Concentration* | .34 | − .17 | − .36 | 1.00 |

version of the model best fits the observed historical phenomena. Perhaps most typical, however, is the multiple regression approach, in which we statistically "isolate" the effects of each predictor variable (and groups of them) in our model, one at a time.

It should be noted, however, that as we shift to these more elaborate analytical tools, we often move away from the orientation that characterizes a creative experimental strategy. Let me illustrate with an imaginary example whose detail is not excessive, given the importance of this point to my overall argument.[13] In the columns in table 1 are the magnitudes of war and of three hypothetical predictor variables for twenty observation periods, and below them are some of the statistical characteristics of those four distributions.

Under the traditional mode, one would begin—or, unfortunately, also end—by examining the product-moment correlation matrix (table 2). It turns out that all of the predictors show a *positive*, but weak association with war, and equally weak, but *negative* associations with each other. From this, the orthodox inference would be that all three predictors rise and fall with war over time, but that their impact on war is far from impressive.

Suppose, however, that one then reverted to the simpler mode, and examined these associations via a set of 2 x 2 contingency tables, as shown in table 3. When we examine this type of display, we tend to ask fewer questions about mere covariation and begin to pose

Table 3.  Contingency Table Analyses

| *Stratification* | | War | |
|---|---|---|---|
| | | *Hi* | *Lo* |
| | *Hi* | 4 | 0 |
| | *Lo* | 8 | 8 |

| *Polarity* | | War | |
|---|---|---|---|
| | | *Hi* | *Lo* |
| | *Hi* | 4 | 0 |
| | *Lo* | 8 | 8 |

| *Concentration* | | War | |
|---|---|---|---|
| | | *Hi* | *Lo* |
| | *Hi* | 4 | 0 |
| | *Lo* | 8 | 8 |

more experimental questions. For example: which conditions *have* to be present (i.e., are necessary) for war levels to be high, and which have to be present for those levels to remain low? Or, can a high or low level on one or more of the predictors "guarantee" high or low magnitudes of war? That is, is any one, or combination of them, sufficient by itself?

As the tables show, the frequency distributions in our imaginary case are identical, and the chi-square value of 3.33 is significant at the .07 level for all of them. Experimentally speaking, then, if we had hypothesized that it is *necessary* for stratification or polarity or concentration to be high in order for war levels to be high, we would have been wrong. That is, for eight of the twenty observation periods, we get high war levels with low levels of these three predictor variables. Conversely, if we had hypothesized that it was *sufficient* for any one of them to be high for war to be high, we would have been quite right. That is, each is high in only four of the twenty periods and in each of those periods, war is also high, and war is never low when any one of the predictors is high. To put it another way, despite the rather weak correlations, we nevertheless find that four of our hypotheses were correct (when any predictor is high, war will be high), and none were incorrect (war is never low when any of the predictors is high). In addition, in sixteen of the twenty periods in which any of the predictors was low, there is no clear pattern, since half of these were high war periods and half were low on war. In sum, despite the crudeness of our dichotomous indicators and the simplicity of the analysis, the contingency table clarifies the relationship and thus illuminates a facet of the experimental problem that might have gone unnoticed in the search for mere correlation.

Returning to statistical analysis once more, the important point is not only that we exercise whatever isolation and control we can in a particular investigation. What *really* makes the difference in the longer run is whether we can design a *sequence* of experiments such that we may eventually differentiate between those conditions that play an important role in shaping a set of outcomes and those that merely *appear* to do so. The reasoning is nicely articulated in Platt's "Strong Inference" article (1964), which warns against the mere accumulation of correlational findings. The essential idea is to move systematically from analysis to analysis, always trying to design the next one such that the strongest possible inferences about the "causal" process can be made. In his language, we try to move as quickly as possible toward "the critical experiment," by which he means the one that permits us to reject all but one remaining alternative explanation. This requires us, of course, to think in more cumulative long-run terms, rather than in terms of a series of disconnected and quite discrete experiments. The concept of meta-experiment seems to convey the essential point as we expand our horizon from a single investigation to a series of clearly connected investigations that add up to a coherent research strategy.

## Simulations

In addition to the comparative case study strategy and the use of statistical, post hoc manipulations, there is a third way in which a fair degree of experimental control can be achieved: the simulation. As indicated in the opening of this section, simulations may be differentiated along several dimensions, one of which is the relative role of humans and machines in generating one's data (Singer 1965a). At one end of that continuum is the simulation in which humans are assigned roles as officials, ministries, nations, etc., and permitted to act out those "roles" in a free and unstructured environment. In the middle are simulations in which these roles are acted out in a more structured and preprogrammed environment, with some of the more important outcomes generated by the interaction of the players' decisions and the programmed computer routines. Those routines may, in turn, reflect the hunches and suspicions of the researcher or may actually rest upon referent world findings; ordinarily it is a mix of the two (Guetzkow et al. 1963).

Toward the other end of the continuum is the all-machine simulation, in which no role players are used at all, and the magnitude and variation of *every* input is fully controlled by the researcher. Even if we choose to inject one or more stochastic elements into the simulation, we know their magnitude and place in the simulation, and can modify them at will (Naylor 1971).

At first blush, the use of human players seems attractive, as they offer a diversity, richness, and realism that is not easily generated by the computer. And in terms of generalizability, these are assets that are not to be ignored. Furthermore, if the players happen to be actual policy makers (rather than students, for example) one could argue that we not only get realistic behavioral inputs and outputs from them, but can even approximate a laboratory experiment. While these considerations are by no means negligible, the loss of effective control is a serious one. First, when a foreign ministry official moves from his natural setting into a laboratory-type setting, the new environment is likely to have a systematic but unknown effect on his behavior. Second, in the laboratory, he knows that the consequences of his decisions will be of minor importance, whereas in his official role they could be earth-shaking. Third, a key element in the behavior of bureaucrats is the realization that they must live with and work with their colleagues tomorrow, next week, and next year. This constraint is seldom present in the laboratory or simulation setting. Thus, if our objective is to isolate, observe, and measure the effects of each stimulus that might be accounting for the variation in our outcome variable, the use of human players is not an attractive option.

On the other hand, as we noted above, such control is easily achieved in the all-machine simulation. One can work with inputs (and outputs) that range in veridicality from the purely speculative to the thoroughly grounded. Whether the input be a set of facts, a number of correlations, or a coherent submodel, its closeness to reality is itself a matter of considerable controllability.

Another important virtue of the computer simulation is that it permits an exciting approximation to the *replication* of one's experiments. One of the key differences between the ideographic and nomothetic styles is that devotees of the former are inclined to tell us that contingent or speculative history is a waste of time, or worse. There is, we are told, no point in asking "what if" questions, since what has happened is already in the past. One (admittedly extreme) implication of this view is that what *did* happen is what *had* to happen, and that nothing else *could* have happened. Such an overdetermined view has ominous consequences in that it not only stifles creative speculation about the past, but would also prohibit a form of computer simulation that holds a great deal of promise.

That form might be thought of as "replaying history" such as to achieve some of the greatest virtues of a controlled experiment. Without going into much detail, let me summarize the possibilities of reconstructing—and thus replicating—the conditions and events out of the past. As indicated above, one may use this strategy even in the absence of much existential and correlational knowledge, with testing for the internal consistency of one's models as the major objective. But mathematical and logical manipulation is only one of the payoffs in computer simulations.[14]

If such simulations are preceded by an adequate (if undefined) number of comparative and longitudinal historical studies, we then are provided with the basic experimental ingredients: (a) a sufficient data base; (b) a fairly clear picture of the statistical regularities and relationships among our variables; (c) some idea as to where in time these relationships change in direction or magnitude; and (d) a fair sense of which predictor variables are most powerful in accounting for the variance in our observed outcomes.

With such an empirical and conceptual base, we can then go on to the "reconstruction of history" to which we alluded earlier. One strategy is to set all of the initial conditions of the referent system as of the beginning of the historical process, and then put the simulation in motion. Then, as each change in the predictor variables occurs in the simulation (which is, we hope, matching the actual observed events from the past), their combined effects should lead to the predicted fluctuations in the outcome variable. These events should, in turn, impinge on the predictors if we utilize a feedback model, and move the system into its next temporal cycle.

Depending on the solidity of our model and our data, the computer output should match rather closely the historical realities that have already been recorded. But if we examine a fairly long time span (such as the century and a half of the Correlates of War project), that goodness of fit will not last for the entire run. Conversely, we can expect that the way in which the variables shape the direction and magnitude of our outcomes will shift over time. Their relative potency may change, the sequence in which they interact with each other may change, and the pattern of that interaction is likely to change.

Now some scholars will urge that this very inconstancy of the relationships among predictors, and between them and our outcomes, is what makes social science impossible. If the causal sequence changes from epoch to epoch or case to case, it is argued, how can we discover or articulate behavioral generalizations or speak of law-like regularities? Admittedly, this is one of the harsh realities that makes social science in general, and experimentations in particular, often more difficult than in the physical and biological fields. But the problem is far from insoluble, and the computer simulation offers a promising solution.

In the straight longitudinal study, relying on statistical manipulation as the major control device, it is difficult (and very time-consuming) to identify the inflection points at which variables and relations among them undergo change. But in the simulation, we can accomplish five things. First, as we watch the historical "events" unfold, we can quickly spot these inflection points. Secondly, having done so, we can—on the basis of our prior empirical findings—estimate what those changes were. Third, we can then modify our model and its parameters accordingly, via a simple set of program instructions. Fourth, we can rerun the longer historical period to ascertain whether these changes were of the correct type and injected at the appropriate juncture. Fifth, if not, we continue to experiment until the printout once again fits the historical realities.

In sum, then, the all-machine simulation—if based on sufficient empirical and theoretical work—gives us a remarkably close parallel to the laboratory experiment. With it, we can try out a wide variety of ideas, run them and rerun them against historical reality, and eventually emerge with a fairly good fit between the simulation and the reality. In other words, we can isolate and control for the effects of all sorts of possible stimuli, constantly improving our model until it finally plays out the historical drama. It may not be as rich in detail as that found in the historians' narratives, and it may be more numerical than our more verbal colleagues might prefer, but it can, in principle, be very close to the "real thing."

## Conclusion

For too long, we in the macro-social sciences have labored under the handicap of a severe inferiority complex. That sense of inferiority is, I would submit, far from justified. But, like our colleagues in the physical and biological sciences, as well as our nonscientific brethren, we have accepted all too readily a number of dubious myths.

One of these is the notion that social phenomena are too complex to ever be comprehended by the human mind, whereas physical and biological phenomena are not. Another is that social phenomena are nearly impossible to observe, partially because they are largely symbolic and intangible, and partially because they occur across too broad a spatial and temporal domain. A third is that even if we could observe these phenomena, they are too subtle and fast moving to permit operational measurement. A fourth is that most social phenomena cannot be put into the laboratory, and since science is only done in the laboratory, there can be no social science. While these epistemological myths are overstated here for emphasis, their milder versions pervade much of the scholarly literature, not to mention the belief systems of most of the world's cultures. As I have tried to indicate in the paper at hand, none of them is well founded. There are difficulties, to be sure, but this is true of every area of investigation.

Further, we could readily find many of the so-called "natural" scientists who would also dispute these myths. The galaxies are complex, yet astronomers continue to expand our understanding of their dynamics. Elementary particles are hardly visible to the naked eye, yet physicists continue to observe them and trace their behavior. Impulses in the central nervous system move at incredible speed, yet biochemists continue to improve their grasp of the way in which that system operates. And, tornadoes or cold fronts can hardly be brought into the laboratory, yet meteorologists measure their characteristics and are increasingly able to predict their effects. To put it bluntly, the distinctions among the sciences are severely overdrawn, and we need to recognize the great potentialities of scientific method for the understanding of human phenomena.

Of course, our inferiority complex arises not only out of naive beliefs as to what is possible. They also arise out of the very real fact that we have, to date, not done nearly as well as the physical and biological sciences. In some crude way, one might estimate that we are where the physical sciences were about 200 years ago, and where the biological sciences were 50 years ago. Our models are primitive, our procedures are inadequate, and our research strategies are often incoherent. But this is less a function of the innate inaccessibility of social phenomena to scientific inquiry, and more a function of our beliefs to that effect.

Furthermore, these myths and beliefs are not, in turn, natural to the human condition. Humanity has been governed for thousands of years by elites who have a vested interest in perpetuating our ignorance. Because ignorance about social phenomena helps to keep us in a state of thralldom, these elites—and counterelites—have created, sanctioned, or enforced a combination of taboos and constraints that account for a large part of our contemporary ignorance.

While it is incumbent on all human beings to resist and reject these taboos and constraints, scientists have an additional obligation. Those in the physical and biological sectors should learn enough to recognize that their work is inherently no different than ours, and they should stop acting like magicians engaged in occult and esoteric activities which only the initiated can comprehend. But, most important, we in the social sciences must set ourselves free from those epistemological—as well as ideological—fetters that keep us in a state of perceived inferiority and make it unlikely that we will "crack" some of the most important problems facing humanity. Fuller utilization of the experimental mode may not guarantee our success, but it should make our recurrent failures of the past a bit less likely in the future.

# VI

# Indicator Construction
# and Data Acquisition

Throughout this volume, considerable attention has been paid to the clarification of key concepts and to the conduct of research that revolves around those concepts. It is, however, one thing to sharpen up, sort out, or reinterpret such concepts, and quite another to use them in the search for empirical regularities or historically accurate models. There is a critical intermediate step embracing the twin activities of index construction and data acquisition; some might suggest that these are disparate activities, but as the article below makes clear, they are highly interdependent.

In the construction of an index or indicator, we begin with an abstract concept that seems critical to a given theoretical question, go on to define it in verbal terms, and then ask three important questions. First, we ask whether variations in this phenomenon across time and space leave some sort of directly observable trace; in our field the answer is almost always "no." We then ask whether there is some other phenomenon that rises and falls with the one that concerns us and *does* leave a directly observable trace; this happens on rare occasions. But if the answer is again negative, we begin to construct what is often called an "auxiliary theory" by asking what other phenomena exist that might either "cause" or be "caused" by the one that continues to elude us. If we can think of one, can argue persuasively that it does lead to, or result from, the phenomenon of interest—in other words, articulate the causal linkages involved—and then ascertain that it does leave an observable trace, we may well have come up with an indicator that will prove to be both reliable and valid.

As is well known, simple repetition of the measuring procedures will help establish their *reliability*, but *validity* of our indicators is much more difficult to establish. This is true enough when the data set that is generated by our procedures need not go through any complex transformations or conversions. In the text for chapter 12, for example, the procedures for generating the data are fairly complex, but once the set is completed, the indicator rests on a very simple arithmetic computation. But for other indicators, the transformation must be more complex, especially if we are using data that describe nations or relations between pairs of nations in order to construct, for example, a description of the *system* of nations. While space limitations preclude the inclusion here of any papers describing the more complex index construction procedures, chapter 14 in part VII summarizes one such effort. Among others are M. D. Wallace and Singer (1970), Ray and Singer (1973), and Bueno de Mesquita (1975). Volume II will have several papers describing the construction of such indices, as well as several in which they are utilized for analytic purposes.

# 12

# The Diplomatic Importance of States, 1816-1970: An Extension and Refinement of the Indicator

## With Melvin Small

*Returning to a fairly typical problem of converting the scattered traces of historical events into a scientifically useful data set, this article sets forth one of the more interesting and controversial of our efforts.[1]*

In an earlier issue of this journal [*World Politics*], we presented our findings on the composition of the interstate system, along with the diplomatic importance or "status" attributed to each member by the others in the system (Singer and Small 1966a). Covering the period between the Napoleonic Wars and the onset of World War II, we set out both to calculate the ranking of the states every five years during those 125 years, and to make explicit the criteria by which system membership and status ranks were established. Our major motivation was to identify the empirical domain within which our own research would go forth and to develop certain indicators which were relevant to the Correlates of War project; it also seemed likely that these data might be of use to others in the scholarly community.[2]

In extending the project beyond World War II and up to a more recent date, we faced not only the requirement to gather additional diplomatic representation data, but also the opportunity to reconsider some of our original indicators. In this supplementary report, therefore, we will not only present the additional data, but will also use the occasion as an opportunity to recapitulate (and where necessary, modify) the procedures and rationale behind our proposed index of diplomatic importance. Worth noting at the outset is the fact that we are not the only ones with certain reservations about the index. A number of our colleagues have, in spoken (if not written) word, raised some questions about its validity. Some of the criticisms can only be termed foolish, but most of them have struck us as eminently reasonable.[3] In the opening section, we will address ourselves to the question of validity; in later sections we will summarize our revised procedures, compare them to those originally employed, and then follow with a recapitulation of the resulting indicator values.

## Diplomatic Representation as an Indicator of Importance

In the original study we argued that the relative importance that the states in the system attributed to one another could be inferred from the number and rank of the diplomatic missions accredited and dispatched to each of their capitals. The reasoning was that the decision to locate, maintain, or abolish a mission of any particular rank in any foreign capital reflected a wide variety of considerations within and between the several governments, and that the sum total of such missions would represent some consensus as to how important the recipient state was to all the others in the system. In other words, we treated the numerous and continuing decisions of whether or not to send diplomatic missions to foreign capitals as a sort of running sociogram, illuminating each state's relative diplomatic importance to the membership of the system at large. The resulting scores seemed, in our judgment, generally to vindicate that assumption, and to reflect the changing—as well as the stable—fortunes of the system's members over the nineteenth and twentieth centuries.

On the other hand, the problem of face validity remained far from solved. Not only were we somewhat dissatisfied with some of the rankings, but we also concluded that the reasoning behind the index needed to be stated in more detailed and vigorous fashion. One of the purposes of this paper is to do exactly that; but before doing so, a few words as to the utility of such an indicator might be helpful.

What can one do with an adequate measure of diplomatic importance? At its simplest, such an index would help to distinguish among states with high, medium, and low diplomatic involvement vis-à-vis the others in the system, and thus differentiate between central and peripheral subsystems. Second, such an index would permit us to test a variety of hypotheses regarding the relationship between the diplomatic importance of a state and its foreign policy behavior, interaction, and relationship patterns. A third type of use might be to measure the discrepancy between a state's diplomatic importance and its capabilities—in order to test hypotheses, for example, which relate status discrepancies to foreign policy actions. Other uses come to mind, and are being followed in the Correlates of War project, but enough has been said to indicate that our interests are not merely antiquarian or encyclopedic.

Aside from the question of utility, what are the probabilities of constructing a valid and reliable index of diplomatic importance? A useful point of departure is to note that every effort to "measure" some social phenomenon requires us to infer back from what we *can* observe to what we cannot—or do not—observe in any direct fashion. We use words, numbers, and pictures as representations of the referent ("real") world, and make inferences about the referent world phenomenon on the basis of the symbols we use to represent it.

What we seek here is a rather general reflection of the relative importance of each state member to the others in the system during a given half-decade. One way to clarify the limitations of the proposed indicator is to spell out some of the things we are *not* trying to measure. First, we are not trying to measure power, capability, or influence.[4] These characteristics of a state will certainly affect its diplomatic importance, but they are not identical with it. And, as suggested above, the very magnitude of the difference between importance and these other attributes remains a critical area of inquiry. Second, we are not proposing to measure "relative acceptance" or any other deviation in a country's score between what it *does* receive and what it *should* receive, given its geographical centrality, size, power base, or other intrinsic attribute.[5] Third, we are not (at least for the time being) interested in measuring the importance of one particular state to another particular state. To measure a specific dyadic relationship with sufficient precision would require much more evidence than will be offered here. Thus, no inferences should be—or can be—made about China's importance to the United States from the absence of their respective embassies in Peking and Washington (an example which is often suggested by critics of our proposed indicator). To extend that point a bit further, we are not trying to measure a state's importance in a particular region or in the context of a specific substantive problem. The index is intended to be *general* as to place and context, not specific. Nor are we interested here in measuring the short-run fluctuations in a state's diplomatic importance. Rather, the objective is to estimate the more slow-moving importance scores as they rise and decline in response to gross and general trends in international politics.

Further, we are not trying to measure the precise interval between two states that fall close to one another in our rank orderings. Even though we compute and present the raw and normalized interval-scale scores of the states, we urge users not to interpret these scores too literally. To emphasize the imprecision of these values, we eschew the convention which shows a tie by giving the equal scorers a fractional rank position, such as 7.5 for those which tie for seventh place in a given period. Rather, we rank them as seven and eight arbitrarily, by their state code number. For the same reason, we also convert those two sets of interval scores into grouped ordinal scores, dividing the membership of the system into quintiles, each of which contains approximately one-fifth of the members in the given observation year.

Returning, then, to what we *do* seek to measure, we reason as follows: First, most governments do not establish diplomatic missions in the capital (or principal) cities of *all* other sovereign members of the system. They send missions to only a fraction of the other states; as a matter of fact, that fraction has been a rather consistent figure, ranging from a low of 37 percent in 1849 to a high of 60 percent in 1827, when the system was considerably smaller. This means that, over the past 155 years, we usually find missions from only about 45 percent of the other states in the capital of the average state.

What accounts for this deviation from universality? We begin with the awareness that each government has a given propensity to exchange missions with each of the others in the system, in accordance with its judgment of their relative importance to its own state. Reflecting geographical and logistical distance, economic interdependence, cultural affinities, alternative modes of intercourse via third-party nations or organizations, and so forth, that set of judgments will, at the very outset, assure a less than universal exchange of missions. On top of this original estimate of importance, each government must also contend with a variety of resource limitations. These would include: a perceived limitation of funds and personnel in general; a lack of diplomats familiar with the language, culture, etc., of a possible diplomatic partner; and the reluctance of diplomats to accept certain posts, on grounds of remoteness, climate, housing, cuisine, servants, and ambiance. These limitations require that governments husband their scarce personnel and funds, and thus further reduce the likelihood that all will have missions in all. If the decision to exchange missions were simply a function of perceived relative importance in the context of limited resources, we *could* interpret our indicator as reflecting the relative importance of each state to every other state, and thus make reasonable inferences at the *dyadic* level.

But intervening between the judgment of another state's relative importance and the dispatch of a mission, there is a second set of inputs into the prospective sender's decision process. We refer to political constraints and incentives, some of which can occasionally be potent enough to outweigh the original judgment. These could include not only the political eagerness or reluctance of the potential partner, but: (a) domestic pressures favoring or opposing the establishment or perpetuation of a given bond; or (b) the urgings of other influential governments favoring or opposing such a bond. Although we would not argue that the original judgments as to the relative importance of a given state are completely apolitical, they are usually made within the context of the foreign ministry, and thus normally reflect a degree of detached expertise. But when special interest groups or foreign governments intrude into the process, we can expect an occasional deviation from what the bureaucratic consensus would have been.

Although it is often suggested that such "political" incentives or constraints are a twentieth-century innovation, the precedent goes back at least to the 1820s and 1830s. As the South American revolutions of that period succeeded in replacing monarchies with republics, the United States was eager to see the legitimization of the new governments. The more autocratic regimes of Europe (particularly Russia, Austria, and Prussia) were quite opposed, however, and such states as Britain and Holland found themselves caught between the two sets of pressures. And while many Europeans did eventually exchange missions with many of the American states, the Holy Alliance was able to slow down the rate of recognition. To some extent, such political pressures were again generated following the revolutions of 1848, but not to the extent found in the current century with the rise of the Communist regimes. This time, however, the United States has been on the other side, urging—with appreciable success—the *withholding* of recognition from the USSR in the 1920s and 1930s, and from China in the 1950s and 1960s, to take the more dramatic examples. Even in 1970, with missions in 87 percent of the system's members, the U.S. (and many of its allies) withheld official recognition from Albania and Mongolia—as well as China—on political grounds.

The effects of such extranormal pressures will usually lead to depressed importance scores for the states whose isolation is sought by one or another of the major powers. Whether these "lower-than-expected" scores can be thought of as valid indicators of the holders' diplomatic importance depends upon the reasoning behind the measure, and this leads to the second part of the causal inference loop which we see as linking the indicator with the concept and with the referent world. One interpretation would have it that the recipient's score has been contaminated by extraneous considerations and that we therefore have a threat to our indicator's validity. Another interpretation—and the one which informs the argument at hand—is that the net score *does* reflect the recipient's importance. In one way or another, every government is faced periodically with the need to estimate, or reestimate, how "important" it is to exchange missions with every other one in the system. That relative importance is reflected in its willingness to: (a) allocate limited resources to a given diplomatic bond; (b) incur the costs of overcoming domestic or foreign opposition to such a bond; and (c) sacrifice one set of attractive bonds in order to maintain or establish another set of more or less equally attractive ones.

We might think of those recurrent national choices as constituting a slowly changing and ongoing plebiscite among all the system's members, in which the separate governments must weigh a myriad of considerations in determining how important it is for them to have or not have a formal and reciprocated diplomatic presence in each of the other world capitals. To put it another way, the number (and/or rank) of missions in each state is a resultant of all the decisions concerning relative importance that have been made in the months and years preceding each observation year. Those several decisions, which cannot be reliably or economically observed, predict to (or "cause") the total number of ambassadors, ministers, and chargés d'affaires accredited to a given state in any half-decade.

Carrying the argument a step further, the importance indicator may also be interpreted in a *pre*dictive, as well as a *post*dictive fashion. In that case, our causal inference is that the diplomatic importance of a state will be high if it has diplomatic bonds with many other states and low if it has few such bonds. While the essentiality of such missions may decline with the improvement in communications technology, or the increase in multilateral contacts via the IGOs, or shifts from bureaucratic to summit diplomacy, the relative ability of states to be important to others at a given time will clearly be a function, *inter alia*, of their place in the global communication network. If we consider diplomatic bonds as channels in such a network, and each capital as a node, a node into which a great many channels flow will be more critical and salient to the overall network than a node at which very few such channels intersect. That, too, is diplomatic importance.

In sum, then, our measurement argument is that the number of diplomatic missions found in a given national capital at $t_1$ will be both a *consequence* of the relative importance attached to that nation by the others in the system at $t_0$, and a *cause* of its relative importance at $t_2$.

## Modifying the Indicator

In the original report, we spelled out our measurement and coding procedures in considerable detail, carrying the reader step by step from data acquisition through the varieties of index construction. Here, we will recapitulate the general procedures briefly, going into detail only where modifications or clarifications seem to be in order. On the basis of our own experience with the indicator (in its several forms) plus the comments offered by others, we find three sets of problems which call for further explication. These are: (a) the post-1945 inflationary trend toward greater use of ambassadors and the relative decline in the numbers of ministers and envoys; (b) the degree to which diplomatic missions are exchanged in a purely reciprocal and symmetric fashion; and (c) the extent to which the indicator should reflect the importance of the states *from* whom the missions are sent. Let us examine these three problems in that order, and then summarize our revised coding and scaling procedures.

*The Problem of Post-1945 Inflation*

The original scores, it will be recalled, were computed in several ways. The first of these was the composite score, and it reflected not only the *number* of accredited missions in the recipient nation, but the *ranks* of those missions. Adhering to the *règlements* of Vienna (1815) and Aix-la-Chapelle (1818), we divided the missions into three ranks: ambassador, envoy or minister (whether accredited to the head of state or the foreign ministry), and chargé d'affaires; consular officials were not counted. The host state received three points for each ambassador, two for each minister, and one for each chargé. Such a scheme makes perfect sense as long as there is considerable differentiation, and the post-Napoleonic pattern did indeed hold for about 130 years. But on the eve of World War II we already had some signs that the pattern was breaking down. By 1950, as table 1 indicates, diplomatic "inflation" had clearly begun to take its toll. If more and more governments replaced ministers with ambassadors, scores based on the rank of the missions would begin to lose their discriminatory power. Examining eleven states representing the middle and major powers which have been in the system since its inception, we find that the ambassadorial rank accounted for about 15 percent of their diplomatic missions until the 1930s. But on the heels of World War II, that figure rose sharply, and by 1965 it approached the 90 percent level.[6]

Faced with this situation, we considered and tried several alternative measures (including budget share, proportions of secretariat

Table 1. Percentage Distribution of Diplomatic Ranks Received in Sample Capitals, 1816-1965

|            | 1816  | 1844  | 1874  | 1904  | 1930  | 1950  | 1965  |
|------------|-------|-------|-------|-------|-------|-------|-------|
| Ambassador | 15.0  | 7.8   | 10.3  | 14.8  | 17.5  | 42.5  | 88.2  |
| Minister   | 72.4  | 69.8  | 80.2  | 80.2  | 72.6  | 53.4  | 5.5   |
| Chargé     | 12.6  | 22.4  | 9.5   | 5.0   | 9.9   | 4.1   | 6.3   |
| TOTAL      | 100.0 | 100.0 | 100.0 | 100.0 | 100.0 | 100.0 | 100.0 |

Note: The eleven states in the sample, all members of the central system, were Britain, France, Prussia or Germany, Sardinia or Italy, Holland, Belgium, Austria, Switzerland, Denmark, Sweden, and the United States.

personnel, and elected officerships in various intergovernmental organizations) and found them quite invalid on their face; the reasons will be obvious to students of international organization and need not be reiterated here. Similarly, we quickly discarded the idea of weighting missions according to their staff size, their budget, or the value of their buildings.[7] Following those brief experiments, we returned to our raw data to see if it really made any difference whether we included the diplomatic rank of each mission received. With a mixture of chagrin and relief, we found that such a refinement made almost no difference in the rank orderings of the states. The smaller states, having originally received more low-ranking than high-ranking diplomats, suffer little by this change in coding rules. And the "top dogs," having so many missions of *all* ranks, lose little by the modification; only such states as Turkey, which often receive fewer missions than such middle powers as Holland or Denmark, but those frequently at the ambassadorial level, sustain any appreciable loss. As a matter of fact, the rank correlation between the weighted and unweighted scores for the period of 1816–1940 was .99, suggesting that we had invested considerably more time and money in data acquisition and computation than was necessary. The empirical lesson is that one's indicators can be too *refined* as well as too *crude*.

## The Problem of Asymmetric Representation

A second problem came to light once our data were all in and assembled into a machine-readable nation-by-nation matrix. We found that about 10 percent of our dyadic diplomatic bonds were asymmetrical. That is, while $X$ may have sent an envoy to $Y$, $Y$ was reported as not having reciprocated; the asymmetric pattern was coded accordingly.

The problem is, first, to identify the various ways in which such reported asymmetries can come about, and second, to settle upon a reasonable scheme for coping with them. In principle, there should be no such asymmetries, since the formal rules and established procedure make it clear that negotiations on the granting of diplomatic *recognition* should ultimately lead to an *exchange of diplomatic missions*. But there are several ways in which deviations can and do occur.

First, on some occasions, one of the parties will be embarrassed by a shortage of funds or personnel, and will accredit one minister or ambassador to two or even three governments. He or she will *reside* in only one of these capitals, but will have a staff in the other(s) and will visit on a regular basis. In both the original coding and here, we score on the basis of missions established and staffed, regardless of whether the *head* of the mission is responsible for missions in additional neighboring states. That source of reported asymmetries, then, is of no consequence here. Second, the logistics and bureaucratic politics within governments could be such as to make for lengthy delays in the dispatch of a representative. This is usually true of only one party, and we no longer assume an asymmetry, but code $Y$'s mission as if it were already in $X$ once $X$'s has been established in $Y$. At worst, this coding convention could lead to a slight acceleration of the date at which X picks up an additional point. Given the temporal imprecision of our index, the effect of this change is inconsequential. Third, diplomatic lists are usually prepared by the protocol office in a foreign ministry and then made available to governmental and nongovernmental users of those lists, including those who collate and publish them. Somewhere along that tenuous administrative chain, occasional errors of omission (and commission) would not be surprising. Under the revised procedures, we explicitly recognize that such errors can occur, and again utilize the assumption of perfect symmetry.

A fourth source of asymmetry could, however, be quite "real": A government could intentionally delay the dispatch of its representative, or recall him for an appreciable period of time. In very rare instances, the political realities might even lead to an *agreed* temporary asymmetry. But given the brevity of such possible periods of asymmetry in almost all of these cases, we are again justified in coding as if the bond were reciprocal at all times. A fifth possible source comes to mind, but it need not be seriously considered: the unilateral decision of one government to establish a mission in another's capital city without benefit of either negotiation or reciprocity. We have heard suggestions that the more aggressive states might engage in this practice as an indirect way of gaining visibility, influence, or importance, but we find no evidence of that practice now or in the past century-and-a-half.

To summarize, then, we now treat all the asymmetries that turn up in the historical record as irrelevant, recognizing that they are either temporary aberrations or the consequence of reportorial errors. The effect of this modification is to rectify the slightly understated scores of those states which were at the disadvantaged end of the reported asymmetries. How do the scores generated by these slightly different sets of coding criteria compare? The mean *tau* value for the correlation between the presymmetrized and the revised rankings is .83; it would be even higher were it not for the first three observation periods, whose data inadequacies produce rank-order coefficients of .63, .53, and .60 respectively. Notwithstanding the similarity in the original and revised rank scores, we are persuaded that the revision, calling for an assumed reciprocity throughout, provides us with an indicator whose validity is appreciably enhanced.

*The Problem of Differentiating Among Senders*

A third problem *looks* most serious, but turns out to be negligible in historical fact. One of the more credible threats to the face validity of our index is that it assigns one point to the recipient state, regardless of whether the embassy or legation has been set up by Burma or Britain, Yemen or Yugoslavia. The alert critic might then suggest that we remedy this obvious deficiency by weighting each mission—not by its rank on the ambassador-minister-chargé ladder—but by the diplomatic importance of the *sending government*. This is readily accomplished by a simple iterative procedure, in which the computer is programmed not merely to count the number of entries alongside each state's name in the state-by-state matrix for each observation year, but to multiply each such entry by the number of missions found in each sending state's row. Thus, for 1950, Argentina would receive 40 points for the Spanish mission and 70 for the United States' mission in Buenos Aires, rather than just one point for each. Consequently, the states that are highly valued by those with the higher diplomatic importance scores will themselves receive a higher score than if most of their partners were middle- and low-ranking.

As suggested at the opening of this section, this procedure might indeed appear to make "more sense," but empirically it makes virtually no difference. The distribution of missions around the globe is, and has been, such that the nonweighted and weighted scores never show a rank correlation lower than .90 (1840); for 1935 the *tau* value is .96, and the mean for our 31 sets of observations is .94. The only discernible result of weighting is to raise slightly the scores of the states that exchange fewer missions, but try to make them "count" by concentrating on the top-ranked system members. Thus, we can repeat a conclusion which we stated in the original article: The iterative weighting scheme adds virtually nothing to the validity of our index, but raises its computational cost considerably.[8]

*Scoring Procedures Summarized*

Having discussed the three major problems encountered in trying to devise a valid measure of diplomatic importance, let us now briefly summarize the coding procedures. For each diplomatic bond, as manifested by the exchange of missions at the chargé level or above, the host state receives one point. (Mere recognition, which may precede the dispatch or exchange of missions by several years, is not sufficient.) These observations are taken once per half-decade, producing thirty-one sets of readings when the compilation is updated to 1970. Given the generally slow rate of change in the scores, the researcher who is working with *annual* data may either use the same score for each of the four following years or, better still, interpolate, with little cause for concern. As long as the missions are at the rank of chargé d'affaires or higher, the host state receives one point; as reported above, differentiating among the three standard ranks makes virtually no difference up through the 1940s, and by 1950 almost all missions are at the embassy rank. For similar reasons, we find it neither necessary nor economical to differentiate according to the importance score of the sender.[9]

Once the total number of missions in each system member's capital has been recorded for each observation year, we have that state's raw importance score. To permit comparability across the years, in view of the rather steady increase in the size of the system, we normalize those scores by converting them into percentage form. Thus, the normalized score for each state is simply determined by ascertaining what percentage of the rest of the system's members have established diplomatic bonds with it in each half-decade. The top figure can range from 1.00 for several periods in the nineteenth century to a low of .82 for Italy in 1920; the lowest score is .00, for Rhodesia in 1970.

Finally, to reemphasize our earlier point that neither of these interval-scale figures be taken too literally, we also aggregate the states into quintile groupings for each observation year. That is, even though we compute and present cardinal and ordinal scores, the user must understand that such numbers offer only an approximate indication of each state's position; we are not suggesting, for example, that India, having two more bonds than Canada in 1965, is exactly two points (or .017) more "important" than the latter. Even the quintile scores must not be overinterpreted; our intention here is merely to provide one possible measure of the states' gradual ascents and declines in importance over the past century-and-a-half.

## Data Sources

A generally accepted rule of thumb concerning quantification in the macro-social sciences is that the further back in time one goes in search of reliable data, the more difficult the problem becomes. The United Nations Secretariat, for example, and that of the League before it, have systematically compiled a large body of statistical information by which their member states might be described and compared along a wide variety of dimensions. National governments, industrial firms, and business associations have likewise begun the systematic compilation and publication of all sorts of figures in the past several decades. Unfortunately, what holds for certain economic and social data does not necessarily hold for diplomatic data, even if we leave aside matters of reliability and validity. The problem of ascertaining the presence or absence of diplomatic representation in national capitals for the sample years since 1945 has turned out, surprisingly, to be almost as acute as it was for the previous 130 years. As pages 251-52 and footnote 22 of the original article indicate, we were able to find most of the needed information for the earlier period in the *Almanach de Gotha*, and the gaps were filled without too much difficulty by recourse to fewer than a dozen additional sources. Since World War II, however, things have not been quite as simple.

Although many foreign ministries do publish one or more lists per year showing the states *in* which their government maintains an embassy, legation, etc., or *from* which they receive such missions, one can readily appreciate the effort of assembling over one hundred such lists for each sample year and then comparing and collating the information. Thus, we felt it would be more economical to find one or more single sources from which the missions sent by or received in a large number of states might be ascertained.

Unfortunately, the *Almanach de Gotha*, which had weathered everything from Napoleon to World War I, did not survive the Nazi era and ceased publishing in 1940. In 1951, two different diplomatic yearbooks were published which offered detailed lists of the representatives accredited to each government, but, for reasons unknown to us, publication ceased in 1952, making it necessary to find alternate sources for 1955, 1960, 1965, and 1970 (see *Diplomatic Year-Book* 1951 and *World Diplomatic Directory and World Diplomatic Biography* 1951). Of course, our task was eased immeasurably once we decided to abandon interrank discrimination and to score solely on the presence or absence of missions.

For these four data points we used the *Europa Year-Book*, *The Statesman's Year-Book*, and the *Code Diplomatique*. For the earlier years, the first of these proved to be the most useful, since *The Statesman's Year-Book* did not provide relatively complete listings until the mid-sixties. In addition, we corresponded with a number of foreign ministries and were thus able to fill some of the gaps in these three publications. Finally, we were able to compare our results with those provided by East, who has collated all the separate listings from several of the postwar editions of *The Statesman's Year-Book*. Despite the diversity of our sources, however, we feel as confident about our figures for the post-World War II period as we did about those for the earlier span.[10]

## Identifying Interstate System Members

So much for coding procedures, data sources, and the rationale behind the measures. Let us turn now to the equally critical matter of identifying those national political entities which constituted the interstate system during the period under study, and whose diplomatic importance we seek to measure. Since the criteria for inclusion in the system were carefully spelled out in the original paper and updated in Russett *et al.*, they will here be dealt with only briefly (Russett, Singer, and Small 1968). From 1816 to 1920, a state was considered a member of the system if it had a population of at least 500,000 and recognition from our two "legitimizers," England and France. From 1920 to the present, a state qualified for membership if it had the requisite 500,000 population and recognition from *any* two major powers, *or* if it was a member of the League of Nations or the United Nations, for however brief a period.

There were, however, the inevitable exceptions. Thus, even though they lacked the diplomatic recognition or membership in international organizations, five states were nevertheless classified as members of the system: Nepal from 1920, Mongolia from 1921, Yemen from 1926, Saudi Arabia from 1927, and Rhodesia from 1966. On the other hand, five states which did meet our criteria were *not* classed as independent members of the system. India, despite her membership in the League, was excluded until 1947; Byelorussia and the Ukraine were excluded, since their membership in the United

Nations was merely the result of a political bargain arranged at Yalta; and Manchoukuo and Slovakia clearly failed on the grounds that they exercised virtually *no* control over their foreign policies.[11]

## The Results: Diplomatic Importance Scores

In table 2 we show the diplomatic importance scores of all members of the system for selected years of the post-World War II period. Given the exceedingly unsettled state of the world during the war and immediately after its termination, we do not show any figures for 1945; thus we move from 1940, the final reading in the original paper, to 1950 as the first meaningful set of data for the period under study here. For each of the years, we divide the states into quintiles, as before, and show the total number of diplomatic bonds for each state. In addition, we have again controlled for change in the size of the system to permit comparison across time; this normalization is achieved by dividing each state's total score by the size of the system, less one, that year. Therefore, a score of 1.00 would mean that *all* the others in the system had missions in that state's capital that year; the U.S. score for 1950 means that 93 percent of them had missions in Washington that year. Rounding to two places (with decimal points removed) frequently creates the appearance of tied scores, but we have retained the rank positions reflected by the three-place figures. These scores are based on the state of affairs at the beginning of the half-decade; thus the 17 new states which entered the system *during* 1960 and the three states which entered the system *during* 1965 are not included in our tabulation or used in computing normalized scores until the following observation years.

## Table 2. Diplomatic Importance Ranks and Scores by Half-Decade, 1950-1970

| | 1950 | | | | |
|---|---|---|---|---|---|
| Rank | Missions Re- ceived | Normal- ized Score | Rank | Missions Re- ceived | Normal- ized Score |
| 1 United States | 70 | 93 | 39 Guatemala | 25 | 33 |
| 2 France | 70 | 93 | 40 Costa Rica | 25 | 33 |
| 3 United Kingdom | 67 | 89 | 41 Rumania | 25 | 33 |
| 4 Belgium | 62 | 83 | 42 Bolivia | 24 | 32 |
| 5 Italy | 61 | 81 | 43 Hungary | 24 | 32 |
| 6 Holland | 58 | 77 | 44 Nicaragua | 22 | 29 |
| 7 Denmark | 54 | 72 | 45 Australia | 22 | 29 |
| 8 Argentina | 51 | 68 | | | |
| 9 Norway | 51 | 68 | 46 Haiti | 21 | 28 |
| 10 Switzerland | 50 | 67 | 47 Honduras | 21 | 28 |
| 11 Sweden | 50 | 67 | 48 Bulgaria | 21 | 28 |
| 12 U.S.S.R. | 45 | 60 | 49 South Africa | 21 | 28 |
| 13 Chile | 44 | 59 | 50 Iraq | 21 | 28 |
| 14 Brazil | 43 | 57 | 51 Pakistan | 21 | 28 |
| 15 Egypt/U.A.R. | 42 | 56 | 52 Paraguay | 20 | 27 |
| | | | 53 Syria | 20 | 27 |
| 16 Mexico | 41 | 55 | 54 Luxembourg | 19 | 25 |
| 17 Spain | 40 | 53 | 55 Afghanistan | 17 | 23 |
| 18 Czechoslovakia | 39 | 52 | 56 Saudi Arabia | 16 | 21 |
| 19 Cuba | 38 | 51 | 57 Iceland | 15 | 20 |
| 20 Turkey | 38 | 51 | 58 Israel | 15 | 20 |
| 21 Poland | 36 | 48 | 59 China | 15 | 20 |
| 22 India | 35 | 47 | 60 Ireland | 14 | 19 |
| 23 Canada | 34 | 45 | 61 Thailand | 14 | 19 |
| 24 Venezuela | 34 | 45 | | | |
| 25 Portugal | 34 | 45 | 62 New Zealand | 13 | 17 |
| 26 Dominican Rep. | 33 | 44 | 63 Ethiopia | 12 | 16 |
| 27 Ecuador | 33 | 44 | 64 Jordan | 12 | 16 |
| 28 Colombia | 32 | 43 | 65 Philippines | 12 | 16 |
| 29 Peru | 32 | 43 | 66 Liberia | 10 | 13 |
| 30 Finland | 32 | 43 | 67 Albania | 9 | 12 |
| 31 Iran | 32 | 43 | 68 Burma | 8 | 11 |
| | | | 69 Indonesia | 8 | 11 |
| 32 Greece | 30 | 40 | 70 Ceylon | 7 | 9 |
| 33 Panama | 29 | 39 | 71 Nepal | 4 | 5 |
| 34 Uruguay | 29 | 39 | 72 North Korea | 3 | 4 |
| 35 Lebanon | 29 | 39 | 73 South Korea | 3 | 4 |
| 36 Yugoslavia | 28 | 37 | 74 Mongolia | 2 | 3 |
| 37 Salvador | 26 | 35 | 75 Yeman Arab Rep. | 1 | 1 |
| 38 Taiwan | 26 | 35 | | | |

## Table 2. Diplomatic Importance Ranks and Scores by Half-Decade, 1950-1970 *(Cont.)*

| | 1955 | | | | |
|---|---|---|---|---|---|
| Rank | Missions Received | Normalized Score | Rank | Missions Received | Normalized Score |
| 1 United Kingdom | 77 | 92 | 43 Colombia | 33 | 39 |
| 2 United States | 76 | 90 | 44 Guatemala | 32 | 38 |
| 3 Italy | 76 | 90 | 45 Bolivia | 32 | 38 |
| 4 France | 74 | 88 | 46 Hungary | 32 | 38 |
| 5 Holland | 68 | 81 | 47 Bulgaria | 32 | 38 |
| 6 Sweden | 65 | 77 | 48 Panama | 31 | 37 |
| 7 Belgium | 63 | 75 | 49 Paraguay | 31 | 37 |
| 8 West Germany | 63 | 75 | 50 Rumania | 31 | 37 |
| 9 Denmark | 63 | 75 | 51 Thailand | 30 | 36 |
| 10 Switzerland | 62 | 74 | | | |
| 11 Spain | 61 | 73 | 52 Honduras | 29 | 35 |
| 12 Norway | 60 | 71 | 53 Salvador | 29 | 35 |
| 13 Argentina | 58 | 69 | 54 Philippines | 29 | 35 |
| 14 Austria | 58 | 69 | 55 Iraq | 28 | 33 |
| 15 Brazil | 55 | 65 | 56 Costa Rica | 27 | 32 |
| 16 India | 55 | 65 | 57 Luxembourg | 27 | 32 |
| 17 Mexico | 54 | 64 | 58 Afghanistan | 27 | 32 |
| 18 U.S.S.R. | 54 | 64 | 59 Haiti | 26 | 31 |
| | | | 60 Nicaragua | 26 | 31 |
| 19 Yugoslavia | 52 | 62 | 61 Ethiopia | 26 | 31 |
| 20 Japan | 52 | 62 | 62 South Africa | 26 | 31 |
| 21 Chile | 51 | 61 | 63 China | 25 | 30 |
| 22 Poland | 51 | 61 | 64 Taiwan | 25 | 30 |
| 23 Canada | 50 | 60 | 65 Burma | 24 | 29 |
| 24 Egypt/U.A.R. | 50 | 60 | 66 Iceland | 23 | 27 |
| 25 Turkey | 49 | 58 | 67 Saudi Arabia | 22 | 26 |
| 26 Pakistan | 49 | 58 | 68 Ireland | 21 | 25 |
| 27 Czechoslovakia | 48 | 57 | 69 Jordan | 21 | 25 |
| 28 Venezuela | 44 | 52 | 70 Ceylon | 21 | 25 |
| 29 Iran | 44 | 52 | | | |
| 30 Portugal | 43 | 54 | 71 Libya | 19 | 23 |
| 31 Finland | 43 | 51 | 72 New Zealand | 19 | 23 |
| 32 Cuba | 41 | 49 | 73 Liberia | 12 | 14 |
| 33 Indonesia | 41 | 49 | 74 Yemen Arab Rep. | 12 | 14 |
| 34 Greece | 40 | 48 | 75 Albania | 11 | 13 |
| | | | 76 East Germany | 10 | 12 |
| 35 Peru | 38 | 45 | 77 South Vietnam | 9 | 11 |
| 36 Lebanon | 38 | 45 | 78 Cambodia | 8 | 10 |
| 37 Ecuador | 36 | 43 | 79 Mongolia | 7 | 8 |
| 38 Uruguay | 36 | 43 | 80 North Korea | 7 | 8 |
| 39 Dominican Rep. | 35 | 42 | 81 Nepal | 7 | 8 |
| 40 Syria | 35 | 42 | 82 Laos | 6 | 7 |
| 41 Israel | 35 | 42 | 83 North Vietnam | 5 | 6 |
| 42 Australia | 35 | 42 | 84 South Korea | 3 | 4 |

## Table 2. Diplomatic Importance Ranks and Scores by Half-Decade, 1950-1970 *(Cont.)*

| | 1960 | | | | |
|---|---|---|---|---|---|
| Rank | Missions Received | Normalized Score | | Missions Received | Normalized Score |
| 1 Italy | 82 | 92 | 46 Ecuador | 37 | 42 |
| 2 United States | 80 | 90 | 47 Afghanistan | 36 | 40 |
| 3 United Kingdom | 80 | 90 | 48 Salvador | 35 | 39 |
| 4 Holland | 77 | 87 | 49 Iraq | 35 | 39 |
| 5 France | 75 | 84 | 50 Guatemala | 34 | 38 |
| 6 Sweden | 73 | 82 | 51 Haiti | 33 | 37 |
| 7 Austria | 71 | 80 | 52 Costa Rica | 33 | 37 |
| 8 Denmark | 71 | 80 | 53 Bolivia | 33 | 37 |
| 9 West Germany | 69 | 78 | 54 Burma | 33 | 37 |
| 10 Belgium | 67 | 75 | 55 Philippines | 33 | 37 |
| 11 Japan | 65 | 73 | 56 Australia | 33 | 37 |
| 12 Yugoslavia | 63 | 71 | | | |
| 13 Switzerland | 62 | 70 | 57 Panama | 32 | 36 |
| 14 Spain | 62 | 70 | 58 Paraguay | 32 | 36 |
| 15 Norway | 62 | 70 | 59 Sudan | 32 | 36 |
| 16 India | 61 | 69 | 60 Ethiopia | 31 | 35 |
| 17 Argentina | 60 | 67 | 61 Tunisia | 31 | 35 |
| 18 Czechoslovakia | 58 | 65 | 62 Honduras | 30 | 34 |
| 19 Egypt/U.A.R. | 58 | 65 | 63 Bulgaria | 29 | 33 |
| | | | 64 Jordan | 29 | 33 |
| 20 Brazil | 56 | 63 | 65 Nicaragua | 28 | 31 |
| 21 Poland | 55 | 62 | 66 Luxembourg | 27 | 30 |
| 22 U.S.S.R. | 55 | 62 | 67 Saudi Arabia | 27 | 30 |
| 23 Finland | 55 | 62 | 68 China | 27 | 30 |
| 24 Cuba | 54 | 61 | 69 Iceland | 26 | 29 |
| 25 Turkey | 54 | 61 | 70 Morocco | 26 | 29 |
| 26 Israel | 53 | 60 | 71 Cambodia | 24 | 27 |
| 27 Mexico | 52 | 58 | 72 Ghana | 23 | 26 |
| 28 Portugal | 52 | 58 | | | |
| 29 Canada | 51 | 57 | 73 New Zealand | 22 | 25 |
| 30 Greece | 50 | 56 | 74 Ireland | 20 | 22 |
| 31 Pakistan | 50 | 56 | 75 South Africa | 20 | 22 |
| 32 Chile | 49 | 55 | 76 Nepal | 20 | 22 |
| 33 Venezuela | 47 | 53 | 77 Libya | 19 | 21 |
| 34 Iran | 47 | 53 | 78 Malaysia | 18 | 20 |
| 35 Indonesia | 47 | 53 | 79 Albania | 17 | 19 |
| 36 Lebanon | 45 | 51 | 80 Liberia | 16 | 18 |
| 37 Thailand | 45 | 51 | 81 Laos | 15 | 17 |
| | | | 82 South Vietnam | 15 | 17 |
| 38 Uruguay | 43 | 48 | 83 South Korea | 14 | 16 |
| 39 Rumania | 43 | 48 | 84 East Germany | 12 | 13 |
| 40 Taiwan | 42 | 47 | 85 Mongolia | 10 | 11 |
| 41 Hungary | 40 | 45 | 86 Yemen Arab Rep. | 8 | 9 |
| 42 Colombia | 39 | 44 | 87 North Korea | 8 | 9 |
| 43 Peru | 39 | 44 | 88 North Vietnam | 8 | 9 |
| 44 Ceylon | 39 | 44 | 89 Guinea | 5 | 6 |
| 45 Dominican Rep. | 38 | 43 | | | |

Table 2. Diplomatic Importance Ranks and Scores by Half-Decade, 1950-1970 *(Cont.)*

| Rank | Missions Received | Normalized Score | Rank | Missions Received | Normalized Score |
|---|---|---|---|---|---|
| | | 1965 | | | |
| 1 United States | 112 | 93 | 48 Peru | 49 | 40 |
| 2 United Kingdom | 112 | 93 | 49 Uruguay | 49 | 40 |
| 3 France | 111 | 92 | 50 Tunisia | 49 | 40 |
| 4 Holland | 109 | 90 | 51 Syria | 49 | 40 |
| 5 West Germany | 102 | 84 | 52 Ceylon | 49 | 40 |
| 6 Sweden | 102 | 84 | | | |
| 7 Italy | 101 | 83 | 53 Jordan | 46 | 38 |
| 8 Belgium | 95 | 79 | 54 Saudi Arabia | 46 | 38 |
| 9 Japan | 95 | 79 | 55 China | 46 | 38 |
| 10 India | 89 | 74 | 56 Ethiopia | 45 | 37 |
| 11 Canada | 87 | 72 | 57 Afghanistan | 45 | 37 |
| 12 Switzerland | 87 | 72 | 58 Guinea | 44 | 36 |
| 13 Israel | 85 | 70 | 59 Colombia | 42 | 35 |
| 14 Austria | 84 | 69 | 60 Mali | 42 | 35 |
| 15 U.S.S.R. | 83 | 69 | 61 Australia | 42 | 35 |
| 16 Egypt/U.A.R. | 83 | 69 | 62 Philippines | 40 | 33 |
| 17 Denmark | 82 | 68 | 63 Senegal | 39 | 32 |
| 18 Norway | 79 | 65 | 64 Guatemala | 38 | 31 |
| 19 Yugoslavia | 76 | 63 | 65 South Vietnam | 38 | 31 |
| 20 Lebanon | 75 | 62 | 66 Ecuador | 37 | 31 |
| 21 Pakistan | 75 | 62 | 67 Luxembourg | 37 | 31 |
| 22 Poland | 74 | 61 | 68 Taiwan | 37 | 31 |
| 23 Spain | 71 | 59 | 69 Haiti | 36 | 30 |
| 24 Czechoslovakia | 70 | 58 | 70 Dominican Rep. | 36 | 30 |
| 25 Brazil | 69 | 57 | 71 Salvador | 36 | 30 |
| | | | 72 Panama | 36 | 30 |
| 26 Finland | 67 | 55 | 73 Libya | 36 | 30 |
| 27 Argentina | 66 | 55 | 74 Burma | 36 | 30 |
| 28 Sudan | 66 | 55 | 75 Laos | 36 | 30 |
| 29 Turkey | 65 | 54 | | | |
| 30 Greece | 64 | 53 | 76 Bolivia | 35 | 29 |
| 31 Ghana | 62 | 51 | 77 Zaire | 35 | 29 |
| 32 Indonesia | 62 | 51 | 78 Nicaragua | 34 | 28 |
| 33 Iraq | 61 | 50 | 79 Costa Rica | 34 | 28 |
| 34 Hungary | 59 | 49 | 80 Paraguay | 33 | 27 |
| 35 South Korea | 59 | 49 | 81 Liberia | 33 | 27 |
| 36 Mexico | 57 | 47 | 82 Cameroun | 33 | 27 |
| 37 Portugal | 57 | 47 | 83 Iceland | 32 | 26 |
| 38 Rumania | 57 | 47 | 84 Malaysia | 32 | 26 |
| 39 Chile | 55 | 45 | 85 Honduras | 31 | 26 |
| 40 Nigeria | 55 | 45 | 86 Dahomey | 31 | 26 |
| 41 Morocco | 55 | 45 | 87 Cambodia | 31 | 26 |
| 42 Cuba | 54 | 45 | 88 Ireland | 30 | 25 |
| 43 Algeria | 53 | 44 | 89 Ivory Coast | 28 | 23 |
| 44 Iran | 52 | 43 | 90 New Zealand | 28 | 23 |
| 45 Bulgaria | 51 | 42 | 91 Cyprus | 27 | 22 |
| 46 Thailand | 51 | 42 | 92 Nepal | 26 | 21 |
| 47 Venezuela | 49 | 40 | 93 Togo | 24 | 20 |

## Table 2. Diplomatic Importance Ranks and Scores by Half-Decade, 1950-1970 *(Cont.)*

### 1965

| Rank | | Missions Received | Normalized Score | Rank | | Missions Received | Normalized Score |
|---|---|---|---|---|---|---|---|
| 94 | Tanzania | 24 | 20 | 108 | Malagasy | 17 | 14 |
| 95 | Niger | 23 | 19 | 109 | East Germany | 16 | 13 |
| 96 | Upper Volta | 23 | 19 | 110 | Chad | 16 | 13 |
| 97 | Sierra Leone | 23 | 19 | 111 | Kuwait | 16 | 13 |
| 98 | Congo | 23 | 19 | 112 | North Vietnam | 16 | 13 |
| 99 | South Africa | 23 | 19 | 113 | Zambia | 13 | 11 |
| 100 | Yemen Arab Rep. | 22 | 18 | 114 | North Korea | 13 | 11 |
| | | | | 115 | Central African R. | 12 | 10 |
| 101 | Albania | 21 | 17 | 116 | Rwanda | 12 | 10 |
| 102 | Gabon | 21 | 17 | 117 | Burundi | 10 | 8 |
| 103 | Kenya | 21 | 17 | 118 | Jamaica | 9 | 7 |
| 104 | Mongolia | 21 | 17 | 119 | Trinidad-Tobago | 9 | 7 |
| 105 | Somalia | 19 | 16 | 120 | Malawi | 9 | 7 |
| 106 | Uganda | 18 | 15 | 121 | Malta | 2 | 2 |
| 107 | Mauritania | 17 | 14 | | | | |

### 1970

| Rank | | Missions Received | Normalized Score | Rank | | Missions Received | Normalized Score |
|---|---|---|---|---|---|---|---|
| 1 | United Kingdom | 122 | 92 | 31 | Greece | 68 | 51 |
| 2 | Holland | 119 | 89 | 32 | Sudan | 68 | 51 |
| 3 | France | 119 | 89 | 33 | Algeria | 67 | 50 |
| 4 | Belgium | 117 | 88 | 34 | Lebanon | 67 | 50 |
| 5 | Switzerland | 117 | 88 | 35 | Ethiopia | 66 | 50 |
| 6 | United States | 115 | 86 | 36 | Hungary | 64 | 48 |
| 7 | Sweden | 114 | 86 | 37 | Morocco | 63 | 47 |
| 8 | Canada | 113 | 85 | 38 | Mexico | 62 | 47 |
| 9 | Italy | 110 | 83 | 39 | Ghana | 62 | 47 |
| 10 | West Germany | 106 | 80 | 40 | Nigeria | 60 | 45 |
| 11 | Japan | 103 | 77 | 41 | Indonesia | 60 | 45 |
| 12 | India | 103 | 77 | 42 | Chile | 59 | 44 |
| 13 | Austria | 98 | 74 | 43 | Tunisia | 59 | 44 |
| 14 | Denmark | 97 | 73 | 44 | Australia | 58 | 44 |
| 15 | Pakistan | 96 | 72 | 45 | Venezuela | 55 | 41 |
| 16 | Yugoslavia | 95 | 71 | 46 | Mali | 55 | 41 |
| 17 | U.S.S.R. | 92 | 69 | 47 | Iran | 54 | 41 |
| 18 | Norway | 92 | 69 | 48 | Thailand | 53 | 40 |
| 19 | Rumania | 91 | 68 | 49 | Guinea | 52 | 39 |
| 20 | Spain | 88 | 66 | 50 | Syria | 52 | 39 |
| 21 | Egypt/U.A.R. | 86 | 65 | 51 | Ceylon | 52 | 39 |
| 22 | Argentina | 85 | 64 | 52 | Peru | 50 | 38 |
| 23 | Israel | 85 | 64 | 53 | Uruguay | 50 | 38 |
| 24 | Poland | 83 | 62 | 54 | Senegal | 50 | 38 |
| 25 | Czechoslovakia | 80 | 60 | 55 | Kenya | 50 | 38 |
| 26 | Finland | 80 | 60 | | | | |
| 27 | Bulgaria | 78 | 59 | 56 | Portugal | 49 | 37 |
| | | | | 57 | Afghanistan | 49 | 37 |
| 28 | Brazil | 75 | 56 | 58 | Taiwan | 49 | 37 |
| 29 | Turkey | 72 | 54 | 59 | Jordan | 48 | 36 |
| 30 | South Korea | 71 | 53 | 60 | Cuba | 47 | 35 |

## Table 2.  Diplomatic Importance Ranks and Scores by Half-Decade, 1950-1970 *(Cont.)*

| | 1970 | | | | |
|---|---|---|---|---|---|
| Rank | Missions Re-ceived | Normal-ized Score | Rank | Missions Re-ceived | Normal-ized Score |
| 61  Tanzania | 47 | 35 | 98   Zambia | 34 | 26 |
| 62  Iraq | 47 | 35 | 99   Nepal | 34 | 26 |
| 63  China | 47 | 35 | 100  South Vietnam | 34 | 26 |
| 64  Malaysia | 47 | 35 | 101  Somalia | 33 | 25 |
| 65  Zaire | 46 | 35 | 102  Congo | 31 | 23 |
| 66  Colombia | 45 | 34 | 103  North Korea | 31 | 23 |
| 67  Saudi Arabia | 45 | 34 | 104  Upper Volta | 30 | 23 |
| 68  Ivory Coast | 43 | 32 | 105  Niger | 29 | 22 |
| 69  Kuwait | 43 | 32 | 106  Sierra Leone | 28 | 21 |
| 70  Philippines | 43 | 32 | 107  Togo | 28 | 21 |
| 71  Luxembourg | 42 | 32 | 108  Chad | 28 | 21 |
| 72  Cameroun | 42 | 32 | | | |
| 73  Libya | 42 | 32 | 109  Malagasy | 26 | 20 |
| 74  Panama | 41 | 31 | 110  Albania | 25 | 19 |
| 75  Dominican Rep. | 40 | 30 | 111  Central African R. | 25 | 19 |
| 76  Salvador | 40 | 30 | 112  North Vietnam | 25 | 19 |
| 77  Ecuador | 40 | 30 | 113  Ireland | 24 | 18 |
| 78  Burma | 40 | 30 | 114  South Africa | 24 | 18 |
| 79  Guatemala | 39 | 29 | 115  Gabon | 23 | 17 |
| 80  Paraguay | 39 | 29 | 116  Burundi | 23 | 17 |
| 81  Liberia | 39 | 29 | 117  Yemen Arab Rep. | 23 | 17 |
| 82  Uganda | 39 | 29 | 118  Malawi | 22 | 17 |
| | | | 119  Jamaica | 21 | 16 |
| 83  Costa Rica | 38 | 29 | 120  Trinidad-Tobago | 20 | 15 |
| 84  Cyprus | 38 | 29 | 121  Rwanda | 18 | 14 |
| 85  Dahomey | 38 | 29 | 122  Botswana | 17 | 13 |
| 86  Nicaragua | 37 | 28 | 123  East Germany | 16 | 12 |
| 87  Bolivia | 37 | 28 | 124  Barbados | 15 | 11 |
| 88  Laos | 37 | 28 | 125  Guyana | 14 | 11 |
| 89  Iceland | 36 | 27 | 126  Lesotho | 13 | 10 |
| 90  Mongolia | 36 | 27 | 127  Mauritius | 13 | 10 |
| 91  Cambodia | 36 | 27 | 128  Gambia | 12 | 9 |
| 92  Mauritania | 35 | 26 | 129  Yemen People's R. | 12 | 9 |
| 93  Singapore | 35 | 26 | 130  Equatorial Guinea | 11 | 8 |
| 94  New Zealand | 35 | 26 | 131  Swaziland | 5 | 4 |
| 95  Haiti | 34 | 26 | 132  Maldive Islands | 3 | 2 |
| 96  Honduras | 34 | 26 | 133  Rhodesia | 0 | 0 |
| 97  Malta | 34 | 26 | | | |

The foregoing data, plus those found in the earlier paper, permit one to ascertain which states were in which approximate position vis-à-vis others in any given half-decade since the Congress of Vienna. For some theoretical purposes, such cross-sectional pictures of the system's hierarchy can be quite useful; but for others, it would be more valuable to have a longitudinal picture, and were space available, such a table would be presented. Potential users may request the data for "Diplomatic Importance Score of Each Nation by Quintile during each Half-Decade, 1816–1970" from the Archive, as mentioned in note 9.

## Conclusion

The general impression, as one scrutinizes the scores and rankings in table 2, is that we have come fairly close to "tapping" the concept of diplomatic importance. By and large, the major powers always cluster at the top; the "pariah" states and their satellites score somewhat lower than their better-established opposite numbers; the nonaligned states outrank their NATO and Warsaw Pact counterparts; the smaller but centrally placed states show up higher than might be expected; and the more peripheral actors systematically fall into the lower quintiles. Further, the longitudinal picture is quite satisfactory: The peripheral states move up on the diplomatic importance scores as they industrialize and/or seek an increasingly active role in the system; those which suffer defeat (or great damage) in war show the expected decline and vice versa; and the newly independent states begin near the bottom of the listing but move up as their potential is developed and recognized.

On the other hand, the index does produce some readings that might seem out of place, and they also merit attention. One apparent anomaly is the tendency of certain smaller states of Western Europe to hover near or at the top of the rankings during most of the post–World War II period, above the USSR, China, India, or Japan. Partly, this is due to the reluctance of governments to sever long-established ties, and partly to the fact that the interstate system is still centered in Europe. In addition, Belgium, Holland, and Switzerland are major trading states as well as hosts to a variety of international organizations, while Italy also provides the seat of the Vatican, making it an important focal point for the Catholic countries of the world. The position of Soviet Russia, then, below these smaller Western states, should come as no surprise.

Further, as we have already emphasized, we are not trying to measure size, military capability, or industrial potential, even though such factors will affect the scores. Moreover, as a revolutionary (and therefore pariah) state in a conservative and capitalist-dominated system, the Soviet Union's score will inevitably reflect the fear and hostility of other members of the system, plus the systematic efforts of the major Western powers to keep her in isolation. The same may be said, but more forcefully, of Communist China. Not only are her capabilities considerably fewer than the Western press suggests, and her energies largely directed toward internal development, but the United States has, until very recently, systematically discriminated against and tried to isolate this latest challenger to the old diplomatic order.

Having noted these possible discrepancies between the computed scores and what might have been "expected," we remind the reader that, as a first systematic attempt, any index such as this will certainly have some deficiencies. More important, there will be disagreement as to whether deviations from the expected are indeed discrepancies. That disagreement will, in turn, depend upon both the folklore out of which our expectations arise and the clarity and face validity of the reasoning behind the measuring procedures. Though there is little we can do about the former, we hope that our performance on the latter is adequate. In any event, we regard the argument made here to be considerably more rigorous and explicit than that found in the original paper.

Finally, some may feel that we have taken on an impossible task: trying to reflect, in a single indicator, a complex state of affairs which emerges from a variety of background factors. It is clear that we have not produced a simple proxy indicator, with a one-to-one association between the observed phenomenon and some single unobserved condition in the empirical world. But the very diversity of the factors that affect the measure and the very complexity of the decision processes that produce the outcome may well be viewed as an asset. When we can, by parsimoniously observing a single set of traces, tap the resultant of a very complex set of interactions, we have progressed on the measurement front. And what holds for the GNP of a nation, the IQ of a schoolboy, the earned-run average of a baseball pitcher, or the force of a moving object would seem to hold for the diplomatic importance of a state.

We realize, however, that such single-index measures of complex phenomena are never fully satisfactory in reliability and validity, and that they usually undergo improvement as they are put into use and their inadequacies become evident. As the science of world politics develops, we trust that the measure at hand will not only prove useful to many researchers, but will experience whatever improvements and refinements turn out to be necessary.

# VII

# Testing Some
# Preliminary Models

In many ways, everything that has been covered up to this point in the volume has been preliminary to the real activities of social science. The generation of social science knowledge is a complex process characterized by a sequence of discrete steps whose original distinctiveness is then blurred by a variety of feedback loops. But once the problem is defined, the key concepts well articulated, the indices constructed, and the data acquired, we turn to the analysis of the data in order to look for, or confirm the existence of, certain patterns and regularities. Here again, there is plenty of controversy.

Perhaps the central argument is over the relationship between correlational and explanatory knowledge. Leaving aside those who cannot tell the difference (and all of us are in that situation once in a while), the question is essentially one of priorities and of the bases upon which we can make causal inferences. As I see it, one school of thought holds that we move from correlational to explanatory knowledge in a systematic, building-block fashion. The point of followers of this school is that the more we know about which factors rise and fall with our observed outcomes, across time and cases, the closer we are to explaining those outcomes. But the counterpoint is that correlation and covariation, whether the analysis embraces one or several variables on the predictor side of the equation, remain just that. One can, it is argued,

223

discover covariations unto eternity and yet make no progress toward explanation. This noble objective, it follows, requires some sort of a priori "theory" that is set up in formal language (verbal, mathematical, diagrammatic, electronic) and then subjected to efforts at disconfirmation.

While I share the hope that we will some day be developing and disconfirming highly formal models as a matter of routine, our field is still some distance from that august state. Not only do we know very little about what phenomena rise and fall together; we also know little about which phenomena rise and fall in a given *single* pattern. That is, we must have observed and measured the outcome phenomena and their variation across time and across cases before a serious effort at explaining that variation can be undertaken. Further, we must observe and measure those variables that are expected to play an explanatory role, and then see whether *their* values rise and fall systematically with the outcome variable that is to be explained.

Of course, even if the predictor variables do show a high correlation—singly or in combination—with the outcome, this could be mere coincidence, with no causal or explanatory inferences permissible. Conversely, a number of promising explanatory variables may show no correlation with the outcome, and thus be rejected, merely because the model omitted some additional key variable that, when included, might interact with the others in such a way as to produce the elusive correlation. To know which variable is missing from the equation, which ones to drop out, and how to combine them, requires a considerable understanding of the phenomena at hand—as well as a modicum of luck—but to speak of this understanding as a "theory" in this context is still premature. As our multivariate models give an increasingly good fit across a long and wide empirical domain, and are able to cope with allegedly different historical and cultural settings, we can begin to take them more seriously. As that goodness of fit increases, along with the persuasiveness of the argument that leads us to *expect* that fit, we come closer to approximating the construction and verification of a theory in the scientific sense.

# 13

# Alliance Aggregation and
# the Onset of War, 1815-1945
## *With Melvin Small*

*Regardless of one's epistemological (and aesthetic) preferences about the proper route to theory, most would agree that world politics and peace research today are much more in the exploration and discovery phase than in the verification and confirmation phase. To the extent that this is true, the search for correlational knowledge is a highly useful activity. This paper was the first analysis to emerge out of the Correlates of War project, following a number of papers devoted to early speculation, index construction, and presentation of data sets.[1] As such, it has all the weaknesses of the bivariate analysis, especially when conducted by relative neophytes, which my coauthor and I were at the time. I include it here not only for sentimental purposes, but also because it addresses an interesting question, converts that question into operational language, and then examines the results in a manner that is tentative and exploratory, yet systematic. While an investigation such as this is a far cry from either a compelling theory of war or a persuasive piece of policy guidance, in my judgment it does constitute an indispensable step toward those ends.*

## A Framework for Inquiry

In any search for the "causes" of international war, there are at least four possible levels of analysis at which we might focus our

225

attention: the individual, the subnational interest group, the nation, and the international system. Furthermore, each of these four possible classes of empirical referent may be examined in terms of its *structural* attributes or in terms of its *behavior*. That is, the individual, the interest group, the nation, or the system is an object of analysis which reveals relatively *static* properties such as size, composition, organization, power, or capacity for change, and relatively *dynamic* properties such as activity level, aggressiveness, cooperativeness, responsiveness, initiative, or communicativeness. In addition to these two sets of attributes, an individual or a social organization will reveal *relationship* attributes vis-à-vis other actors at the same or other levels of organizational complexity. Nations, for example, may be geographically near or distant, more or less interdependent economically, politically hostile or friendly, ethnically or industrially similar, and so forth. In sum, we may look for the causes of war in structure, behavior, or relationship at—or across—many levels of social organization. Combining these three classes of variables with the four suggested levels of analysis, we can postulate at least twelve different classes of information one might examine in any systematic search for those factors most often associated with war.

Of course, the moment these twelve categories are filled in with illustrative variables, it becomes evident that the structural-behaviorial-relational trichotomization is not always clear-cut; one might argue, for example, that an individual personality attribute, such as rigidity, or a national one, such as autocracy, is more a behavioral than a structural property. At the least, we must recognize that we may have to infer one set of attributes from the observation of another set.

Regardless of the level of organization (or class of variable) at which we look, we must make at least two epistemological assumptions: (1) that explanatory variables will be found in more than one place, the exact number being a function of one's theoretical predilections; and (2) that the interaction of two or more such classes of variables will have more explanatory power than the mere correlation of any single class of variable with our dependent variable: the incidence of war. Which particular levels or classes one gives priority to is likewise a matter of individual judgment, with two considerations deserving attention in that selection. First, there is the question of parsimony, and this should lead to a preference for variables that are at the more general rather than the more idiosyncratic end of the continuum. Second, certain classes of possible predictors to events such as war seem to get considerable attention in the scholarly literature, at the expense of others of intuitively equal significance. On the basis of these considerations, and with the intention of turning later to other possible predictors (and combinations thereof), we focus here on one cluster of *structural* variables at the *systemic* level of analysis: alliance aggregation.

## Alliance Aggregation as a Predictor to War

Without going into the quagmire of terminological and normative dispute which has characterized much of the theoretical literature on the balance of power, we can nevertheless note that its defense or justification clearly rests on the assumption that the stability of the international system can be maintained without reliance on superordinate political institutions.[2] In the words of M. A. Kaplan (1957b), it postulates a system which is "subsystem dominant"; that is, one in which most authority is found at the national actor, or subsystemic level, rather than at the supranational or systemic level. The same notion is conveyed by the international lawyers' distinction between a system in which most of the authority lines are horizontal and one in which they tend to be vertical in direction (Falk 1959).

In the absence of significant legal or political institutions at the supranational level, the preservation of relative stability and the survival of the nations are seen as depending upon the presence or absence of one or more of the following phenomena, depending in turn upon the theoretical predilections or national outlook of the observer: For the nations themselves, the phenomena are their restraint and limit of ambition, their similarity of values, their approximate parity, the absence of permanent friendships and hostilities, or their willingness to coalesce against a challenger. For the system, these conditions might be the absence of alliances, the presence of a minimum number of alliance coalitions, the approximate parity of the coalitions, the fluidity and impermanence of these coalitions, or a high level of normative consensus. That some of these requirements are vague and that others are inconsistent seems not to discourage those who consider supranational institutions as unnecessary. In one fashion or another, they would rely upon what might be characterized as the diplomatic equivalent of Adam Smith's "invisible hand," a mechanism whereby the individual pursuit of individual interests redounds to the advantage and stability of the community as a whole.

Central to this notion is the understanding that the invisible or unseen hand will function only to the extent that all nations are free to deal and interact with all others as their national interests dictate. Thus, it is assumed that every dyadic relationship will be a mixture of the cooperative and the conflictful, with political, economic, ideological, and other issues all producing different interest configurations for each possible pair of nations. The net effect, it is believed, is such a welter of crosscutting ties and such a shifting of friendships and hostilities that no single set of interests can create a self-aggravating and self-reinforcing division or cleavage among the nations; A and B may well have competitive economic interests in the Middle East, but harmonious strategic interests in the Caribbean, while B and C's political interests may coincide in regard to West Africa and clash in an international organization setting.

It follows from this sort of a model that anything which restrains or inhibits free or vigorous pursuit of the separate national interests will limit the efficacy of the stabilizing mechanism. And among those arrangements seen as most likely to so inhibit that pursuit are formal alliances. Nations in the same alliance are less free to compete with their allies in such spheres of incompatibility, and less free to cooperate with outsiders in areas of overlapping interests.[3] Just how *much* freedom to pursue normal interests is lost by an allied nation is, of course, most difficult to measure. Although some approximation of the degree of inhibition—or loss of interaction opportunity— can be gleaned from the text and associated documents of a given alliance treaty, a fuller appreciation would require a laborious examination of the treaty's context, and the motivations, relative power, and performance of the signatory nations. Despite the obvious simplifications, however, a differentiation based on the documents themselves is not without some merit, and we will therefore distinguish all the alliances examined as to whether they are military, neutrality, or entente commitments; the specific coding rules are outlined in a later section.

Be that as it may, if each alliance commitment reduces, to *some* degree, the normal interaction opportunities available to the total system, and the loss of such interaction opportunities is supposed to inhibit the efficacy of the balance-of-power mechanism, we should find that as the system's interaction opportunities diminish, war will increase in frequency, magnitude, or severity. Moreover, if the alliance configurations show less and less partial overlap, and they instead increasingly reinforce a tendency toward a very few (but large-sized) coalitions, the system's loss of interaction opportunities becomes even more severe. Carried to its extreme condition, this tendency culminates in a completely bipolarized system, with interaction opportunities reduced (theoretically, at least) to one; each nation would then have only friends or foes, and few relationships in between these two extremes. On the other hand, if there are no alliances in the system at all, these interaction opportunities will be equal to the total number of pairs or dyads possible with a given total number of nations in the system; this would be equal to $N(N-1)/2$.

There are, of course, several other lines of reasoning by which one might be led to predict that alliance commitments will negatively affect the stability of the international system, but they are largely variations on the present theme and several have been presented elsewhere (Deutsch and Singer 1964). Thus, rather than dwell any longer here on the plausible reasons why alliance aggregation *should* correlate with the onset of war, it might be more useful to ascertain the extent to which it does. In order to put this proposition to the historical test, however, a number of preliminary steps are essential. These are the following:

1. Articulate the hypothesis in the various forms it might reasonably take.
2. Delineate the empirical world in time and space from which the evidence will be gathered.
3. Describe the procedures by which the chaotic welter of historical fact is converted into data.
4. Present the raw data which emerge from the above operations.
5. Ascertain the strength and direction of any correlations which would tend to confirm or disconfirm the various hypotheses.
6. Interpret the results of this search for correlations.

In the sections which follow, the above procedures will be described in appropriate detail.


## The Basic Hypotheses

Having articulated the reasons for examining the relationship between alliance aggregation and war, we can now spell out in more detail the hypotheses to be tested. In the next section, we can then move on to a specification of the procedures by which the key variables were converted from their widely scattered verbal state to collated and codified numerical form.

The hypotheses may be thought of as falling into two general classes, both of which belong to the systemic level of analysis. The first concerns alliance aggregation and the consequent loss of inter-action opportunities in general; that is, it ignores the specific nature of the alliance configurations which are produced, and looks merely at the system's *aggregate* loss of such normal opportunities. The second of these is as concerned with the specific configurations as it is with the aggregate loss of normal dyadic interaction, and focuses on the extent to which the alliance commitments produce a bipolar-ized system. Bipolarization may thus be thought of as a special case of alliance aggregation.

### Alliance Aggregation and the Magnitude or Severity of War

Looking first at the matter of general alliance configurations, and the extent to which they reduce normal interaction opportunities, we may articulate the first basic hypothesis: *The greater the number of alliance commitments in the system, the more war the system will experience.* The second hypothesis pays more attention to specific alliance configurations, and thus reads: *The closer to pure bipolarity the system is, the more war it will experience.*

In order to put these propositions to the test, we must first identify the empirical world within which the postulated relation-ships are to be sought. Let us describe and justify the world which we have selected, but a preliminary indication of the basic procedure might best precede that. Basically, the method to be employed is a trend analysis. After developing several different measures of alliance aggregation and several measures of the onset of war, we will exam-ine the extent to which the two sets of variables rise and fall together over time.

As to the empirical domain in which the longitudinal data will be compared, the problem is to examine a span of time which is not restricted to the all-too-recent, and therefore most salient, period upon which much theorizing in international relations seems to be based. On the other hand, if we go too far back we may well find ourselves examining international environments of such disparity that generalizations embracing them become foolish and irrelevant.

For the contemporary scholar, there does seem to be a chronological cutting point which provides a sufficiently extensive empirical world while nevertheless permitting a reasonable degree of comparability. We refer to the period opening with what we normally recognize as the beginning of the modern international system (the Congress of Vienna) and closing with the Japanese surrender in Tokyo Bay. Despite the many changes in the pattern and process of international relations during that 130-year period, we find a remarkable constancy. The national state was the dominant actor and the most relevant form of social organization; world politics were dominated by a handful of European powers; the Napoleonic reliance upon the citizen's army endured, with all of its implications for public involvement in diplomacy; the concept of state sovereignty remained relatively unchallenged; and while technological innovation went on apace, the period postdates the smoothbore and predates the nuclear-missile combination. In sum, it seems reasonable to conclude that this period provides an appropriate mixture of stability and transition from which generalization would be legitimate. As to whether such generalization might be extended beyond 1945 and into the present, we would be skeptical, but this is, of course, an empirical question, and one to which we will return in our conclusion.

Stated in the preceding rather general form, the hypotheses immediately raise a number of important conceptual and methodological problems. In addition to the procedures for operationalizing "number of alliance commitments" or "closer to pure bipolarity" (the independent variables) and "more war" (the dependent variable)—and these will be articulated in the next section—there are three relevant concerns of substance: (1) the time lag between the presence of a given number or percentage of alliance commitments and its effect in the form of international war; (2) the differentiation between separate regions of the world, especially between the "central" and the "peripheral" portions of the system; and (3) the differentiation between distinctive time periods in our 130 years, especially that between the nineteenth and twentieth centuries.

Let us look first at the matter of time lag. If, indeed, there *is* any relationship between the loss of interaction opportunities and war, that relationship must take a certain amount of time to make itself felt; the system certainly cannot be expected to respond immediately to a specific increase or decrease in interaction opportunities. Not only do we not find in the literature any compelling reason for assuming a given response time, but that response time might well differ for, let us say, different decades.[4] Consequently, each year's interaction opportunity measures have been correlated with the war indices for not only the following year ($Y + 1$), but for the following three ($Y + 3$) and five years ($Y + 5$) as well; for example, if a given alliance aggregation index for 1851 is relatively high, we want to know whether its effect is felt by 1852, by 1854, or 1856. That is, our dependent variables for 1851 will reflect the amount of war which began in 1852, the amount which began between the beginning of 1852 and the end of 1854, and the amount which began between the beginning of 1852 and the end of 1856.

Two points of clarification are in order here. First, note that we are distinguishing between the amount of war which *began* in the specified time period, regardless of how long it endured, and the amount of war which the system experienced during that period. Second, we are looking at the amount of war which began at any time *within* three time periods of increasing length: within one, three, or five years, not during 1852, or 1854, or 1856 alone. Thus all forms of the basic hypothesis will be tested under three different chronological conditions.

Beyond the refinement of the hypothesis in order to account for varying time lags, we should also refine it to permit its testing within several different time- and space-bound worlds. That is, if we recognize the extent to which theorizing about diplomatic history has been dominated by European-centered scholars and practitioners from the Western world, it seems prudent to wonder whether a given relationship might be found in one region but not in another. Combining that awareness with a recognition that it was not until relatively recent times that the international system could be treated as a more or less single and interdependent one, it makes perfect sense to look for a point in time at which the non-European nations "joined" that central system. The most reasonable such point seems to be that which closed out World War I and marked the birth of the League of Nations; this organization, while its pretensions to universality were never fulfilled, quite explicitly included many non-European members and concerned itself with all continents. Thus, while treating the post-1920 system as a single one, we look upon the pre-1920 epoch as having both a central, Europe-oriented system and a peripheral one. Consequently, all sets of correlations will be examined in two systemic contexts. The first will be called the *total system* and will include all "independent" nations which existed during any part of the entire 130-year period. The second context will be one in which we "shuck off" the peripheral nations prior to

1920, in order to eliminate the statistical "noise" generated by the less important and least active nations. This we will call the *central system*, and its composition is the same as the total system's for the final 25 years, but smaller for the first 105 years.

Further, we do not restrict attributed membership in the central system to European nations only, nor do all European nations fall into the central category for the pre-League period. In order to qualify for inclusion in the central system during that earlier period, a nation must either be located in Europe or deeply involved in relatively durable relationships with European nations. Given the difficulty of operationalizing this latter phenomenon and given the high degree of consensus among historians, we have adhered closely to that consensus.[5] To be more specific, we have *excluded* a number of European nations from our pre-League central system in line with the following criteria. Outside of Prussia and Austria, the German states are excluded because their 1815 treaty of confederation sharply restricts their diplomatic independence; for example, they are prohibited, formally and effectively, from alliances which might be directed at other members of the confederation. As for the Italian states other than Sardinia, they, too, enjoy few of the perquisites of real independence prior to their unification in 1860. Modena, Parma, Tuscany, and the Two Sicilies are closely linked by dynastic ties to Austria and turn out to be little more than satellites of Vienna. As to the Papal States, the French and Austrian guarantees effectively preclude them from any significant degree of normal diplomatic interplay.[6]

Turning to the considerations which led us to *include* several non-European nations in (and exclude others from) the pre-League central system, only a few political entities even qualify (by population and recognition criteria) as independent nations at all (if we forget Latin America for the moment) and almost none of these are regularly involved in Continental diplomacy or with the Continental powers abroad. In Asia and Africa, for example, only China, Japan, Persia, Siam, Ethiopia, Korea, and Morocco meet the population and diplomatic recognition requirements between 1815 and 1920.[7] They are, of course, considerably more independent than the subordinate German and Italian states, and they do occasionally interact with the European powers (for example, Persia in the 1850s and Siam in the 1880s), but they remain largely unrelated to the wars and treaties of Continental diplomacy. China and Japan, however, are brought into our central system in 1895 as a consequence of the Sino-Japanese War. As to Western Hemisphere nations, the same considerations apply. Aside from the United States after the Spanish-American War, the Americas are even less involved in Continental affairs than the Asian and African nations. Between 1815 and our cutoff date of 1920 there are no alliance ties with a European power and there are only two international wars involving Europe in Latin America: that between France and Mexico in 1862-1867 and that involving Spain with Bolivia, Chile, and Peru in 1865-1866. And there are no cases of Latin American nations engaging in European wars.[8]

In sum, then, we treat the post-1920 international system as a relatively interdependent one, but divide the pre-League system into two parts: the central and the peripheral. The search for correlations between alliance aggregation and war is thus conducted in two somewhat different empirical worlds so that we may, in one, ignore those political entities which qualify as independent nations, but which may hardly be thought of as active participants in international politics. For the pre-League period, then, the following nations are treated as members of the *central system*, as of the year indicated; it should be noted that Sardinia, Prussia, and Serbia become, respectively, Italy in 1860, Germany in 1871, and Yugoslavia in 1919, and that Austria and Hungary are treated as a single nation until 1918. Those in the left-hand column are members throughout the entire period.

| | |
|---|---|
| Austria-Hungary | Greece—1828 |
| Denmark | Belgium—1830 |
| England | Serbia—1878 |
| France | Romania—1878 |
| Holland | China—1895 |
| Portugal | Japan—1895 |
| Prussia | United States—1899 |
| Russia | Norway—1905 |
| Sardinia | Bulgaria—1908 |
| Spain | Albania—1914 |
| Sweden | Czechoslovakia—1919 |
| Switzerland | Poland—1919 |
| Turkey | Finland—1919 |

The following nations are excluded from the pre-1920 central system and treated as members of the *peripheral system* only, between the dates shown. The earlier date marks its qualification as a sovereign nation and the latter, if any, marks either its disqualification (via federation for the seven German and the five Italian states, or annexation for Morocco and Siam) or its entry into the central system (marked by an asterisk); needless to say, the precise date at which the population criterion was met cannot always be shown, and others might select a year or two later or earlier.

Baden, 1815–1870

Bavaria, 1815–1870

Hanover, 1838–1870

Hesse-Electoral, 1815–1866

Hesse-Grand Ducal, 1815–1867

Mecklenburg-Schwerin, 1843–1867

Saxony, 1815–1867

Württemberg, 1815–1870

Modena, 1842–1860

Papal States, 1815–1860

Parma, 1851–1860

Tuscany, 1815–1860

Two Sicilies, 1815–1861

Morocco, 1847–1911

Korea, 1888–1905

Ethiopia, 1898

Persia, 1855

United States, 1815–1899*

China, 1860–1895*

Japan, 1860–1895*

Brazil, 1826

Colombia, 1831

Mexico, 1831

Peru, 1837

Chile, 1839

Argentina, 1841

Venezuela, 1841

Bolivia, 1848

Guatemala, 1849

Ecuador, 1854

Haiti, 1859

Salvador, 1875

Uruguay, 1882

Santo Domingo, 1887

Siam, 1887

Paraguay, 1896

Honduras, 1899

Nicaragua, 1900

Turning to the post-1920 setting, in which we drop the distinction between central and peripheral systems, we find the following additional (not previously listed) nation members and their dates of qualification for entry into the total system:

Estonia, 1920

Latvia, 1920

Lithuania, 1920

Hungary, 1920

Luxembourg, 1920

Liberia, 1920

South Africa, 1920

Australia, 1920

New Zealand, 1920

Canada, 1920

Afghanistan, 1920

Nepal, 1920

Mongolia, 1921

Costa Rica, 1920

Panama, 1920

Ireland, 1921

Saudi Arabia, 1927

Iraq, 1932

Yemen, 1934

Cuba, 1934

Egypt, 1936

In addition to these spatial differentiations, a case can be made for an explicit chronological differentiation. Contemporary theoreticians are, all other things being approximately equal, more likely to argue from recent than from remote diplomatic events. Therefore, they may well be basing their postulated correlation between alliance aggregation and war on twentieth-century diplomatic history while tending to forget the nineteenth. To ascertain whether or not this has been the case, we have explicitly divided our 130-year epoch from Vienna to Tokyo Bay into two distinct periods, with the turn of the century marking the break. As to selecting this cutoff point rather than one closer to the midpoint, a number of considerations seemed relevant. First of all, there seemed to be an appreciable qualitative difference between World War I and the wars that preceded it. And bearing in mind the fact that time lags of up to five years are used, we must of necessity use a cutoff year no later than 1908. Secondly, the period *prior* to World War I is markedly different from that preceding most other wars, in that it produced a sharp and clear confrontation between the Central Powers and the Allies, and this bipolarization was well under way by 1902. To be sure, some of the alliances contracted before 1899 (Triple and Dual alliances) transcend both periods, but in order to evaluate their effects, we would have had to go back to 1879. Had we chosen this date, we would have eliminated from the nineteenth-century pattern those several interesting, though ephemeral, configurations of the 1879 to 1899 period which had little relationship to the post-1900 world. Moreover, only after 1900 does the rate of alliance activity show that marked increase which culminates in the grouping of France, England, Russia, and Japan into several interlocking alliances and ententes which by 1908 had resolved itself into the pre–World War I bipolarization.

Finally, there appears to be a marked difference in the amount and rate of diplomatic and military activity between the nineteenth and twentieth centuries, so that while 1899 does not represent an exact chronological midpoint, it is probable that the eight-five years prior to 1900 represent an approximate equivalent of the forty-five postcentury years in terms of "diplomatic time."

To summarize this part of the discussion, then, our hypothesis will actually be put to the test in eighteen different forms, in order to differentiate among: (1) three different time lags, for (2) six different time-space systems. In matrix form, we would want to show the correlation between our several alliance indices and wars beginning for each of the spatial-temporal cells in table 1.

Table 1.  Spatial-Temporal Domains and Time Lags

| | | Time Lags or Spans | | |
|---|---|---|---|---|
| Period | System | *Y + 1* | *Y + 3* | *Y + 5* |
| 1815-1945 | Central only | | | |
| 1815-1945 | Total | | | |
| 1815-1899 | Central only | | | |
| 1815-1899 | Total | | | |
| 1900-1945 | Central only | | | |
| 1900-1945 | Total | | | |

*Alliance Aggregation and the Frequency of War*

Up to this point we have been discussing a relationship which, however interesting, may possibly not be getting at the basic theoretical proposition. That is, we have been assuming that any positive relationship existing between aggregate alliance commitments and war would be revealed in the correlation between our various alliance indices in a given year and certain indices of the *magnitude* or *severity* of war in certain years immediately following. It could be argued that the existence of a statistically significant correlation between interaction opportunity losses and the severity or magnitude of war is really, by indirection, a *dis*confirmation of the hypothesis. The reasoning might be that not only do magnitude or severity seldom covary with frequency, but that they are more likely to vary inversely. A glance at figures for sickness, auto or industrial accidents, or battle casualties, for example, would show that the *least* serious events occur most frequently, and that in their most disastrous form these phenomena occur much less often. As a matter of fact, this is precisely what Richardson (1960b) found in his *Statistics*

Table 2.  Frequency Distribution of all International Wars, 1815-1945, by Size, Duration, Magnitude, and Severity (N = 41)

| | No. of participants | | Months duration | | Magnitude in nation-months | | Severity: battle deaths in thous. | |
|---|---|---|---|---|---|---|---|---|
| | *Range* | *Freq.* | *Range* | *Freq.* | *Range* | *Freq.* | *Range* | *Freq.* |
| High | 21-26 | 1 | 61-84 | 2 | 750+ | 1 | 10,000+ | 1 |
| Med.-high | 16-20 | 0 | 46-60 | 4 | 151-750 | 3 | 1001-10,000 | 1 |
| Medium | 11-15 | 1 | 31-45 | 1 | 31-150 | 8 | 101-1000 | 7 |
| Med.-low | 6-10 | 2 | 16-30 | 5 | 5-30 | 25 | 11-100 | 13 |
| Low | 1-5 | 37 | 0.5-15 | 29 | 1-5 | 4 | 1-10 | 19 |

*of Deadly Quarrels.* Classifying deaths on the basis of a $\log_{10}$ scale, he found that in 282 cases of mass violence between 1820 and 1945, deaths were distributed as follows:

| | |
|---|---|
| $3 \pm \frac{1}{2} - 188$ | $6 \pm \frac{1}{2} - 5$ |
| $4 \pm \frac{1}{2} - 63$ | $7 \pm \frac{1}{2} - 2$ |
| $5 \pm \frac{1}{2} - 24$ | |

Likewise, if we look at his observed frequency of ninety-one wars classified by the number of participants, a similar distribution holds:

| | |
|---|---|
| 2- 42 | 7- 3 |
| 3- 24 | 8- 2 |
| 4- 8 | 9- 1 |
| 5- 7 | 10- 0 |
| 6- 3 | 20- 1 |

Our own results reveal the same pattern, even though our more stringent criteria for war produced a much smaller number of cases. Whether the seriousness of war is measured in terms of number of participants, duration, or battle-connected military deaths, the same inverse correlation between frequency and seriousness is found, as shown in table 2.[9]

Given this rather critical observation, it certainly behooves us to pay as much attention to the correlations between interaction opportunity and the *frequency* of war as to those between such phenomena and the *magnitude* or *severity* of war. This we shall do in the sections which follow.

### Operationalizing the Variables

In order to put any hypothesis to the empirical test, of course, one must at the very least demonstrate a correlation between the independent and dependent variables. Though a positive correlation between alliance aggregation and war, high enough not to have occurred by sheer chance, cannot be interpreted as a demonstration of any causal connection, the search for such a correlation is a necessary first step. That the presence or absence of covariation between alliances and war is not a mere artifact requires considerable subsequent analysis, but the first order of business, and that which concerns us here, is whether the hypothesized correlations are indeed borne out by the historical evidence.

This enterprise, in turn, cannot be launched until the constructs have been operationalized—until the researcher has converted the ambiguous verbal labels into variables whose shifting presence or absence or strength can be repeatedly observed and recorded. That is, we must devise explicit and visible procedures by which the welter of events and conditions may be coded, sorted, and classified in so reliable a fashion that other scholars will, in applying the identical coding procedures to the same body of information, come up with almost exactly the same data. Whether these highly reliable procedures do, however, produce data which index the qualitative variables we seek is another matter. Whereas the relative *reliability* of our measures is easily established, their *validity* always remains a matter of some dispute. Recognizing, then, that the search for operational (or machine-readable) variables may well lead to the observation of phenomena quite remote from those about which we seek to generalize, let us turn to the procedures used here.

### Magnitude and Severity of War: The Dependent Variables

Before examining the frequency and distribution of our *independent* variables, we had better know what it is they are supposed to be predicting to. In the overall project of which this study is a small part, war is one of the major dependent variables; the object is to ascertain which structural, relational, and behavioral phenomena at which levels of social organization most strongly correlate with war. War, however, means many things to many people, and as a consequence, some definition and operationalization are essential; a full and detailed treatment of the problem is presented elsewhere (Singer and Small 1972), but a brief recapitulation is clearly in order here.

First of all, there are many deadly quarrels (to borrow Richardson's quaint phrase) which are not normally thought of as war: riots, murders, assassinations, pogroms, executions, duels, punitive expeditions, retaliatory strikes, and so on. Even when the deadly quarrel endures and involves nations, many ambiguities remain. How many nations must be involved, for how long, and with how many men or arms? And what is a nation? Secondly, even if we agree upon the meaning of war, there are several different classes of war, each having different relevance to the search for meaningful generalization about the international system.

In order to handle these ambiguities and inconsistencies, a two-step coding procedure was used. First, adapting from the schema found in *A Study of War* (Wright 1942, app. 20), four classes of war were differentiated: international, imperial, colonial, and civil. The criterion here is strictly one of the political-legal status of the participants. Thus, an *international* war [which has been called an interstate war in subsequent studies] is one in which at least one participant on each side is an independent and sovereign member of the international system, with a population exceeding 500,000 and enjoying diplomatic recognition from our two legitimizers, Britain and France. If only *one* side includes one or more independent system members, then the war is classified as imperial or colonial, depending on the political status of the adversaries, as follows. When the dominant (and usually there is only one) adversary is a more or less independent political entity, but *not* a qualified system member by our criteria, the war is classified as *imperial;* examples might be Serbia before 1878, Persia before 1855, or a Pathan tribe. When the dominant adversary is an entity which not only fails to qualify as a system member but which is also an ethnically different people formerly or presently under the suzerainty of the system member(s) against which it is fighting, the war is seen as *colonial;* examples of such wars might be the Russo-Polish ones of 1831 and 1863 or the Spanish-Cuban of 1868–1878. Wars of this latter category would generally fall, in contemporary parlance, under the rubric of wars of national independence. Finally, a *civil* (or internal) war is one between a system member's government and such subnational factions as are able to engage in armed resistance, insurgency, or revolution. Of course, any war may *become* an international war by the intervention of one or more independent members of the international system, and the classification of a war may therefore change between its onset and its termination.[10]

However, not all international wars are of equal interest to us here, nor is reliable information on all of them available. Thus, we exclude those wars in which the best estimate of total battle-connected deaths is less than 1,000.[11] Using these criteria of war type and casualty threshold, we find that there were forty-one international wars in the total international system between 1815 and 1945; if we ignore the pre-Versailles peripheral system, that number drops to twenty-four.

Having identified those international wars which interest the student of international relations as he examines the effects of alliance patterns, the next point to note is that these wars differ markedly in their duration, magnitude, and intensity. Thus, the correlation of alliance aggregation with mere war frequency would be of limited interest (if not downright misleading) and further gradation is clearly necessary. This gradation is achieved in the first instance by use of the nation-months-of-war measure, so that the simple *magnitude* of each war is the sum of the months which all nations individually experienced as participants in the war; other political entities, even though they participate in a qualifying war, do not contribute to that war's nation-months if they fail to meet the recognition and population criteria for system membership.

A second-order refinement is also necessary, on the recognition that a nineteenth- or twentieth-century British war-month holds rather different implications for the international system than, for example, a Bulgarian war-month. This differentiation could be recognized by introducing several different factors as modifiers. We might want to classify the nations by power, status, or size, and then weight their nation-months by the consequent absolute or relative score. But no such satisfactory index yet exists, especially when it must be applied not only to the early nineteenth century but to many non-European powers for which we have little accurate data at present. We have, therefore, resorted to the simple distinction between major and minor powers and calculated their wars and nation-months of war separately. Though the major-minor dichotomy may be too primitive for some theoretical purposes and not too readily operationalized, diplomatic historians have found it quite useful for centuries. Moreover, despite the invisibility of their criteria, they show near unanimity in the classification results.[12] Thus, our major powers and the dates during which they enjoyed that status are:

Austria-Hungary, 1815- 1918
Prussia or Germany, 1815- 1918, 1925- 1945
Russia, 1815- 1917, 1922- 1945
France, 1815- 1940
Britain, 1815- 1945
Japan, 1895- 1945
United States, 1899- 1945
Italy, 1860- 1943

A final point regarding our nation-months (magnitude) measure concerns the chronological placing of our forty-one wars. It should be reiterated here that our major concern must be not with the amount of war *going on* in the given year or years following each year's level of alliance aggregation in the system, but with the amount of war which *commenced* within that one-, three-, or five-year period. Our interest is in measures reflecting the *onset* of war. That most of the nation-months of World War II, for example, occurred during 1942 and 1943 is of much less interest in this study than the fact that they commenced in 1939.

In addition to nation-months as an index of the magnitude of war, at least one other factor seems to justify consideration. That factor we will call *severity* and it will be measured by the number of battle-connected deaths of military personnel sustained by all participants in any given war. As with the identification and classification of our wars, a full treatment of the problems encountered in locating, evaluating, and converting the casualty information into reliable data is provided in our forthcoming volume, and again only a brief summary is offered here. There have, of course, been several prior efforts to collect data on war casualties (Bodart 1916; Dumas and Vedel-Peterson 1923; Sorokin 1937; Klingberg 1945; Richardson 1960b; and Urlanis 1971), but none provides a fully satisfactory compilation, even for the primitive statistical purposes encountered in this undertaking. All are partially guilty of employing either shifting or invisible criteria of classification, and as a consequence, several different sets of such figures were collected and then our own best estimates finally used. For each nation in each international war, we calculated (and estimated) two types of deaths: (1) military personnel who died, or were reported as permanently missing, as a consequence of malicious acts of the enemy; and (2) military personnel who died from accidents, wounds, disease, or exposure during the period of hostilities. Note that, in partial contradistinction to Richardson's criteria, we did *not* include: (1) civilians of participating nations who died as a result of enemy actions (and to have included this category in our World War II figures would not have changed appreciably the fact that almost half of all deaths in our forty-one wars were accounted for by this single holocaust); (2) such civilians who died from exposure or disease; (3) neutral civilians; and (4) those children who might have been born had there been no war. Battle-connected deaths of military personnel, thus, will provide our index of each war's severity.[13] ...

*Alliance Aggregation: The Independent Variable*

Shifting our attention now from the outcome, or dependent variable, to the predictor, or independent variable, what procedures might be used to operationalize and quantify the extent to which alliance commitments reduced the interaction opportunities available to the international system? The problem here is somewhat more complex than that confronted in regard to the magnitude and severity of war, since a modest inferential leap is required. Referring back to the rationale behind our general hypotheses, we argued there that the effect of each alliance of any type was to reduce the extent to which the pluralistic, self-regulating mechanism could operate effectively. And two different lines of reasoning were suggested, depending upon the intervening constructs selected. In one, we concentrated upon the loss of interaction opportunity due to aggregate alliance commitments of all nations in the system; this may be thought of as a simple subtractive procedure. In the other, we examined the loss of interaction opportunity due to the bipolarizing effect of these alliance commitments. To put it briefly, there should be a difference between the effects of a structure which reflects a crazy-quilt pattern of all sorts of overlapping alliance membership and one in which that membership approaches or reaches a state in which only a very few easily distinguishable coalitions merge. There may, of course, be a close interdependence between these two conceptually distinct conditions, since it is perfectly plausible to assume that alliance building is by and large an activity directed *against* other nations and other existing or anticipated alliances. If such is the case, then, the mere aggregation of alliance commitments may well move the system in the direction of some minimum number of coalitions and hence *toward* bipolarity. We will revert to this matter when we present our data, and will then have some evidence for the extent to which these two conditions covary.

Returning, then, to our operationalizing procedures, let us look first at the aggregate measure of interaction opportunity loss, in its various forms. Perhaps the most orderly procedure would be to begin with an overview of the large number of alliance ties that interest us in an analysis such as this. The typology is based upon: (1) the nature of the obligation or commitment undertaken toward one ally by another; and (2) the nature of the signatories in terms of whether they are major or minor powers.

As to the first dimension, three classes of alliance commitment are considered. Class I, which will be called a *defense pact*, commits each signatory to intervene with military force on behalf of the other(s). Class II, which is called here a *neutrality or nonaggression pact*, commits each to refrain from military intervention against any of the other signatories in the event that they become engaged in

war. Class III, labeled *entente*, merely requires that the signatories
consult with one another in the contingent eventuality. It should be
noted here that these classifications are based upon the treaty text
itself and not upon the way in which the alliance was adhered to in
actual practice.[14]

Perhaps a brief justification of our reliance on written alliances in
general and their texts in particular is in order. Admittedly, other
phenomena would reveal more fully the friendship-hostility, close-
distant, or dependent-independent dimensions of international relationships, but two considerations are relevant here. First, it seems
perfectly reasonable to assume that the decision to undertake such
an alliance commitment does indeed reflect and respond to many of
these more specific, prior relationships. Moreover, one cannot argue
that the commitments are undertaken in a frivolous manner, with
little awareness of the implications or little intent to honor them. On
the basis of our earlier analysis of such commitments, we found, for
example, a significant positive correlation between alliance membership and war involvement on the side of the alliance partner. Second,
there are some serious obstacles to getting at the more complex
phenomena surrounding alliance formation. For example, much of
this could be ascertained via content analysis of diplomatic communications, yet the availability of all, or a representative sample of,
such documents is problematical; and that method is still a costly
and time-consuming one. Moreover, other research groups are moving
ahead on the "automation" of content analysis, and there is little
point in duplicating that important pioneering venture at this juncture (Holsti *et al.* 1969).

Turning to the second dimension, there is the matter of the
signatories' power status. Here our interest is in whether a given
alliance tie—and every multilateral alliance is treated, for analytical
purposes, as if it were a number of separate bilateral ones—is between
two major powers or between two minors, or between a major and a
minor. Combining the two sets of dimensions, then, we see that nine
types of bilateral alliance commitment are possible.[15]

As should be quite evident by now, it is no simple matter to
identify all alliances of all relevant types for 130 years and ascertain
their scope, membership, and duration. For a study of this type,
based as it is on what aims to be the complete population of events
rather than a sample thereof, this requirement is mandatory. Let us
summarize, therefore, the coding rules which are developed in greater
detail in the above-cited paper. First, only those alliance commit-

ments embodied in a formal, written treaty, convention, or executive agreement were included, whether or not it was secret at the time. Among those which were excluded were: (1) collective security agreements, such as the League Covenant and the United Nations Charter; (2) charters and constitutions of international organizations such as those of the Universal Postal Union, International Labour Organization, or the Danube River Commission; (3) treaties of guarantee to which all relevant powers registered their assent, such as the Belgian Neutrality Agreement of 1839, the Washington Conference Treaties of 1921–1922, and the Locarno Pacts of 1925; (4) agreements limited to general rules of behavior, such as the Kellogg-Briand Pact and the Geneva Conventions; (5) alliances which were consummated during, or less than three months before, a war in which any of the signatories participated, unless the alliance endured beyond the formal treaty of peace; (6) any alliances contracted during the two world wars, whether or not the signatories were belligerents; and (7) any alliance which did not include at least two members of our system.

In addition to these problems of ambiguity regarding inclusion or exclusion, there was the matter of chronological coverage. The effective inception date is almost always stipulated in the text or associated documents; if not, the date of ratification was used. In those few cases for which formal termination is not clear, we have relied upon a consensus of the historical monographs available. Finally, renewals were not counted as separate treaties unless the specific commitments were changed, as from entente to defensive alliance. . . .

Once all of the relevant alliances were discovered, classified, and counted, it was a simple matter to complete the operationalization of our aggregate interaction opportunity indices. For each year, we merely converted the raw numbers of each type of alliance into a percentage figure, so that we ended up with a list of the five following independent variables:

1. Percentage of all nations having at least one alliance *of any class* with any type of nation, major or minor.
2. Percentage of all nations having at least one *defensive* pact with any type of nation.
3. Percentage of *major* powers having at least one alliance *of any class* with another major power.

4. Percentage of major powers having at least one *defensive* pact with another major.

5. Percentage of major powers having at least one alliance *of any class* with any *minor* power.

In addition to these five measures of aggregate interaction opportunity loss[16] we also sought a measure of the extent to which the various alliances created a degree of bipolarity in the system for each year. Here the procedure was a bit more complicated, and to balance off manageability with relevance, the computations were only made for *defensive* pacts among *major* powers. The first step was to calculate the maximum number of dyads that could be formed from among the population of major powers, using the formula $N(N - 1)/2$. Then we calculated the percentage of these which had been exhausted, via the following steps. All defensive pact links were counted and the target(s), if any, of each identified; either a single nation or all members of a given alliance can be classified as targets. Next, we eliminated all linkages that were no longer possible: (1) those between members within each alliance; (2) those between members of opposing alliances; and (3) those between a target nation and all members of the alliance directed against that target nation. For any nation which was neither a target nor an alliance member, the maximum number of linkages still open was then counted, using the rule that it might contract an alliance with other nonallied or nontarget nations, plus either all members of the largest alliance, or all the nonallied target(s), whichever was the larger number. Once the number of feasible remaining defensive alliance links was ascertained, that number was divided into the original number that would have been possible in the absence of any such alliances, to give the percentage of major power defensive alliance ties exhausted.

One problem that confronted us was the occasional ambiguity regarding the target nation of a given alliance. That is, in 48 of our 130 years, there was sufficient disagreement among historians as to whether or not there is any target at all. In those cases, we computed an alternative bipolarity index. As in other places where professional consensus was used in place of a costly and complex operationalizing procedure, our authorities are identified in the basic descriptive article (Singer and Small 1966b). In the tables, therefore, two sets of bipolarity indices and two sets of correlations are shown, and in the next section the intercorrelations between them are also shown. Let us illustrate (figure 1) this procedure by reference to the alliance

Figure 1.   Major Power Alliance Configurations, 1913.

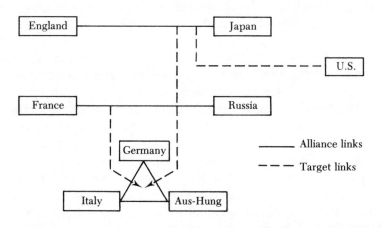

configuration of 1913; in that year, there were eight major powers, offering a maximum of twenty-eight possible linkages.

In the diagram, we see that twenty-one (or 75 percent) of those twenty-eight possible linkages were exhausted by alliances or by the logic of the targets as follows:

| *By Alliance (5)* | *By Target (14)* | |
|---|---|---|
| England-Japan | England-Italy | France-Germany |
| France-Russia | England-Germany | France-Austria |
| Austria-Germany | England-Austria | Russia-Italy |
| Austria-Italy | Japan-Italy | Russia-Germany |
| Germany-Italy | Japan-Germany | Russia-Austria |
| | Japan-Austria | Japan-United States |
| | France-Italy | England-United States |

Two more linkages are exhausted because if the United States allied with Germany, Austria-Hungary, and Italy, it obviously could no longer ally with France and Russia.

Before leaving this section, one more procedure needs to be described. Just as we ran correlations for three different time lags during which the onset of war could be measured, we felt that there was no *a priori* justification for assuming that our alliance data for a single year gave us the best independent variable. It could just as readily be argued that the system's alliance patterns are best reflected in their average magnitude over a longer period of time; for example, the duration of a given configuration might be as important as its magnitude. Therefore, three separate indices for each year and each independent variable were computed, showing that year's index, an average for that year plus the two preceding years, and an average for that year plus the four preceding years. Thus, for 1908 we have indicators on the independent variable side for 1908, the 1906–1908 average, and the 1904–1908 average. While all correlations have been run, only the three-year average is reported. (The remaining figures may be requested from the authors.)

These, then, represent our effort to convert the chaotic welter of historical facts or impressions on wars and alliances into relatively operational and machine-readable variables. The rigorous social scientist may well argue that intuition and apparent consensus among historians was permitted too large a role, while the diplomatic historian may hold that we have forced a large number of discrete events and unique relationships into too few Procrustean categories. Be that as it may, we have sought the most reasonable balance between reliability and validity, and urge others to examine and perhaps improve upon the detailed coding procedures outlined in the descriptive papers cited earlier.


## Observed Correlations

With our operationalizing procedures out of the way, and our raw data's legitimacy more or less established, we can now turn to the many alternative correlations which were sought and/or found. Because of our uncertainty as to which represented the best measure and because of the low marginal cost of the additional measures, we developed and gathered data on a multiplicity of indices for both the dependent and the independent variables. Therefore, prior to an examination of the correlations between our independent and dependent variables, it might be helpful to look *within* each of these groups, summarize their intercorrelations, and ascertain the extent to which each of our seven independent variables and our five dependent ones seem to be measuring the same phenomena.


### Comparing the Dependent Variables

It will be recalled that we collected our data in such form as to permit the measurement of both the amount of war *underway* in any given year and the amount which *began* in any given year. In this study, however, concerned as we are with the extent to which alliance aggregation predicts to the *onset* of war, we will only present the data showing the number, magnitude, and severity of wars *beginning* in a given year. For a number of theoretical and methodological reasons, the underway data will be reserved for a separate and later paper.

The reader will also recall that the exploratory nature of the study demanded that we allow three different time lags during which a given alliance pattern's "effects" could be measured. That is, uncertain as to how long it took for the hypothesized consequences of alliances to be felt, we gathered data to show the effects within one year, within three years, and within five years following each year's alliance configuration. Thus, if we are looking, for example, at the alliance data for 1868, those various indices were all correlated with the data for wars which began in 1869, which began between January 1869 and December 1871, and those which began between January 1869 and December 1873. Once these data were in, however, it became clear that, if any alliance effects were to be found, they had largely made themselves felt within three years, especially in the twentieth century.[17] Thus, only the $Y + 3$ correlations will be shown in the tables here.

As table 3 reveals, whether we look at the total international system or the central system alone, there is indeed an impressively

Table 3. Correlations Among Dependent Variables: The Onset of War Within Three Years of Each Year's Alliance Aggregations, 1815-1945

|  | Total System | | | | Central System | | | |
|---|---|---|---|---|---|---|---|---|
|  | N-m war begun—all | N-m war begun—majors | Battle deaths—all | Battle deaths—majors | N-m war begun—all | N-m war begun—majors | Battle deaths—all | Battle deaths—major |
| N-m war begun—all |  |  |  |  |  |  |  |  |
| N-m war begun—majors | 95 |  |  |  | 96 |  |  |  |
| Battle deaths—all | 97 | 96 |  |  | 98 | 97 |  |  |
| Battle deaths—majors | 97 | 97 | 99 |  | 98 | 98 | 99 |  |
| No. wars begun | 34 | 35 | 28 | 27 | 52 | 54 | 49 | 47 |

Note: All coefficients are significant at .01 level.

high correlation among most of these dependent variable indicators.[18] It is patently evident that we were overly concerned. That is, whether we look at the total system or the central system, and whether we look at all nations or major ones only, the correlation coefficient between nation-months and battle deaths is only a shade less than one. (Unity, of course, would show that the indices were all measuring precisely the same thing.) The only low, but nevertheless still significant, correlations are between the magnitude and severity measures on one hand and the frequency ones on the other. Given the distributions described earlier, this was to be expected.

*Comparing the Independent Variables*

Comparing the alliance aggregation figures to one another is a somewhat more complex matter than that involving the war data. Here, we have not only the standard spatial and chronological subsets, but the various combinations of signatory status and alliance class. Further, there is the distinction between aggregate commitments and those which generate our two alternative indices of bipolarity. In addition to these latter, which, as indicated earlier, are based solely on the polarization among the major powers, there are: (1) all classes of alliance among all nations; (2) all classes of alliance among major powers; (3) defense pacts among all; (4) defense pacts among majors; and (5) all alliances between majors and minors. As noted earlier, we are not examining here the extent to which neutrality pacts and ententes "predict to" war, inasmuch as the count on these is somewhat misleading; that is, neutrality or entente commitments were counted only when no defense pact existed between the nations in any dyad. In other words, only the highest class of commitment between each pair was counted.

As table 4 reveals, there exists a very impressive intercorrelation among these several alliance measures. In the central system, every indicator correlates strongly with every other, and in the total system, the only absence of correlation is that between the initial and the alternative bipolarity figures on the one hand, and the all-allied and all-in-defense-pact figures, on the other. This lack of significant correlation need not surprise us, given the fact that the bipolarity measures reflect major power cleavages only. Again, but to a considerably lesser extent than with war, we are tapping approximately the same structural phenomena.

## Table 4. Correlations Among Independent Variables: Annual Alliance Aggregations, 1815-1839

| | Total System | | | | | | Central System Only | | | | | |
|---|---|---|---|---|---|---|---|---|---|---|---|---|
| | % nations in alliance | % nations in defense pact | % majors in alliance | % majors in defense pact | % majors allied with minors | Major bilateral defense exhausted—a | % nations in alliance | % nations in defense pact | % majors in alliance | % majors in defense pact | % majors allied with minors | Major bilateral defense exhausted—a |
| % nations in defense pact | 74 | | | | | | 80 | | | | | |
| % majors in alliance | 50 | 53 | | | | | 77 | 74 | | | | |
| % majors in defense pact | 32 | 60 | 81 | | | | 58 | 83 | 81 | | | |
| % majors allied with minors | 64 | 61 | 64 | 59 | | | 80 | 70 | 42 | 33 | | |
| Major bilateral defense exhausted—a | 00 | −01 | 47 | 57 | 26 | | 54 | 53 | 47 | 57 | 51 | |
| Major bilateral defense exhausted—b | 45 | 50 | 60 | 68 | 67 | 58 | 57 | 70 | 60 | 68 | 48 | 58 |

Note: All but two coefficients are significant at .01 level

Having digressed for the important purpose of ascertaining the extent to which our many different measures tend to tap the same phenomena, we may now move on to the primary concern of the study: the extent to which alliance aggregation in its various forms predicts to war.

### Total System, 1815-1945

In order to make more comprehensible the many pairs of correlations within our six different systemic settings, a brief recapitulation would seem to be in order. The correlations will be so presented in

**Table 5. Total System, 1815-1945: Correlations Between Alliance Indicators and Magnitude, Severity, and Frequency of War Beginning Within Three Years**

|  | % of All in any Alliance | % of All in Defense Pact | % of Majors in any Alliance | % of Majors in Defense Pact | % of Majors with Minor | Bipolarity Initial | Bipolarity Alternate |
|---|---|---|---|---|---|---|---|
| Nation-months war–all | *30* | −05 | 05 | 06 | 17 | 08 | 13 |
| Nation-months war–majors | *28* | −01 | 10 | 04 | 22 | 14 | 18 |
| Battle deaths for all | *34* | −01 | 11 | 01 | 21 | 15 | 19 |
| Battle deaths for majors | *31* | −01 | 12 | 04 | 21 | 17 | 21 |
| Number of wars | 07 | −01 | 06 | 04 | 18 | −03 | 01 |

the separate tables as to identify: (1) the international system or portion thereof which is under examination; (2) the time period for which it is being examined; (3) the specific independent variables being used; and (4) the specific dependent variables. As we indicated earlier, a great many more correlations were run than are reported here; among those not shown here are: (1) eight of the nine *r* values for each cross-correlation, with only the three-year average for alliance indices and the three-year lag for war indices correlated in the text and accompanying tables; (2) all neutrality pact and entente data, with only the defense pact and all alliance class categories shown in the text; and (3) all data dealing with war actually under way, with only the data on *onset* of war shown in the text. Contrary to some practice, we will include all *r* values in each table, even those which are not equivalent to statistically significant levels; those which equal or exceed the .01 level requirement will be italicized. As to sequence, we begin with the total system for the entire 1815- 1945 period, and then drop the peripheral nations and concentrate on the central system only for the same full period. Next we look at the total system in the nineteenth century, and then move on to the central system only for that eighty-five- year period. Finally, we examine the twentieth-century total system and central system in that order.

Turning, then, to our first and most comprehensive empirical world—that of the total international system for the entire

**Table 6.  Central System, 1815-1945: Correlations Between Alliance Indicators and Magnitude, Severity, and Frequency of War Beginning Within Three Years**

| | % of All in any Alliance | % of All in Defense Pact | % of Majors in any Alliance | % of Majors in Defense Pact | % of Majors with Minor | Bipolarity Initial | Bipolarity Alternate |
|---|---|---|---|---|---|---|---|
| Nation-months war–all | *33* | 11 | 06 | –02 | *34* | 12 | 16 |
| Nation-months war–majors | *34* | 14 | 11 | 03 | *34* | 15 | 13 |
| Battle deaths for all | *35* | 12 | 11 | 01 | *34* | 15 | 18 |
| Battle deaths for majors | *35* | 14 | 12 | 04 | *34* | 17 | 20 |
| Number of wars | 19 | 07 | 05 | –03 | *28* | –07 | 16 |

1815-1945 period (shown in table 5)—we find one set of consistently high correlations. That is, the grossest of the independent variables—percentage of *all* nations in at least one alliance of *any* class—shows significant correlations with all four of the magnitude and severity indicators, but not with the number of wars beginning within three years. On the major power side, however, no such findings emerge. As a matter of fact there are no other sufficiently high *r* values at all for this total system-entire period setting, although the major with minor correlation approaches that level.

*Central System, 1815- 1945*

Let us now take the first of several steps in the direction of increasingly restrictive empirical worlds, and shuck off all the peripheral system nations, leaving the central system only, but still for the entire time period. The picture is pretty much the same, as we see in table 6; that is, the percentage of all nations in any class of alliance correlates strongly with all four magnitude (nation-months of war) and severity (battle deaths) indices. Again, defense pacts among all, or among majors only, do not show a high covariation; but in this more restrictive setting, the percentage of majors having at least one alliance of any kind with a minor power does predict significantly to all the war measures. Note that even the frequency measure corre-

**Table 7.  Total System, 1815-1899: Correlations Between Alliance Indicators and Magnitude, Severity, and Frequency of War Beginning Within Three Years**

|  | % of All in any Alliance | % of All in Defense Pact | % of Majors in any Alliance | % of Majors in Defense Pact | % of Majors with Minor | Bipolarity Initial | Bipolarity Alternate |
|---|---|---|---|---|---|---|---|
| Nation-months war–all | −16 | −16 | −23 | *−34* | −21 | *−32* | −23 |
| Nation-months war–majors | −04 | 01 | −26 | −14 | −01 | −2̄3 | −19 |
| Battle deaths for all | −27 | −23 | *−38* | *−42* | *−33* | *−33* | *−28* |
| Battle deaths for majors | −26 | −19 | *−41* | *−38* | −27 | *−30* | −25 |
| Number of wars | −00 | 01 | −10 | −05 | 05 | −21 | −12 |

lates, albeit modestly, with the major-minor measure, but not with any of the other alliance indicators.

### Total System, 1815–1899

As suggested in a previous section, it seemed useful to inquire as to whether the relationship between alliance commitments and war might be stronger or weaker in different epochs; thus we have not only divided our total population into central and total systems, but have also divided it into nineteenth- and twentieth-century systems. Let us therefore shift from the full population (that is, total system, entire 130-year period) and examine the total system up through 1899 only. A brief glance at table 7 indicates that this concentration upon the nineteenth-century total system exercises a striking effect on our correlations. That is, we no longer find alliance aggregation in general predicting to war, and those *r*s that are close to significant are all in the *negative* direction. And when we move over to include major powers only, their general alliance involvement does indeed show a strong—but negative—correlation with both the severity measures; the same holds for major-minor alliances vis-à-vis battle deaths for all. As to our initial bipolarity measure, we find relatively strong correlations vis-à-vis one of the magnitude measures and both of the severity measures.

Table 8. Central System, 1815-1899: Correlations Between Alliance Indicators and Magnitude, Severity, and Frequency of War Beginning Within Three Years

| | % of All in any Alliance | % of All in Defense Pact | % of Majors in any Alliance | % of Majors in Defense Pact | % of Majors with Minor | Bipolarity Initial | Bipolarity Alternate |
|---|---|---|---|---|---|---|---|
| Nation-months war—all | −19 | −14 | −15 | −08 | −16 | −19 | −14 |
| Nation-months war—majors | −20 | −14 | −19 | −09 | −13 | −17 | −16 |
| Battle deaths for all | *−45* | *−45* | *−44* | *−45* | *−33* | *−34* | *−30* |
| Battle deaths for majors | *−46* | *−41* | *−48* | *−42* | *−30* | *−32* | *−28* |
| Number of wars | −05 | −02 | −03 | 07 | −04 | −20 | −06 |

Although the statistically alert reader may already anticipate what our *post*-1900 correlations will look like, it would be premature either to present them next or to offer an interpretation of the above rather consistent negative correlations. Rather, let us stay in the same nineteenth-century time frame, but again shuck off the nations of the peripheral system and look exclusively at the nineteenth-century central, or European, state system.

## Central System, 1815–1899

Here, as table 8 makes evident, the same nineteenth-century pattern continues. That is, all of the strong correlations are in the negative direction, with the severity indices again most sensitive to alliance aggregation. Worth observing is that every one of the alliance indicators correlates strongly and inversely with all battle deaths and with major-power battle deaths arising from war beginning within three years of the alliance condition.

## Total System, 1900–1945

We can now look at some of the evidence that should have been anticipated once the nineteenth-century data were contrasted to data

Table 9.  Total System, 1900-1945:  Correlations Between Alliance
Indicators and Magnitude, Severity, and Frequency of War Beginning
Within Three Years

| | % of All in any Alliance | % of All in Defense Pact | % of Majors in any Alliance | % of Majors in Defense Pact | % of Majors with Minor | Bipolarity Initial | Bipolarity Alternate |
|---|---|---|---|---|---|---|---|
| Nation-months war—all | 53 | 43 | 24 | 05 | 43 | 15 | 28 |
| Nation-months war—majors | 46 | 48 | 35 | 16 | 47 | 24 | 36 |
| Battle deaths for all | 56 | 48 | 29 | 08 | 46 | 19 | 31 |
| Battle deaths for majors | 51 | 48 | 31 | 13 | 45 | 23 | 36 |
| Number of wars | 18 | 29 | 50 | 26 | 54 | 27 | 26 |

for the entire period. That is, if alliances and war show some modest
positive correlations for the entire 130 years and somewhat stronger,
but *negative* correlations for the first 85 years, we may logically
expect positive and somewhat stronger $r$s for the twentieth-century
data. This indeed is what we find in table 9, despite the fact that our
$N$ of only 45 years raises the $r$-value requirement to a coincidental
.45. Thus, the percentage of all nations in any class of alliance, as
well as in defense pacts, correlates highly with all four magnitude and
severity measures in every case but one (.43 with nation-months of
war for all). Likewise, the major-minor figure predicts well to three
of these four dependent variables. On the bipolarity side, however,
none of the correlations are high enough to be interesting.

*Central System, 1900–1945*

Turning to the last of our empirical worlds (table 10), the pattern
is essentially the same for the central as for the total twentieth-
century system. Though defense pacts among all do not predict to
war compellingly in this case, alliances in general among all do, as do
major-minor alliances in three of the four cases. Again, the bipolarity
correlatings are all moderately in this direction, but as in the total
system, they still fail to satisfy the .01 requirements.

Table 10.  Central System, 1900-1945:  Correlations Between Alliance
Indicators and Magnitude, Severity, and Frequency of War Beginning
Within Three Years

| | % of All in any Alliance | % of All in Defense Pact | % of Majors in any Alliance | % of Majors in Defense Pact | % of Majors with Minor | Bipolarity Initial | Bipolarity Alternate |
|---|---|---|---|---|---|---|---|
| Nation-months war–all | *45* | 04 | 23 | 05 | 42 | 14 | 27 |
| Nation-months war–majors | *49* | 17 | 35 | 18 | *47* | 24 | 36 |
| Battle deaths for all | *50* | 09 | 29 | 09 | *46* | 19 | 32 |
| Battle deaths for majors | *50* | 13 | 31 | 14 | *45* | 23 | 36 |
| Number of wars | 25 | −02 | 24 | −05 | 40 | −05 | 02 |

## Summary and Interpretation

Given the material with which we worked, the data-making
operations, and the observed correlations between and among our
many variables, what can we now say regarding the basic hypothesis?
Do alliance aggregations in general, or bipolarity tendencies in particular, correlate in any meaningful way with the onset of international
war in the nineteenth and twentieth centuries?

Assuming that our measures are as valid and reliable as claimed,
the evidence seems to be relatively unambiguous. We say relatively
because there are two quite distinct and incompatible patterns, but
the incompatibility is easily resolved by dividing the entire historical
epoch into two periods. That is, if we look at the twentieth-century
segment only, the hypothesis is rather strongly confirmed. (Taking
the seven independent variable indicators and the four measures of
war magnitude and war severity, for both the central and the total
systems, we have fifty-six opportunities for a strong positive correlation to appear. Our results show such a correlation on seventeen of
these occasions.) Looking first at the alliance aggregation measures,
for both the central and the total systems, we find that the percentage of all nations in the system having at least one alliance with any
other nation predicts to the amount of war on all eight of the
possible occasions. And the percentage of major powers having at

least one alliance with a minor does likewise on six of the eight possible occasions. Defense pact aggregation does so on three of the eight possible occasions. Combining this powerful tendency with the fact that there are quite a few more correlations that are only slightly weaker and that not a single negative correlation appears, we may only conclude that the well-accepted hypothesis has indeed been borne out by our historical evidence.

Does the hypothesis do as well in an earlier epoch? Clearly not. To the contrary, on all eight of the possible occasions for a positive correlation to turn up between gross alliance aggregation and the magnitude or severity of war in the nineteenth century, the correlation was negative. And if the same matrix were constructed for defense pacts, seven of the eight turn out to be negative. Furthermore, if we look at all classes of alliance among major powers only for the nineteenth century, all eight correlations are again negative, four of them strongly so. Even if we focus on major-power defense pacts for both of these nineteenth-century systems, five of the eight negative correlations meet our rather stringent threshold criteria. Finally, all eight of the war correlations with major-minor alliance percentages are negative, three at the .01 equivalent level. The observed relationship between alliance aggregation and the onset of war in the nineteenth century, then, is clearly a negative one, and shows a distribution which is diametrically opposed to, and almost as strong as, that found for the twentieth century.

To what extent is the alliance aggregation pattern repeated when we try to predict to war from *bipolarity*? In general, the same tendencies appear, but with somewhat lower coefficient values. That is, if we look at both the initial and the alternative indices of major-power bipolarization, and correlate them with our four magnitude and severity indices in both forms (central and total) of the twentieth-century system, all sixteen $r$s are positive, but only twelve of these are in significance ranges better than .1 (not .01). Any doubt as to the general tendency is dispelled, however, when we examine the nineteenth-century total and central systems. As with alliance aggregation, every one of the $r$ values is negative, with eight of the sixteen meeting the .01-level requirement.

Given the extraordinarily low probability of such correlations occurring in such consistent form by sheer chance, we have no choice but to conclude that alliance aggregation and bipolarization do indeed have a meaningful relation to the onset of war. But it is important to note the theoretical implications of these relationships. It is certainly clear that formal alliance patterns do not exercise a uniform impact over time. To the contrary, both alliance aggregation and bipolarity covary strongly with the amount of war that follows within three years during the twentieth century, and correlate *inversely* to almost the same degree during the nineteenth century.

Regardless of the war-onset measure we use, the pattern is similar. Whether it is nation-months of war or battle-connected deaths, whether the data are for the total system or the central one only, and whether they reflect all members of the system or major powers only, when alliance aggregation or bipolarity in the nineteenth century increases, the amount of war experienced by the system goes down, and vice versa. And in the twentieth century, the greater the alliance aggregation or bipolarity in the system, the more war it experiences.

Now the cautious or skeptical reader may say that "it depends" upon what we mean by "amount of war," and ask whether the same picture emerges when we look at the sheer *number* of wars. As a matter of fact, it does, but not quite as impressively. That is, almost all of our independent variables correlate negatively with the number of wars beginning within the $Y + 3$ period during the nineteenth century, and positively during the twentieth century. And the five exceptions out of the fourteen opportunities are barely perceptible: we find *r*s of .01, .05, and .07 for the nineteenth, and - .02 and - .05 for the twentieth. Moreover, if there were any concern that it is the sheer magnitude and severity of the two world wars that accounts for the twentieth-century positive correlation, it should be noted that when the *number* of wars begun is used as the dependent variable, the *r* values for percentage of all nations in alliances of any class are .18 and .25. For all major power alliances, these are .50 and .24, and for major-minor alliances, they are .54 and .40, for the total and central systems respectively.[19] In sum, whether we measure amount by number of wars, the nation-months involved, or battle deaths incurred, alliance aggregation and bipolarity predict strongly away from war in the nineteenth century and even more strongly toward it in the twentieth. One might say that those who generalize about the effects of alliance activity—and most postulate a destabilizing effect, especially in regard to bipolarity—have been so preoccupied with more recent history that they have neglected the patterns which obtained in an earlier, but by no means incomparable, period; one recent exception is Waltz (1964).

It is obvious that correlation and causality are rather different things, and that correlation at a high level is *necessary* to the establishment of a causal relationship, but not at all *sufficient*. Unless a logically tight and empirically correct linkage between the independent variables and the dependent ones can be presented, and competing explanations can be disconfirmed, we have established something less than causality. Thus, it seems appropriate to conclude on a cautious note, by indicating the sorts of substantive and methodological question which remain.

For example, are we able to demonstrate a close empirical and chronological connection between specific alliances and specific wars? At this juncture, our data are not in the form which would permit a direct answer, but we do have some results of a tangential nature. That is, if we look at the frequency with which a given nation belongs to any alliance within three years prior to any war, and compare that figure to the frequency with which it participates in any war, we find that for all 82 of our nations over the 130-year period, the correlation is .60; and for the 67 central-system members, the figure is a very high .72. But this still doesn't establish a causal connection. Again, there is the simple, but not unreasonable, argument that national decision makers will tend to step up their alliance-building activities as they perceive the probability of war to be rising. This might well account for our twentieth-century correlations, and we have, as yet, produced no evidence to contravene the hypothesis.

Beyond this, even though we have uncovered a compelling relationship between alliances and the onset of war, the magnitude of that relation still remains an empirical question, and it may well be that other factors will account for much more of the variance than these two sets of variables. As a matter of fact, if we use the statistical rule of thumb which permits us to say that the amount of variance accounted for by a given independent variable—the coefficient of determination—is approximately the square of the product-moment correlation, we see how limited the alliance effect may be. With the twentieth-century (positive) correlations averaging out at .29 and the nineteenth-century (negative) ones averaging out at .26, these alliance factors may be interpreted as accounting for somewhere between 8.4 and 6.8 percent of the variance.[20]

Furthermore, a number of qualifications and caveats regarding some of our independent variables come to mind. As to the five different alliance aggregation indices, we did indeed cover a wide range of possibilities, using all classes of alliance, as well as defense pacts alone, using all nations as well as major powers alone, using six different spatio-temporal forms of the international system, and using nine different lead and lag combinations, but the exploration nevertheless remains incomplete. Again, though we have gathered data on neutrality pacts and on ententes, data on these classes of alliance have not been processed for use here, and it may well be that their presence and absence might shed further light on the alliance-war relationship. Another possibility worth examining might be that of *changes* in alliance aggregation; that is, each year's increments or decrements vis-à-vis the previous year or years might reveal a discernible pattern that either strengthens or challenges the tendency discovered in this study. Likewise, an investigation into the *rates* of change might produce some valuable results. Finally, a closely related systemic property is that of the number of individual alliance changes and shifts made in a given year or more by all nations in the system. This measure we call lateral mobility, and some preliminary work on it is already underway.

Similar thoughts occur when our bipolarity measures are considered. First of all, the measure itself reflects the degree of cleavage among major powers only, and while one would intuitively expect the total system to partially parallel the major power subsystem, we have no hard evidence that it does. Moreover, the measure is by no means as compelling an indicator of bipolarization as it might be. Since embarking on this project we have discovered in the sociometry and graph theory literature some promising alternative operations by which such cleavage might be measured; some of these operations require that we first develop a better procedure for identifying alliance targets, while others do not.[21] In the same vein, it immediately occurs to us that bipolarity by itself may not be as interesting or compelling a predictor as when it is combined with one or more additional variables. For example, it might well pay to examine the joint effects of polarity and parity: Is high bipolarity more likely to precede the onset of war when the two coalitions are approximately equal in power and capability or when a clear disparity exists?

Or, it might well be that the traditional theory overlooks a simple but crucial element: Can the invisible hand ever function within so small a population? Certainly a large numerical discrepancy exists between the thousands of buyers and sellers in an economic marketplace and the 82 actors in our pre-1945 total system or the 120-odd ones in the postwar system. It might turn out that hypotheses generated from models of oligopoly or duopoly will stand the empirical test more successfully than those generated by a free and open market model.

Then, again, there is the matter of structural or cultural context. Is it not possible that the structural variable utilized here—alliance aggregation—is in turn responsive to other systemic properties, and that its predictive power is a function of its interaction with such variables? To put it another way, are nations as likely to respond to short- and middle-range security requirements and make alliances on that basis alone, when the diplomatic culture is increasingly ideological or less homogeneous, or when the structure of the system is more rigid or its supranational aspects are increasing? Similarly, it can be argued that our approach is entirely too formal, and that emphasis might better be placed on other indices of international relationship: diplomatic communication, trade, tourism, or less formal and perhaps unwritten indicators of reciprocal commitment. Though these suggestions would carry us beyond our immediate concern here, they are certainly well taken.

A final concern is that raised in a thoughtful critique (Zinnes 1967) regarding the extent to which this analysis really "tested the balance-of-power theory." As the title of this paper and its specific sections makes clear, we are not testing *the theory*, but only one basic proposition which we believe can be deduced from it; moreover, to grace the conceptual and empirical chaos of the balance-of-power literature with the label "theory" is much too generous. Within that critique, however, a specific problem of considerable importance *is* raised, and it merits a brief discussion. As we understand the criticism, it concerns the validity of our independent variable, and questions whether our alliance aggregation and alliance involvement indicators really reflect the diminution of cross-pressures as implied in our theoretical argument. Our argument, it will be recalled, is that each alliance commitment undertaken by a nation reduces its interaction opportunities, and thus the interaction opportunities available to the entire system; as these diminish, we reason that the allied nation is now "less free to compete with its new allies and less free to cooperate with nonallies." The randomized cross-pressures on it give way, to some extent, to pressures that are likely to be more discriminatory and systematic. That is, the nation is now less likely to treat all others in a neutral fashion, but will tend to remove some of them from the neutral category and treat them more nearly as friends or as opponents. Given what we know about reciprocity in diplomatic behavior, it follows that those nations which are now treated in a nonrandom fashion will respond more or less in kind. The original randomized pressures (impinging on it from many directions) will now come in upon the newly allied nation from more parallel or polarized directions, with a net loss of pluralistic cross-pressures in the system as a whole.

The criticism is that this model, while a reasonable interpretation of the classical formulation, ignores the fact that cross-pressures are *not* reduced unless the "nations belong to one and only one alliance" (Zinnes 1967, p. 7). It goes on further to contend that in only 22 of our 130 years does that condition hold, and that our various indicators are therefore not theoretically valid. The assertion here, as we understand it, is that multiple alliance commitments do not necessarily diminish the cross-pressures, and may, under some conditions, even increase them. While the question is an empirical one, neither we nor others have yet sought to test it against evidence, and we must therefore fall back on logical analysis. In principle we would expect the assertion to hold in only an extremely limited set of cases: those in which a nation belongs to two alliances which are clearly *directed against one another.* And the only case in our population which clearly satisfies this unlikely condition is that of Italy, which belonged to both the Triple Alliance and the Entente (in a fragile sort of way) during the period leading up to World War I.

Even if there were other cases of such multiple membership in conflicting alliance groupings, however, the criticism would not hold. That is, it would only hold if the international system were composed solely of those two alliance memberships; as long as the system is larger than the five nations hypothesized in the critique, the assertion fails to stand. This is so because the allied nation, in its dealings with nations outside the two conflicting alliances, will not be as free as a nonallied nation would be in dealing with these more remote system members. In sum, we consider our independent and our intervening variables to be valid, and therefore remain satisfied that we have indeed examined a proposition which is central to the classical balance-of-power paradigm.[22]

These considerations bring us, therefore, back to the points raised at the outset of the paper. In any search for the "causes" of war, the quest for correlates may lead us not only into attributes of the international system, but into attributes of the more war-prone nations, their preconflict and prewar relationships, and their prewar behavior and interaction. It is our working assumption that any theory of the causes of war will include all four sets of independent variables. But we urge that considerable exploration of systemic properties be given high priority. Unless we understand the environment within which internation conflict occurs, and can ascertain the approximate effect of that environment, there is no meaningful way of establishing the controls which are essential to any experimental inquiry. And if we look upon this quantitative approach to diplomatic history as a sequence of ex post facto, natural world experiment, the importance of such controls cannot be exaggerated.

# 14

# Capability Distribution, Uncertainty, and Major Power War, 1820-1965

*With Stuart A. Bremer*
*and John Stuckey*

*If social science research were conducted "by the book," this part would include a paper that brings the investigation in chapter 13 together with related ones, and then extends, clarifies, and generalizes on the basis of the further investigations. That is, in the view of those of us who deem the inductive emphasis most appropriate at this stage in the growth of our science, each study should be expected to build upon and then go beyond several more limited studies along the same road. But scientific research is quite unlike mathematics or philosophy, for example, and will remain so until much later in the enterprise. As long as the experimental and empirical work is uppermost in our minds, we usually conduct it through the vehicle of a "project." Projects involve not only several people; they involve individuals whose concerns and commitments are not identical with those of the principal investigator. Most of them, of course, are graduate students who are passing through a particular university and project. Not only do they have diverse priorities but, since the project director's responsibility is to help educate these students as well as to conduct research, he or she cannot run the project like an assembly line. Thus we seldom turn out our findings in a neat and linear fashion, building step by inexorable step to the final synthesis. And even without these conflicting priorities, the progress would be less than beautifully linear. When we know so little about a phenomenon as complex as international war, and have so many equally plausible hunches, our research is bound to follow a pattern all too similar to the well-known "random walk."*

*Thus this paper was selected because it typifies a promising next step, once the underbrush has been partially cleared via bivariate analyses.[1] It is still very close to the exploration-discovery end of the research spectrum, and quite distant from the verification-disconfirmation end toward which we hope to move. Some, of course, think that we should be working in the latter region now, but the path of science is strewn with the bones of "theories" that died of malnutrition in their first few steps. Given the importance of our enterprise and our commitment to the long haul, we prefer a more prudent, though time-consuming, strategy, and refuse to send an underfed infant into the inhospitable and demanding environment of causality, explanation, and theory. When they have been reasonably nourished with evidence and their mettle has been tested against the hard facts of empirical reality, it will be time enough to send our models forth to claim adult status as scientific theories.*

*This paper is included, then, because it illustrates the ways in which multivariate analyses can move us beyond those of a bivariate sort and closer to the formalization and testing of more rigorously theoretical formulations. Whether this analysis, in turn, will bring us to the brink of an important discovery, we cannot say. I think that in due course it will, but it could also meet a less auspicious fate and disappear into that special scientific limbo reserved for studies that were never on the right track. Thus a paper such as this could turn out to have been a useful building block, an inefficient digression, or an utterly useless caper. In any event, it is illustrative of the project's earlier and middle phase and, regardless of its ultimate destiny, represents one view of the way we might go in trying to identify the causes of war.*

In any systematic effort to identify the immediate or remote sources of international war, one has a variety of more or less equally reasonable options. First of all, one can focus either on the behavior of the relevant governments, or on the background conditions within which such behavior occurs. And if one leans toward ecologically oriented models—as we do—the choice is between the attributes of the nations themselves and the attributes of the system or subsystem within which the nations are located. Further, one may choose to focus on the structural attributes of the nations or the system, or on their cultural or physical attributes.

In the Correlates of War project, we have recently begun to examine the behavioral patterns of nations in conflict, in order to ascertain whether there are recurrent patterns which consistently distinguish between those conflicts which eventuate in war and those which do not (Leng and Singer 1970). But even though we contend that no model is adequate unless it includes such behavioral and interactional phenomena, we also believe that behavior cannot be understood adequately except in its ecological context.

Hence, the first two phases of the project have been restricted to the attributes of the system and those of the nations and pairs of nations that comprise the system. In the process, we have found it necessary to allocate more energy to data generation and acquisition (not to mention data management) than to data analysis, and in addition to making these data sets available via the International Relations Archive of the Inter-University Consortium for Political Research, we have published a fair number of them (Singer and Small 1966a; 1966b; Russett, Singer, and Small 1968; Small and Singer 1969; 1970; Wallace and Singer 1970). In due course, three handbooks will be published, embracing respectively the fluctuating and cumulative incidence of war (Singer and Small 1972), the changing structure of the international system since the Congress of Vienna, and the capabilities of the states which constitute that system (Small forthcoming). We prepare these volumes not only to make our data as widely available as possible, but also in order to explain why and how we construct our most important measures. That is, unlike some other social science sectors, the international politics field finds very little data of a ready-made nature, requiring those of us in that particular vineyard to first convert our concepts into operational indicators, prior to any analysis. And even though we still have some major index-construction and data-generation tasks before us, we have not been completely inattentive to the possibilities of some modest theoretical analyses (Singer and Small 1966c; 1968; Singer and Wallace 1970; M. D. Wallace 1971; Bremer, Singer, and Luterbacher 1973; Gleditsch and Singer 1975; Skjelsbaek 1971). These partial and tentative analyses are, of course, essentially of a brush-clearing nature, preliminary to the testing of more complex and complete models.

The report at hand falls into that same brush-clearing category, designed to help us sort out some of the dominant regularities in the international system, and to aid in evaluating a number of equally plausible, but logically incompatible, theoretical formulations. To be quite explicit about it, we suspect that anyone who takes a given model of war (or most other international phenomena) very seriously at this stage of the game has just not looked at the referent world very carefully. Just as our colleagues in the physical and biological sciences have found that nature is full of apparent inconsistencies and paradoxes, requiring a constant interplay between theoretical schemes and empirical investigations, we believe that the complexities of war and global politics will require more than mathematical rigor and elegant logical exercises. So much, then, for the epistemological case on which we rest our research strategy. In the Conclusion, we will address ourselves to the equally important normative case, but let us turn now to the investigation at hand.

## The Query and Its Rationale

Our concern here is to ascertain the extent to which the war-proneness of the major powers, from 1820 through 1965, can be attributed to certain structural properties of the subsystem which they constitute. The first of these properties is the distribution of national capabilities within it at given points in time, and the second is the direction and rate of change in that distribution between any two of those points in time.

Before presenting our measures and analyses, however, it is pertinent to ask why one might expect to find any relationship between the distribution of "power" on the one hand, and the incidence of war, on the other. Without either tracing the discussion as it has unfolded in the literature of diplomatic history and international politics, or developing a full articulation of our own line of reasoning, we may nevertheless summarize what looks to us like a fairly plausible set of considerations.

### The Major Powers' Preoccupation with Relative Capability

We begin with the assumption that the foreign policy elites of all national states are, at one time or another, concerned with their nation's standing in the power and/or prestige pecking order.[2] For any given nation at any given time, certain ranking scales will be of considerably greater salience than others, as will the relative position of one or another of their neighbors. Normally, we would not expect the decision makers of Burma to worry very much about their nation's military-industrial capability vis-à-vis that of Bolivia, or find the Swedish foreign office attending to the rise in Afghanistan's diplomatic prestige. Nor would it be particularly salient to the Mexican defense ministry that Australia's preparedness level had risen sharply over the previous half-decade. That is, the salience of a given nation's rank position on a given power or prestige dimension will only be high for the foreign policy elites of those other nations that are relatively interdependent with the first, and are "in the same league."

But we are talking here only about major powers, which—almost by definition—are highly interdependent one with the other, and clearly in the same upper strata on most of the recognized power or prestige dimensions. This becomes more evident if we indicate which states comprise the major power subsystem during the different periods of the century and a half which concerns us here. While the data introduced in a later report will indicate how valid the classification is, we emphasize that our criteria—quite intentionally—are less than operational. That is, rather than define the major power subsystem over time in terms of certain objective power and/or prestige indicators, we adhere to the rather intuitive criteria of the diplomatic historians. On the other hand, the consensus among those who have specialized in the various regions and epochs is remarkably high (especially from 1816 through 1945), and it leads to the following.

As the post-Congress period opens, we find Austria-Hungary, Prussia, Russia, France, and Britain constituting this select subsystem. Italy joins the group after unification in 1860, as does Germany as the successor state to Prussia in 1870. The two non-European newcomers are Japan in 1895, following its victory over China, and the United States, after defeating Spain in 1898. These eight continue as the sole major powers until World War I, which sees the dismemberment of the Austro-Hungarian empire, and the temporary loss of position for Germany (from 1918 to 1924) and Russia (from 1917 to 1921). World War II leads to the temporary elimination of France (from 1940 to 1944) and the permanent (i.e., at least through 1965) elimination of the Axis powers of Italy, Germany, and Japan. As the victors in that war, Britain, Russia, and the United States continue as members of the major power category; France regains membership in 1945, and China qualifies as of 1950.

It should not be difficult to argue that these states become major powers by dint of close attention to relative capability, and remain so in the same way. Of course, mere allocation of attention to their power and prestige vis-à-vis others will not suffice. They must begin with a solid territorial and demographic base, build upon that a superior industrial and/or military capability, and utilize those resources with a modicum of political competence.[3] Nor would it be difficult to argue that all of the major powers are sufficiently interdependent, directly or indirectly, to warrant treatment as a discernible subsystem. To a very considerable extent, during the epoch at hand, the policies of each impinge on the fate of the others; and as Campbell (1958) has urged in another context, this condition, plus a similarity of attributes, permits us to think of them as a single social system. We could, of course, go on to construct and apply a number of indices which might reflect the similarities and the interdependence of the major powers, but such an exercise is probably not necessary here.

If, then, we can assume that the states which constitute this oligarchy (Schwarzenberger 1951) do indeed represent the most powerful members of the international system and that they are in relatively frequent interaction with one another, the next question is the extent to which they all collaborate to preserve the status quo, or conversely, vie with one another for supremacy. Our view is that neither extreme holds very often, and that the cooperative and competitive interactions among them fluctuate markedly over time. Further, as Langer (1931), Gulick (1955), Kissinger (1957), and others have demonstrated, even when they work together to impose a common peace, they keep a sharp eye on their relative capabilities. Each major foreign office is, at a given point in time, deeply concerned with the growth of some of their neighbors' strength and the decline of others'. Moreover, yesterday's allies are often tomorrow's rivals or enemies. Even as domestic political power has passed from the hands of the kings, kaisers, czars, and emperors to party bureaucrats and elected bourgeois rulers, the instability of coalitions has abated but slightly. Despite the inhibitory effects of articulated ideologies, competition for public office, and all the demagoguery which comes in the train of popular diplomacy, major power relationships continue to shift, albeit more slowly.

## The Role of Uncertainty

It is, however, one thing to argue that the distribution and redistribution of relative capability will turn out to be a major factor in the behavior of national states, and quite another to predict the strength—and direction—of its relationship with war. As a matter of fact, we contend that a rather strong case can be made for two alternative, but incompatible, models. In each of these models, capability configurations represent the predictor or independent variables, and decision-makers' uncertainty serves as the (unmeasured) intervening variable. By uncertainty we mean nothing more than the difficulty which foreign policy elites experience in discerning the stratifications and clusters in the system, and predicting the behavior of the other members of that system.

How does uncertainty link up with capability patterns on the one hand and with war or peace, on the other? Considering the latter connection first, those who believe that it is *un*certainty which usually makes for war will argue that most war is the result of misjudgment, erroneous perception, and poor predictions. The opposing view is that high levels of *certainty* are, on the contrary, often at the root of war, and that the major inhibitor to war is a *lack* of clarity, order, and predictability. When relative capabilities are difficult to appraise, and when coalition bonds are ambiguous, outcomes are more in doubt, and it is that very uncertainty which helps governments to draw back from the brink of war (E. B. Haas and Whiting 1956, p. 50).

Shifting from the possible link between uncertainty and war to that between capability distributions and such uncertainty, both schools of thought tend to converge. Here, the assumption is that three different variables will affect uncertainty in the system: the extent to which capabilities are highly concentrated in the hands of a very few nations, whether the distribution is changing toward higher or lower concentration, and the rate at which relative capabilities are moving. The model, as we see it, holds that uncertainty levels will rise when: (a) capabilities are more equally distributed and not concentrated; (b) the direction of change is toward such equal distribution and away from high concentrations; and (c) when there is high fluidity, rather than stability, in capability distributions.

To summarize, we find two contending models of more or less equal plausibility. One, which we might call the "preponderance and stability" model, holds that war will *in*crease as the system moves away from a high and stable concentration of capabilities. The other, which might be called the "parity and fluidity" model, holds that war will *de*crease as the system moves away from such a high and stable concentration and toward a more ambiguous state of approximate parity, coupled with a relatively fluid movement of the nations up and down the power hierarchy.

For the moment, we will leave these models in their preoperational and verbal form. Then, after describing the measures and the resulting data in some detail, we can return to their formal articulation and to an examination of the extent to which each fits the empirical world of the past century and a half. It should, of course, be emphasized that even if our design were flawless, our measures impeccable, and our analyses beyond reproach, the findings would nevertheless be far from conclusive. First of all, there is Popper's dictum (1965) regarding the disconfirmability, as opposed to the confirmability of empirical generalizations. Second, we must stress that the generalizations being tested here are very gross and undifferentiated. This, we believe, is as it should be in the early stages of a particular line of theoretical investigation, but we recognize at the same time that a more refined set of tests, with attention to additional variables and tighter analytical controls, is ultimately required.

## The Variables and Their Measurement

Space limitations and the conventions of scientific reporting usually preclude a fully detailed description of the precise operations by which one's verbalized constructs are converted into machine-readable data. This is especially unfortunate when most of these constructs or variables are not found in ready-made operational form (such as votes) and have not yet achieved even partial acceptance as reliable and valid indices (such as gross national product). But as we noted at the outset, we have been neither bashful nor niggardly in publishing our data, and we can therefore refer to those separate studies in which our rationale, procedures, and results are presented in greater detail. Thus, we will describe and justify our measures in only the briefest fashion here, beginning with the outcome variable (war) and then moving on to our predictor variables: concentration, change in concentration, and movement.

### The Incidence of War

We begin by distinguishing among interstate, extrasystemic, and civil wars; the latter two are of no concern here, and we deal only with those of the first type in which at least one major power was an active participant and in which each side sustained at least 1,000 battle-connected fatalities. The particular index used in the analysis at hand is a reflection of the magnitude of war underway, as measured in nation-months of such major power interstate war. And since our time unit is the half-decade, we measure the warlikeness of each such period as the average annual amount of war underway during that period. The war data for each of the 29 periods from 1820 to 1965 are shown in table 1.[4]

## National Capabilities

To this juncture, we have alluded to power, strength, and capability, but have sidestepped any definitions; that delicate chore can no longer be avoided. As one of us (Singer 1963a) emphasized some years ago, power is to political science what wealth is to economics, but not nearly as measureable. The focus there was on the influence *process*, and the range of strategies appropriate to each basic type of internation influence situation; relative capabilities, or the bases of power, were by and large ignored.

Recently, several serious efforts to convert the intuitive notions of national capability or power base have appeared (German 1960; Fucks 1965), but rather than examine them or compare our approach to theirs, we will merely summarize our measures here. In a later volume we plan to discuss the several existing efforts, indicate the theoretical reasoning behind our own measures, and present our data in considerable detail.

We begin with six separate indicators, combine them into three, and then combine those into a single power base or war potential (Knorr 1956) score for each nation every half-decade. The six fall into three groupings of two dimensions each. The *demographic* dimension includes, first, the nation's total population, and second, the number of people living in cities of 20,000 or larger. The *industrial* dimension embraces both energy consumption (from 1885 on) and iron or steel production. The energy may come from many sources, but is converted into coal ton equivalents, and the iron/steel production is based on the former only until 1895, at which time we shift to steel alone. The third pair of measures are *military* expenditures and armed forces size, excluding reserves.

As to the more obvious validity questions, we carefully considered the need for separate indicators of social organization, national unity and motivation, and technical skills, but concluded that each of those was adequately reflected in one or more of the six specific indices. Closely related to the choice of indices and subindices is the matter of their relative contributions to a nation's power base. And while we are still experimenting with a number of weighting and interaction-effect schemes, our tendency is to treat them as equally important, and additive in their effect. In line with these tentative assumptions, we first compute the total score (in people, tons, dollars, etc.) for the system, and then ascertain each nation's percentage share. This has the virtue of normalizing all of our data, reduces the computational problems associated with fluctuating currency conversion rates, avoids that of changes in purchasing power, and puts the figures into ideal form for the computation of our concentration-distribution scores, to which we will turn in a moment.

In addition, since the validity of the composite six-dimensional score is a long way from being demonstrated, we computed these percentage share scores not only for all six dimensions combined, but for the three two-dimensional indices of demographic, industrial, and military capability, and then for each of the six separately. There are, thus, ten power indices for each nation every half-decade, but only the *composite* scores are utilized in our analyses here.

### The Distribution of Capabilities

In our discussion of the impact of certainty and uncertainty on the incidence of major power war, we indicated that capability distributions should exercise a strong effect on these certainty levels. How do we measure CON, or the extent to which these capabilities are concentrated or diffused among the nations which comprise the major power subsystem?

Once more, the measurement problem is sufficiently complex to warrant reference to a fuller statement elsewhere (Ray and Singer 1973). To summarize here, we have been struck with the empirical inadequacy of several measures of inequality which have been rather widely used, and have thus devised our own.[5] To operationally measure the concentration of capabilities (within the grouping of from five to eight major powers) we proceed as follows. First, we compute the standard deviation of the *observed* percentage shares. Second, we divide that figure by the *maximum* standard deviation of the percentage shares that is possible for a given N; that maximum would occur if one nation held 100 percent of the shares, and the others had none at all. The resulting index ranges from zero (reflecting perfect equality in the distribution) to 1.0 (in which case one nation holds 100 percent of that capability), and—if our interpretation of the relevant data is correct—should turn out to be high in face validity. The concentration scores are listed in table 1, along with the war data and the change and movement measures, to which we now turn.[6]

## Movement and Change of Capability Distributions

Having dealt with the measurement of our outcome variable and the key predictor variable, we can now shift to the indices which reflect change across time in the latter. As the scores in table 1 make clear, the distribution of power in the major power subsystem is by no means a static thing. How do we measure such shifts?

Two rather distinct indices are employed. The first is a straightforward reflection of the extent to which the concentration index has gone up or down during the period (usually five years) between any two observations. We call it simply change in concentration, or ΔCON. The second is a bit more complex, and it reflects the number of percentage shares which have been exchanged between and among the major powers during each period, whether or not that redistribution leads to a change in the rank ordering.

We begin by comparing the percentage of capability shares held by each of the nations at the beginning and the end of the half-decade. If, for example, the top-ranked nation held 30 percent of the composite capability shares at the beginning of a half-decade, and the other four held, respectively, 25, 20, 15, and 10 percent, and the distribution at the end of the period were 35, 25, 15, 15, and 10, there would have been a movement of 10 percentage shares. That is, the top nation picked up 5 percentage shares, number three lost 5, and the remaining three scores remained constant. But in order to make the movement index (called MOVE) comparable across all 30 periods in our 150 years, with the size (and composition) of the subsystem changing from time to time, it must be normalized. That normalization is achieved by dividing by the *maximum possible* amount of movement or redistribution. That maximum, in turn, would occur if the lowest-ranked nation picked up all the shares between the two observations, and ended up with 100 percent of them. Thus, our denominator is computed by subtracting the lowest nation's score from 100 percent and multiplying that difference by two, since whatever it gained will have been lost by the others.[7]

It is now time to mention two irregularities that must be dealt with in computing our capability distribution and war measures. First, as already noted, the major power subsystem (as we define it) gains and loses members at several points during the century and a half under study. This not only requires us to normalize for its size when measuring capability distributions, but also to eliminate the distortions that could arise in measuring change or movement between two observations that are based on dissimilar subsystem membership. We do this by counting only the movement of shares between and among nations which were members at both observation points, and thus avoid any artifact which could arise merely because the 100 percent is divided among a smaller or larger population at the separate data points.

The second irregularity stems from the fact that we would get rather distorted indices of relative capability if we measured the military, industrial, and demographic strengths during the two world wars. Thus, in place of the 1915, 1940, and 1945 observation years, we use 1913, 1938, and 1946, respectively. But this makes several of our interobservation intervals longer or shorter than five years. For the war measure, as mentioned earlier, we solve that problem by converting each period's total nation months of interstate war underway into an *average annual* index. For the change in concentration and the movement measures—which are essentially rate of change measures—we merely divide all the interobservation scores by the number of years which have elapsed between them; this again produces an average annual index.

Having now summarized, albeit briefly, the ways in which we convert our separate war and capability concepts into operational indices, we can present the resulting figures. In table 1, then, we list the CON, ΔCON, MOVE, and WAR indices for each of the twenty-nine observation points embraced in the study. Bear in mind that CON is the only one of our indices which is measured at a *single* point in time; the change and movement indices reflect the average annual magnitudes during the period immediately following the CON observation, and the amount of war is also that underway during the years immediately following that observation. However, a variety of time lags and leads will be introduced when we turn to our analyses, resulting in re-alignments across the rows as we move the various columns upward and downward.

Table 1. Capability and War Indices

| Period Beginning $(T_o)$ | CON $(T_o)$ | Average Annual $\Delta$CON $(T_0 \to T_1)$ | Average Annual MOVE $(T_0 \to T_1)$ | Average Annual Nation-Months of WAR Underway $(T_0 \to T_1)$ |
|---|---|---|---|---|
| 1820 | 0.241 | −0.15 | 0.40 | (2.92) |
| 1825 | 0.233 | 0.17 | 0.47 | 6.68 |
| 1830 | 0.242 | 0.02 | 0.41 | 0.00 |
| 1835 | 0.243 | −0.22 | 0.88 | 0.00 |
| 1840 | 0.232 | 0.50 | 0.60 | 0.00 |
| 1845 | 0.257 | 0.06 | 0.28 | 6.40 |
| 1850 | 0.260 | 0.34 | 0.67 | 9.36 |
| 1855 | 0.276 | 0.07 | 0.38 | 17.24 |
| 1860 | 0.280 | −0.49 | 0.82 | 16.82 |
| 1865 | 0.255 | −0.45 | 1.23 | 12.98 |
| 1870 | 0.233 | −0.15 | 0.46 | 5.44 |
| 1875 | 0.225 | 0.02 | 0.34 | 3.52 |
| 1880 | 0.226 | −0.36 | 0.53 | 2.64 |
| 1885 | 0.208 | −0.10 | 0.65 | 2.12 |
| 1890 | 0.203 | 0.39 | 0.55 | 0.00 |
| 1895 | 0.223 | −0.41 | 0.67 | 0.00 |
| 1900 | 0.202 | 0.09 | 0.93 | 4.32 |
| 1905 | 0.207 | 0.10 | 0.37 | 3.40 |
| 1910 | 0.212 | −0.14 | 0.74 | 8.47 |
| 1913 | 0.208 | 2.34 | 1.69 | 87.06 |
| 1920 | 0.371 | −2.49 | 1.26 | 0.00 |
| 1925 | 0.247 | −0.13 | 0.80 | 0.00 |
| 1930 | 0.241 | −0.25 | 2.57 | 6.68 |
| 1935 | 0.228 | −0.37 | 2.23 | 8.73 |
| 1938 | 0.217 | 2.50 | 2.82 | 123.97 |
| 1946 | 0.417 | −3.10 | 1.88 | 0.00 |
| 1950 | 0.293 | 0.76 | 0.99 | 103.34 |
| 1955 | 0.331 | −0.56 | 1.36 | 0.52 |
| 1960 | (0.303) | (0.09) | (1.21) | 0.44 |

Note: For display convenience, the values of $\Delta$CON and MOVE have been multiplied by 100. The original values were used in all computations. Figures shown in parentheses ( ) are shown for information only; they are not used in the univariate statistics of table 2 or in the CON LEADS models.

## Examining the Data

Before we get to our analyses and the testing of the contending models, certain characteristics of the several data sets merit a brief discussion. Our motives are twofold. The careful examination of one's data series, time plots, and scatter plots is, in our judgment, an important prerequisite to the conduct of statistical analyses. In

## Table 2.  Descriptive Statistics

|  | CON | ΔCON | MOVE | WAR |
|---|---|---|---|---|
| **Entire span ($N = 28$)** | | | | |
| Mean | .250 | −.0007 | .0096 | 15.36 |
| Median | .237 | −.0012 | .0071 | 3.92 |
| Maximum | .417 | .0250 | .0282 | 123.97 |
| Minimum | .202 | −.0310 | .0028 | 0.0 |
| Standard deviation | .0504 | .0105 | .0069 | 32.33 |
| Range | .215 | .0560 | .0254 | 123.97 |
| Auto-correlation | .21 | −.58 | .63 | −.15 |
| Secular trend (beta) | .30 | −.09 | .66 | .32 |
| (b) | .0004 | −.00002 | .0001 | .2501 |
| **19th century ($N = 14$)** | | | | |
| Mean | .244 | −.0005 | .0058 | 5.94 |
| Median | .242 | −.0004 | .0050 | 4.48 |
| Maximum | .280 | .0050 | .0123 | 17.24 |
| Minimum | .208 | −.0049 | .0028 | 0.0 |
| Standard deviation | .0201 | .0028 | .0026 | 6.08 |
| Range | .072 | .0099 | .0095 | 17.24 |
| Auto-correlation | .62 | .18 | .01 | .72 |
| Secular trend (beta) | −.24 | −.37 | .17 | −.01 |
| (b) | −.0002 | −.0005 | .00002 | −.0042 |
| **20th century ($N = 14$)** | | | | |
| Mean | .257 | −.0009 | .0315 | 24.78 |
| Median | .226 | −.0014 | .0113 | 3.86 |
| Maximum | .417 | .0250 | .0282 | 123.97 |
| Minimum | .202 | −.0310 | .0037 | 0.0 |
| Standard deviation | .0692 | .0149 | .0078 | 44.07 |
| Range | .215 | .0560 | .0245 | 123.97 |
| Auto-correlation | .13 | −.60 | .50 | −.32 |
| Secular trend (beta) | .61 | −.14 | .56 | .18 |
| (b) | .0020 | −.0001 | .0002 | .3849 |

Note: The autocorrelation coefficient shown is first-order only. For the separate century series, each variable was divided according to its lag-lead relationship in the ADD/CON LEADS model. Thus the statistics shown above for the nineteenth century include the CON observation at 1885,  ΔCON and MOVE 1885-1890, and WAR 1890-1894. The twentieth- century series begins with the following observation on each variable.

addition, there are the well-known constraints which one's data distributions can impose in the selection and interpretation of the statistical analyses employed. The relevant summary statistics for our four variables are shown in table 2.[8]

Looking at the measures of central tendency, we note that the differences between the means and medians for our three predictor variables are quite small in all three time spans. This suggests that these variables do not have seriously skewed distributions. The same cannot be said for the war variable, however. The mean nation-months of war figure for the twentieth century is 24.78, while the median value is only 3.86, indicating that the distribution is positively skewed. This condition is no doubt due to the extreme values associated with World War I, World War II, and the Korean War.

Examining the measures of dispersion (range and standard deviation), we find that, as one might expect, all of our measures vary less in the nineteenth century than in the twentieth. With one exception these differences are not serious, and that exception is the war variable. Again we find the three large wars in our series exerting a disproportionate influence on the distributional properties of the war variable. The standard deviation of war in the nineteenth century is 6.08, while the comparable figure for the twentieth century is 44.07. Although Chauvenet's criterion (Young 1962) might cast some doubt on the analyses associated with such outliers, we feel that the brush-clearing nature of this work suggests neither the transformation nor the elimination of these data points. We realize, however, that these values may weaken the predictive power of our models, particularly in the twentieth century.

Two additional descriptors will also be important when we turn to our analyses. One of these is the *autocorrelation* coefficient, reflecting the extent to which each successive value of a given variable is independent of, or highly correlated with, the prior value of that same variable. For the entire time span, several of our indices show rather high autocorrelations, with $\Delta$CON at - .58 and MOVE at .63. These turn out, however, to be quite different when we examine the centuries separately, suggesting further that these epochs are divided by more than a change in digits. Now we find that CON shows a .62 autocorrelation in the earlier epoch but only .13 in the present. The two indices of redistribution are negligibly autocorrelated in the nineteenth, but discernibly so (-.60 and .50) in the twentieth. As to the amount of war underway in each half-decade, there is a high .72 correlation between successive periods in the earlier century, but a low -.32 in this century. We will return to the implications of these in the context of our multivariate analyses, but we should point out here that the important consideration is not so much that of autocorrelation of the indices, but of the autocorrelations of the differences between the predicted and observed values (i.e., residuals) of the outcome variable.

Then there is the closely related problem of secular trends. If one's variables are steadily rising or falling during the period under study, they can produce statistical associations that are largely a consequence of such trends. Hence the widespread use of "first differences" and other techniques for detrending in the analysis of time series data. How serious is the problem in the study at hand? If we standardize each variable and regress the resulting series on the year of observation, also standardized, we can then estimate the trend of our various series by comparing the resulting slopes (or beta weights, which of course are equal to the product-moment correlation coefficients).

For the entire time span, MOVE shows the steepest slope, with a standardized regression coefficient of .66; CON and WAR are moderately steep with coefficients of .30 and .32 respectively. In the nineteenth century, $\Delta$CON (- .37) and CON (- .24) show downward slopes, MOVE is slightly positive (.17), and WAR (- .01) shows virtually no trend whatever. CON develops a sharp positive trend (.61) in the twentieth century, as does MOVE (.56). The other variables show weak twentieth-century trends, - .14 for $\Delta$CON and .18 for WAR.

Before turning to our analyses, one additional data problem requires brief attention. Important, from both the substantive and methodological viewpoints, is the extent to which the predictor variables covary with each other, and these coefficients are shown under the correlation matrices in tables 4, 5, and 6. For the entire span, the product-moment correlation between CON in one period and $\Delta$CON in the next is - .71; that between CON and $\Delta$CON during the preceding half-decade is .47. When CON is correlated with the amount of movement in the subsequent half-decade, we find a coefficient of .21, and it is .50 when correlated with the half-decade preceding it. As to the two indices which reflect the durability of capability distribution, any suspicion that they might be tapping the same phenomenon is quickly dispelled; the correlation between $\Delta$CON and MOVE is a negligible .08. When we turn to our multivariate analyses and discuss the problem of multicollinearity, these correlations as well as those that obtain within the separate centuries will be examined further.

## The Bivariate Analyses

With our theoretical rationale, index construction, and data summaries behind us, we can return to the query which led to the investigation in the first place: What are the effects of capability distribution and redistribution on the incidence of war involving the members of the major power subsystem? We approach the question in two stages, the first of which is a series of bivariate analyses. These are employed not only because it seems useful to know as much as possible about such relationships prior to the examination of more complex models, but also because the theoretical argument suggests that CON, ΔCON, and MOVE should exercise independent—as well as combined—effects on decision-maker uncertainty and on war. From there, we will move on to a number of multivariate analyses, in which we compare the war fluctuation patterns *predicted* by several additive and multiplicative models against the patterns which were actually *observed.*

We begin in a direct fashion and ask whether there is any discernible association between our several measures of capability distribution on the one hand, and fluctuations in the incidence of war, on the other. Bear in mind that: (a) CON is measured as of the first day (more or less) of every fifth year (except for the 1913, 1938, and 1946 substitutions noted earlier); (b) ΔCON and MOVE are measured between two successive readings of CON; and (c) WAR is measured during the period immediately following either the observation of CON or the second of the two observations on which ΔCON and MOVE are based. (A typical set of observations would be: ΔCON and MOVE from 1 January 1840 to 1 January 1845; CON at 1 January 1840; and WAR from 1 January 1845 through 31 December 1849.) The working assumption here is that whatever independent effects each of the predictor variables will have upon the incidence of war will be felt within the subsequent half-decade. In the multivariate analyses, we will experiment with these time lags and leads, and in a follow-up study (when our annual data are in) we will further explore the effects of different, and more precisely measured, time lags and leads.

Turning, then, to the product-moment correlations between these predictor variables and major power interstate war, we examine the coefficients reported in table 3. If those who view high concentration, upward change in concentration, and low movement as conducive to decisional certainty (and thus to low levels of war) are correct, we should find negative correlations for the CON-WAR and ΔCON-WAR association and positive ones for the MOVE-WAR association. Conversely, if the world is closer to the model articulated by those who see low concentration, downward change in concentra-

Table 3.  Bivariate Correlation Coefficients ($r$) and Coefficients of Determination Between Capability Indices and WAR in Succeeding Time Period

| | Average Annual Nation-months of War Underway$_{t_1 \to t_2}$ | | | | | |
| | Total Span (N = 28) | | 19th Century (N = 14) | | 20th Century (N = 14) | |
| | $r$ | $r^2$ | $r$ | $r^2$ | $r$ | $r^2$ |
|---|---|---|---|---|---|---|
| $CON_{t_0}$ | −.10 | .01 | .81 | .66 | −.23 | .05 |
| $\Delta CON_{t_0 \to t_1}$ | −.38 | .14 | .19 | .04 | −.41 | .17 |
| $MOVE_{t_0 \to t_1}$ | .34 | .12 | −.01 | .00 | .24 | .06 |

tion, and high movement as conducive to uncertainty (and thus to low levels of war), the signs would be just the opposite. What do we find?

Examining the total century and a half first, it looks as if the preponderance and stability school has the better of the predictive models. While correlation coefficients of − .10, − .38, and .34 are not impressively high, all three are in the direction predicted by that particular model.[9] But as we have already intimated, there seem to be intuitive as well as empirical grounds for treating the centuries separately. Not only have many historians noted the transitional role of the 1890s, but several of our own analyses to date (Singer and Small 1966c; 1968; Small and Singer 1969) reinforce that impression.[10] Our suspicions are further reinforced when we compute the correlations for the centuries separately. We now find that those who recommend high concentration and low movement in order to reduce the incidence of war do not do quite so well. In the twentieth century, the signs are all in the direction predicted by their model, while for the nineteenth century (or more precisely, the period ending with the 1890–1895 observations), the signs are reversed.[11]

Before leaving the bivariate analyses, however, a brief digression is in order that we might check for the presence and effect of cross-lag correlations. Here the search is not for the impact of the predictor variable on the outcome at subsequent observations, but for the impact of the "outcome" variable on chronologically subsequent values of the putative "predictor" variable. In the case at hand, we expected to find a number of cross-correlations, and some did indeed turn up. That is, when we correlated the amount of war underway in any period against the concentration measure in the subsequent period, we found a coefficient of .80 for the full 150 years, .52 for the nineteenth century, and .81 for the twentieth. Similarly, for the impact of prior war on ΔCON, the coefficients were - .66, - .51, and - .68; and for its effect on MOVE, they were .30, .46, and .17. Most of these are sufficiently strong to suggest the need for reexamining the extent to which our capability indices predict to subsequent war when the effects of *prior* war have been removed. Hence, we predicted the CON, ΔCON, and MOVE measures from preceding levels of war; the variance in those measures which could *not* be so explained (i.e., residual variance) was then used as a relatively less biased predictor of war in the following half-decade.

For the entire period, the residual correlation between CON and WAR is a negligible .01, the effect on the nineteenth-century coefficient is to reduce it from .81 to .65, and for the twentieth, the association drops from - .23 to - .03. As to the relationship between the residuals of ΔCON and WAR, the coefficients drop from - .29 to - .01, from .18 to - .03, and - .34 to - .06, for the full and the separate epochs respectively. The impact on the predictive power of MOVE, however, is to strengthen rather than reduce it. The full span's coefficient rises from .34 to .45, and those for the nineteenth century rise from - .01 to - .17, and from .23 to .41, respectively.[12]

Having emphasized the importance of such a cross-lag correlation check, however, we would now back off and argue that residuals should *not* be used in either the bivariate analyses at hand or in the multivariate ones which follow in the next section. That is, our theoretical concern here is exclusively with the effect of the concentration and redistribution of capabilities upon the incidence of war in the following period, regardless of what produced those capability configurations. Thus, while the war-to-capability association must be kept in mind, it is of minor consequence in the analyses at hand. We will, however, return to it in later reports, in which a number of feedback models will be put to the test.

Thus we conclude this section on the associations between capability concentrations and major power interstate war by noting that the evidence is, for the moment, quite divided. While high concentration and changes toward it do—as the preponderance and stability school suggests—tend to reduce the incidence of war in the current century, such is clearly not the case in the previous century. Those patterns are much closer to what is predicted by the peace through-parity-and-fluidity model. Let us turn, then, to a more detailed and complex scrutiny of the question.

## The Multivariate Analyses

With the bivariate analyses and some very tentative conclusions behind us, we can now turn to the multivariate models and consider the possible *joint* effects of capability configurations on the incidence of major power war. We do this via the consideration of four different versions of our model, reflecting those of an additive and those of a multiplicative type, and distinguishing between those in which we measure CON before ΔCON or MOVE and those in which CON follows ΔCON and MOVE chronologically. Before examining the several models and the extent to which they match the historical realities, we consider the rationale behind each type.

Looking at the additive-multiplicative distinctions first, let us think of our three predictor variables as if they were merely binary in nature, with 1 reflecting a high value of each and 0 reflecting a low value. Let us assume, further, that war will result if the variables, singly or in combination, reach a threshold of 1 or more. If their effects are additive, it is clear that we will have wars as long as *any one* of them is equal to 1. On the other hand, if their effects are *multiplicative, all* of them must equal 1, since a 0 value on any one of them will give us a product of 0. Another way to look at this distinction is to think of the road to war as having either fixed or flexible exits. In the multiplicative case, there are several exits, since we only need to have a low value (i.e., 0) for *any* one of them to avoid war; hence the flexibility of exits from the road to war. In the additive case, however, the exits are quite fixed; unless *every* one of the predictors is low (i.e., 0), war will result. We might also think of the additive version as a "marginal" one, in that the magnitude of each variable can only exercise a marginal effect on the probability of war, whereas the magnitude of each in the multiplicative case can be determining, at least in the negative sense.[13]

In addition to considering additive and multiplicative versions of the basic model, we need to consider the chronological sequence in which the variables are combined in accounting for the incidence of war. In the bivariate analyses, since the effects of each predictor variable upon war were measured separately, this was no problem. But here, especially since we already know that there is some interdependence among the three predictors, that sequence becomes critical. Unless we want to assume that the capability configurations could exercise their impact later than five years after being observed—which we do not—there are two major options. In one, we measure CON at 1870 (for example), $\Delta$CON and MOVE between 1870 and 1875, and WAR from 1875 through 1879; we call this the CON LEADS version. In the other, we measure CON at 1875, with $\Delta$CON and MOVE observed between 1870 and 1875, and WAR again measured during the 1875–1879 period; this is the CON LAGS version.

Thus, the basic model can be represented in four different forms:

ADD/CON LEADS: $\text{WAR}_{t_{1 \to 2}} = \alpha + \beta_1 (\text{CON}_{t_0}) + \beta_2 (\Delta\text{CON}_{t_{0 \to 1}}) + \beta_3 (\text{MOVE}_{t_{0 \to 1}}) + \epsilon$

ADD/CON LAGS: $\text{WAR}_{t_{1 \to 2}} = \alpha + \beta_1 (\Delta\text{CON}_{t_{0 \to 1}}) + \beta_2 (\text{MOVE}_{t_{0 \to 1}}) + \beta_3 (\text{CON}_{t_1}) + \epsilon$

MULT/CON LEADS $\text{WAR}_{t_{1 \to 2}} = \alpha \times (\text{CON}_{t_0}^{\beta_1}) \times (\Delta\text{CON}_{t_{0 \to 1}}^{\beta_2}) \times (\text{MOVE}_{t_{0 \to 1}}^{\beta_3}) \times \epsilon$

MULT/CON LAGS $\text{WAR}_{t_{1 \to 2}} = \alpha \times (\Delta\text{CON}_{t_{0 \to 1}}^{\beta_1}) \times (\text{MOVE}_{t_{0 \to 1}}^{\beta_2}) \times (\text{CON}_{t_1}^{\beta_3}) \times \epsilon$

where $\alpha$ = estimated constant term, or intercept; $\beta$ = estimated regression coefficient, and $\epsilon$ = error term, or unexplained variance. How well do the several versions predict to the actual historical pattern of major power interstate war? In table 4 we show the following for each version of the model: the multiple regression coefficient ($R$), the multiple coefficient of determination ($R^2$), and the corrected multiple coefficient of determination ($\bar{R}^2$), as well as the beta weights, or standardized regression coefficients ($b$), and the squared partial correlation coefficients ($r^2$) between each of the separate predictor variables and war, controlling for the other two.[14]

The overall impression is that all four versions of the preponderance and stability model do moderately well in predicting to the incidence of war. Every one of the signs is in the direction predicted by that model, with high CON and upward $\Delta$CON preceding low levels of war (i.e., negative correlations with war) and high movement predicting to high levels of war. But the direction of the signs is a relatively crude index; how close is the fit between predicted and observed war levels?

Here we see that the two additive versions of the model, accounting as they do for 31 and 30 percent of the variance, do

Table 4. Predictive Power of Four Versions of the Capability-War Model, ENTIRE SPAN ($N = 28$)

| Version | MULTIPLES | | | CON | | $\Delta$CON | | MOVE | |
|---|---|---|---|---|---|---|---|---|---|
| | $R$ | $R^2$ | $\overline{R^2}$ | $b$ | $r^2$ | $b$ | $r^2$ | $b$ | $b^2$ |
| ADD/CON LEADS | .56 | .31 | .23 | −.28 | .04 | −.61 | .20 | .45 | .20 |
| ADD/CON LAGS | .55 | .30 | .22 | −.18 | .02 | −.33 | .11 | .46 | .18 |
| MULT/CON LEADS | .43 | .19 | .09 | −.27 | .04 | −.57 | .15 | .21 | .04 |
| MULT/CON LAGS | .43 | .18 | .08 | −.22 | .03 | −.28 | .07 | .24 | .05 |

$R$   = Multiple correlation coefficient
$R^2$ = Coefficient of multiple determination
$\overline{R^2}$ = Corrected coefficient of multiple determination
$b$   = Standardized regression coefficient
$r^2$  = Squared partial correlation coefficient

Correlations among the predictor variables:

| $\Delta$CON $_{t_0 \to t_1}$ | 1.00 | | −.71 | | .47 | |
|---|---|---|---|---|---|---|
| MOVE$_{t_0 \to t_1}$ | .08 | | .21 | | .50 | |
| | $\Delta$CON$_{t_0 \to t_1}$ | | CON$_{t_0}$ | | CON$_{t_1}$ | |

fairly well, whereas the multiplicative versions do not do as well. But this is only true before we correct for the degrees of freedom lost or gained by the number of observations and the number of predictor variables. When we introduce those corrections, none of the versions turns out to be particularly powerful in accounting for the observed levels of war. We also note that it makes little difference whether we

Table 5. Predictive Power of Four Versions of the Capability-War Model, 19TH CENTURY ($N = 14$)

| Version | MULTIPLES | | | CON | | $\Delta$CON | | MOVE | |
|---|---|---|---|---|---|---|---|---|---|
| | $R$ | $R^2$ | $\overline{R^2}$ | $b$ | $r^2$ | $b$ | $r^2$ | $b$ | $r^2$ |
| ADD/CON LEADS | .85 | .73 | .65 | .85 | .72 | .29 | .19 | −.38 | .00 |
| ADD/CON LAGS | .85 | .73 | .65 | .96 | .71 | −.31 | .17 | −.39 | .00 |
| MULT/CON LEADS | .72 | .52 | .38 | .73 | .52 | .16 | .04 | −.08 | .01 |
| MULT/CON LAGS | .72 | .52 | .38 | .83 | .50 | −.35 | .13 | −.08 | .01 |

Correlations among the predictor variables:

| $\Delta$CON$_{t_0 \to t_1}$ | 1.00 | | −.14 | | .49 | |
|---|---|---|---|---|---|---|
| MOVE$_{t_0 \to t_1}$ | −.46 | | .19 | | −.12 | |
| | $\Delta$CON$_{t_0 \to t_1}$ | | CON$_{t_0}$ | | CON$_{t_1}$ | |

observe CON before or after the two redistribution indices (ΔCON and MOVE). As to the predictive power of the separate indices, the impact of CON in the additive versions is consistently less than that of ΔCON and MOVE; in the multiplicative versions, this pattern is less clear. In sum, however, it is noteworthy that a model could predict as well as this one does, given the already apparent differences between the nineteenth- and twentieth-century systems. One indication of its overall predictive power is revealed in figure 1; the observed war values are shown as o's and those predicted by the ADD/CON LEADS version are shown as plus signs. What we see, in the distance between each pair of half-decade points, is that our fit is considerably better for the earlier than for the later epoch. More specifically, while it seems to predict fairly well to the occurrence and nonoccurrence of war, it seriously underestimates the war levels generated by the two world wars and the Korean War, for example.

Do the several versions of our model do better when we examine the two centuries separately? As tables 5 and 6 indicate, their predictive power is impressively high for the nineteenth century and rather low for the twentieth; this disparity would account for the mixed results in the overall time span. In table 5, reflecting the

**Figure 2.** ADD/CON LEADS Model, Nineteenth Century.

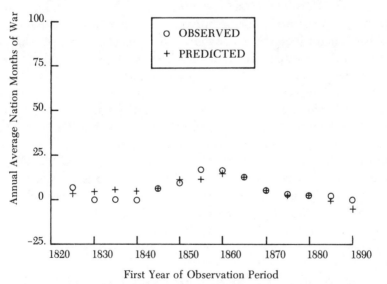

First Year of Observation Period

Table 6. **Predictive Power of Four Versions of the Capability-War Model, 20TH CENTURY ($N = 14$)**

| Version | MULTIPLES | | | CON | | $\Delta$CON | | MOVE | |
|---|---|---|---|---|---|---|---|---|---|
| | $R$ | $R^2$ | $\overline{R^2}$ | $b$ | $r^2$ | $b$ | $r^2$ | $b$ | $r^2$ |
| ADD/CON LEADS | .59 | .35 | .15 | −.50 | .12 | −.85 | .29 | .44 | .19 |
| ADD/CON LAGS | .56 | .31 | .10 | −.31 | .07 | −.32 | .10 | .45 | .17 |
| MULT/CON LEADS | .68 | .46 | .30 | −.81 | .31 | −1.11 | .46 | .37 | .18 |
| MULT/CON LAGS | .64 | .41 | .23 | −.58 | .24 | −.24 | .07 | .42 | .18 |

Correlations among the predictor variables:

| $\Delta CON_{t_0 \to t_1}$ | 1.00 | | −.75 | | .49 | |
|---|---|---|---|---|---|---|
| $MOVE_{t_0 \to t_1}$ | .14 | | .16 | | .51 | |
| | $\Delta CON_{t_0 \to t_1}$ | | $CON_{t_0}$ | | $CON_{t_1}$ | |

earlier epoch, we find that the additive versions are once again considerably more powerful than the multiplicative ones. More important, however, are the differences among the corrected coefficients of determination. This very conservative index shows that the additive versions account for at least 65 percent of the variance in our outcome variable (WAR) in the first of our two epochs.

As to the twentieth century, the multiple coefficients of determination ($R^2$) are far from negligible, but unlike the findings for the entire period and the nineteenth century, here we find the multiplicative version to be more powerful than the additive one. This is not only quite consistent with our bivariate results, but is understandable in the context of our interpretation of multiplicative models. That is, the − .23 correlation between CON and WAR in the twentieth century suggests that there is *some* association between the two, and an examination of our scatter plots showed that while most war did occur when CON was low, there were several periods in which CON was low, but *no* war occurred. To put it another way, low CON was *necessary* in order for large wars to occur, but it was far from sufficient. The multiple-exit interpretation would suggest, then, that the absence of a downward change in CON (i.e., − ΔCON), a high MOVE, or the effect of some unmeasured intervening variable(s) nevertheless permitted the low CON state of affairs to remain a peaceful one.

Looking at the beta weights, we find that all the signs but one are in the directions predicted by the parity-fluidity school's version of the model in the nineteenth century, and by the preponderance-stability version in the twentieth. That exception occurs in the nineteenth-century ADD and MULT models, when we observe CON after ΔCON and MOVE in the unfolding of events. Whereas a change toward higher concentration makes for more war when CON itself leads, it makes for less war (as the preponderance-stability school would predict) when CON follows behind ΔCON and MOVE. This result is a consequence of the high autocorrelation (.62) in CON in the nineteenth century.[15]

Returning to the other beta weights, we ask which of the separate indicators exercises the strongest impact. In the nineteenth century, CON is by far the most potent variable in the regression equation, with all $r^2$ values greater than .50. This is, of course, fully consonant with the bivariate findings, as is the negligible strength of the movement index. And, as noted above, the effect of ΔCON (when we control for CON and MOVE) is a moderately strong and positive one when CON leads the redistribution measures, and almost as strong but negative when CON follows in the chronological sequence. In the twentieth century, on the other hand, we find that all three predictor variables exercise approximately the same impact.[16] And whereas the additive versions give the better fit in the earlier epoch, the multiplicative ones do better in the current century. As a matter of fact, the MULT/CON LEADS version shows fairly strong predictive power, with an $R^2$ of .46 and partial $r^2$s of

**Figure 1.**  ADD/CON LEADS Model, Full Time Span.

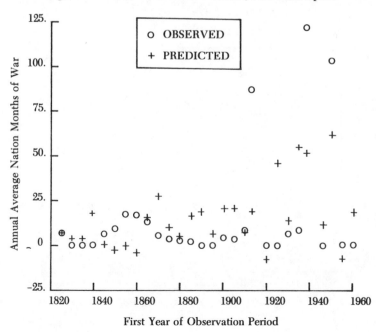

First Year of Observation Period

.31 and .46 for CON and ΔCON, respectively. Again the bivariate and multivariate analyses point quite consistently in the same direction.[17]

An examination of figures 2 and 3 will not only reaffirm, but strengthen, the above statistical results. Plotted on the same scale as figure 1, these indicate the discrepancy between the levels of war predicted by the ADD/CON LEADS model and the amounts that actually occurred in each half-decade. The deviations (i.e., the distances between o and + for each half-decade) are remarkably small in the nineteenth century, but much less consistent in the twentieth-century plot. The parity-fluidity school is thus strongly vindicated in the earlier epoch, while those who look to peace-through-preponderance-and-stability have the better of the argument in the later one.

A close look at table 7 permits us to see more specifically wherein the amount of war predicted by the models deviates from that which actually occurred. Note, by way of introduction, that even though the same basic model is employed (i.e., ADD/CON LEADS, reflected in the first line in tables 4, 5, and 6), the difference in the predictions made by the full-span model and those for the separate centuries is a result of the difference in signs, as already

Figure 3.    ADD/CON LEADS Model, Twentieth Century.

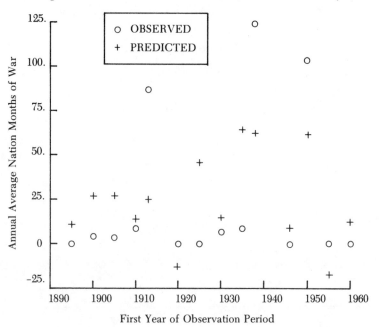

Table 7.  Observed Levels of War and Levels Predicted by ADD/CON LEADS Model: Entire Time Span and Separate Centuries

| | Average Annual Number of Nation-Months Under Way | | | |
|---|---|---|---|---|
| *Period Beginning* | *Observed* | *Full-Span Model Predictions* | *19th-Century Model Predictions* | *20th-Century Model Predictions* |
| 1825 | 6.68 | 6.72 | 4.80 | |
| 1830 | 0.0 | 3.51 | 4.78 | |
| 1835 | 0.0 | 3.44 | 6.06 | |
| 1840 | 0.0 | 17.79 | 4.39 | |
| 1845 | 6.40 | 0.36 | 6.32 | |
| 1850 | 9.36 | −2.54 | 10.23 | |
| 1855 | 17.24 | −0.20 | 12.41 | |
| 1860 | 16.82 | −4.35 | 15.33 | |
| 1865 | 12.98 | 14.87 | 12.32 | |
| 1870 | 5.44 | 27.10 | 5.92 | |
| 1875 | 3.52 | 9.31 | 2.69 | |
| 1880 | 2.64 | 5.06 | 1.89 | |
| 1885 | 2.12 | 16.03 | −0.43 | |
| 1890 | 0.0 | 16.84 | −3.51 | |
| 1895 | 0.0 | 6.35 | | 10.16 |
| 1900 | 4.32 | 20.44 | | 26.92 |
| 1905 | 3.40 | 20.15 | | 27.39 |
| 1910 | 8.47 | 7.47 | | 11.91 |
| 1913 | 87.06 | 18.96 | | 25.62 |
| 1920 | 0.0 | −7.29 | | −11.95 |
| 1925 | 0.0 | 45.64 | | 46.28 |
| 1930 | 6.68 | 13.56 | | 15.36 |
| 1935 | 8.73 | 54.36 | | 64.54 |
| 1938 | 123.97 | 51.70 | | 63.13 |
| 1946 | 0.0 | 11.83 | | 9.12 |
| 1950 | 103.34 | 61.94 | | 62.24 |
| 1955 | 0.52 | −7.36 | | −16.90 |
| 1960 | 0.44 | 18.45 | | 13.12 |

mentioned. That is, since the best-fitting equation for the entire span has the same signs as that which is nearly the best for the twentieth century, it therefore imposes *its* predictions on the nineteenth century.[18]

Shifting to the columns for the war levels predicted by the parity-fluidity (nineteenth century) and preponderance-stability (twentieth century) models, a number of specific discrepancies merit explicit comment. Working our way down, we first note that the model underestimates—or more accurately, lags in predicting—the amount of war in the 1820- 1840 period. From there on to the end of the nineteenth century, the fit is fairly good, giving us our estimated standard error of 3.60, which is a function of the actual discrepancy between the predicted and the observed values.

Moving into the later of our two eras, the twentieth-century model tends to overestimate the levels for 1925-1929 and 1935-1937, to underestimate the magnitudes of World War I, World War II, and the Korean War, and to overestimate the final decade's warlikeness. This latter discrepancy may well be accounted for by the coding rules used for this particular study, excluding as they do the appreciable levels of *extra*systemic war which marked that period. In general, the twentieth-century model spreads out the total amount of war more evenly, rather than predicting the radical fluctuations which do in fact occur; the standard error of the prediction is 40.48. For both centuries, of course, the inclusion of additional variables would have given us a better fit, but our objective was not so much to create or discover a best-fitting model as it was to *test* an *a priori* one.


Conclusion


Before we summarize the results of these analyses, it is important to make very explicit the tentative nature of our findings. Nor is this a mere genuflection in the direction of scientific custom. The study is preliminary in several fundamental meanings of the word.

First, there are the standard problems associated with any "first cut" investigation. Among these are: (a) the absence of any prior analyses of the same type; (b) the possibility of inaccuracies in our data, and as Morgenstern (1963) reminds us, the sources of error may indeed be considerable; and (c) the lack of any hard evidence against which the validity of our predictor variables might be measured. In this vein, our use of the composite index of capability may possibly conceal certain important differences that could be revealed by each of the separate (demographic, industrial, and military) indices.

Secondly, the reliance on quinquennial observations might well account for an untoward portion of the results, in both the positive and negative sense of the word. The cutting points between the half-decades can so distribute the capability and war scores that, by accident alone, they may fall into either the "right" or "wrong" time period. Had we used a measure of the amount of war *begun* in a given period, that problem would have been even more accentuated;

by measuring war underway, we minimize but do not eliminate the dangers of such an artifact. And any *annual* fluctuation in the predictor variables is concealed. In addition, the fixed interval between observations forecloses the use of briefer or longer spans in experimenting with various lag and lead relationships. In a follow-up study, when our annual capability data are available, we will have much more flexibility in our design, and will be able to ascertain whether the quinquennial time units do indeed represent a source of distortion in the results.

Third, our use of the single nation as our object of analysis may not only be an inaccurate reflection of who the "real" actors are, but produce distorted measures of capability and its distribution. Fourth, as we noted, our decision to defer the analysis of the feedback loops which connect *prior war to concentration* as well as *concentration to subsequent war* leaves our analysis of the problem far from complete. Fifth, it may well be that these findings will continue to hold as we reexamine our model's applicability to the major subsystem, but turn out to be quite inapplicable to the power and war dynamics of other subsystems or the international system as a whole. Finally, it should be emphasized that this investigation is at the systemic level only and that no inferences can be made as to which particular nations, blocs, or dyads become involved in war resulting from the distribution or redistribution of capabilities.

With these caveats in mind, let us summarize what we have done in the investigation at hand, and what we think has been discovered. To recapitulate the theoretical argument, we have synthesized from the literature two distinct and incompatible models of the way in which the distribution and redistribution of capabilities affects the incidence of major power war. One, which we see as a formal and integrated version of the classical balance-of-power viewpoint (E. B. Haas 1953), predicts that there will be less war when there is: (a) approximate parity among the major nations; (b) change toward parity rather than away from it; and (c) a relatively fluid power hierarchy. The other, reflecting the hegemony view, predicts that there will be less war when there is: (a) a preponderance of power concentrated in the hands of a very few nations; (b) change, if any, toward greater concentration; and (c) a relatively stable rank order among, and intervals between, the major powers. Even though a variety of intervening variables may be introduced as the link between such capability configurations and the preservation of peace, we suggest that decisional uncertainty is a parsimonious and appropriate one, and is implied in many of the traditional analyses. While both schools agree that parity and fluidity increase that uncertainty, only the first would hold that such uncertainty makes for peace; the preponderance and stability school sees uncertainty as leading to war.

These two sets of predictions have been consolidated into a single basic model incorporating the three predictor variables (capability concentration, rate and direction of change in concentration, and the movement of capability shares among the powers) and the outcome variable (amount of interstate war involving major powers). But the classical theorizers were less than precise in their formulations, and said little in regard either to the sequence in which the variables should exercise their effects, or the way in which those effects might combine, making it necessary to construct alternative representations. Since an examination of only the most obvious version would be less than a fair test, we articulated and tested four versions: an additive and a multiplicative form with the measurement of concentration prior to the measurement of its change and movement, and an additive and multiplicative one with concentration measured after change and movement.

The first test of all four versions was for the entire century and a half since the Congress of Vienna, and it showed the preponderance and stability school's predictions to be closer to historical reality than those of the parity and fluidity school. But even though the correlations were all in the direction predicted by the preponderance school, their goodness of fit was not very impressive. Then, on the basis of prior findings, as well as a number of visual and statistical examinations of the data, we divided the century and a half into two separate eras of equal length, and retested the models.

This time, the predictions of the *parity and fluidity* school turned out to be correct in the direction of their associations and strong in their fit with nineteenth-century reality. Particularly powerful was the additive form of the model with concentration measured prior to its redistribution. And, not surprisingly, given the results of the full 150-year analyses, the twentieth-century findings matched the predictions of the *preponderance and stability* school. But whereas the corrected coefficient of determination $(\bar{R}^2)$ for the parity model in the earlier era was .65, the best of those for the preponderance model in the contemporary era was .31.

Bearing in mind the opening paragraphs in this section, as well as the relatively clear empirical results, we conclude that the concentration of major power capabilities does indeed exercise an impact on the incidence of war, and that its impact has been a radically different one in the past and present centuries. As to possible explanations for these radical differences, space limitations preclude any lengthy consideration. For the moment, though, we might speculate that uncertainty—our unmeasured intervening variable—plays a different role in the two centuries. When diplomacy was still largely in the hands of small elite groups, the uncertainty factor (allegedly resulting from an equal distribution of power, and fluidity in the rank orderings) may have been modest in both its magnitude and its effects. Schooled in the accepted norms of the game, these professionals might be uncertain as to exactly who ranked where, but nevertheless fairly confident as to general behavior patterns. The shared culture made it relatively clear what each would do in given— and familiar—situations of conflict or crisis, and their relative freedom of action made it easier to conform to such regularized expectations.

By the turn of the century, however, industrialization, urbanization, and the democratization of diplomacy may have begun to erode the rules of the game. Conventional definitions of the national interest were no longer widely accepted at home, and political oppositions and interest groups could make certain foreign policy moves difficult and costly to a regime. The increasing need to mobilize popular support as well as material resources meant that the vagaries of domestic politics would intrude more fully into a nation's diplomacy. And a grasp of other nations' domestic politics has never been a strong point in the foreign offices of the world. Hence, the normal uncertainties of the "balance-of-power" system were aggravated by these additional uncertainties, meaning that the probability of war could only be kept within bounds when power configurations were exceptionally clear and the pecking order was quite unambiguous. This is, of course, only one of several possible interpretations, and a highly speculative one at that.[19] In due course, then, we hope to bring more solid evidence to bear on the power-war relationships which are reported here; in that context, a number of technological, sociological, and political hypotheses will receive due consideration.

Given our findings and the associated caveats, are any policy implications worth noting? On the one hand—as our critics continue to remind us—such macro-level phenomena as the distribution of military-industrial capabilities are not exactly susceptible to short-run policy control. In this, as in other of our analyses to date, the independent variables are indeed "independent" as far as immediate human intervention is concerned. They change rather slowly, and worse yet, they seldom seem to change in response to conscious and intelligent planning.

On the other hand, a fuller understanding of these structural conditions is much to be valued. Not only do they appear to exercise a powerful impact on the peacefulness of the international system, but they also constitute some of the major constraints within which men and groups act and interact. Despite the views of Rapoport (1970a) and others that "there is no lack of knowledge about 'what men could do' to insure peace," we are struck with the evidence to the contrary.

Closely related is the familiar issue of how similar the world of the 1970s and 1980s is to that of the 1816–1895 or 1900–1965 periods. If the system has changed drastically on one or more occasions in this century, or is likely to do so in the near future, how relevant are the results of historical analyses? Our findings in the Correlates of War project to date suggest rather strongly that: (a) today's world *is* different from that of the nineteenth century; but (b) the most discernible changes occurred around the turn of the century and not with World War I or II or with the advent of nuclear weapons and ballistic missiles. For the moment, then, all we can say is that it behooves us to treat all such alleged transformations as empirical questions, and to ascertain the extent to which such changes have affected the probability of war. We suspect, as noted above, that the twentieth-century system *is* a less stable and less easily understood one than the nineteenth, and that we *are* experiencing different types of war brought on by differing conditions. But it may also have given us the knowledge and skills that make it more tractable to us than the nineteenth century was for those who sought to understand and control the international politics of that era.

In saying this, however, we have no illusions that social scientific discoveries related to war (or other problems of social justice) will inevitably be utilized to better the lot of humanity (Singer 1970). Knowledge can not only remain *un*applied; it can also be *mis*applied. But that is no justification for eschewing knowledge. Rather, our job is to ask the most important questions, seek the answers in the most efficient and rigorous fashion, publish our findings and interpretations in an expeditious fashion—and act on them in a forthright manner. As we see it, peace research—especially on the structural conditions that make for war—*is* peace action of a critical sort. Thus, as we continue to press for the policy changes that we *suspect* may improve man's chances for survival and dignity, we nevertheless continue that research which will permit us to replace mere suspicion with relatively hard knowledge.

*"Capability Distribution, Uncertainty, and Major Power War, 1820–1965," by J. David Singer et al., is reprinted from* Peace, War, and Numbers, *Bruce M. Russett, editor, © 1972, pp. 19–48, by permission of the Publisher, Sage Publications, Inc.*

# 15

# Foreign Policy Indicators:
# Predictors of War in
# History and in the
# State of the World Message

*With Melvin Small*

*Throughout, I have spoken of the vision that nurtures many peace researchers—the hope that our findings and insights might be put to practical use. That use is, of course, a delicate matter, and one on which there is much disagreement. In addition to some of the normative and ideological issues raised earlier in this volume, there are very real limits on the applicability of the actual research once it has been done.*

*Taking the two system-level analyses presented in chapters 13 and 14 as examples, one can see the difficulty. Suppose, in the first instance, that we had found a* really *strong positive association between alliance aggregation and the incidence of war in the current century. Should this lead foreign policy elites to shun alliances? If so, which types of alliances, with which types of partners, and at what point during, or before, a conflict sequence? And even if these empirical questions were already answered, should the decision makers believe that the pattern will hold in the future? How should they respond to the probabilistic nature of our findings, given their usual concern with a highly specific "point prediction"? Similarly, in the second of these papers, what do the elites or counterelites do with the discovery that high-capability concentrations were closely associated with war in the nineteenth century? Do they promptly seek to accelerate the industrialization and military preparedness of the weaker nations and cut back on that of the stronger? How about their own preparedness, especially if a lower capability would improve the distribution?*

*On top of these constraints, there is the matter of whether intervention is possible. Even if desirable, to what extent can we—establishment or antiestablishment—hope to change and shape those predictor variables that seem to be affecting the likelihood of war? A fair percentage of such variables may have a great deal of explanatory and predictive power (desirable from a* pure *science point of view), but may be barely manipulable (undesirable from an* applied *science point of view). Sometimes this is because the changing values of such variables are due to events and conditions of the past, over which we no longer have any control; sometimes it is because we can only modify these variables so slowly as to make their manipulation worthless in the short run; and sometimes we just have no idea as to what factors, in turn, shape and affect those that we want to change, and we are therefore unable to get at them.*

*These considerations have, unfortunately, led a good many people to condemn the policy science–peace research approach, and a belated awareness of them has led others to drop out of peace research after an initial, but naive, enthusiasm. While I defer to no one in my belief that rigorous research will, in the* long *run, reduce the incidence of war by reducing the error rate in foreign policy prediction, I also see some short-run gains. One is the usefulness of habituating foreign policy elites and their critics to the scientific mode. Just reading and thinking about some of the more creative and rigorous books and articles in world politics can lead to a greater intellectual sophistication and, quite likely, an awareness that there is room for improvement in the way problems are currently analyzed. Similarly, the experience might serve to alert them to new factors and the relationships among them, expand their conceptual repertoires, and even suggest ways in which they might begin to clarify, operationalize, and measure those factors of a more familiar sort.*

*In addition, studies such as those discussed above can certainly serve to challenge some unquestioned assumptions and raise doubts about some widely accepted models and metaphors. As should be apparent, none of our research yet comes close to the degree of scientific rigor and social relevance that I think possible, but I believe that steady progress is being made in that direction. In the interim, it is possible that some of our work might play a marginally useful role in the short run, and that consideration led us to prepare this paper.[1] It was first presented to a panel on international indicators at the American Political Science Association meetings in 1972; a few weeks later, Melvin Small presented it in Rome at a conference arranged by the Italian Foreign Ministry. Following that conference (replete with a formal banquet and liveried footmen in marbled halls) we compressed the paper, ultimately examining only three of the propositions about the maintenance of peace from the first several "state of the world" messages. Once completed, the paper was submitted to* Foreign Affairs *and* Foreign

Policy. *Even with a brief statistical primer attached, neither of these august reviews found the manuscript attractive, but it was shortly thereafter accepted by Edward Quade and his Rand Corporation associates for the more avant-garde* Policy Sciences.

Among the several "movements" of the past decade, one of the more interesting and durable is the social indicators movement. In an effort to cope with the increasing complexities of social planning, as well as with the increasing militance of the socially disadvantaged, practitioners and academics have sought to develop more effective tools for the planning, executing, and evaluating of social policy. Central to that enterprise has been the effort to convert many of the vague notions associated with "quality of life" into more precise and operational language. As a result, we now have quantitative indicators which are designed to tap or reflect not only such tangible conditions as "full employment" or "national product," but more elusive conditions such as the job satisfaction, health care, educational achievement, and environmental quality of a given population.[2]

As these illustrations make clear, the historical origins are found largely in the area of economic activity, with such measurement occurring in the "softer" sectors only in the more recent period. While it is likely, for reasons that will become clear as this paper unfolds, that some of us may have gone overboard in our enthusiasm for these more contemporary indicators, they have already begun to demonstrate their utility.[3] In the foreign policy sector, on the other hand, the utility of indicators has been largely ignored. Outside of the thoughtful exhortations of scholars such as Bobrow, one finds little explicit attention to the kinds of indicator that might be developed, or the ways in which they might improve the efficacy and/or humaneness of national foreign policies (Bobrow and Schwartz 1968; Bobrow 1969; 1970). In the article which follows, we hope to focus attention on some of the possible applications of foreign policy indicators and to illustrate the potential that may already lie close at hand.

## Indicators and Their Foreign Policy Applications

In this opening section we cover a number of preliminary points before turning to our specific assignment. First, we attempt to define what we mean by indicators, how they are devised and evaluated, and how they may be differentiated. We then go on to summarize their possible roles in the policy process. Following these preliminaries, we will turn to a more specific application of certain indicators that, while devised for basic research, may turn out to be useful for applied prognosis as well.

## Indicators as Proxies

When we speak of indicators in the context of social phenomena, it is useful to distinguish between two different usages of the term. The first and most familiar usage is in the sense of a proxy, surrogate, symptom, representation, measure, or index. That is, many of the concepts that we use in describing social phenomena do not have easily observed empirical referents. Rather, we make an inferential leap of greater or lesser magnitude from some trace or proxy, which we *do* observe, back to the phenomenon of interest, which often remains unobserved. The condition or event in which we are interested may be unobserved because it has occurred in the past and is gone from sight, or is spread over too broad a space, or has too many component elements, or is sufficiently intangible as to lie beyond the human senses. To illustrate, we may infer the severity of a war from the battle-deaths estimates that are compiled afterward, or the industrial capability of a nation from its steel production, or the material quality of life from infant mortality rates, or the ego strength of an individual from his responses to certain projective tests, or the efficacy of a therapeutic treatment from the patients' average stay in hospital.

In other words, we try to "operationalize" the more elusive concept or variable by devising a procedure through which its presence, strength, or rate of change might be indirectly measured or inferred. If the same operation or procedure, applied to the same phenomenon, gives the same "reading" regardless of who conducts it or when, we say that the index or indicator is a *reliable* one. But devising reliable indicators is only part of the struggle to "observe the unobservable." More difficult and ambiguous is the *validity* of an indicator: the extent to which it really does tap or reflect the phenomenon we claim to be getting at and measuring. Whereas reliability is easily demonstrated by repeated observational tests, validity always remains partially a matter of judgment. There are, however, some ways in which we can go beyond mere assertion as to the validity of an indicator. One is the extent to which an alternative indicator of the allegedly identical phenomenon gives us a set of readings which are highly correlated with those produced by the original indicator. For example, caloric intake might correlate highly (but negatively) with infant mortality, suggesting that both might be valid indicators of material quality of life; or the energy consumption of a nation might correlate highly with its steel production, strengthening our confidence in the validity of both as possible indicators of industrial capability.

A second strategy in the search for validity is to ascertain whether the readings on our indicator conform to what one's model or "theory" would predict. If, for example, our model predicts that the "diplomatic interdependence" of pairs of nations should increase as their trade increases, and the number of nations with whom they both have diplomatic relations does indeed increase following a rise in their trade, we have some grounds for believing that the number of nations with whom both members of each pair have relations is a valid indicator of their diplomatic interdependence.

But when all is said and done, the most important test is that of "face validity": Are competent specialists persuaded that the indicator really taps the unobserved phenomenon? And that usually rests, in turn, on the extent to which we believe that: (a) changes in the unobserved phenomenon of interest lead to, or cause, commensurate changes in the value of the indicator; (b) changes in the value of the proxy or trace that serves as the indicator will lead to, or cause, commensurate changes in the actual event or condition of interest; or (c) the values of the variable and its alleged indicator at least rise and fall together, despite the absence of any causal link. In the latter case it may merely be that some third factor exercises an equally strong impact on both the variable and its indicator.

### Indicators as Predictors

Shifting now from the use of indicators as proxies for, or traces of, some less readily observed phenomenon, there is a second and more complex role for social indicators. This is the predictive or early warning role, in which the indicator continues to serve as a proxy or reflection of some unobserved phenomenon, while at the same time it also predicts the changes in the magnitude of some *subsequent* phenomenon. That is, its magnitude is supposed to rise and fall with the magnitude of both the subsequent phenomenon and the *indicator of* that latter event or condition. While an indicator, when used for proxy purposes, is usually measured after (or simultaneous with) changes in the phenomenon it supposedly reflects, it is measured beforehand when used for predictive purposes.

More important than temporal sequence, however, is the extent to which our predictor covaries with *another indicator* rather than the extent to which it covaries with some unobserved phenomenon. While this makes it easier to ascertain the degree of covariation, it also means that we must now deal with the problems of reliability and validity of the indicators at *each* end of the chain. These reliability and validity links are illustrated in the following diagram, in which time runs from left to right and observability runs from top to bottom.

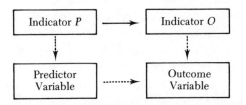

The broken vertical lines leading down from the indicators to the variables emphasize that the latter will often lie below some threshold of direct observability, and their presence or strength will thus have to be inferred from the presence and strength of the indicators which we devise to represent them. The solid line between indicators *P* and *O* reminds us that it is a simple matter to observe the correlation or covariation between our predictive and outcome indicators.

But the very simplicity of ascertaining the correlation between indicators can often mislead us into thinking that we have, by that operation, ascertained the predictive, and perhaps even the causal, connection between the unobserved phenomena themselves. If we are merely inferring a *predictive* relationship between the variables, the only (!) threat to that inference lies in the validity and the reliability of our two indicators. But if we want to infer, from a strong correlation between indicators *P* and *O*, that changes in the predictor variable *cause* changes in the outcome variable, all sorts of additional difficulties arise. Since, however, our concern here is not with explanation and causality, but only with the more manageable problem of early warning and prediction, we can sidestep these philosophical issues for the nonce. Suffice to say, then, that the weak dotted line conveys the tenuousness of any causal link between the two variables, as well as the extent to which the predictive link between them depends on the quality of their respective indicators.


## The Policy Uses of Indicators

Bearing in mind these two meanings of indicator, as well as the dangers of overinterpretation, let us next mention some of the ways in which each type of indicator might be used for policy purposes. They may, of course, be useful not only in: (a) the formulation of policy; but in (b) the monitoring of its execution; and (c) the evaluation of its success.

In the formulation stage, we may use indicators in both their proxy and predictor roles. The former are used to tell us something of the state of the world at the moment, and the direction and rate of change in the conditions and events of interest. The latter may help us to predict which outcomes are most likely to arise out of those conditions, and thus, which of them should be perpetuated (or modified) in order to arrive at (or avoid) some future outcome. In the monitoring stage, we rely primarily on proxy indicators, hoping that they can tell us whether or not the assigned or agreed actions have been executed, and how close certain of the transition conditions are to those expected and thought of as necessary to a successful outcome. And in the evaluation stage, we again turn to proxy indicators to measure the success of the policy, by observing the discrepancy between the ultimate outcome and that which we had predicted and preferred. Moreover, such objective evaluation can be utilized for self-correcting feedback purposes, and provide the basis for change in our predictive models. That is, if the magnitude of the outcome indicator is not as predicted, we know that the appropriate predictor conditions were not those that the model led us to believe, and that other preconditions will have to be established to arrive at the desired outcome. Needless to say, if the indicator is not a valid one, or if the numbers are fictitious, reliance on them can be disastrous. In the Vietnam War, for example, U.S. personnel appear to have not only inflated such indicators as body counts and truck interdictions, but, worse yet, assumed that they were valid indicators of military success.

For predictive indicators to be of much use, however, they must not only satisfy the measurement criteria of reliability and validity. Whereas the historian or political scientist is often satisfied with the construction of an indicator that merely meets these two criteria—on the assumption that it will in due course be scientifically useful—the policy maker must demand more. He or she must be satisfied that it is also a *dependable* predictor. Either through his own experience, or on the basis of highly credible academic research, he must be persuaded that, in a reasonably large number of cases, the indicator turns out to be a solid predictor. Now, some will ask *how* solid a job of prediction the indicator or index must do before it becomes useful in the policy process. Some officials will insist on 100 percent performance, and will shy away from any indicator unless there is a demonstrated correlation of 1.0 between it and the hoped for, or feared, outcome. The purist would, for example, refuse to take seriously a prediction that increased military pressure by A leads to increased diplomatic resistance from B unless that association has *always* occurred.

This seems overly conservative in two ways. First, it ignores the hard fact that foreign offices are always playing the odds, and no matter how unconscious the operation may be, the estimation of probabilities goes into almost all predictions. Second, this very tendency to think probabilistically reflects an important reality of the political world: Very few events or conditions *are* certain. It is not only the state of our knowledge about diplomatic behavior and the changing state of the global system; it is also that *some* degree of randomness will always inhere in these phenomena. Thus, we urge that at this early stage in the development of solid knowledge about international politics, we set more modest and realistic standards. We are not prepared to state what the performance level of an indicator should be in order to take it seriously, but we would point out that, if track records *were* kept, most of us would hope to do better than the two-out-of-three score of U.S. experts on nonroutine predictions.[4]

## Predictive Indicators in the State of the World Message

So much, then, for the usefulness of foreign policy indicators in the abstract. Let us shift now to a more specific real world context, in which we find some promising signs of an increased role for such indicators. Reference is to the "state of the world" message inaugurated by President Nixon and his special assistant for national security affairs, Henry Kissinger.

The first of these was presented to the Congress, and the wider world at home and abroad, at the beginning of Nixon's second year in the White House (18 February 1970). Entitled *U.S. Foreign Policy for the 1970s: A New Strategy for Peace*, it represented both a report on the administration's first year of foreign policy stewardship and a statement of predictions and preferences regarding the near and middle future. Linked in style and timing to the traditional State of the Union message, it was quickly dubbed—with official encouragement—the "state of the world" message. The second, third, and fourth ones (25 February 1971, 9 February 1972, and 3 May 1973) were similar in form and orientation to the first, and like their predecessor, carried the peace theme in the subtitle.

While there is always some tendency to dismiss such reports as self-serving propaganda and political smokescreen, these state of the world messages obviously have other purposes as well.[5] In addition to assuring the Congress, the media, and the domestic public of the administration's competence, patriotism, farsightedness, and commitment to peace, the document also meets two other important needs. One is that of communicating a range of signals to other governments, friendly and otherwise, and to some of the world's intergovernmental organizations, in a fairly general and noncommittal fashion. The other is to provide guidance and legitimation to U.S. officials in Washington and in the field.

Finally, although the authors may not have so intended, the state of the world message provides, in one place, the sort of general overview of world politics that policy analysts may examine for a variety of purposes. One might, by techniques ranging from those of biblical exegesis to quantitative content analysis, search for all sorts of patterns, trends, deviations, inconsistencies, subtle clues, blunt warnings, articulated and unarticulated premises, and so forth.[6] Our purpose is more limited, and our technique quite simple.

Given the persistence of the "peace" theme in all four messages to date, we sought to tap the administration's collective views as to which particular events and conditions make for peace, conflict, and war in the modern global system and its subsystems. More specifically—and even allowing for the possibility of intentionally misleading statements or deliberately vague interagency compromise phrases—the document offers an excellent opportunity to identify the sorts of indicators used by this administration, implicitly or explicitly, to predict to, or away from, war. Once these indicators have been "teased out" of the document, we might then be able to convert them into more operational language and then ascertain the extent to which they *have* been dependable predictive indicators in the past. That is, given the tendency of the U.S. and other foreign policy establishments to base their forecasts on "lessons of the past" and what "history tells," it is not inappropriate to ask how closely those "lessons" conform to the systematically observed regularities.

In so doing, however, we cannot overemphasize the tentative nature of this comparison. First, despite a conscientious effort to avoid it, we may have misinterpreted the phraseology of these reports, and attributed a position to the administration which is not justified. This danger is more real when dealing with preoperational statements, and as foreign policy makers begin to speak in more precise terms, via the explicit use of indicators, the possibility of misinterpretation will, of course, decline. Second, we are looking here at only a small part of the historical evidence: that which has been generated by a single research enterprise, the Correlates of War project at The University of Michigan. When the work of such scholars as North and Rosecrance and their colleagues is brought to bear, a more adequate test of these historical predictions (or postdictions) will be possible (see Choucri and North 1975; Rosecrance 1963).[7] And, third, given the tentative nature of the results emerging from these projects, it would be premature to claim that we have really pinned down the historical correlations to which we refer.

What we have attempted here, then, is a two-step operation involving these reports. First, we have selected from them a number of predictive statements which embody, if only implicitly, the idea of early warning indicators in the area of war and peace. These are statements which predict that certain preconditions will increase the probability of war for the international system, its regions, or certain specific nations. Second, we have translated these statements into more operational language, using the indicators which had been devised earlier for the Correlates of War project. Rather than spell out the reasoning and procedures behind each of these indicators here, we will cite the book or article in which that information can be found.[8] And, third, we have asked—in a tentative and illustrative fashion only—how regularly the predictor indicators and the war outcomes have been associated in the manner postulated by the administration. Thus, in each of the following sections, we will offer the predictive statement as it appears in one of the state of the world reports, summarize how we convert the predictor variable into an operational indicator, and examine the extent to which it has been correlated with war over the century and a half from the Congress of Vienna through 1965.[9]

*Acceptance of War Leads to More War*

Let us turn now to the first of the predictors we have selected for discussion from the state of the world messages. One of the more widely accepted propositions in the folklore of international politics is that war begets war, on the premise that: (a) the victorious initiator of war will seek to repeat his success; (b) that another will be encouraged by the example; or (c) that the defeated party will, alone or with others, move as soon as feasible to settle old scores. In any event, we find in the 1972 report (p. 148) the proposition that "the resort to military solutions, if accepted, would only tempt other nations in delicately poised regions of tension to try the same."

The predictor variable, like most of those used in diplomacy, can be interpreted (and thus operationalized) in several ways. At one extreme, we can merely ask whether wars come in bunches like epidemics. At the other, we can set up increasingly restricted conditions and ask, for example, whether initiators of wars are more likely to do so again when they have emerged victorious and/or unchallenged; since the number of versions of this hypothesis is quite large, and we hope to examine them in a fairly exhaustive fashion in a subsequent paper, here we will look at just a few versions for purposes of illustration.

In its simplest form, then, we can interpret "resort to military solutions" to mean war in general. Historically, does war lead to more war? During the 150 years from 1816 through 1965, 93 serious international wars began (wars with 1,000 or more battle deaths). How often were such wars followed by another within the same or subsequent year?[10] It turns out that 53 (57 percent) of the 93 wars were so followed by another war. But what does this tell us about war contagion? For instance, how likely is it that those 53 wars would have been followed shortly by another war, on the basis of chance alone?

To test this "null" hypothesis (that it was mere chance), we use the year as our unit of analysis, and ask whether those years during which international war began were more likely to be followed by another war in the same or subsequent year than were those years in which no war began. It turns out that the 93 wars in our study began in 70 different years. Of those 70 war years, 51 saw the onset of one war, 16 saw two wars begin, two years saw three wars, and one year was cursed with the onset of four. Of the 51 single-war years, 22 were followed by at least one war in the subsequent year. Those 22,

Table 1a.  **Frequency with Which War Years Are Followed by War Years, 1816-1965**

|  |  | War year? | | |
|---|---|---|---|---|
|  |  | *Yes* | *No* | |
| War | Yes | 41 | 40 | $\chi^2$ = 1.11 |
| follows? | No | 29 | 40 | $Q$ = 0.17 |
|  |  | 70 + | 80 | = 150 |

Table 1b.  **Nineteenth Century**

|  |  | War year? | | |
|---|---|---|---|---|
|  |  | *Yes* | *No* | |
| War | Yes | 31 | 21 | $\chi^2$ = 2.00 |
| follows? | No | 14 | 18 | $Q$ = 0.31 |
|  |  | 45 + | 39 | = 84 |

Table 1c.  **Twentieth Century**

|  |  | War year? | | |
|---|---|---|---|---|
|  |  | *Yes* | *No* | |
| War | Yes | 10 | 19 | $\chi^2$ = 0.26 |
| follows? | No | 15 | 22 | $Q$ = 1.13 |
|  |  | 23 + | 41 | = 66 |

plus the 19 multiple-war years, make a total of 41 years in which war that began in one year was followed by at least one more beginning in the same or subsequent year. That is, while 41 war years were followed by subsequent war years, this also holds for 40 nonwar years. This is a negligible difference and could easily have occurred by chance alone. Turning the question around, we can ask how many war and nonwar years were followed by nonwar years. Here it turns out that 29 of the war years and 40 of the nonwar years were not followed by the onset of a new war in the next year. And while this difference is greater than the first—and is in the direction predicted by the president's message—it is nevertheless far from impressive.

Using the contingency table (table 1a) to summarize these figures, we set up two columns, at the bottom of which we show that 70 of the 150 years studied were marked by the onset of one or more serious wars, while 80 were not. Next we set up two rows, so that we can divide the two columns between those years that were followed by war and those that were not. With the four figures (plus the column totals and *their* sum, as a check on our arithmetic, and for later purposes of estimating the statistical significance of our results) we can calculate the extent to which the observed distribution deviates from pure randomness. That is, if the phenomena being examined were completely random, and without some meaningful pattern, all four cells would contain approximately the same number of cases, or about 37 or 38. Thus, by visual inspection alone, we see that the 41–40 difference between war and nonwar years followed by war years is not particularly great, whereas the 29–40 difference seems somewhat sharper. But if we calculate more precisely the strength of association, we find a Yule's $Q$ score of only 0.17. And, since we can occasionally get low $Q$s which are nevertheless statistically significant, as well as high $Q$s by chance alone, we compute the deviation from randomness as reflected in a coefficient such as $\chi^2$ (chi-square) and then check it out in a significance table. In this case, the $\chi^2$ value of 1.11 is so low that we conclude it could easily have emerged by sheer chance.

But this is, after all, much too primitive a test of the administration's hypothesis, and a number of more refined ones seem to be called for. To illustrate, given the possibility that there are important differences between the nineteenth and twentieth centuries, it makes sense to test the war-begets-war hypothesis for the two periods separately. In the nineteenth (table 1b), where 45 of the 84 years (1816 through 1899) saw the onset of war, 31 of them were indeed soon followed by another war, whereas only 14 were not. While not dramatic, this is certainly in the direction postulated by the state of the world message. In the twentieth, on the other hand (table 1c), where 25 of the 66 years (1900 through 1965) saw the onset of war, only 10 were followed by another war year, whereas 15 were not. This is contrary to the prediction, but again, not overwhelmingly so. Rather than rely on visual inspection of these two sets of figures, though, we once more invoke the $Q$ and $\chi^2$ formulae, which take account of the figures in all four cells of each century's matrix. And, as we would suspect from the very probable $\chi^2$ values of 2.00 and 0.26 respectively, the $Q$ values are also sufficiently low (0.31 and 0.13) to confirm that the historical pattern was quite weak in each of the centuries separately.

But this may still be too crude an interpretation of the administration's proposition. Perhaps the phrase "if accepted" may well be

Table 2.  Frequency with Which Wars in Which Victim Was Not
Aided Are Followed by War

|  |  | Victim aided? | | | |
|---|---|---|---|---|---|
|  |  | *Yes* | *No* | | |
| War | Yes | 6 | 15 | | $\chi^2 = 0.12$ |
| follows? | No | 7 | 22 | | $Q = 0.11$ |
|  |  | 13 | + 37 | = 50 | |

essential to an understanding of the authors' meaning: that the
victim of armed attack was not promptly and vigorously joined by
others who came to its defense. Thus, we now ask how frequently we
find such cases followed by subsequent resort to force. Restricting
ourselves to the 50 interstate wars which mark the 1816-1965
period (thus excluding the colonial and imperial wars, which rarely
engaged third parties), our table 2 matrix shows that 13 were marked
by such intervention on the side of those who were attacked, while
37 were not.[11] Since six of the 13 former cases (46 percent) were
soon followed by another war and 15 of the 37 latter were (41
percent), it would appear to make little difference whether "resort to
military solutions" was accepted by the rest of the nations in the
system or not. That is, wars in which the victim is left to fight alone
are not significantly more likely to be followed by more war than
those in which the victim of armed attack *is* joined by others.

Alternatively, "accepted" could be interpreted to mean that the
initiators were permitted to emerge victorious, and that under *those*
conditions, war might beget more war. Here again (table 3a) the
evidence is mixed. Thus, of the 50 interstate wars in our population
of cases, the initiators "won" 34 of them.[12] In 12 of those 34 cases
(35 percent), renewed interstate warfare broke out in the near
future. Conversely, on those 16 occasions in which the initiator did
*not* win, the number followed by war was 9 (56 percent). While this
is a higher proportional figure, the $Q$ value of 0.40 is not quite
enough to justify the counterconclusion that peace is best preserved
by permitting the initiator to win.

In this context, we might again ask whether the historical evidence is more solid in one or the other of our two centuries. In the
nineteenth, which saw 27 of the 50 interstate wars (table 3b), 19
were won by the initiator. But only 6 of those 19, or 32 percent,
were followed by war, while 6 of the 8, or 75 percent, which were
*lost* by the initiator were so followed. Here, the $Q$ coefficient is a
rather strong 9.73, and the $\chi^2$ of 4.30 *is* strong enough to permit a

**Table 3a. Frequency with Which Wars in Which Initiator Wins Are Followed by War**

|  |  | Initiator wins? | |  |
|---|---|---|---|---|
|  |  | *Yes* | *No* |  |
| War | Yes | 12 | 9 | $\chi^2 = 1.96$ |
| follows? | No | 22 | 7 | $Q = 0.40$ |
|  |  | 34   +   16   = 50 | | |

**Table 3b. Nineteenth Century**

|  |  | Initiator wins? | |  |
|---|---|---|---|---|
|  |  | *Yes* | *No* |  |
| War | Yes | 6 | 6 | $\chi^2 = 4.30; p < 0.05$ |
| follows? | No | 13 | 2 | $Q = 0.73$ |
|  |  | 19   +   8   = 27 | | |

**Table 3c. Twentieth Century**

|  |  | Initiator wins? | |  |
|---|---|---|---|---|
|  |  | *Yes* | *No* |  |
| War | Yes | 7 | 2 | $\chi^2 = 1.03$ |
| follows | No | 8 | 6 | $Q = 0.45$ |
|  |  | 15   +   8   = 23 | | |

rejection of the null hypothesis: $p < 0.05$ means that it had a probability of less than 5 percent of occurring by sheer chance. The interesting thing, however, is that the pattern is quite the opposite of that predicted by the administration. In other words, for the nineteenth century, wars that the initiator *lost* were more likely to be quickly followed by another.

What about the twentieth century? Table 3c shows 7 of the 15 (47 percent) wars *won* by the initiator in this century were soon followed by war, while only 2 of the 8 (25 percent) in which the initiator *lost* were so followed—making for a pattern just the reverse of the nineteenth-century experience. However, in this century, the relationships, while supporting the administration's prediction, are not strong enough to permit ready acceptance of the hypothesis that the initiator's being allowed to win is more likely to lead to another war.

Table 4. Frequency with Which Wars in Which Victim Was Aided Successfully Are Followed by War

|  |  | Victim aided successfully? | |  |
|  |  | *Yes* | *No* |  |
| War | Yes | 5 | 1 | $\chi^2 = 0.31$ |
| follows? | No | 4 | 3 | $Q = 0.58$ |
|  |  | 9   + | 4   = 13 |  |

So far, we have found little support for the notion that wars in which the victim nations are defended by other nations are less likely to be followed by another war than wars in which the victim is *not* defended. The same holds for the notion that defeating the initiator will inhibit the prompt beginning of other wars. But there are further questions that we may ask. For example, among those specific cases in which the victim nation *is* defended by others, are the wars that are won by the initiator more likely to be followed by war? The answer comes as something of a surprise to those of us raised on the ideas of collective defense and collective security. As table 4 shows, in the 13 cases that were marked by military support of the victim, the initiator was turned back 9 times. But in 5 of those cases, the system saw additional war in the same or following year. On the other hand, if the initiator prevailed despite military support for his victim (it happened 4 times), there is only one case in which additional war occurred. The $Q$ coefficient of 0.58 comes close to suggesting that, if peace be the sole concern, it is better for the initiator to win.

Another way to look at this question is to shift from the aggregated systemic level of analysis, and to focus on the specific nations themselves. Here we ask whether those nations which initiated war turn out to initiate another war within the following ten years. As table 5 indicates, it matters a great deal whether the initiator emerged victorious or not. That is, of the 73 nations that were on the initiating side, only 13 of them were initiators again within the decade. But 12 of those 13 had won the first war, and the high $Q$ and $\chi^2$ values show that this is a very strong and statistically significant relationship; that is, such a $\chi^2$ had less than a 2 percent probability of occurring by chance alone.

Further evidence as to the effect of victory is seen in table 6, where the coefficients are even more persuasive. Here, we see that of the 98 nations that were on the side which was attacked, only 11 of

**Table 5. Frequency with Which Initiators of War Soon Initiate Another War**

|  |  | Initiators win? | |  |
|---|---|---|---|---|
|  |  | *Yes* | *No* |  |
| Initiates | Yes | 12 | 1 | $\chi^2 = 5.82; p < 0.02$ |
| another war? | No | 34 | 26 | $Q = 0.80$ |
|  |  | 46 + | 27 = 73 |  |

them turned around and initiated war within the decade. But again, 10 of those 11 future initiators, even though often caught unprepared, nevertheless emerged on the winning side.

In sum, these two analyses suggest that it is not so much that war begets war, since very few nations initiate wars in the decades following prior war experience, but that *victorious* war begets war, and this finding is certainly consonant with the administration's hypothesis. More generally, we see that the simple proposition is in fact a rather complex one, and that the alternative ways of interpreting and testing it (via many alternative indicators) lead to rather different conclusions. The evidence, then, is far from complete, and in a subsequent paper we intend to examine the epidemiology question in considerably greater detail.

*Weakness Leads to War*

A close corollary of the proposition that the global community's *acquiescence* in the initiation of war will lead to more war is that which tells us that relative *weakness* leads to war. This may be interpreted as a national level prediction, with weaker nations being more vulnerable and therefore more likely to *have* to fight in self-defense; it may also be interpreted in systemic terms, with weakness

**Table 6. Frequency with Which Victims of Attack Soon Initiate Another War**

|  |  | Victim wins? | |  |
|---|---|---|---|---|
|  |  | *Yes* | *No* |  |
| Initiates | Yes | 10 | 1 | $\chi^2 = 6.77; p < 0.01$ |
| another war? | No | 43 | 44 | $Q = 0.82$ |
|  |  | 53 + | 45 = 98 |  |

ón the part of the "peace loving" (or "status quo") nations serving as a temptation to the stronger. This type of predictive statement finds repeated expression in all four of the administration's reports on the state of the world. It appears in particularly crisp language in the first of these: "Peace requires strength. So long as there are those who would threaten our vital interests and those of our allies with military force, we must be strong. American weakness could tempt would-be aggressors to make dangerous miscalculations" (p. 4). And the theme is echoed in 1972: "American weakness would make no contribution to peace. On the contrary, it would undermine prospects for peace" (p. 155).

In discussing the relationship, past or predicted, between war-proneness and national power or strength, we quickly come face to face with the familiar question of "what is power?" In a forthcoming volume, we will discuss that question in painstaking detail, but here we must be brief. First, there is the difference between a nation's power *base* or *potential* on the one hand, and military preparedness or other indices of force *in being*, on the other. Second, the bases of power have changed across time. Third, a nation's capacity to exercise influence may range considerably across space. The indicator we employ here is a very general one, and that limitation should be kept in mind as the discussion unfolds.

We use a straightforward measure in which we combine six factors: steel production, energy consumption, urban population, the square root of total population, armed forces size, and military expenditure. For more thorough analyses, we use several different combinations and weightings of these six, but here we will merely compute each nation's share of each element's distribution in the system, and then compute the average of its percentage shares. Thus, if a nation has 8 percent of the system's armed forces, steel production, and urban population, and 12 percent if its military expenditures, energy consumption, and total population (converted to its square root), its composite score would be 10 percent. In the analysis at hand, restricted only to the major powers for the 150-year period, the rankings and scores turn out to be remarkably close to those that a diplomatic historian might expect; in other words, the face validity of the indicator—as a reflection of general power potential—appears to be quite high. (For a more restricted test, and perhaps one more appropriate to the administration's argument, we might want to use the military dimensions only, or better yet, an indicator which reflects the fraction of overall capabilities that has been allocated to military preparedness.)

## Table 7. Relative Capabilities of Major Powers Prior to Their Entry into Inter-State Wars

| | Above Major Power Average | | Below Major Power Average | |
|---|---|---|---|---|
| | *Steady or Rising* | *Falling* | *Steady or Rising* | *Falling* |
| France | Franco-Span, 1823<br>Navarino Bay, 1827<br>Crimean, 1854<br>Franco-Mex, 1862<br>Franco-Pruss, 1870 | Roman Repub, 1849<br>*Ital Unif, 1859*<br>Sino-French, 1884 | *WW I, 1914* | *WW II, 1939*<br>Korean, 1951<br>Sinai, 1956 |
| Britain | Anglo-Persian, 1856 | Navarino Bay, 1827<br>Crimean, 1854<br>*WW I, 1914* | | *WW II, 1939*<br>Korean, 1950<br>Sinai, 1956 |
| Germany | *WW I, 1914*<br>*WW II, 1939* | | 2nd Schles-Holstein, 1864<br>Seven Weeks, 1866<br>*Franco-Pruss, 1870* | 1st Schles-Holstein, 1848 |
| Aust-Hung | | | Ital Unif, 1859 | Austro-Sardin, 1848<br>Roman Repub, 1849<br>2nd Schles-Holstein, 1864<br>*Seven Weeks, 1866*<br>*WW I, 1914* |
| Italy | | | Italo-Roman, 1860*<br>Italo-Sicil, 1860*<br>*WW I, 1915* | Seven Weeks, 1866<br>Italo-Turk, 1911<br>Italo-Ethiop, 1935<br>WW II, 1940 |
| Russia | Crimean, 1853<br>Russo-Jap, 1904<br>*Russo-Jap, 1939*<br>Russo-Finn, 1939<br>*WW II, 1941* | Navarino Bay, 1827<br>Russo-Turk, 1828<br>Russo-Hung, 1956 | *WW I, 1914* | Russo-Turk, 1877 |
| U.S. | | *WW I, 1914*<br>*WW II, 1939*<br>Korean, 1950 | | |

Table 7. Relative Capabilities of Major Powers Prior to Their Entry into Inter-State Wars *(Cont.)*

|        | Above Major Power Average | | Below Major Power Average | |
|--------|--------------------|---------|--------------------|---------|
|        | *Steady or Rising* | *Falling* | *Steady or Rising* | *Falling* |
| China  |                    |         | Korean, 1950<br>Sino-Indian, 1962 |         |
| Japan  |                    |         | Russo-Jap, 1904<br>*WW I, 1914*<br>Manchurian, 1931<br>Russo-Jap, 1939<br>WW II, 1941 | Sino-Jap,<br>1937 |
| Total  | 13                 | 12      | 16                 | 18      |

Notes: (1) Italics—Attacked by another major.
      (2) Dates—Year of Entry
      (3) *—New in system and no prior measurement of its capability.

Using this composite indicator, *does* it turn out that major powers are more likely to get into war, or to be attacked, when they are: (a) nearer the bottom of the capability scale; or (b) experiencing a decline in relative power? In table 7, we present a rough summary of where each major power stood vis-à-vis the others in that subset on the eve of its serious interstate wars, as well as the direction in which its capabilities tended to be moving, in regard to the average score of the majors at that time.

In summarizing so large a body of information in such a table, we must emphasize several limitations. First, as already noted, our composite capability measure is still a tentative one whose validity is far from conclusive. Second, we are still refining the data on which the indicator is based. Third, specification of initiators and defenders in war is by no means self-evident, and as we complete our historical reconstruction of the events leading up to each war, there may be revisions as well as refinements in our classifications. With these caveats in mind, we look at table 7, which lists the capability status of each major power on the eve of its entries into interstate wars over the 150 years under study.

Of the total of 59 war entries, 34 occurred when the combatant state was weaker than the average major power, while only 25 occurred when it was above the average on the composite capabilities indicator (see column totals in tables 7 and 8). To the extent that we have a valid indicator of strength and that the average score consti-tutes a reasonable cutting point between the weaker and the stronger, the administration's prediction finds some historical sup-

Table 8. Relative Capability Frequencies of Major Power Participants

|  | Above | Below |  |  |
|---|---|---|---|---|
| Steady or rising | 13 | 16 | $\chi^2$ | 0.10 |
|  |  |  | $Q$ = | 0.14 |
| Falling | 12 | 18 |  |  |
|  | 25   + | 34   = 59 |  |  |

port. Next, we ask whether that pattern is reinforced by the association between the nation's war experiences and the rise, stability, or decline in their capability scores (see totals in table 7 and rows of table 8). Here we find virtually no difference: 30 occur when the major power's score is falling, and 29 when it is either rising or holding steady. As to the combined "effect" of both scores, the 13-12 and 16-18 figures reinforce the impression that present strength is moderately important and that direction of change is of minor consequence. On the other hand, the U.S. experience is unique in that all three of its wars (since joining the major power class) began while it was in the upper half, but on the decline.

It is, of course, one thing to participate in a serious war and quite another to be more or less *compelled* to do so, as a result of another power's initiation of hostilities. Thus, we now move on to refine our inquiry, and ask how frequently the *victims* of military assault by another major power were on the high or low side of the major power average, and whether their shares of the capability pie were rising, holding steady, or falling. As the $Q$ value of 0.20 and the $\chi^2$ of 0.09 in table 9 show, this version of the administration's proposition stands up even less well. Among the 9 major power victims, 5 were above average in capability while 4 were below, and 5 were steady or rising while 4 were falling. These cell entries are as near

Table 9. Relative Capability Frequencies of Major Power Victims of War Initiation

|  | Above | Below |  |  |
|---|---|---|---|---|
| Steady or rising | Crimean Russo-Jap (04) Russo-Jap (39) | WWI Fr-Pruss. | $\chi^2$ = 0.09 |  |
| Falling | Ital. Unif. Korean | WWII Seven Weeks | $Q$ = 0.20 |  |
|  | 5   + | 4   = 9 |  |  |

Table 10.  Relative Capability Frequencies of Victims Versus
Initiators in Major Power Wars

|  | Victim Stronger | Victim Weaker |  |
|---|---|---|---|
| Steady or rising |  | Crimean Fr-Pruss. |  |
|  |  |  | $\chi^2 = 0.51$ |
| Falling | Ital. Unif. Russo-Jap (04) Russo-Jap (39) Korean | Seven Weeks WW II WW I | $Q$ cannot be calculated when any cell is empty |

equality as possible, given the $N$ of 9. Historically, therefore, we conclude that when major powers have fought one another, the victim nation is no more likely to be below the average major power capability scores than above, and no more likely to be falling in its share of the composite capabilities than it is to be rising or holding steady.

Once again, though, there are alternative ways to operationalize, and put to the test, these state of the world propositions. In this case, it may be more important to compare those who were attacked to their *attackers*, rather than to *all* the other major powers; and the figures in table 10 show that such a modification does make a modest difference. That is, in the 9 major-major wars, we find that the victim was weaker than the attacker in just over half the cases, and that is a negligible difference. On the other hand, all of the 4 that *were* stronger than their attackers were *declining* in relative capabilities, as were 3 of the 5 that were weaker, and this pattern lends some credence to the state of the world argument. To put it in its strongest sense, we find no cases of a major power being attacked by another when the first was both stronger than, and rising vis-à-vis, the potential attacker.

This does not, of course, wrap up the argument. So far, we have only examined the capability–war relationship when war *did* occur. It is equally crucial to examine those cases in which war did *not* occur. Thus, in table 11, we summarize all the half-decade experiences of all the major powers, and ask two simple questions.

First, how many major power half-decades are characterized by an above average military–industrial capability, and second, how many of them were followed by entrance into one or more wars of any type? As the frequency distributions show, there were somewhat more below-average than above-average cases (94 to 84), but many more peaceful than warlike cases (126 to 52). More important, when

Table 11. Frequencies with Which Major Powers Were Below Average in Capabilities and Entered into War

|  |  | Below average? | | |
|  |  | Yes | No | |
| Entered | Yes | 31 | 21 | $\chi^2 = 1.37$ |
| war? | No | 63 | 63 | $Q$   = 0.19 |
|  |  | 94   +   84 | = 178 | |

we put the two sets together, we find that capability makes very little difference. Whereas more of the warlike cases (31 to 21) involve below-average majors, the nonwar cases include just as many above as below capability scores. And as the weak $Q$ value of 0.19 and the $\chi^2$ of 1.37 make clear, the pattern is much too close to random to justify any interpretation either way.

Similarly, if we look (table 12) not at capability scores for these major power periods, but ask whether or not they were *preceded* by a fall in strength, the same essential picture emerges. That is, of the 80 nation periods preceded by a fall in capability, 29 (33 percent) were followed by war involving those majors which fell in relative capability, while 20 (25 percent) of those 80 that rose in capability were also followed by war. Again, the $Q$ value of 0.18 reveals only very weak support of the proposition, although in the predicted direction.

In sum, we have found very little support for the administration's "weakness leads to war" proposition. While our limited historical experiment tends to confirm the belief that when major power wars occur, the victim nation was falling in capability relative to the initiator, we cannot say much about the likelihood of *getting into* war from knowing anything about capability and direction of change. That is, major powers seem to be as likely to get into war when their capability is above the major power average as when it is below it, and they seem as likely to get into war when their capability is rising as when it is falling.

*Alliances Help to Deter War*

As intimated in the previous sections, the likelihood of war and the nature of its outcome will depend not only upon the relative strength of the would-be initiator and its victim. The capabilities of allies can often be conclusive. But it is usually too late to begin

Table 12.  Frequency of War Entry by Major Powers at Times of Declining Relative Capability

|  |  | Capability falling? | | |
|---|---|---|---|---|
|  |  | *Yes* | *No* | |
| Entered | Yes | 29 | 20 | $\chi^2 = 1.18$ |
| war? | No | 60 | 60 | $Q = 0.18$ |
|  |  | 89 + | 80 = | 169 |

forming alliances once war has begun, or even on its eve; as a matter of fact, of the 177 formal alliances established during the 150 years under study, only 8 were consummated during, or within the three months preceding, hostilities. This tendency, by itself, suggests that practitioners have generally shared the administration's view that "we must build an alliance strong enough to deter those who might threaten war" (1970, p. 27).

Such an inquiry requires three different foci. First, is the international system less war-prone when alliance levels are high? Second, are the nations which join into most alliances also the ones which experience the least war? Third, does high alliance involvement on the eve of war make a nation less likely to be drawn into that war?

Before examining the historical correlations between alliance levels and war, we should summarize the operations and reasoning behind our indicators. Despite the relative ease of identifying all formal alliances (at least after the archives are opened) and differentiating among their types, ours represents the first published effort to convert that diplomatic information into machine-readable, quantitative, indicators.[13] First, we only include *written* treaties of alliance between and among sovereign states. Second, we differentiate among: (a) defense pacts, in which the signatories contract to *fight alongside* one another if either is "attacked"; (b) neutrality or nonaggression pacts, in which the obligation is to *not fight against* the other; and (c) ententes, which oblige the signatories to *consult* in the event, or imminent likelihood of, hostilities. Third, we exclude: (a) such highly asymmetric alliances as in treaties of guarantee; (b) collective security arrangements such as the League and the U.N., in which the potential attacker may well be one of the signatories; and (c) general declarations of nonviolent behavior, such as the Kellogg-Briand Pact or the Geneva Conventions.

With all alliances, members, and dates recorded, we then combine the information in order to measure, for each year, what percentage of the *system's* members are in one or more alliances of each type;

## Table 13. Correlations Between Alliance Aggregation and Onset of War

| Predictors | No. of Wars | Nation-Months | Battle Deaths |
|---|---|---|---|
| | % | % | % |
| *Total time span* | | | |
| Nations in any alliance | 0.00 | 0.27 | 0.26 |
| Nations in defense pacts | −0.01 | 0.05 | −0.01 |
| Majors in any alliance | 0.01 | 0.20 | 0.20 |
| Majors in defense pacts | 0.00 | 0.11 | 0.09 |
| *Nineteenth century* | | | |
| Nations in any alliance | 0.03 | −0.09 | −0.24 |
| Nations in defense pacts | 0.00 | 0.10 | −0.23 |
| Majors in any alliance | −0.21 | −0.18 | −0.34 |
| Majors in defense pacts | −0.16 | −0.28 | −0.45[*] |
| *Twentieth century* | | | |
| Nations in any alliance | 0.00 | 0.23 | 0.21 |
| Nations in defense pacts | −0.02 | 0.05 | 0.04 |
| Majors in any alliance | 0.34 | 0.31 | 0.28 |
| Majors in defense pacts | 0.19 | 0.12 | 0.04 |

[*]Less than 5% probability of occurring by chance alone.

these are our alliance *aggregation* indicators. For each *nation*, we ascertain the number of alliance commitments of each type it has with different classes of nations each year, in order to get its alliance *commitment* index.

Looking at the question first in its most general form (before going on to a more refined analysis), we ask whether high alliance aggregation levels do indeed lead to low levels of war in the system, and vice versa. In table 13 we show the "product-moment" correlations between the various alliance and war indicators for the entire time span, and then for each of the centuries separately. If most of the high alliance aggregation periods were followed by high amounts of war, and the low alliance periods were followed by low amounts of war, these correlations would be positive, and would range from about +0.50 up to a maximum possible value of +1.00. Conversely, if these high alliance aggregation levels were followed by the *least* warlike three-year periods, the correlation coefficients would show a *negative* sign, and again could in principle approach a value of −1.00. And if these alliance and war levels are temporally associated in a largely random fashion, the coefficient values would be close to zero. Further, as with the contingency table analyses, we are interested in

Table 14. Correlations Between Major Power Alliance Involvement and War Experience

| Predictors | No. of Wars per Year | Months of War per Year | Battle Deaths per Year |
|---|---|---|---|
| All alliances | 0.60 | −0.39 | 0.13 |
| All defense pacts | 0.42 | −0.45 | 0.07 |
| All neut. pacts | 0.25 | −0.07 | −0.47 |
| All ententes | 0.67* | 0.01 | 0.49 |
| Alliances with majors | 0.00 | −0.26 | −0.49 |
| Defense with majors | −0.03 | −0.37 | −0.28 |
| Neut. with majors | 0.11 | −0.23 | −0.58 |
| Ententes with majors | 0.00 | 0.08 | −0.66 |
| Alliances with minors | 0.68* | −0.35 | 0.31 |
| Defenses with minors | 0.51 | −0.43 | 0.16 |
| Neut. with minors | 0.28 | 0.00 | −0.40 |
| Ententes with minors | 0.60 | −0.01 | 0.62 |

*Less than 5% probability of occurring by chance alone.

both the strength of the association and the likelihood—reflected in the "statistical significance" level of the correlation coefficients—that the higher ones did not occur by chance alone.

Turning to table 13, then, we find that the patterns are very close to random for the *total* time span; regardless of which indicators we use for the predictor and outcome variables, the highest correlation we find is a weakly positive one of 0.27. Skipping to the twentieth century alone, the signs are again by and large positive, and thus in the direction opposite to that predicted by the administration, but with a somewhat more consistent pattern. For example, when most of the *major* powers are in one or more alliances, the following periods tend to be fairly warlike, as measured by the frequency of wars begun as well as by their magnitude in nation-months or their severity in battle-connected deaths. But even the 0.34 correlation had more than a 5 percent probability of occurring by chance alone.

Reverting to the nineteenth century, however, we find a reasonably clear congruence between the state of the world report's propositions and the historical record. Here, most of the correlation coefficients are negative, but only one of the 12 had less than a 5 percent probability of emerging by chance alone. So far, then, the administration's view is closer to that found in the previous century than in the current one, but none of the patterns is particularly strong.

Turning now from a consideration of the alliance-war relation-ship in the entire interstate system, we examine the more restricted grouping of major powers only. In this case, the query is whether those majors which had the highest levels of alliance participation during their entire tenure in the system were also those which experienced the lowest incidence of war involvement. Here, we can say nothing about a possible causal connection because these nations could, for example, have had most of their alliance participation in one time period and their war involvement quite a few years later or earlier. In any event, if the administration's hypothesis is correct, most of the correlation coefficients should be strong and negative. As table 14 indicates, the alliance– war relationship is again quite confused.

On the other hand, there is a very consistent and rather strong *positive* association between the *number* of alliances each of the majors had and the number of wars that each experienced, con-trolling for the length of time that they belonged to the major power subsystem. But this seems to hold only for alliances with *minor* nations, since these indices of alliances with other *majors*—and these were quite rare—show an essentially random association with their war proneness. Further, it matters considerably whether our indi-cator is the *frequency* with which allied powers get into war, or the *amount* of war they experience. That is, when we correlate their alliance involvement with the magnitude and severity of war which they experience, we find most of the coefficients to be negative, as postulated. However, none of these is sufficiently strong to have had a less than 5 percent probability of occurring by chance alone.

Despite the consistency of the positive and negative signs, we must avoid overinterpreting them. As noted earlier, such coefficients tell us nothing of the temporal sequence: once more a nation could have most of its alliance involvement in one historical epoch and its wars in another. Thus, a more realistic test for the proposition that alliances deter war is to examine the extent to which high alliance involvement is closely *followed* by low war experience for the nations, and vice versa.

What we examine next is the frequency with which major power membership in one or more alliances in a given year is followed by entry into interstate war during that same year or within the two following years. As the matrix in table 15 shows, there is virtually no discernible pattern. Of the 648 major power alliance membership years, 116 (18 percent) are followed by war entry of the alliance members, while 532 (82 percent) are not. Even though this looks as

Table 15. Frequencies with Which Majors Belonged to Alliances and Then Entered into War

|  |  | In alliance? | | |
|  |  | *Yes* | *No* | |
| Entered | Yes | 116 | 44 | $\chi^2 = 0.03$ |
| war? | No | 532 | 195 | $Q = 0.02$ |
|  |  | 648 + | 239 | = 887 |

if alliance membership reduces war experience, we next note that of the 239 nation-years *not* marked by alliance membership, 44 are nevertheless followed by entry into war and 195 are not. These percentages are also 18 percent and 82 percent respectively, identical to those for years in which these nations were in alliances. The similarity of these ratios is confirmed when we compute the $\chi^2$ and $Q$ coefficients, each of which is negligible. In other words, membership in alliances seems to have had little effect on the historical likelihood of major powers getting into war or remaining at peace.

Finally, the historical association between alliance membership and war participation may be examined in terms of the effect of *joining* an alliance rather than merely *being* in one. In other words, does the *formation* of alliances turn out to predict decreases in the war proneness of nations, particularly the major powers? In table 16, we present the familiar four sets of frequencies, beginning with the number of years in which any of the majors did or did not join a new alliance. We then divide those frequencies according to whether those joining and nonjoining years were or were not followed by entry into an interstate war. We reiterate in passing that we do not count those few alliances which were entered into during, or less than three months before, a war; this is to eliminate the confounding effects of those alliances which are created in order to fight, rather than deter, a war.

Table 16. Frequencies with Which Majors Joined Alliances and Then Entered into War

|  |  | Joined alliance? | | |
|  |  | *Yes* | *No* | |
| Entered | Yes | 31 | 129 | $\chi^2 = 2.6$ |
| war? | No | 104 | 623 | $Q = 0.18$ |
|  |  | 135 + | 752 | = 887 |

As the $Q$ and $\chi^2$ coefficients indicate, the pattern is far from dramatic, but what association we do find is in the direction opposite to that predicted. Of the 135 alliance entries by major powers, 31 (23 percent) were followed by their entry into war, and 104 (77 percent) were not. However, note that of the 752 nation-years which did *not* see major power alliance entries, only 129 (17 percent) were followed by entry into war by those nations, while 623 (83 percent) were not. In other words, those powers which entered into alliances were somewhat more likely to subsequently get involved in war than those major powers which did not. But the association is far from a statistically significant one.

We have, therefore, some tentative evidence that, historically, alliances have not prevented war. As a matter of fact, our more realistic tests of the temporal sequence between alliance involvement and war suggest that, in the case of alliance *membership*, major powers are as likely to get into war while participating as not, and, in the case of alliance *formation*, major powers are more likely to get into war subsequent to joining alliances than not. At best, then, it seems that the creation of alliances has done little to keep major powers out of war.


## Conclusion


In our effort to illustrate ways in which contingent predictions ("if——, then,——") in foreign policy might be improved via the use of operational indicators, we have merely scratched the surface. First of all, we have selected such predictions from only one set of documents reflecting a single nation and a single government. Second, we have only selected a fraction of those which could be examined in the light of a small part of a single research project. Third, all of the contingent predictions are of a simple bivariate nature, with a single predictor variable; and while many practitioners and researchers tend to think in essentially bivariate terms, a moment's pause reminds us that few outcomes in international politics are likely to be "determined" by a single factor.

Furthermore, we have addressed ourselves primarily to the *prediction* problem in policy making and have ignored many other critical issues, ranging from the decisional setting through effective policy implementation. Nor have we wrestled with the differentiation between factors which might have a great deal of predictive or explanatory power and those which, while not theoretically powerful, may offer greater opportunity for conscious and timely human intervention.[14]

On the other hand, this modest exercise should convey an idea of the possibility that we may indeed "learn from history." To begin, if we can frame our policy prediction statements in more precise language, we are already part way to the construction of reliable and valid indicators. If we can begin to approach history in a systematic and rigorous fashion, rather than merely ransack it for arguments and analogies that are convenient at the moment, we can begin to accumulate a fair amount of existential and correlational knowledge. If we can assimilate that knowledge through a multitheoretical taxonomy, we can begin to develop modest islands of explanatory knowledge. If that knowledge can be integrated into alternative theories, these can be put to further historical test. And, from the more successful and accurate theories, additional predictions can be made. A sequential scenario such as this might, in due course, lead to the conditions sought by the conscientious policy maker. These were put nicely in the first state of the world message, "Our actions must be the products of thorough analysis, forward planning, and deliberate decision. . . . We must know the facts: intelligent discussions . . . and wise decisions require the most reliable information available. . . . We must know the alternatives: we must know what our real options are, and not simply what compromise has found bureaucratic acceptance" (pp. 17-18).[15]

Having sounded this moderately sanguine note, however, it now behooves us to back off and face up to some of the more critical issues that confront the applied scientist. First, there is the question of whether social scientists *should* be concerned with the policy implications of their research. Should we actively emphasize those implications, ignore them, or intentionally conceal them, to take the three dominant views? Further, should we make them available to some governments and not to others? To some political parties and not to others? To some agencies or bureaus and not to others? In the short run, of course, these remain fairly academic questions, given the paucity of our correlational and predictive (not to mention explanatory) knowledge, and the skepticism of foreign office types the world over.[16]

But as (and if) the proposed trend continues, and our knowledge base becomes more solid, these can emerge as increasingly salient questions. To respond in an indirect fashion, we have no illusions that all the disasters that befall mankind are a consequence of ignorance or incompetence; nor do we urge that if we merely understood more fully the consequences of our actions, life would be less nasty, brutish, or short. Similarly, we do not suggest that there is little difference between the "good guys" and the "bad guys" in classifying nations, regimes, agencies, or individuals. But we would nevertheless argue that an applied social science is an essential concomitant of any related efforts to move toward a world of peace, prosperity, and justice.

Further, the same extension and diffusion of knowledge that can permit *policy makers* and their interpreters to become more sophisticated and insightful regarding the issues which confront them, can also serve to disenthrall the *general citizen*. Whether cheerleader, naysayer, or merely the victim of governmental decisions, the man in the street can become a more critical and knowledgeable participant in the governmental process. And, in doing so, he will increasingly blunt one of the major weapons of demagogues, bigots, and warmongers: the combined ignorance which permits the leader, as well as the led, to believe the most ill-founded and foolish propaganda.

This consideration leads us, with some reluctance, to the unattractive issue of pseudoscience or "scientism." Not only the general citizen and the politician, but the specialists in foreign and defense ministries are always in danger of being taken in by research that *looks* like science. To some extent, the universities, but more often the "think tanks" and industrial research firms, are well populated with "number jugglers" whose reports have a decidedly scientific aura to them. The background factors that make for shoddy work are all too familiar: (a) today's strategic analyst or Middle East specialist was yesterday's expert on traffic safety or water pollution; (b) a large fraction of the organization's business comes from a mission-oriented client with the consequent political pressures; and (c) time pressures often guarantee a quick and dirty job on contract research.[17]

But most often, the source is simple ignorance at the client's end as well as at the researcher's end. This need not be surprising, given the durability of the "three-culture problem" in today's world. Sir Charles Snow (1961) reminded us of the gulf between the scientific culture and the humanistic culture, but he neglected to emphasize that those of the former class are no less ignorant of the social sciences than those of the latter; engineers, physicists, and systems analysts often have even more erroneous notions about social systems (and how to study them) than poets, lawyers, or businessmen.

Thus, we conclude with an emphasis on not only the familiar need for more research, but the less familiar one of the need for a very different kind of "education for world affairs." In the primary and secondary schools, in colleges and graduate schools, and perhaps more critically, in the public and private discussion of public policy questions, it is essential that we move out of the prescientific era. Superstition was of little use in understanding the weather or estimating the strength of a tunnel, and medieval notions of human physiology were of little help in diagnosing and curing disease. Why should we hope that such primitivism will suffice in the solution of foreign policy problems? Given the destructive effects of bureaucratic politics, as well as the mix of good intentions and bad, there is no need to compound the felony with so large a measure of ignorance. Surely we can do better.

# Notes

Chapter 1. Individual Values, National Interests, and Political Development in the International System (pp. 3-23)

1. One critic accuses most modern social scientists as failing to see that politics is, at least in potential, "an instrument of reason, legitimately dedicated to the improvement of social conditions." See Bay (1965: 44).
2. Easton (1953: 220), for example, urges that one effect of more rigorous methodology is to impose upon political science "an obligation to re-examine and revise the way moral theory has been studied." As a matter of fact, two members of the original panel had already published important books representing a conscious effort to evaluate social science in terms of fundamental ethical criteria and to apply such knowledge to an improvement in the human condition; see Etzioni (1968) and Kelman (1968). A useful anthology on the relationship between contemporary social needs and the *physical* and *biological* sciences is N. Kaplan (1965).
3. While we would prefer to refer here to the global, rather than the international system, the relevant data sets are almost inevitably restricted to, and arranged in terms of, national states and their citizens only. See Singer (1969a).

4. Lest there be any misunderstanding, these statements are to be read in the most probabilistic sense. I see social events as a mix of the deterministic, the stochastic, and the voluntaristic, with several or many factors normally necessary to account for their incidence. This view recognizes that even the most regular and recurrent patterns have their exceptions, and that we are always playing, to some extent, the "numbers game." See Singer (1970).

5. One frequently heard reason is that the data are seldom available, but I would disagree; a combination of diligent research in the archives and monographs, plus some ingenuity in the construction of measures—even if only ordinal or nominal, rather than interval in nature—should remove many of these difficulties. A second is that these systems allegedly change radically over time and are so different across time as to be virtually incomparable. My only response to that allegation is that the nature and magnitude of those differences is an empirical question, and one to be examined, rather than assumed away.

6. Closely related, but often overlooked, is the fact that what may enhance the values of an overwhelming majority in *one* system may be quite detrimental to a few or many in a neighboring or distant system. Only if we believe that "morality stops at the water's edge" can we take group or national interest arguments seriously.

7. Some of the possibilities and pitfalls of the survey approach are evident in the careful and suggestive *Reports on Happiness* (Bradburn and Caplovitz 1965). Also relevant are W. A. Scott (1959), Albert (1956), and F. R. Kluckhohn (1960).

8. One fundamental issue, which has long engaged our best economists, but which we sidestep here in the need for brevity, is that of the transitivity and dominance of preferences for the individual, and *within* the group. Among the treatments of this class of problems are: Arrow (1951), Dahl and Lindblom (1953), Black (1958), and Buchanan and Tullock (1965).

9. Among those who have explicitly dealt with this question are: Lasswell and Kaplan (1950), Angell (1951), Bay (1958), Russett et al. (1964), and Braybrooke (1968).

10. By way of an interim report, if we control for the population of the nations in the system, there is a very modest increase in the incidence of battle-connected deaths over the past century-and-a-half. See Singer and Small (1972). Some sources of data on domestic violent deaths are: Richardson (1960b), Rummel (1963), Feierabend and Feierabend (1966), Tanter (1966), and Gurr (1967).

11. A very tentative reading of the infant mortality data shows a less consistent downward trend than might have been expected, with upswings in certain nations appearing in the wake of rapid urbanization.

12. While verbal speculation on the meaning of liberty and freedom is almost endless, there has been little effort to operationalize the concept; a suggestive exception is Oppenheim (1960).

13. The Lorenz curve shows graphically the actual distribution in terms of cumulative percentages; for example, that 5 percent of the population suffer 20 percent of the infant mortalities; 10 percent account for 35 percent of them, and so on, and that perhaps the most privileged 40 percent only experience 3 percent of them. The area represented by the difference between this curve and the perfect equality line (running at 45 degrees out from the origin of the vertical and horizontal axes) gives the index of inequality, and is usually computed by the Gini or Schutz equations. See Alker and Russett (1964), and Ray and Singer (1973).

14. In a longitudinal analysis, of course, this distinction often becomes blurred, since the statistical associations between *predictor* variables and the intrinsic development indicators are often based on varying time lags, while the same instrumental variables used as an *indicator* would be correlated against the intrinsic value *without* any such lag.

15. Two summaries of a wide variety of indicators (with data) are Banks and Textor (1963) and Deutsch (1960); suggestive treatments of the problem in general are Almond and Coleman (1960), Pye (1966), Huntington (1965), Holt and Turner (1966) and Cutright (1963). The papers presented at the August 1971 Workshop on Indicators of National Development—at Lausanne under the direction of Stein Rokkan—promise a real improvement in the subtlety and solidity of such measures in the near future; Taylor and Hudson (1972), and Russett et al. (1964).

16. As to the widely shared view that maximum citizen participation in the political decision process is indicative of high development, some serious problems present themselves. If the choices are defined in advance by a relatively unrepresentative elite, or if participation is little more than ritualized public acclamation for the wisdom of the rulers, for example, such participation may be an index of modernization, but not of development. A similar problem arises with some of the dimensions in Deutsch's (1961) mobilization indicators, since several of them say less about citizen control over his destiny than about the ease with

which he can be manipulated by elite dominance of educational and communication facilities.

17. Particularly relevant here is the view that all social systems are essentially coalitions of greater or lesser cohesiveness and integration, and that there probably never has been the sort of unity—voluntary or coerced—which is assumed by some textbook writers and practitioners, especially the unity they attribute to societies other than their own.

18. A recent article on social and cultural pluralism in the *American Journal of Sociology* turned out to have indicators (with one exception) which are measures of ethnic, religious, and linguistic *heterogeneity*, rather than pluralism, at least as it is understood in sociology and political science. See Haug (1967).

19. The loyalty problem is particularly intriguing in the bureaucratization context, since if rationality is to replace superstition, we will have to find some alternative to the superstitious belief in the moral infallibility of tribal (i.e., national) saints and deities.

20. Closely associated with decisional effectiveness and control is the point made by some of the "conservative" economists: that a politically developed system is one in which the number of "political" decisions is minimized and the number of "economic" ones is maximized. In their view of *political* decisions, the will of the majority is imposed on the minority, but in *economic* ones, each individual allegedly is free to decide for himself. The principle strikes us as a sound one, but there always remains the extent to which unequal distributions of power make a mockery of individual choice.

## Chapter 2.    Threat-Perception and the Armament-Tension Dilemma (pp. 27–47)

1. There is considerable evidence that this has not necessarily been the view held by other, and more influential, presidential advisers.

2. The writer would question M. A. Kaplan's (1957a) classification of today's system as "loose bipolar" as overemphasizing the influence of the "universal actor" (UN), the "nonbloc actors" (neutrals), and the other bloc actors (Soviet and Western allies). Significantly, the "tight bipolar" model is characterized as having "a high degree of dysfunctional tension," and one which "will not be a highly stable or well integrated system."

3. For a suggestive, but abstract, treatment of the foreign-policy

decision-making process, see Snyder, Bruck, and Sapin (1954). Probably the most comprehensive discussion of the United States process is found in Snyder and Furniss (1954). Also valuable is Macmahon (1953). For the Soviet process, see Fainsod (1954) and Kulski (1954).

4. This phrasing is used to distinguish the writer from those who might posit the existence of some *objectively* definable national interest.

5. This would concur with the conclusion of most students of Soviet foreign policy (Fainsod 1954; Kulski 1954; B. Moore 1950); but for the opposing emphasis see Huszar (1955) and Leites (1956).

6. "Disarmament" as used in this paper refers to any step in the process of reduction of a nation's military capabilities—thus the distinction between partial and total disarmament.

7. For such evaluations see Bernard et al. (1957), Cantril (1950), and Dunn (1950).

8. The quote is from the testimony of M. Q. Sibley, of the University of Minnesota, an active pacifist. It should be added that the pacifist begins from an even more fundamental premise: Violence and the tools of violence are themselves immoral and under no circumstances justifiable. This aspect of pacifism will not be discussed here.

9. Obviously, there are other considerations behind these movements, such as fear of nuclear retaliation in a war "not of their making," costs, increasing fallout, and the search for domestic political issues, but these merely supplement, rather than negate, their basic reasoning.

10. However, after the alleged cut had been negatively interpreted by Dulles, Wilson, and most of the press, Governor Stassen called a special news conference to praise the step as an "initiative we wanted them to take" (*New York Times*, May 19, 1956, p. 1).

11. Van Dyke asks "why states propose disarmament" and enumerates the following: to save money, to reduce tensions and the danger of war, and to achieve a propaganda advantage. "Of these, only the first is well reasoned and fully compatible with the . . . objective" (1957, pp. 233- 41).

12. Recent French proposals have emphasized the merit of this sort of inspection and verification.

13. See, however, Melman (1958).

14. For a more detailed discussion of this approach see the proposals of Clark and Sohn (1960).

## Chapter 3.   Internation Influence: A Formal Model (pp. 48–67)

1. This paper was originally prepared for the International Studies Division of the Institute for Defense Analyses, and is now released for publication. The views expressed are not necessarily those of the Institute, the Arms Control and Disarmament Agency, or the Department of Defense. The author wishes to thank Caxton C. Foster for his assistance both at the conceptual and the graphic level, and Lloyd Jensen for help in surveying the literature on social power.

2. The worlds of the diplomatic past and the experimental present may both be called analogous to that of the diplomatic present in that neither is an exact replication, yet each has a number of important similarities to it. In some respects, one might even find that the small group experiment provides a closer replication of the present international system than does the international system of the eighteenth or nineteenth centuries. See Singer (1961c).

3. Throughout this paper, we will often use the singular personal pronoun to denote a nation, but it will always be understood that the nation is not a person and is not capable of perceiving, predicting, and preferring in the literal psychological sense. Thus all designations will, unless otherwise specified, refer to those who act for and on behalf of, the nation: the foreign policy decision makers. We are not, however, accepting the proposition of the "methodological individualists," who deny the empirical existence or conceptual legitimacy of the group or nation. Their point of view is articulated in F. H. Allport (1924), while two persuasive refutations are Nagel (1961) and Warriner (1956).

   On the choice of the nation-as-actor, see Wolfers (1959) and Singer (1961b).

4. This definition is tentatively employed in Dahl (1957); Dahl tends to use "power" and "influence" interchangeably. The emphasis on change or modification is also retained by French and Raven (1959).

5. We will use this word in its generic sense, rather than in the various specialized ways found in such psychological theories as conditioning, learning, and S-R.

6. "Power" may be measured in a multitude of ways: relative or absolute, perceived or objective, potential or present; and many criteria may be used in making such measurements. Furthermore, the distinction between "fate control" and "behavior

control" made by Thibaut and Kelley (1959) is quite relevant here. Thus, the U.S. certainly has the power to decide the ultimate *fate* of Cuba, for example, but lacks the power to exercise effective and continuing control over Cuba's day-to-day *behavior*.

7. See Waltz (1959) and the review article based on it: Singer (1960).

8. Among the outcomes to be considered are those which might impinge on the domestic setting or upon one's allies or any Nth powers.

9. One quite successful attempt has been made to draw an analytic distinction between punishment and denial, but it seems less relevant here. Glenn Snyder (1959; 1961) refers to retaliation as punishment, while denial refers to the costs inflicted upon B (the deterree who was not deterred) while trying to gain his military objective.

10. Some suggestive versions of such a technique are advocated in R. C. Snyder and Robinson (1961, pp. 30- 34).

11. D. Katz (1960). Note that this does not preclude the use of influence by ambiguity; it calls for clarity regarding A's preferences but permits ambiguity regarding A's behavior if B does not comply. Highly suggestive in this regard is Schelling (1960b).

## Chapter 4. Escalation and Control in International Conflict: A Simple Feedback Model (pp. 68- 88)

1. This is an expanded version of an earlier paper entitled "A Cybernetic Interpretation of International Conflict" in Rizzo and Gray (1970).

2. The analysis suggested here does not of course necessarily apply to every conceivable internation conflict. While most such conflicts are, in my judgment, matters of routine incompatibilities between and among traditionally defined national interests, some do indeed raise legitimate issues of justice and morality. Unfortunately, we have not yet developed any generally accepted criteria for distinguishing between the two types of case, and even if we could, nationalistic appeals would often overwhelm them.

3. Among the studies which deal with public response to foreign policy moves, at least in the U.S., are Deutsch and Merritt (1965) and Rosenau (1963; 1967).

4. An important (and hopeful) exception to this generalization would be those cases in which the psychic mobilization has been too hysterical, has gone on too long, or has otherwise rested on a less than credible base; in such cases, the domestic opposition, or some sector of it, might possibly push the "ins" toward a *less* bellicose position.

5. For the sake of simplicity here, I not only assume that there is a viable opposition in most nations but that the political spectrum is largely based on a two-faction, quasi-pluralistic division, with one or the other in power at a given time. These are, of course, drastic simplifications, but do not affect the argument at hand.

6. A similar interpretation is offered by Thorstein Veblen (1919, p. 3) in looking at the extent to which the Spanish-American and other wars were forced upon the respective governments: "The more that comes to light of the intimate history of that episode, the more evident does it become that the popular war sentiment to which the administration yielded had been somewhat sedulously 'mobilized' with a view to such yielding. . . . So also in the case of the Boer war. . . . And so again in the current European war . . . here again it is a matter of notoriety that the popular sentiment had long been sedulously nursed and mobilized to that effect, so that the populace was assiduously kept in spiritual readiness for such an event."

7. As I write these lines, the radio newscast tells us that "American aircraft carried out fifty-two sorties in the Hanoi-Haiphong area" but that the "Vietcong terrorists continued their campaign of intimidation against unarmed civilians in an effort to disrupt the forthcoming democratic elections!" Propaganda in the name of patriotism is of course a virtue.

8. For a cross-national range of interpretations of the media's role in foreign policy, see B. C. Cohen (1963), Kruglak (1963), Reston (1966), Nimmo (1964), and Hale (1964).

9. The Vietnam War has led to a number of excellent U.S. studies which illustrate the naturalness of the process by which those who stand to gain from the escalation or continuation of the conflict drift into behavior which contributes to such escalation; see Barnet (1970), L. Lewin et al. (1967), and Janeway (1968).

10. The fact that some members of the middle elite (including political officeholders) do eventually get off the bandwagon in no way contradicts the model. They seldom do so until the conflict has reached its apogee and shows little tendency to decline; recent examples might be Germany in 1944, France in 1957, and the U.S. in 1970.

11. In almost every government agency or corporation, there is a controller (or comptroller) whose major assignment is to watch budgetary income and outgo and to issue warnings when they tend to get out of balance, or look as if they might do so. Perhaps every foreign ministry ought to have an analogous officer whose sole responsibility is to watch for those trends which signal a potential loss of diplomatic maneuver.

12. There is an extensive literature on bipartisanship in U.S. foreign policy, but it tends to look at only one part of the problem. Revering the traditional doctrine that "politics must stop at the water's edge" in the name of patriotism, it seldom notes the frequency with which bipartisanship produces a conspiracy of silence. Since foreign policy is rarely an issue in national or local elections, the electorate is most unlikely to hear any criticism (thoughtful or otherwise) of the regime in this regard (W. Miller 1967; Waltz 1967). And when it *is* an issue, the parties usually seek to outdo one another in simplistic appeals.

13. They could probably get some reinforcement in this task from the more alert and concerned consumers of national media. One possible mechanism might be the establishment of some sort of readers' pressure group which could single out certain newspapers and periodicals from time to time, publicize the more serious distortions which they perpetuate, and try to organize "subscribers' strikes." If such errors of fact and interpretation were called to the attention of publishers and editors by a readership which is in a position to impose a temporary boycott, some progress might be made. And since much of the propagandistic material in the newspaper and radio reports must be traced to the wire services, these transmitters might then begin to demand higher standards from UPI, AP, Reuters, Tass, and the rest.

14. In an earlier paper (Singer 1969a), this projection is discussed at some length, but the evidence by which it may be vindicated or rejected has not yet been assembled. For an interpretation of the opposing evidence, see Deutsch (1969).

15. The past decade has seen the establishment of several peace research centers around the world, usually associated with such universities as London, Oslo, and Michigan. The recently created International Peace Research Institute in Stockholm, while financed largely by the Swedish Government, may approximate the Wright scheme on the physical science side by publishing reports on disarmament inspection methods, etc. The Pugwash Continuing Committee is also, at this writing, preparing a memorandum on the creation of such an agency. Also relevant is the

annual *Report on the World Social Situation*, published by the United Nations Department of Economics and Social Affairs.

16. Law firms (sometimes foreign) occasionally handle governments' cases before international legal tribunals, and the lessons from those experiences might be applicable to these essentially non-legal conflicts.

## Chapter 5.  The Strategic Dilemma: Probability Versus Disutility (pp. 91–100)

1. An interesting philosophical question is raised here by asking whether the decision is a result of objective external phenomena or the subjective preferences and predictions of those "making" the decision. I would say both.

2. The lack of comparability arises because types I and II are classified by Kahn (p. 126) in terms of the *behavior to be deterred*, while III is described in terms of *what the deterrer* will do "to make the aggression unprofitable."

3. Kahn uses the word "defender" here, but it is perfectly evident that weapons technology has so corrupted traditional notions of defense that the victim's reaction must be about 75 percent retaliatory and offensive, and only about 25 percent defensive. On this matter see Singer (1961d).

4. These, and other criticisms, may have been valid when Kahn first began to lecture on strategy, but they are now very dead horses. Perhaps he educated the rest of us too well!

5. For a less sophisticated but highly pungent attack on the strategy see Loosbrock (1960).

6. In his own whimsical fashion, Kahn has capitalized this and many other phrases, allegedly for purposes of emphasis, but I hope he will pardon my refusal to be an accomplice in slogan making.

7. Since I am unable to discern any appreciable difference between his analysis of types II and III, and am already short of space, I will attempt no further discussion of this latter. It should be noted, however, that he makes an excellent case against the use of tactical nuclear weapons in type II or III situations where limited war becomes a factor.

8. His position is not altogether clear on this, however. In one place, he argues that "nonmilitary defense may have an impor-

tant role in deterring the Russians from extremely provocative behavior, but this is different from deterring an attack on the United States" (p. 115, n.5).

9. For a detailed and thoughtful explanation of his proposals, see Appendices II, III, and IV, pp. 597–640. On the physical and social implications of an attack on the United States see Hirshleifer (1956), Michael (1955), Rosow and Phelps (1959), U.S. (1959), and Tiryakian (1959).

10. It should be noted that his concern here is not with being able to continue the war but with postwar rebuilding. He assigns a very low probability to a "broken-backed" war of long duration and predicts truce negotiations "a few days" after an opening exchange (pp. 107, 219). This prediction is more likely to be true if those empowered to negotiate survive such an exchange.

11. Elsewhere (p. 528) he recognizes the unsettling effect of this, and suggests that "the main destabilizing effect of type II deterrence can be handled in part by not keeping the first strike forces on alert." Thus, he is again confronted with a dilemma: If you want the threat to be credible, you have to be provocative, and if you don't want to be provocative, you can't make it credible.

12. Some other points of possible vulnerability in preventing the development of a counterforce capability might be in keeping charts and guidance systems inaccurate, or limiting the yield in warheads. Another technique for reducing the Soviet expectation of surprise attack might be to dismantle our "soft" close-in IRBM sites—even before Atlas and Titan are operational and deployed.

13. That Kahn himself is aware of the possibility of nonreconcilable demands is indicated in a section called "The Conflicting Objectives" (pp. 531–39), but he never really wrestles with the dilemmas posed, despite a consideration of alternatives to a credible first-strike capability (pp. 539–50). This is another of the many examples of the book's basic inconsistency: His main thrust is on behalf of developing this capability, but he then covers himself by suggesting that it may not do all the things he claimed for it earlier in the study.

14. At first, I was surprised that Klaus Knorr, in his foreword, commends Kahn's "masterly command of method" and his "step-by-step presentation." But then we are reminded that the book was written at Princeton's Center of International Studies, giving Professor Knorr many months of contact with the author and his mode of expression. And even then, he does refer to the

fact that these "lectures in book form" have retained "some of the informality of the original presentation." A gracious understatement!

## Chapter 7. Inspection and Protection in Arms Reduction (pp. 113–130)

1. The author is indebted to Inis L. Claude, Jr., and Karl Deutsch for their comments on an earlier draft of this paper.

2. "Most" is used to suggest that certain groups in some nations would find disarmament *dis*advantageous to themselves. But this does not mean that they necessarily fail to see the advantages to their nation as a whole; thus many senior Western military officers have undertaken disarmament-oriented assignments with a high degree of skill and energy. Such is not, however, nearly as true of certain groups of civilian scientists with a vested interest in such elements as nuclear energy.

3. The probability-utility model is discussed below under "Deterrence of Violations."

4. It is beyond the scope of this paper to consider the pros and cons of arms control or stable deterrence *vs.* arms reduction or elimination. Suffice to say that the former are seen as preliminary stopgap measures which may well provide the bridge between a relatively uncontrolled competition for quantitative and qualitative superiority in weaponry and the beginnings of genuine reductions and prohibitions on existing and future capabilities. Elsewhere, this relationship is spelled out in considerable detail; see Singer (1962a; 1962b).

5. It is ironical, but all too frequently true, that national governments use a double standard in setting the requirements for policies that are intended to do the same thing: provide for national security. Thus, they ask that the information-producing effectiveness of a disarmament or arms control inspectorate exceed that of their own national intelligence operations, and that the deterrent effect of such arrangements far exceed those of their national military capabilities.

6. A lesser, but not irrelevant, concern is that of evasions which *are* promptly detected. In that type of case, the symmetries of the reduction schedule may be expected to prevent any strategic imbalance.

7. In an early draft of a working paper on inspection, J. B. Phelps and R. S. Leghorn note that "an inspection system should not only be able to ascertain the truth in spite of efforts to conceal it, but it should help the inspected nation to display the truth

when it wants to." See, also, the Phelps paper in Summer Study on Arms Control (1961). To put it another way, nations act largely on the basis of the other's intentions, and these are inferred from information regarding the other's capabilities.

8. A persuasive case for maintaining and sharpening the distinction between nuclear and nonnuclear weapons has been made by Read (1960).

9. One possible exception is that the *early warning* and communication requirements for a system of arms control, where each side has some stipulated level of nuclear-missile weapons (200 is a popular figure), might be greater and more costly than those needed for the inspection of a *prohibition* on the production of such weapons. A second, and more obvious one, is that of nuclear warheads, whose production or testing is more easily detected than stockpiling. Note, however, that unless such weapons are taken out of hiding and deployed they are of little military use.

10. The pioneering effort was by Seymour Melman (1958). Other valuable studies are by Feld *et al.* (1959); Kalkstein and Phelps in Frisch (1961); Feld, Pool, and Bohn in Brennan (1961); and Wiesner (1961).

11. A corollary is Wiesner's observation that, "as the inspection system is developed, the probable error . . . will decrease, and consequently the size of the legal force (remaining in national hands) can be decreased with safety . . ." (Wiesner 1961, p. 137). Here again we see the critical relationship between the disarmament rate and the growth of the control agency. On the other hand, *evasion* schemes may be improved over time and the inspectorate may become lazy or subverted.

12. Simulation and gaming of inspection systems may well offer a fruitful technique for such investigation, and the author is currently involved in the design of such a study. See the ingenious pioneering effort of Robert H. Davis *et al.* (1961).

13. Quite obviously, all these (and other) techniques will be used by the separate *national* intelligence agencies in order to verify and supplement the work of the control agency.

14. In inspection for tax evasion or unlawful merger or collusion, this is a highly developed technique. See, for example, two early studies of the FTC operation: Henderson (1924) and the doctoral dissertation by Blaisdell (1932).

15. Of course, such an arrangement would increase espionage opportunities, and might well encounter resistance as a result.

16. It is clear that the inspectorates will have to keep to a minimum the number of "false detections," in order to prevent an overloading of the agency and governmental communication nets, and to maintain the latter's confidence in the system. The graduated classification procedure is intended to help inhibit false detection and to permit the filing of low-warning reports when the inspector is relatively unsure of his evidence.

17. In this particular case, the procedure could be in three steps: aerial reconnaissance, ground inspection, and earth sampling. Unless each produces reassuring information, the next step is executed, until a reasonably certain conclusion is reached and reported. See U.S. (1960, pp. 47 ff.).

18. On the matter of the competence of, and precedence for, international administrative regulation, see Henkin (1958, chap. 7). Such procedures raise a delicate problem of "due process," and national ratifications of the agreement or treaty permitting interrogation, etc., will require carefully drafted limitations and protections.

19. For precedent and legal considerations, see Wright (1952), Hudson (1934), Finch (1952), and Parker (1952).

20. For an analysis of these and other self-help responses to alleged violations, see Iklé (1961) and Hammond (1962).

21. An important exception is the study by Clark and Sohn (1960). See also Singer (1958, 1961a).

22. A further response delay could be built into this arrangement by physically separating some or all of the warheads from their delivery vehicles.

23. For these and other implications of a zone-by-zone inspection system, see Sohn and Frisch (1961).

24. The assumption is that the numbers of weapons in each category that are transferred to control agency depots will be based on agreed percentages of pretransfer inventories and on a phasing-out schedule for the dismantling or converting of production facilities.

25. As one observer put it, ". . . detecting violations is not enough. What counts are the political and military consequences of a violation once it has been detected, since these alone will determine whether or not the violator stands to gain in the end" (Iklé 1961, p. 208). Also germane, in a larger sense, is the nature of the positive attractions of the overall system and the incentives for maintaining the disarmament program. For example, the inspection personnel might also play a useful dual role as safety observers, quality control consultants, informal communication

links, etc. Conversely, normal peaceful activities could be used for inspection purposes as well, i.e., equip some portion of the world's commercial airliners with aerial photography equipment as an inexpensive means of regular coverage of inspection zones.

26. The more secure the remaining weapons are, the fewer that will be needed to inflict "unacceptable" punishment on the violating adversary. Unfortunately, however, the more secure they are, the less likely the control agency is to know their numbers and locations.

27. Violation attempts not approved by national governments may seem unlikely, but we need only note the frequency with which subordinates in governmental agencies violate regulations to which their superiors intend to adhere, on the assumption that such behavior constitutes loyalty.

28. For a critical evaluation of deterrence, see Singer (1962a). A more complete and formal analysis is in Singer (1962c).

29. Address to General Assembly, October 3, 1960; General Assembly Official Records, *Plenary* . . . , p. 320 (U.S. 1960, p. 276); and United Nations Document A/C. I/L. 249, October 13, 1960 (U.S. 1960, p. 298). See also Vladimirov (1960).

30. See Department of State Press Release 73, February 18, 1960, and UN Document TNCD/7, June 27, 1960 (U.S. 1960, pp. 50, 130); and U.S. (1962). The same view is implied in the September, 1961, disarmament declaration to the U.N., which referred to "the disbanding of all national armed forces and the prohibition of their re-establishment in any form whatsoever, other than those required to preserve internal order and *for contributions to a United Nations Peace Force.*" (U.S. Dept. of State Publication 7277, 1961, p. 11.) Under the present charter, it is probably wise to accept this limited and semiadequate arrangement, but a disarmament treaty which amended the charter should eliminate the veto which each nation has regarding the transfer of its forces to United Nations control.

31. It should be borne in mind, however, that the word "control" in Russian (as well as in French) means inspection, examination, checking, etc., but does not imply supervision or enforcement.

**Chapter 9. The Outcome of Arms Races: A Policy Problem and a Research Approach (pp. 145- 154)**

1. A suggestive exception, with some data, is Huntington (1958); for a differing view on the European race prior to World War I, see

Moll (1968). See also the brief discussion and tabular materials in appendix 22 of Wright (1942 or 1965).

2. See Abelson (1963) for a suggestive derivation and extension of the Richardson model, and for an explicit rejection of the model, see Alker (1968).

3. For an interesting discussion and some data, see the exchange between Richardson and Horne in *Nature* (1951).

4. Among the studies which focus on the domestic economic incentives behind arms expenditures are: Walton (1916), Cobden (1867), Hirst (1937), and Perlo (1963). Also relevant is the literature on budget increment as a function of prior appropriations or expenditures; see Davis, Dempster, and Wildavsky (1966), for example.

5. A promising approach to ascertaining responsiveness and symmetry is found in Chase (1968b, pp. 93–95).

## Chapter 11. The Historical Experiment as a Research Strategy in the Study of World Politics (pp. 175–196)

1. Originally presented at the 1973 meetings of the International Political Science Association in Montreal, Canada. I should like to thank Karl Deutsch, Stuart Bremer, Elaine Morton, Donald Campbell, Anatol Rapoport, and Jean Laponce for their helpful comments, and the National Science Foundation for its support under grant no. GS-28476X2.

2. Representative of that view is Etzioni (1965, p. 88): "There probably will never be a science of international relations as there is one of physics or chemistry, if for no other reason that experiments are practically impossible and the number of cases is too small for a rigorous statistical analysis." And even so creative and catholic a scholar as Paul Lazarsfeld (1949, p. 378) alleges that survey methods "do not use experimental techniques." On the other hand, in a 1965 paper (p. 155), Holsti and North actually allude to the possibility of transforming history "into something approaching a laboratory of international behavior," and a similar point is made by Snyder (1963). In sociology, two of the early proponents of the experimental mode were Greenwood (1945) and Chapin (1947).

3. Elsewhere, I have spelled out in greater detail my views on the more promising strategies for explaining war in general (Singer 1971a), as well as the strategy being pursued in the Correlates of War project in particular (Singer 1972a).

4. Some would differentiate between these two versions of the field experiment. When the researcher merely waits for a condition or event that is probably coming anyway, we refer to a "natural" field experiment; illustrative is the Simon and Stern (1955) study on the effects of TV upon voter turnout. When the researcher consciously injects the stimulus condition, we refer to a "contrived" field experiment.

5. On the detailed procedures of observation, measurement, and index construction in the Correlates of War project, see Small and Singer (1969; 1973), Singer and Small (1972), Wallace and Singer (1970), and Ray and Singer (1973).

6. As a matter of fact, the laboratory experimenter must face several problems that need not concern those of us who conduct historical experiments. Perhaps foremost among these is the problem of experimenter bias. As Rosenthal (1963; 1966) and others have demonstrated, the theoretical biases of the researcher—or laboratory assistants—constitute a recurrent source of distortion in the experimental work of physical and biological, as well as social, scientists. In small-group experiments, for example, the way in which the stimulus is presented can induce systematic bias in the behavior of the subjects. Similarly, the observation and measurement of human or animal responses to a stimulus can be systematically distorted by the expectations of the observer.

7. These are: "*History*, the specific events occurring between the first and second measurement in addition to the experimental variable; *Maturation*, processes within the respondents operating as a function of the passage of time per se (not specific to the particular events), including growing older, growing hungrier, growing more tired, and the like; *Testing*, the effects of taking a test upon the scores of a second testing; *Instrumentation*, in which changes in the calibration of a measuring instrument or changes in the observers or scorers used may produce changes in the obtained measurements; *Statistical regression*, operating where groups have been selected on the basis of their extreme scores; Biases resulting in differential *selection* of respondents for the comparison groups; *Experimental mortality*, or differential loss of respondents from the comparison groups; *Selection-maturation interaction*, etc., which in certain of the multiple-group quasi-experimental designs, such as Design 10, is confounded with, i.e., might be mistaken for, the effect of the experimental variable."

8. A reasonable position on this issue is that taken by Blalock (1961, p. 5): "There appears to be an inherent gap between the

languages of theory and research which can never be bridged in a completely satisfactory way. One *thinks* in terms of ... causes ... but one's *tests* are made in terms of covariations, operations, and pointer readings."

9. Smelser (1968) distinguishes between "parameter variables" and "operative variables" to emphasize this distinction.

10. We should, of course, make clear that history—like all disciplines—contains a wide range of epistemological viewpoints. Illustrative of the growing trend toward greater rigor in that discipline are Rowney and Graham (1969), Lorwin and Price (1972), and Dollar and Jensen (1971).

11. One problem with this comparative case method, however, is the likelihood of ending up with too few cases and too many variables, for a poor N/K ratio; see Deutsch, Singer, and Smith (1965).

12. The theoretical model is articulated in considerable detail in Deutsch and Singer (1964).

13. While this is an imaginary experiment, simplified for illustrative purposes, a fair number of "real" ones have been conducted within the Correlates of War project at Michigan. See, for example, Singer and Small (1968), Singer, Bremer, and Stuckey (1972), and M. D. Wallace (1973). For another imaginary one, see the learning module on "The Scientific Study of Politics" (Singer 1972b). I am indebted to John Stuckey for the illustrations used here.

14. For a simulation that is largely limited to that concern, see Singer and Hinomoto (1965).

## Chapter 12. The Diplomatic Importance of States, 1816–1970: An Extension and Refinement of the Indicator (pp. 199–222)

1. The authors are indebted to the Carnegie Corporation and the National Science Foundation for their support of the overall project, and to those scholars who, in using the original data, were kind enough to communicate a variety of suggestions to us. We would also like to thank David Handley, Kathy Dillon, Vanu Bagchi, and Marsha Stuckey for their assistance in data acquisition, and Stuart Bremer, Raymond Tanter, James Ray, and Harald von Riekhoff for their perceptive comments and suggestions.

2. In addition to several studies now under way in which attributed diplomatic importance serves as one of our independent or intervening variables, others are also utilizing these data. See, for example, M. D. Wallace (1973), Midlarsky (1969), and East (1969). Among others who have done independent studies in this area are Alger and Brams (1967), Bernstein and Weldon (1968), Russett and Lamb (1969), Brams (1969), and Väyrynen (1971). Schwartzman and Araujo (1966), using entirely different indicators of status, came up with a rank-ordering quite similar to our own.

3. One of the former is a witty, if uninformed, commentary in *Encounter* (1966). Our critic, identified only as "R," chose to ignore the text accompanying the tables, leading one to suspect that U.S. elites have used criteria of an extrascholarly nature in selecting overseas recipients of our largesse.

4. In this vein, we are now gathering data by means of which we hope to calculate each state's military-industrial capability twice per decade for the same period, 1816–1970. Although we expect that these capability scores and ranks will show a high positive correlation with the diplomatic importance scores, we also expect some important and interesting exceptions. Two studies which explicitly examine the rank discrepancies produced by the two sets of measures are Wallace (1973) and Ray (1974). In addition, there are some important theoretical implications in the fact that a given state's importance scores and capability scores may be rising or falling at sharply different rates, or perhaps moving in different directions at the same time.

5. For an application of that strategy to data on international trade, see Alker and Puchala (1968); the original index is outlined in Savage and Deutsch (1960).

6. Writing in 1946 (pp. 219–20), diplomat-historian Harold Nicolson noted this inflationary trend when he wrote that "the Vienna *Règlement* (of 1815) did in fact settle the precedence problem for more than a hundred years. It may well be that some future Congress will find itself obliged, in view of the multiplicity of Embassies which have since been created, to adopt a futher *Règlement* under which Ambassadors are classified as of the first, second, or third category. This, it is to be expected, will provoke a most invidious discussion."

7. For an analysis based upon size of mission in the post-World War II era, see Alger and Brams (1967).

8. One indication of how closely the original and the revised indices converge is the magnitude of the coefficient of concor-

dance. The minimum value of Kendall's $W$ when the asymmetric, the weighted, and the nonweighted symmetric scores are correlated is .83 (for 1824); the maximum is .99 (for 1935); and the mean is .96.

9. One other minor detail concerns the special case of the eight German and five Italian states which, prior to 1870, did not qualify for inclusion in the central system. Because the states in these two groupings had close dynastic ties, and were thus *expected* to exchange missions with their sister states, we excluded such missions in the original computation of each of their scores. In retrospect, that *ad hoc* rule seems both arbitrary and unnecessary; *many* groups of nations were in the same position of almost inevitably having to exchange missions. Furthermore, the effect of these more or less automatic missions is a minor one, raising the mean Italian score in 1859, for example, from 11.0 to 14.2, and that of the lesser German states from 8.63 to 13.75. Our data set, which is available at the International Relations Archive of the Inter-University Consortium for Political Research at the University of Michigan, now reflects this revision.

10. See East (1969); for the pre-World War II study, we used the following: *Almanach de Brussels* (Paris 1918); *Almanach de Gotha* (Gotha 1764–1940); *Almanach de Paris* (Paris 1865–1869); *Annuaire Diplomatique et Consulaire de la République Française pour 1899 et 1900* (Paris 1900); *Europa Year-Book* (London 1926–1929); and *The Statesman's Year-Book* (London 1864–1940).

11. Space limitations preclude the listing here of the fluctuating system membership which emerges from the application of these coding criteria; the resulting lists may be found in tables 2.1 and 2.2 of Singer and Small (1972).

## Chapter 13. Alliance Aggregation and the Onset of War, 1815–1945 (pp. 225–264)

1. This study is part of a larger project on the correlates of war, supported by the Carnegie Corporation of New York and the Center for Research on Conflict Resolution at the University of Michigan. We are also grateful to Anatol Rapoport and Keith Smith, with whom we consulted often on conceptual as well as methodological problems. For his efficient aid in data analysis, our thanks go also to Wen Chao Hsieh.

2. Almost all textbooks in the field devote some space to an effort to systematize balance-of-power concepts, with varying degrees of success. In addition, there are several theoretical efforts, among which are Claude (1962), Gareau (1962), E. B. Haas (1953), M. A. Kaplan (1957b), Liska (1962), Deutsch and Singer (1964), and Waltz (1964). Three important efforts to examine the international system in the historical context are Gulick (1955), Langer (1931), and Rosecrance (1963).

3. A recent statement which explicitly expresses these restraints is that by Secretary Rusk in regard to Soviet-American arms control negotiations: "Of course, anything that involves our NATO allies would have to be discussed fully with our NATO allies. We could not, for example, make arrangements ourselves, nor even could the four NATO members now sitting at Geneva be able to make arrangements on control posts throughout the NATO alliance without fullest consideration in NATO."

4. One admittedly intuitive analysis concludes, for example, that "the decision to wage war precedes by one to five years the outbreak of hostilities" (Abel 1941).

5. For a full description of the operations by which nations were coded and classified, see Singer and Small (1966a).

6. There are, of course, a fair number of additional German and Italian states, but they fail to meet our population threshold of 500,000; the classification criteria are discussed below.

7. The population threshold of 500,000 was only established after a fairly exhaustive list of political entities was compiled and it then became evident that almost no nation of a lesser population revealed itself as an active participant. As to recognition, we found that Britain and France almost invariably led the way to recognition by a majority of members of the European state system. Thus, we get a parsimonious criterion which produces almost exactly the same results as would one requiring, let us say, 50 percent of the major power members of the European system to serve as legitimizers; actually these two constituted 40 percent of that group until 1860 and from then until 1895 they constituted 33 percent. Moreover, only Britain and France had sufficiently strong interest in Latin America to justify extending diplomatic recognition to nations in that area. By recognition we mean the accreditation of a representative at or above the rank of chargé d'affaires; neither the consul nor the diplomatic agent qualifies under this scheme.

8. Moreover, there were only three Latin American alliances (Ecuador-Peru, 1860–1861; Colombia-Ecuador, 1864–1865;

and Bolivia-Peru, 1873–1883) which met our criteria of formality, population of the signatories, and consummation in peace time. In general, see Burr (1955).

9. This is a very simple and atheoretical presentation of such distributions. For an indication of the theoretical implication of "mere" distributions, see Horvath and Foster (1963), Weiss (1963), Smoker (1964), and Denton (1966).

10. There is a rapidly burgeoning literature on the subject and it reminds us that very few civil wars remain purely internal for any length of time. See Rosenau (1964), Modelski (1961), and Eckstein (1963).

11. This figure permits us to eliminate many border skirmishes, brief interventions, punitive expeditions, blockades, and bombardments of marginal interest to the international relations student, yet excludes no international war. Where our confidence levels were low and the deaths were estimated to be nearly 1,000, we did, however, include the wars. Three examples of such an occurrence were the French invasion of Spain in 1823, the conquest of the Papal States in 1860, and Spain versus Peru, Chile, and Ecuador in 1866.

12. Some might quarrel with our use of the historians' consensus on the classification of nations into major and minor. One significant point of assurance is found in Morgenthau where approximately the same major-power listing as ours is used (1956, p. 324).

13. As to civilian and military deaths from nonbattlefield engagements, the major possible source is the siege. During the period under study, however, there were few sieges which led to an appreciable number of deaths; see Hargreaves (1948).

14. Elsewhere, we not only spell out the coding rules in greater detail and with illustrations, but give the voluminous bibliography from which our basic information was drawn; see Singer and Small (1966b).

15. Though some scholars tend to differentiate between an alliance and a coalition, the distinction seems unimportant. Gulick, for example, defines an alliance as a "bilateral or trilateral agreement for offensive or defensive purposes," and then defines a coalition as "a similar agreement signed by four or more powers or a conjunction of several alliances directed toward the same end" (1955, p. 78). He alludes to other distinctions, but they make the difference no clearer.

16. We also gathered data for neutrality pacts and ententes, but further refinement of those measures is called for in order to

handle the problem of which alliance commitment takes precedence when a nation belongs to alliances of different classes. Findings based on those measures will be reported subsequently.

17. An interesting point emerges when these various time lags are examined carefully. In the nineteenth century, the effects are seldom fully evident until five years have elapsed, whereas three years suffice in the twentieth century. This pattern strongly suggests that, in contrast to "real" time, "diplomatic" time has indeed speeded up in more recent years. In a subsequent paper, we will report a number of other indications of this time-compression tendency. A suggestive treatment of this problem in social science is W. Moore (1964).

18. A statistical note is in order here. We recognize that our observations do not satisfy the requirements which most statisticians would demand in order to speak of levels of significance. First, we are not sampling here, but are observing the entire population of events. Second our indices—annual readings of alliance aggregation and war onset—obviously are not independent of one another from year to year. Third, the magnitudes are not "normally" distributed, and any normalizing transformation would have distorted a perfectly satisfactory scale. However, one must use some objective and quantitative benchmark by which "strong" relationships may be differentiated from "weak" ones, and by which one may classify these observed relationships as compelling or not. Thus, we have used the Pearson product-moment correlation as our measure of the strength of the observed relationships, and gone on to scrutinize each such correlation value ($r$) to ascertain whether or not we might call it strong or weak. For that purpose, we use Fisher's exact test of statistical significance (two-tailed to allow for negative correlations) and treat all $r$s that exceed the requirements for an .01 level of significance with a given $N$ as strong. For the nineteenth century and an $N$ of 85, that threshold is .25, and for the twentieth and an $N$ of only 45, the threshold requirement goes up to a coincidental .45; values meeting these levels are *italicized*. Note that $r$s are rounded off to only two places and that the decimal point is omitted.

19. To be doubly sure, we also ran these correlations *without* the world war years, with only a minor reduction in the coefficients resulting.

20. Another way of saying this is to reiterate that bivariate analyses can seldom explain (account for) highly complex and obviously multivariate social phenomena.

21. See, for example, Harary (1961), Coleman (1964), Rapoport (1963), Rapoport and Horvath (1961), Berge (1962), and Flament (1963).

22. Furthermore, even though our alliance aggregation index is not responsive to multiple memberships, the alliance *involvement* index presented in an earlier paper *is*, and the correlations between the two indicators when applied to all nations in any alliances and to all in defense pacts are .90 and .87 respectively (Singer and Small 1966b, p. 20).

## Chapter 14. Capability Distribution, Uncertainty, and Major Power War, 1820–1965 (pp. 265–297)

1. Comments on an earlier version of this paper by Karl Deutsch, Melvin Small, Michael Wallace, and James Ray were particularly helpful. We would also like to thank Dorothy LaBarr for her patience and thoroughness in preparing the tables and text, and to acknowledge the support of the National Science Foundation under Grant number 010058.

2. While power and prestige are far from identical, and nations may well have statuses on these two dimensions that are quite inconsistent with each other, there is usually a high correlation between the two. In this paper, we focus only on power, but will deal with prestige (or attributed diplomatic importance) in a later one; for some tentative analyses, see Midlarsky (1969), East (1969), and Wallace (1971; 1972). For more detail on the composition of the international system and its subsystems, see Singer and Small (1966a) and Russett, Singer, and Small (1968).

3. If one accepts the propositions that successful war experience usually leads to increases in national power, and that the more powerful nations usually "win" their wars, the high war involvement and win-lose scores of the major powers offer some evidence that the majors are not only attentive to, but high on relative capabilities (Small and Singer 1970).

4. Despite the modest fluctuations in the size of the major power subsystem, we do not normalize the war measure. Full details of our data-generation and index-construction procedures, and the considerations of validity and reliability upon which the indices rest, along with extensive tabular materials, are found in our forthcoming *Wages of War* (Singer and Small 1972).

5. For example, the Gini is often as sensitive to a changing N as to the allocation of shares, when the N is low. And the Schultz

index, because it sums the ratios of advantage of those above the equal share point, is sensitive only to their shares *as a group* and is not sensitive to the distributions *within* that group. Thus, the index would be the same (.5) for each of the following percentage distributions; 70-20-10-0-0; 70-7.5-7.5-7.5-7.5; and 70-15-15-0-0. The same holds if the index is computed on the basis of those below the equal share point. An alternative approach is that of Brams (1968), and a useful discussion is in Alker and Russett (1964).

6. The formula for computing concentration is as follows:

$$CON = \sqrt{\frac{\sum\limits_{i=1}^{n} (Si)^2 - \frac{1}{n}}{1 - \frac{1}{n}}}$$

where $n$ = number of nations in system, and $Si$ = nation $i$'s share (from .00 to 1.00) of the system's capabilities.

7. The formula for computing movement is as follows:

$$MOVE = \frac{\sum\limits_{i=1}^{n} \left| Si_{t-1} - Si_t \right|}{2 (1 - Sm_t)}$$

where $n$ = number of nations in system, $Si$ = nation $i$'s share of the system's capabilities, $m$ = nation with lowest share of capabilities, and $t, t - 1$ = observation points.

8. As we move into the examination and analysis of our data, we want to acknowledge our debt to Dan Fox of The University of Michigan Statistical Research Laboratory, for the creation of a set of programs particularly suited to time series data management and analysis in the social sciences.

9. Throughout this paper we employ standardized measures of association (correlation coefficients and standardized regression coefficients). Our objective is to evaluate the relative contribution of variables rather than to establish empirical laws, and in this regard we have adopted what Blalock (1961) has called the "quantitative" criterion for evaluating the importance of variables.

10. In this and prior studies we have examined the effects of dividing the 150 years into three or more periods, or of using such salient years as 1871 or 1914 as our cutting point, but the clearest distinctions tend to be found when the 1890-1900 decade is used as our interepoch division.

11. The scatter plots, while not reproduced here, reveal the stronger

linear relationship quite clearly, and in the case of the twentieth-century CON-WAR association, suggest a possible curvilinear pattern; the conversion to logarithmic plots does not, however, produce a linear association. On the other hand, a rank order (rho) correlation of - .53 also suggests that the CON-WAR association in the twentieth century is far from negligible.

12. Given the fact that most of the changes in the size of the major power subsystem occur as the result of high-magnitude wars, we also examined the extent to which such changes themselves might be affecting the value of CON. It turns out—not surprisingly—that whatever decrease is found in the predictive power of CON vis-á-vis subsequent war is already accounted for by prior war; thus there is no need to control for the effects of both prior war *and* change in system size.

13. For an illuminating discussion of the statistical treatment of multiplicative and other interactive models, see Blalock (1965).

14. $\bar{R}^2$ is the coefficient of multiple determination, corrected for degrees of freedom in the following way:

$$\bar{R}^2 = 1 - \left[ \frac{(1 - R^2)(N - 1)}{N - k - 1)} \right]$$

where $N$ = number of observations, and $k$ = number of predictor variables. This index thus conservatively adjusts the goodness-of-fit estimate, penalizing the researcher for a large number of predictor variables and a small number of observations. This rewards parsimony and high $N/k$ ratios; see Ezekiel and Fox (1959, Chap. 17) and Deutsch, Singer, and Smith (1965).

The regression coefficients of the multiplicative models were estimated by means of a $\log_e (X + C)$ transformation on all the variables, where $C = 1.0$ minus the minimum value of variable X. As Russett et al. explain (1964, pp. 311-13), *addition* of these transformed series is equivalent to the *multiplication* of their original values, and permits the researcher to isolate a unique coefficient for each variable's contribution to the combined multiplicative term. Without this transformation, only a gross coefficient for the interactive effect of the three variables could be estimated.

15. The explanation for this phenomenon is somewhat lengthy and several discussions of it may be found in C. Harris (1963). To put the matter briefly, suppose that the true CON measures at $t_0$ and $t_1$ were equal. $\Delta$CON would then be positively related to

the errors in CON at $t_1$ and negatively related to the errors in CON at $t_0$, since $\Delta$CON would under these circumstances be equal to the difference between these error terms. If the simple correlation between WAR and $\Delta$CON were positive, as we have found, then the partial relationship between WAR and $\Delta$CON controlling for CON at $t_0$ would also be positive. This necessarily follows since by controlling for CON at $t_0$ we are controlling for its error as well; thus the partial association between WAR and $\Delta$CON is the equivalent of the relationship between WAR and the error in CON at $t_1$, controlling for the error in CON at $t_0$. As the error in CON at $t_1$ increases, $\Delta$CON will also increase, and since the relationship between $\Delta$CON and WAR is positive, so also must the relationship between WAR and the error in CON at $t_1$ be positive.

However, when we control for CON at $t_1$, rather than at $t_0$, and investigate the relationship between $\Delta$CON and WAR, we are analyzing the relationship between WAR and the error in CON at $t_0$, controlling for the error in CON at $t_1$. As the error in CON at $t_0$ increases, $\Delta$CON will decrease, and since the relationship between $\Delta$CON and WAR is positive, the relationship between WAR and the error in CON at $t_0$ must be negative.

Even though our $\Delta$CON measure is not, as assumed above, simply a function of error, the error components are present and apparently responsible for the observed sign reversal. This reversal supports the positive effect of $\Delta$CON on WAR in the twentieth century, but it also points up some of the problems which may be encountered when both a variable and a first-difference derivation are used in a regression equation.

16. Parenthetically, for those who suspect that the definition of war used here may be too broad in that it embraces *all* interstate war involving major powers, we mention a relevant finding. That is, if we look only at those eight wars in which there is a major power on *each* side, we find that there was a decline in CON during the half-decade preceding all but one of those wars. Since these are almost equally divided between the centuries, they lend some support to the peace through preponderance doctrine.

17. We mentioned earlier the problems of multicollinearity (high correlations among the predictor variables) and autocorrelated error terms. Because our predictor variables are highly correlated in several cases, we omitted one of them at a time and computed the predictions each of our models would have made from each pair of predictor variables, to see the effect of deleting a variable which was highly correlated with another in the equation. The

coefficients from those equations were, predictably, similar in sign and strength to the predictions made from our three-variable models, although they naturally produced somewhat poorer overall results. Had we been interested in finding the "perfect" model we would not have included all three variables each time, but for the purposes of this paper, we considered it useful to present the results for each of the variables in all four variations of the multivariate model. As noted earlier, the correlations between the various predictor variables for each time period are shown beneath tables 4, 5, and 6, respectively.

As to the autocorrelation problem, table 2 shows that several of our variables do exhibit noticeable first-order autocorrelation $r$s: $-.13$ for the 150-year WAR series, and .73 and $-.29$ for the separate centuries. The predictions of our four models do a fair job of explaining, where it exists, the autocorrelation in the war variable. The most highly autocorrelated residual terms result from our nineteenth-century predictions; in the case of the ADD/CON LEADS model, the coefficient of that residual series is .47, which, although sizable, is considerably lower than the amount of autocorrelation in the original series. The coefficients for the residuals of its predictions are .27 for the 150-year span, .47 for the nineteenth century, and $-.13$ for the twentieth.

18. We say "nearly," because we actually get the best fit in the twentieth century with the multiplicative version.

19. It has been alleged (e.g., Bleicher 1971) that one abuses the scientific method by advancing alternative interpretations without supporting data. Our view is that such a practice not only enhances the quality and cumulativeness of science by suggesting possible follow-up investigations, but helps keep our discipline relevant to the real problems of war and peace in the immediate future.

## Chapter 15. Foreign Policy Indicators: Predictors of War in History and in the State of the World Message (pp. 298-329)

1. This is a revised and abbreviated version of the paper originally prepared for the 1972 meetings of the American Political Science Association held in Washington, D.C. We want to acknowledge the important assistance of Hugh Wheeler, the comments and help of John Stuckey, Russell Leng, Stuart Bremer, Catherine Kelleher, and Charles Gochman, and the support of the National Science Foundation under grant no. GS-28476X1.

2. For some examples and discussions, see: UN (1957), Bauer (1966), Sheldon and Moore (1968), Commission on the Social Sciences (1969), U.S. (1969), Duncan (1970), Etzioni (1970), F. R. Harris (1970), and Goldston (1972). One of the earliest efforts to tap a particularly remote social condition is in Bradburn and Caplovitz (1965). And for one attempt to apply social indicators to the quality of life in the global system, see Singer (1971a). A recent bibliography is Wilcox *et al.* (1972).

3. A recurrent theme in the criticism is that expressed by Kristol (1969): "These statistics are organized primarily for management purposes. . . . We can account for public money spent [for example] on mental health, but we haven't the faintest idea whether our mental health is getting better or worse. More than that, we don't even have as yet the conceptual apparatus that would enable us to say what we *mean* by mental health, much less permit us to measure it by a series of index numbers."

   Other criticisms—especially of certain economic indicators—are their failure to reflect inequalities in distribution, the assumption that advertising or military expenditures are social "goods," and their inability to tap the more general concepts of welfare. In response to the latter criticism, one economist retorted: "Producing a summary measure of social welfare is a job for a philosopher-king, and there is no room for a philosopher-king in the federal government" (Okun 1971).

4. In one of the few efforts to estimate such performance, Jensen found that U.S. State and Defense Department respondents scored 67 percent and 63 percent respectively on twenty-five predictions made in 1965 re: diplomatic events which did or did not occur in the next half decade; see Jensen (1972).

   Among the discussions of international event prediction, and tentative efforts to devise predictive indicators, are: Dodd (1945), Bouthoul (1971), Rummel (1969), Vogel (1970), Arosalo (1971), Alcock (1972), and Newcombe and Wert (1973). A different approach is the Delphi method; see Dalkey (1972).

5. James Reston (1970) likened the first one to a maxi-coat in that "it is long, it covers a lot of territory, and it conceals the most interesting parts." Other media reactions included that of David Lawrence (1972), who saw the third report "as one of the most weighty, most serious, and best argued statements of American foreign policy to be made since the end of the Second World War." The Palm Beach *Post-Times* (Feb. 12, 1972), on the other hand, described the same one as "an election year exercise in political propaganda," full of "chest-beating superlatives" set in "gloss and glitter."

6. For a systematic, if somewhat superficial, effort to tap the superpowers' operational codes during the late 1950s, via the State Department *Bulletin, Pravda*, etc., see Singer (1964).

7. Some would say postdiction or retrodiction, but it seems reasonable to speak of prediction, even in the past, as long as we have not yet observed and recorded the unfolding of events or the extent to which the predictor and outcome variables did indeed covary.

8. For the indicators, as well as the rationale and procedures, on the incidence of war at the systemic, regional, pairwise, and national levels, see Singer and Small (1972). As the title dates imply, those wars not ended—or even begun—by December 31, 1965, are not included: the several Indochina Wars, the Six Day War in the Mideast, the Football War, and those in Yemen, Aden, and Angola. A useful summary of the overall project will be found in Singer (1972a).

9. We must differentiate here between the generalizations which can be drawn from a study of comparable cases out of the past, and the sort of dynamic models which can be generated and tested from an examination of the processes which link these cases together as they unfold across time. As Bobrow reminds us (1969, p. 5), without adequate models "we have no more than descriptive trend plots which lack explanatory power and ignore interaction effects."

10. Throughout this section, we use this time span of 1-2 years as a reasonable measure of "following soon," since a longer period would obliterate all distinctions between interwar intervals. That is, with 93 international wars over the century and a half, we get an average of almost two wars every three years, meaning that almost all three-year periods would see war following war. And if we eliminate the 43 imperial and colonial wars, looking only at those 50 which were between sovereign states, there would be an average of one war beginning every three years. See Singer and Small (1972, chap. 9).

11. Interstate wars are differentiated from extrasystemic ones in that the former ($N = 50$) have at least one sovereign state member of the system on each side, whereas the latter ($N = 43$) see system members fighting against colonies and other less-than-sovereign national entities which do not qualify for system membership.

12. We must emphasize that we are only identifying the nations which took the first act of war and initiated military hostilities. This is not always (as in the Franco- Prussian War) the side whose

behavior made the war most likely. To ascertain that with any confidence requires a very detailed and reproducible coding of the events leading up to the war, and we are now engaged in that enterprise; see Leng and Singer (1970). A similar problem exists in identifying the "winner," and for this analysis we merely accept the consensus of the historians who dealt with each of these wars. The Korean War is treated as a "draw"; see Singer and Small (1972, Chap. 14).

13. For details of our coding procedures and the resulting data sets, see Singer and Small (1966b) and Small and Singer (1969).

14. Neither have we examined the policy recommendations that might flow from these tentative findings. That responsibility we will take up in future papers, when focusing more thoroughly on one set of problems at a time.

15. In the first issue of the *Journal of Conflict Resolution* (1957, p. 94), Quincy Wright proposed the establishment of a "world intelligence center" among whose missions would be the measurement of "the changing atmosphere of world opinion [and] the changing condition of world politics." Such a use of foreign policy indicators, whose scores would be published on a weekly or monthly basis by an independent global institute, could appreciably enhance the accuracy and credibility of the facts and help clarify the range of alternatives to which the administration alludes.

16. As to the problems of communication between social scientists and the policymaker, see Burgess (1970, pp. 9–14).

17. These are, of course, impressionistic judgments that could and should be put to the test; a more affirmative view is in Levien (1969).

# Combined References

Abel, Theodore. "The Element of Decision in the Pattern of War," *American Sociological Review*, 7/4 (Dec. 1941), pp. 853-59.

Abelson, Robert. "A Derivation of Richardson's Equations," *Journal of Conflict Resolution*, 7/1 (March 1963), pp. 13-15.

Albert, Ethel M. "The Classification of Values: A Method and an Illustration," *American Anthropologist*, 58 (1956), pp. 22-24.

Alcock, Norman Z. *The Prediction of War*. Oakville, Ont.: Canadian Peace Research Institute, 1972.

Alger, Chadwick. "Comparison of Intranational and International Politics," *American Political Science Review*, 57/2 (1963), pp. 406-19.

——, and Steven J. Brams. "Patterns of Representation in National Capitals and Intergovernmental Organizations," *World Politics*, 19/4 (July 1967), pp. 646-63.

Alker, Hayward R., Jr. "Research Paradigms and Mathematical Politics," in Karl Deutsch and Rudolf Wildenmann, eds., *Social Science Yearbook for Politics*, vol. 5. Munich: Gunter Olzog, 1976.

——. "The Structure of Social Action in an Arms Race." Mimeographed. Cambridge, Mass.: M.I.T., 1968.

——, and Ronald Brunner. "Simulating International Conflict: A Comparison of Three Approaches," *International Studies Quarterly*, 13/1 (March 1969), pp. 70-110.

Alker, Hayward R., Jr., and Donald Puchala. "Trends in Economic Partnership: The North Atlantic Area, 1928-1963," in J. David Singer, ed., *Quantitative International Politics*. New York: Free Press, 1968.

Alker, Hayward R., Jr., and Bruce M. Russett. "On Measuring Inequality," *Behavioral Science*, 9/3 (July 1964), pp. 207-18.

——. *World Politics in the General Assembly*. New Haven: Yale University Press, 1965.

Allport, Floyd H. *Social Psychology*. Boston: Houghton Mifflin, 1924.

Almond, Gabriel A., and James S. Coleman. *The Politics of Developing Areas*. Princeton: Princeton University Press, 1960.

Almond, Gabriel A., and Sidney Verba. *The Civic Culture*. Princeton: Princeton University Press, 1963.

American Friends Service Committee. *Speak Truth to Power*. Philadelphia: American Friends Service Committee, 1955.

Angell, Robert C. "Moral Integration and Interpersonal Integration in American Cities," *American Sociological Review*, 14/2 (April 1949), pp. 245-50.

——. "The Moral Integration of American Cities," *American Journal of Sociology*, 57 Supplement (1951), pp. 1-140.

Aron, Raymond. *The Century of Total War*. Boston: Beacon, 1954.

Arosalo, Uolevi. "East-West Trade as a Potential Indicator of International Tension," *Instant Research on Peace and Violence* (Tampere, Finland), 3 (1971), pp. 120-25.

Arrow, Kenneth. *Social Choice and Individual Values*. New York: Wiley, 1951.

Asch, Solomon E. *Social Psychology*. Englewood Cliffs, N.J.: Prentice-Hall, 1952.

Bales, Robert F. "A Set of Categories for the Analysis of Small Group Interaction," *American Sociological Review*, 15/1 (Feb. 1950), pp. 257-63.

Banks, Arthur S., and Robert B. Textor. *A Cross-Polity Survey*. Cambridge, Mass.: M.I.T. Press, 1963.

Barnet, Richard J. *Who Wants Disarmament?* Boston: Beacon Press, 1960.

——. *The Economy of Death*. New York: Atheneum, 1970.

Bauer, Raymond A., ed. *Social Indicators*. Cambridge, Mass.: M.I.T. Press, 1966.

Bay, Christian. *The Structure of Freedom*. Stanford: Stanford University Press, 1958.

————. "Politics and Pseudopolitics: A Critical Evaluation of Some Behavioral Literature," *American Political Science Review*, 59/1 (1965), pp. 39-51.

Bechhoefer, Bernhard G. *Postwar Negotiations for Arms Control.* Washington: Brookings Institution, 1961.

Beer, Samuel H. "The Comparative Method and the Study of British Politics," *Comparative Politics*, 1/1 (Oct. 1968), pp. 19-36.

Berge, Claude. *The Theory of Graphs.* London: Methuen, 1962.

Bernard, Jessie, Tom H. Pear, Raymond Aron, and Robert C. Angell. *The Nature of Conflict.* Paris: UNESCO, 1957.

Bernstein, Robert A., and Peter D. Weldon, "A Structural Approach to the Analysis of International Relations," *Journal of Conflict Resolution*, 12/2 (June 1968), pp. 159-76.

Black, Duncan. *The Theory of Committees and Elections.* Cambridge, Eng.: Cambridge University Press, 1958.

Blaisdell, Thomas C. *The Federal Trade Commission.* New York: Columbia University Press, 1932.

Blalock, Hubert M., Jr. "Evaluating the Relative Importance of Variables," *American Sociological Review*, 26/1 (Feb. 1961), pp. 866-74.

————. *Causal Inference in Nonexperimental Research.* Chapel Hill: University of North Carolina Press, 1964.

————. "Theory Building and the Statistical Concept of Interaction," *American Sociological Review*, 30/3 (June 1965), pp. 374-80.

Bleicher, Samuel. "Intergovernmental Organization and the Preservation of Peace: A Comment on the Abuse of Methodology," *International Organization*, 25/2 (Spring 1971), pp. 298-305.

Bloch, Ivan de. *The Future of War.* New York: Doubleday & McClure, 1899.

Bloomfield, Lincoln, and Robert Beattie. "Computers and Policy-Making: The CASCON Experiment," *Journal of Conflict Resolution*, 15/1 (March 1971), pp. 33-46.

Bloomfield, Lincoln, and Norman Padelford. "Three Experiments in Political Gaming," *American Political Science Review*, 52/4 (1959), pp. 1105-15.

Bobrow, Davis. "International Indicators." New York: American Political Science Association Meetings, Sept. 1969.

————. *Political and Social Forecasting.* Gaithersburg, Md.: National Bureau of Standards, 1970.

————, and Judah Schwartz, eds. *Computers and the Policy Making Community.* Englewood Cliffs, N.J.: Prentice-Hall, 1968.

Bodart, Gaston. *Losses of Life in Modern Wars*. Oxford: Clarendon Press, 1916.

Boulding, Kenneth. *Conflict and Defense*. New York: Harper, 1962.

Bouthoul, Gaston. "Les Baromètres Polémologiques," *Études Polémologiques*, 1 (1971), pp. 1- 26.

Bowie, Robert R. "Basic Requirements of Arms Control," in Donald G. Brennan, ed., *Arms Control, Disarmament, and National Security*. New York: George Braziller, 1961, pp. 43- 55.

Bradburn, Norman, and David Caplovitz. *Reports on Happiness*. Chicago: Aldine, 1965.

Brams, Steven J. "Measuring the Concentration of Power in Political Systems," *American Political Science Review*, 62/6 (June 1968), pp. 461- 75.

———. "The Structure of Influence Relationships in the International Systems," in James N. Rosenau, ed., *International Politics and Foreign Policy*, 2d ed. New York: Free Press, 1969, pp. 583- 99.

Brandt, Richard. *Ethical Theory*. Englewood Cliffs, N.J.: Prentice-Hall, 1959.

Braybrooke, David. *Three Tests for Democracy*. New York: Random House, 1968.

Bremer, Stuart A. "National and International Systems: A Computer Simulation." Ph.D. dissertation, Michigan State University, 1970.

———, J. David Singer, and Urs Luterbacher. "The Population Density and War Proneness of European Nations, 1816- 1965," *Comparative Political Studies*, 6/3 (Oct. 1973), pp. 329- 48.

Brennan, Donald G., ed. *Arms Control, Disarmament, and National Security*. New York: Braziller, 1961.

Buchanan, James, and Gordon Tullock. *The Calculus of Consent*. Ann Arbor: University of Michigan Press, 1965.

Bueno de Mesquita, Bruce. "Measuring Systemic Polarity," *Journal of Conflict Resolution*, 19/2 (June 1975), pp. 187- 216.

Burgess, Phillip. "International Relations Theory: Prospects, 1970-1995." Los Angeles: American Political Science Association Meetings, Sept. 1970.

Burns, Arthur. "A Graphical Approach to Some Problems of the Arms Race," *Journal of Conflict Resolution*, 3/4 (Dec. 1959), pp. 326- 42.

Burr, Robert N. "The Balance of Power in Nineteenth Century South America: An Exploratory Essay," *Hispanic American Historical Review*, 25 (Feb. 1955), pp. 37- 60.

Burton, John W. "Peace Research and International Relations," *Journal of Conflict Resolution*, 8/3 (Sept. 1964), pp. 281- 86.

Cady, Richard. *Some Notes on the Theory of Arms Races.* Ann Arbor: Bendix Systems Division (BSR 2063), 1966.

Campbell, Donald T. "Common Fate, Similarity, and Other Indices of the Status of Aggregates of Persons as Social Entities," *Behavioral Science*, 3/1 (Jan. 1958), pp. 14-25.

———, and Julian Stanley. *Experimental and Quasi-Experimental Designs for Research.* Chicago: Rand McNally, 1966.

Cantril, Hadley. "The Prediction of Social Events," *Journal of Abnormal and Social Psychology*, 33 (1938), pp. 364-89.

———, ed. *Tensions that Cause Wars.* Urbana: University of Illinois Press, 1950.

Carr, Edward H. *Nationalism and After.* London: Macmillan, 1945.

Carroll, Berenice. "Peace Research: The Cult of Power," *Journal of Conflict Resolution*, 16/4 (Dec. 1972), pp. 585-616.

Caspary, William. "Richardson's Model of Arms Races: Description, Critique, and an Alternative Model," *International Studies Quarterly*, 11/1 (March 1967), pp. 63-88.

Chapin, F. Stuart. *Experimental Designs in Sociological Research.* New York: Harper, 1947.

Chase, Philip. "Control Theory and the Nuclear Arms Race," *Bendix Technical Journal*, 1/3 (1968a), pp. 43-54.

———. "The Relevance of Arms Race Theory to Arms Control," *General Systems*, 13 (1968b), pp. 91-98.

Choucri, Nazli, and Robert C. North. *Nations in Conflict: Prelude to World War I.* San Francisco: W. H. Freeman, 1975.

Clark, Grenville, and Louis Sohn. *World Peace through World Law.* Cambridge, Mass.: Harvard University Press, 1960.

Clark, Grover. *The Balance Sheets of Imperialism.* New York: Columbia University Press, 1936.

Claude, Inis L., Jr. *Swords into Plowshares.* New York: Random House, 1956.

———. *Power and International Relations.* New York: Random House, 1962.

Cobden, Richard. "The Three Panics: An Historical Episode," in *Political Writings.* New York: Appleton, 1867.

Cohen, Benjamin V. "Disarmament and International Law," in U.S. Mission to United Nations Press Release No. 1469, May 3, 1952.

Cohen, Bernard C. *The Press and Foreign Policy.* Princeton: Princeton University Press, 1963.

Coleman, James S. *Introduction to Mathematical Sociology.* New York: Free Press, 1964.

Comfort, Alex. *Authority and Delinquency in the Modern State.* London: Routledge & Kegan Paul, 1950.

Commission on the Social Sciences, National Sciences Board. *Knowledge into Action: Improving the Nation's Use of the Social Sciences.* Washington: National Science Foundation, 1969.

Cutright, Phillips. "National Political Development: Measurement and Analysis," *American Sociological Review,* 28/2 (April 1963), pp. 253-64.

Dahl, Robert A. "The Concept of Power," *Behavioral Science,* 2/3 (July 1957), pp. 201-15.

——, and Charles Lindblom. *Politics, Economics, and Welfare.* New York: Harper, 1953.

Dalkey, Norman. ed. *Studies in the Quality of Life: Delphi and Decision-Making.* Lexington, Mass.: Lexington, 1972.

Davies, David. *The Problem of the Twentieth Century.* New York: Putnam, 1931.

Davies, James. *Human Nature in Politics.* New York: Wiley, 1963.

Davis, Otto A., M.A.H. Dempster, and Aaron Wildavsky. "A Theory of the Budgetary Process," *American Political Science Review,* 60/3 (1966), pp. 529-47.

Davis, Robert H., et al. *Arms Control Simulation.* Santa Monica: System Development Corporation, 1961.

De Jouvenel, Bertrand. *The Art of Conjecture.* New York: Basic Books, 1967.

Denton, Frank H. "Some Regularities in International Conflict, 1820-1949," *Background,* 9/4 (1966), pp. 283-96.

Deutsch, Karl W. *Nationalism and Social Communication.* Cambridge, Mass.: M.I.T. Press, 1953.

——. "Toward an Inventory of Basic Trends and Patterns in Comparative and International Politics," *American Political Science Review,* 54/1 (1960), pp. 34-57.

——. "Social Mobilization and Political Development," *American Political Science Review,* 55/3 (1961), pp. 493-514.

——. *The Nerves of Government.* New York: Free Press, 1963.

——. *Nationalism and Its Alternatives.* New York: Knopf, 1969.

——, and Richard Merritt. "Effects of Events upon National and International Images," in Herbert C. Kelman, ed., *International Behavior: A Social-Psychological Analysis.* New York: Holt, 1965, pp. 132-87.

Deutsch, Karl W., and J. David Singer. "Multipolar Power Systems and International Stability," *World Politics,* 16/3 (April 1964), pp. 390-406.

Deutsch, Karl W., J. David Singer, and Keith Smith. "The Organizing Efficiency of Theories: The N/V Ratio as a Crude Rank Order Measure," *American Behavioral Scientist*, 9/2 (Oct. 1965), pp. 30–33.

Diplomatic Year-Book. London: Diplomatic Press and Publishing Company, 1951.

Dodd, Stuart. "A Barometer of Perceived International Security," *Public Opinion Quarterly*, 9/2 (Summer 1945), pp. 194–200.

Dollar, Charles M., and Richard J. Jensen. *Historian's Guide to Statistics*. New York: Holt, 1971.

Dumas, Samuel, and Knud Otto Vedel-Peterson. *Losses of Life Caused by War*. Oxford: Clarendon, 1923.

Duncan, Otis Dudley. *Toward Social Reporting: Next Steps*. New York: Russell Sage Foundation, 1970.

Dunn, Frederick S. *War and the Minds of Men*. New York: Harper, 1950.

East, Maurice A. "Stratification and International Politics." Ph.D. dissertation, Princeton University, 1969.

Easton, David. *The Political System*. New York: Knopf, 1953.

———. *Systems Analysis of Political Life*. New York: Wiley, 1965.

Eckstein, Harry, ed. *Internal War: Basic Problems and Approaches*. New York: Free Press, 1963.

Edwards, Ward. "Utility, Subjective Probability, Their Interaction, and Variance Preferences," *Journal of Conflict Resolution*, 6/1 (March 1962), pp. 42–51.

Eldersveld, Samuel J. "Experimental Propaganda Techniques and Voting Behavior," *American Political Science Review*, 50/1 (1956), pp. 154–65.

Encounter, "Column," 27 (July 1966), pp. 29–30.

Etzioni, Amitai. *Political Unification*. New York: Holt, 1965.

———. *The Active Society*. New York: Free Press, 1968.

———. "Indicators of the Capacities for Societal Guidance," in Bertram M. Gross and Michael Springer, eds., "Political Intelligence for America's Future," American Academy of Political and Social Science, *Annals*, 388 (March 1970), pp. 25–34.

Eulau, Heinz. *Policy Making in American Cities: Comparisons in a Quasi-Longitudinal, Quasi-Experimental Design*. Morristown, N.J.: General Learning Press, 1971.

Eysenck, Hans J. "War and Aggressiveness," in Tom H. Pear, ed., *Psychological Factors of Peace and War*. New York: Philosophical Library, 1950, pp. 49–82.

Ezekiel, Mordecai, and Karl A. Fox. *Methods of Correlation and Regression Analysis.* New York: Wiley, 1959.

Fainsod, Merle. *How Russia is Ruled.* Cambridge, Mass.: Harvard University Press, 1954.

Falk, Richard A. "International Jurisdiction: Horizontal and Vertical Conceptions of Legal Order," *Temple Law Quarterly,* 32 (1959), pp. 295-320.

Feierabend, Ivo K., and Rosalind L. Feierabend. "Aggressive Behaviors within Polities, 1948-62," *Journal of Conflict Resolution,* 10/3 (Sept. 1966), pp. 249-71.

Feld, Bernard T., et al. *The Technical Problems of Arms Control.* New York: Institute for International Order, 1959.

Finch, Frank A. "An International Criminal Court: The Case Against its Adoption," *American Bar Association Journal,* 38 (1952), pp. 644-48.

Fisher, Ronald A. *Statistical Methods for Research Workers.* London: Oliver and Boyd, 1925.

———, and Ghuean T. Prance. *The Design of Experiments.* London: Oliver and Boyd, 1935.

Flament, Claude. *Applications of Graph Theory to Group Structure.* Englewood Cliffs, N.J.: Prentice-Hall, 1963.

French, John R. P., and Bertram Raven. "The Bases of Social Power," in Dorwin Cartwright, ed., *Studies in Social Power.* Ann Arbor: Institute for Social Research, 1959, pp. 150-67.

Frisch, David H., ed. *Arms Reduction: Programs and Issues.* New York: Twentieth Century Fund, 1961.

Fritz, C. L., et al. *A Modern Information System for the Department of State.* Washington: Department of State, 1967.

Fucks, Wilhelm. *Formeln zur Macht.* Stuttgart, Germany: Deutsch Verlags-Anstalt, 1965.

Galtung, Johan. "Violence, Peace, and Peace Research," *Journal of Peace Research,* 3 (1969), pp. 167-91.

Gareau, Frederic H., ed. *The Balance of Power and Nuclear Deterrence: A Book of Readings.* Boston: Houghton Mifflin, 1962.

Gerard, Ralph W. "The Scope of Science," *Scientific Monthly,* 44/6 (1947), pp. 496-516.

———. "To Prevent Another World War: Truth Detection," *Journal of Conflict Resolution,* 5/2 (June 1961), pp. 212-18.

German, F. Clifford. "A Tentative Evaluation of World Power," *Journal of Conflict Resolution,* 4/1 (March 1960), pp. 138-44.

Gleditsch, Nils Petter. *Fragments of a Theory of Arms Races.* Ann Arbor, Mich.: Bendix Systems Division (BSR 2059), 1967.

———, and J. David Singer. "Distance and International War, 1816-1965," IPRA Fifth General Conference, Oslo, *Proceedings* (1975), pp. 481-506.

Goldston, Eli. *The Quantification of Concern: Some Aspects of Social Accounting.* New York: Columbia University Press, 1972.

Goodman, Leo. "Generalizing the Problem of Prediction," *American Sociological Review,* 17/5 (Oct. 1952), pp. 609-12.

Gorden, Morton. "Burdens for the Design of a Computer Simulation," in Davis Bobrow and Judah Schwartz, eds., *Computers and the Policy-Making Community.* Englewood Cliffs, N.J.: Prentice-Hall, 1968.

Greenwood, Ernest. *Experimental Sociology: A Study in Method.* New York: King's Crown, 1945.

Grundberg, Emile, and Franco Modigliani. "The Predictability of Social Events," *Journal of Political Economy,* 62 (1954), pp. 465-78.

Guetzkow, Harold, Chadwick Alger, Richard Brody, Robert Noel, and Richard Snyder. *Simulation in International Relations: Determinants for Research and Teaching.* Englewood Cliffs, N.J.: Prentice-Hall, 1963.

Gulick, Edward V. *Europe's Classical Balance of Power.* Ithaca: Cornell University Press, 1955.

Gurr, Ted Robert. *The Conditions of Civil Violence: First Tests of a Causal Model.* Princeton: Center of International Studies, Princeton University, 1967.

Haas, Ernst B. "The Balance of Power: Prescription, Concept, or Propaganda," *World Politics,* 5/3 (April 1953), pp. 442-77.

———. *Beyond the Nation State.* Stanford: Stanford University Press, 1964.

———, and Allen S. Whiting. *Dynamics of International Relations.* New York: McGraw-Hill, 1956.

Habermas, Jurgen. *Toward a Rational Society: Student Protest, Science, and Politics.* Translated by Jeremy J. Shapiro. Boston, Mass.: Beacon Press, 1970.

Hale, Oron J. *The Captive Press in the Third Reich.* Princeton: Princeton University Press, 1964.

Hallowell, John. *Main Currents in Modern Political Thought.* New York: Holt, 1950.

Hammond, Paul Y. "Some Difficulties of Self-Enforcing Arms Agreements," *Journal of Conflict Resolution,* 6/2 (June 1962), pp. 103-15.

Harary, Frank. "A Structural Analysis of the Situation in the Middle East," *Journal of Conflict Resolution,* 5/2 (June 1961), pp. 167-78.

Hargreaves, Reginald. *The Enemy at the Gate: A Book of Famous Sieges, Their Causes, Their Progress, and Their Consequences.* Harrisburg, Pa.: Stackpole, 1948.

Harr, John E. *The Anatomy of the Foreign Service: A Statistical Profile.* New York: Carnegie Endowment, 1965.

Harris, Craig, ed. *Problems in Measuring Change.* Madison: University of Wisconsin Press, 1963.

Harris, Fred R., ed. *Social Science and National Policy.* Chicago: Aldine, 1970.

Haug, M. R. "Social and Cultural Pluralism as a Concept in Social System Analysis," *American Journal of Sociology,* 73 (Nov. 1967), pp. 294-304.

Helmer, Olaf, et al. *Social Technology.* New York: Basic Books, 1966.

Henderson, Gerard C. *The Federal Trade Commission.* New Haven: Yale University Press, 1924.

Henkin, Louis. *Arms Control and Inspection in American Law.* New York: Columbia University Press, 1958.

Hirshleifer, Jack. "Some Thoughts on the Social Structure after a Bombing Disaster," *World Politics,* 8/1 (Oct. 1956), pp. 206-27.

Hirst, Francis W. *Armaments: The Race and the Crisis.* London, Cobden-Sanderson, 1937.

Hobbes, Thomas. *Leviathan.* London: J. M. Dent, 1914.

Holsti, Ole R. *Content Analysis for the Social Sciences and Humanities.* Reading, Mass.: Addison-Wesley, 1969.

——, and Robert C. North. "The History of Human Conflict," in Elton B. McNeil, ed., *The Nature of Human Conflict.* Englewood Cliffs, N.J.: Prentice-Hall, 1965, pp. 155-71.

Holsti, Ole R., Richard A. Brody, and Robert C. North. "Violence and Hostility: The Path to World War." Los Angeles: American Psychiatric Association Conference, 1964.

Holsti, Ole R., Robert C. North, and Richard A. Brody. "Perception and Action in the 1914 Crises," in J. David Singer, ed., *Quantitative International Politics.* New York: Free Press, 1968, pp. 123-58.

Holt, Robert T., and John E. Turner. *The Political Basis of Economic Development.* Princeton: Van Nostrand, 1966.

Horne, M. R. "Could an Arms-Race End Without Fighting?" *Nature,* 168 (Nov. 24, 1951), p. 920.

Horvath, Fred. "Psychological Stress: A Review of Definitions and Experimental Research," *General Systems,* 4 (1959), pp. 203-30.

Horvath, William J., and Caxton C. Foster. "Stochastic Models of War Alliances," *Journal of Conflict Resolution*, 7/2 (June 1963), pp. 110-16.

Hovet, Thomas, Jr. *Africa in the United Nations*. Evanston, Ill.: Northwestern University Press, 1963.

Hudson, Manley O. "The Treaty-Making Power of the United States in Connection with the Manufacture of Arms and Ammunition," *American Journal of International Law*, 28 (1934), pp. 736-39.

Huntington, Samuel P. "Arms Races: Prerequisites and Results," *Public Policy*, 18 (1958), pp. 41-86.

———. "Political Development and Political Decay," *World Politics*, 17/4 (April 1965), pp. 386-430.

Huszar, George D.B. *Soviet Power and Policy*. New York: Crowell, 1955.

Hutt, Sidney J., and Corinne Hutt. *Direct Observation and Measurement of Behavior*. Springfield, Ill.: Charles C. Thomas, 1970.

Iklé, Fred C. "After Detection—What?" *Foreign Affairs*, 39 (1961), pp. 208-20.

Intriligator, Michael D. "Some Simple Models of Arms Races," *General Systems*, 9 (1964), pp. 143-47.

Janeway, Eliot. *The Economics of Crisis*. New York: Weybright & Talley, 1968.

Jensen, Lloyd. "Predicting International Events," *Peace Research Reviews*, 4/6 (1972), pp. 1-65.

Jessup, Philip C. *Transnational Law*. New Haven: Yale University Press, 1956.

Kahn, Herman. *A Report on a Study of Non-Military Defense*. Report R-322-RC. Santa Monica: The RAND Corporation, 1958.

———. *On Thermonuclear War*. Princeton: Princeton University Press, 1960.

———, and Anthony J. Wiener. *The Year Two Thousand*. New York: Macmillan, 1967.

Kahn, Herman, et al. *Some Specific Suggestions for Obtaining Early Non-Military Defense Capabilities and Initiating Long Range Programs*. Memorandum RM-2206-RC. Santa Monica: The RAND Corporation, 1957.

Kaplan, Morton A. "Balance of Power, Bipolarity, and Other Models of International Systems," *American Political Science Review*, 51/3 (1957a), pp. 684-95.

———. *System and Process in International Politics*. New York: Wiley, 1957b.

Kaplan, Norman, ed. *Science and Society*. Chicago: Rand McNally, 1965.

Katz, Daniel. "The Functional Approach to the Study of Attitudes," *Public Opinion Quarterly*, 24/2 (1960), pp. 163-204.

Kelman, Herbert C. *A Time to Speak*. San Francisco: Jossey-Bass, 1968.

Kennan, George F. *American Diplomacy, 1900-1950*. New York: Mentor, 1952.

———. *Realities of American Foreign Policy*. Princeton: Princeton University Press, 1954.

Kent, George. "The Application of Peace Studies," *Journal of Conflict Resolution*, 15/1 (March 1971), pp. 47-54.

Kissinger, Henry A. *Nuclear Weapons and Foreign Policy*. New York: Harper, 1957.

Klineberg, Otto. *Social Psychology*. New York: Henry Holt & Co., 1954.

———. *Human Dimension in International Relations*. New York: Holt, 1964.

Klingberg, Frank L. *Historical Study of War Casualties*. Washington: Department of War, 1945.

Kluckhohn, F. R. "A Method for Eliciting Value Orientations," *Anthropological Linguistics*, 2 (Feb. 1960), pp. 1-23.

Knorr, Klaus. *The War Potential of Nations*. Princeton: Princeton University Press, 1956.

Kort, Fred. "Regression Analysis and Discriminant Analysis," *American Political Science Review*, 67/2 (1973), pp. 555-59.

Kriesberg, Louis, ed. *Social Processes in International Relations*. New York: Wiley, 1969.

Krippendorf, Ekkehart. "The State as a Focus of Peace Research," *Peace Research Society Papers*, 16 (1971), pp. 47-60.

Kristol, Irving. "In Search of the Missing Social Indicators," *Fortune* (Aug. 1, 1969), pp. 168-69.

Kruglak, Theodore E. *The Two Faces of Tass*. New York: McGraw-Hill, 1963.

Kulski, Wladyslaw. *The Soviet Regime: Communism in Practice*. Syracuse: Syracuse University Press, 1954.

Landfield, Alvin. "Self-Predictive Orientation and the Movement Interpretation of Threat," *Journal of Abnormal and Social Psychology*, 51 (1955), pp. 434-38.

Langer, William L. *European Alliances and Alignments, 1871-1890*. New York: Knopf, 1931.

Lanzetta, John T. "Group Behavior Under Stress," *Human Relations*,

8 (1955), pp. 29- 52.

Laponce, Jean A. "An Experimental Method to Measure the Tendency to Equibalance in a Political System," *American Political Science Review*, 60/4 (1966), pp. 982- 93.

———. "Experimenting: A Two-Person Game Between Man and Nature," in Jean A. Laponce and Paul Smoker, eds., *Experimentation and Simulation in Political Science*. Toronto: University of Toronto Press, 1972, pp. 1- 15.

Laski, Harold J. *The Dangers of Obedience*. New York: Harper, 1930.

Lasswell, Harold D., and Abraham Kaplan. *Power and Society*. New Haven: Yale University Press, 1950.

Lawrence, David. " 'The London Times' Makes Notable Comments on Nixon's Message," *U.S. News and World Report* (Feb. 28, 1972), p. 92.

Lazarsfeld, Paul. "The American Soldier—An Expository Review," *Public Opinion Quarterly*, 13/3 (1949), pp. 377- 404.

Leary, Timothy. *Interpersonal Diagnosis of Personality*. New York: Ronald, 1957.

Leites, Nathan C. *Operational Code of the Politburo*. New York: McGraw-Hill, 1956.

Leng, Russell J., and J. David Singer. "Toward a Multi-Theoretical Typology of International Behavior." Mimeographed. Ann Arbor: Mental Health Research Institute, 1970.

Levien, Roger. *Independent Public Policy Analysis Organizations: A Major Social Invention*. Santa Monica: The RAND Corporation, 1969.

Lewin, Leonard, et al. *Report from Iron Mountain*. New York: Dial, 1967.

Lijphart, Arend. "Typologies of Democratic Systems," *Comparative Political Studies*, 1/1 (April 1968), pp. 3- 44.

———. "Comparative Politics and the Comparative Method," *American Political Science Review*, 65/3 (1971), pp. 682- 93.

Liska, George. *Nations in Alliance: Limits of Interdependence*. Baltimore: Johns Hopkins Press, 1962.

Loosbrock, John F. "Minimum Deterrence Is a Phony," *Air Force*, 43/10 (Oct. 1960), p. 6.

Lorwin, Val R., and Jacob M. Price, eds. *The Dimensions of the Past*. New Haven: Yale University Press, 1972.

Lotka, Alfred J. "The Growth of Mixed Populations: Two Species Competing for a Common Food Supply," *Journal of the Washington Academy of Sciences*, 22 (1932), p. 461.

Macmahon, Arthur. *Administration in Foreign Affairs.* University, Ala.: University of Alabama Press, 1953.

Madariaga, Salvador de. *Disarmament.* New York: Coward-McCann, 1929.

Masters, Roger D. "World Politics as a Primitive Political System," *World Politics,* 16/4 (July 1964), pp. 595-619.

McClelland, David. *The Achieving Society.* Princeton: Van Nostrand, 1961.

McGuire, Martin C. *Secrecy and the Arms Race.* Cambridge, Mass.: Harvard University Press, 1965.

Meadows, Donella, Dennis L. Meadows, Jorgen Randers, and William W. Behrens III. *The Limits to Growth.* New York: Universe, 1972.

Meehl, Paul. *Clinical vs. Statistical Prediction.* Minneapolis: University of Minneapolis Press, 1954.

Melman, Seymour. *Inspection for Disarmament.* New York: Columbia University Press, 1958.

Merton, Robert K. *Social Theory and Social Structure.* New York: Free Press, 1957.

Michael, Donald. "Civilian Behavior under Atomic Bombardment," *Bulletin of the Atomic Scientists,* 11 (1955), pp. 173-77.

Midlarsky, Manus. "Status Inconsistency and the Onset of International Warfare." Ph.D. dissertation, Northwestern University, 1969.

Milburn, Thomas W., et al. *Non-Physical Inspection Techniques.* Boston: American Academy of Arts and Sciences, 1961.

Miller, Warren. "Voting and Foreign Policy," in James N. Rosenau, ed., *Domestic Sources of Foreign Policy.* New York: Free Press, 1967, pp. 213-30.

Milsum, John, ed. *Positive Feedback.* Oxford: Pergamon, 1968.

Modelski, George. *The International Relations of Internal War.* Princeton: Center of International Studies, Princeton University, 1961.

Moll, Kendall D. *The Influence of History upon Seapower, 1865-1914.* Menlo Park: Stanford Research Institute, 1968.

Moore, Barrington, Jr. *Soviet Politics: The Dilemma of Power.* Cambridge, Mass.: Harvard University Press, 1950.

Moore, Wilbert. "Predicting Discontinuities in Social Change," *American Sociological Review,* 29/3 (June 1964), pp. 331-38.

Morgenstern, Oskar. *On the Accuracy of Economic Observations.* 2d ed. Princeton: Princeton University Press, 1963.

——. *The Question of National Defense.* New York: Random House, 1959.

Morgenthau, Hans J. *Politics among Nations.* 4th ed. New York: Knopf, 1967.

——, and Kenneth W. Thompson, eds. *Principles and Problems of International Relations: Selected Readings.* New York: Knopf, 1956.

Mueller, John, ed., *Approaches to Measurement in International Relations.* New York: Appleton, 1969.

Murphy, Robert E. "Effects of Threat of Shock, Distraction and Task Design on Performance," *Journal of Experimental Psychology,* 58 (1959), pp. 134-141.

Nagel, Ernest. *The Structure of Science.* New York: Harcourt, 1961.

Naylor, Thomas H. *Computer Simulation Experiments with Models of Economic Systems.* New York: Wiley, 1971.

Neunreither, N. "Budget Expenditures as Indices of Political Integration." Brussels: International Political Science Association Meetings, Sept. 1967.

Newcombe, Alan, and James Wert. "The Use of an Inter-Nation Tensiometer for the Prediction of War," *Peace Science Society Papers,* 21 (1973), pp. 73-83.

Nicolson, Harold. *The Congress of Vienna.* London: Folcroft, 1946.

Nimmo, Dan. *Newsgathering in Washington.* New York: Atherton, 1964.

Nogee, Joseph. *Soviet Policy toward International Control of Atomic Energy.* Notre Dame: University of Notre Dame Press, 1961.

Okun, Arthur. "Should GNP Measure Social Welfare?" *Brookings Bulletin,* 8/3 (1971), pp. 4-7.

Oppenheim, Felix E. "Degrees of Power and Freedom," *American Political Science Review,* 54/2 (1960), pp. 437-46.

Osgood, Charles E. *An Alternative to War or Surrender.* Urbana: University of Illinois Press, 1962.

Osgood, Robert. *Limited War.* Chicago: University of Chicago Press, 1957.

Pally, Sidney. "Cognitive Rigidity as a Function of Threat," *Journal of Personality,* 23 (1955), pp. 346-55.

Parker, John J. "An International Criminal Court: The Case for Its Adoption," *American Bar Association Journal,* 38 (1952), pp. 641-44.

Parsons, Talcott. "Order and Community in the International Social System," in James N. Rosenau, ed., *International Politics and Foreign Policy.* New York: Free Press, 1961, pp. 120-29.

Pearson, Karl. *The Grammar of Science.* New York: Meridian, 1957.

Pepitone, Albert, and Robert Kleiner. "The Effects of Threat and Frustration on Group Cohesiveness," *Journal of Abnormal and Social Psychology,* 54 (1957), pp. 192-99.

Perlo, Victor. *Militarism and Industry.* New York: International Publishers, 1963.

Platt, John R. "Strong Inference," *Science,* 146/3642 (Oct. 1964), pp. 347-53.

Pool, Ithiel de Sola. "Public Opinion and the Control of Armaments," in Donald G. Brennan, ed., *Arms Control, Disarmament, and National Security.* New York: Braziller, 1961, pp. 333-46.

Popper, Karl R. *Conjecture and Refutation.* New York: Basic Books, 1965.

Pye, Lucian W. *Aspects of Political Development.* Boston: Little, Brown, 1966.

Rapoport, Anatol. "Lewis F. Richardson's Mathematical Theory of War," *Journal of Conflict Resolution,* 1/3 (Sept. 1957), pp. 249-99.

——. "Mathematical Models of Social Interaction," in R. Duncan Luce, Robert Bush, and Eugene Galanter, eds., *Handbook of Mathematical Psychology,* vol. II. New York: Wiley, 1963, pp. 494-579.

——. "Methodology in the Physical, Biological, and Social Sciences," *General Systems,* 14 (1969), pp. 179-86.

——. "Is Peace Research Applicable?" *Journal of Conflict Resolution,* 14/2 (June 1970a), pp. 277-86.

——. *N-Person Game Theory: Concepts and Applications.* Ann Arbor: University of Michigan Press, 1970b.

——. "Various Conceptions of Peace Research," *Peace Research Society Papers,* 19 (1972), pp. 91-106.

——, and Melvin Guyer. "The Psychology of Conflict Involving Mixed-Motive Decisions." Reprint. Ann Arbor: Mental Health Research Institute, 1969.

Rapoport, Anatol, and William J. Horvath. "A Study of a Large Sociogram," *Behavioral Science,* 6 (Oct. 1961), pp. 279-91.

Ray, James L. "Status Inconsistency and War Involvement among European States, 1816-1970." Ph.D. dissertation, University of Michigan, 1974.

——, and J. David Singer. "Measuring the Concentration of Power in the International System," *Sociological Methods and Research,* 1/4 (May 1973), pp. 403-37.

**Read, Thornton.** *A Proposal to Neutralize Nuclear Weapons.* Princeton: Center of International Studies, Princeton University, 1960.

**Reston, James.** *The Artillery of the Press.* New York: Harper, 1966.

——. "The Nixon Doctrine and Assumptions," *New York Times* (Feb. 20, 1970), p. 40.

**Richardson, Lewis F.** "Generalized Foreign Politics," *British Journal of Psychology*, Monograph Supplement no. 23 (June 1939), pp. 1–89.

——. "Threats and Security," in Tom H. Pear, ed., *Psychological Factors of Peace and War.* New York: Philosophical Library, 1950, pp. 219–35.

——. "Could an Arms Race End Without Fighting?" *Nature*, 168 (Sept. 29, 1951), pp. 567–68.

——. *Arms and Insecurity.* Pittsburgh: Boxwood, 1960a.

——. *Statistics of Deadly Quarrels.* Pittsburgh: Boxwood, 1960b.

**Riggs, Robert E.** *Politics in the United Nations: A Study of United States Influence in the General Assembly.* Urbana: University of Illinois Press, 1958.

**Rizzo, N. D., and W. Gray,** eds. *Unity and Diversity.* New York: Braziller, 1970.

**Rosecrance, Richard N.** *Action and Reaction in World Politics.* Boston: Little, Brown, 1963.

**Rosenau, James N.** *National Leadership and Foreign Policy.* Princeton: Princeton University Press, 1963.

——. *International Aspects of Civil Strife.* Princeton: Princeton University Press, 1964.

——, ed. *Domestic Sources of Foreign Policy.* New York: Free Press, 1967.

——, ed. *International Politics and Foreign Policy.* 1st ed. Glencoe, Ill.: Free Press, 1961. 2d ed. New York: Free Press, 1969a.

——, ed. *Linkage Politics: Essays in National and International Systems.* New York: Free Press, 1969b.

**Rosenthal, Robert.** "On the Social Psychology of the Psychological Experiment," *American Scientist*, 51/2 (1963), pp. 268–83.

——. *Experimenter Effects in Behavioral Research.* New York: Appleton, 1966.

**Rosow, S. M., and John B. Phelps.** *Measures of Destruction: Some Observations on Damage Levels in a General Nuclear War.* Mershon Research Paper no. 3. Columbus: Ohio State University Press, 1959.

Rothstein, Robert L. *Planning, Prediction, and Policy-Making in Foreign Affairs.* Boston: Little, Brown, 1972.

Rowney, Don I., and James Q. Graham, eds. *Quantitative History: Selected Readings in the Quantitative Analysis of Historical Data.* Homewood, Ill.: Dorsey, 1969.

Rummel, Rudolph J. "Dimensions of Conflict Behavior within and between Nations," *General Systems,* 8 (1963), pp. 1-50.

———. "Forecasting International Relations: A Proposed Investigation of Three-Mode Factor Analysis," *Technological Forecasting,* 1 (1969), pp. 197-216.

Russett, Bruce M. *Trends in World Politics.* New York: Macmillan, 1965.

———, and W. Curtis Lamb. "Global Patterns of Diplomatic Exchange, 1963-64," *Journal of Peace Research,* 3 (1969), pp. 37-55.

Russett, Bruce M., J. David Singer, and Melvin Small. "National Political Units in the 20th Century: A Standardized List," *American Political Science Review,* 62/3 (1968), pp. 932-51.

Russett, Bruce M., et al. *World Handbook of Political and Social Indicators.* New Haven: Yale University Press, 1964.

Saaty, Thomas. *Mathematical Models of Arms Control and Disarmament.* New York: Wiley, 1968.

Savage, I. Richard, and Karl W. Deutsch. "A Statistical Model of the Gross Analysis of Transaction Flows," *Econometrica,* 28 (July 1960), pp. 551-72.

Schelling, Thomas C. "Bargaining, Communications, and Limited War," *Journal of Conflict Resolution,* 1/1 (March 1957), pp. 19-36.

———. *The Strategy of Conflict.* Cambridge, Mass.: Harvard University Press, 1960a.

———. "The Threat That Leaves Something to Chance," in *The Strategy of Conflict.* Cambridge, Mass.: Harvard University Press, 1960b.

Schmid, Herman. "Politics and Peace Research," *Journal of Peace Research,* 3 (1968), pp. 217-32.

Schwartz, David. "From Political Theory to Peace Policy," *Peace Research Society Papers,* 11 (1969), pp. 43-46.

Schwarzenberger, Georg. *Power Politics.* New York: Praeger, 1951.

Schwartzman, Simon, and Manuel M. Y. Araujo. "The Images of International Stratification in Latin America," *Journal of Peace Research,* 3 (1966), pp. 225-43.

Scott, Erastus H., ed. *Journal of the Federal Convention.* Chicago: Albert, Scott & Co., 1893.

Scott, William A. "Empirical Assessment of Values and Ideologies," *American Sociological Review*, 24/3 (1959), pp. 299- 310.

Sewell, J. Patrick. *Functionalism and World Politics.* Princeton: Princeton University Press, 1965.

Sheldon, Eleanor, and Wilbert E. Moore, eds. *Indicators of Social Change.* New York: Russell Sage Foundation, 1968.

Sherif, Muzafer, and Caroline W. Sherif. *Groups in Harmony and Tension.* New York: Harper, 1953.

Sherif, Muzafer, and Carl I. Hovland. *Social Judgment.* New Haven: Yale University Press, 1961.

Simon, Herbert A. *Models of Man: Mathematical Essays on Rational Human Behavior in a Social Setting.* New York: Wiley, 1957.

———, and Frederick Stern. "The Effect of Television upon Voting Behavior in Iowa in the 1952 Presidential Election," *American Political Science Review*, 49/2 (1955), pp. 470- 77.

Singer, J. David. "Threat-Perception and the Armament-Tension Dilemma," *Journal of Conflict Resolution*, 2/1 (March 1958), pp. 90- 105.

———. "International Conflict: Three Levels of Analysis," *World Politics*, 12/3 (April 1960), pp. 453- 61.

———. "From Deterrence to Disarmament," *International Journal*, 16/4 (Autumn 1961a), pp. 307- 26.

———. "The Level of Analysis Problem in International Relations," *World Politics*, 14/1 (Oct. 1961b), pp. 77- 92.

———. "The Relevance of the Behavioral Sciences to the Study of International Relations," *Behavioral Science*, 6/4 (Oct. 1961c), pp. 324- 35.

———. "Weapons Technology and International Stability," *Centennial Review*, 5/4 (Fall 1961d), pp. 415- 35.

———. "Stable Deterrence and Its Limits," *Western Political Quarterly*, 15/3 (Sept. 1962a), pp. 449- 64.

———. *Deterrence, Arms Control, and Disarmament: Toward a Synthesis in National Security Policy.* Columbus: Ohio State University Press, 1962b.

———. *Inter-Nation Influence: The Uses and Limits of Threat.* Washington, D.C.: Institute for Defense Analyses, 1962c.

———. "Inter-Nation Influence: A Formal Model," *American Political Science Review*, 57/2 (1963a), pp. 420- 30.

——. "Media Analysis in Inspection for Disarmament," *Journal of Arms Control*, 1/3 (July 1963b), pp. 248–60.

——. "Soviet and American Foreign Policy Attitudes: Content Analysis of Elite Articulations," *Journal of Conflict Resolution*, 8/4 (Dec. 1964), pp. 424–85.

——. "Data-Making in International Relations," *Behavioral Science*, 10/1 (Jan. 1965a), pp. 68–80.

——, ed. *Human Behavior and International Politics: Contributions from the Social-Psychological Sciences.* Chicago: Rand McNally, 1965b.

——. Introduction to J. David Singer, ed., *Human Behavior and International Politics.* Chicago: Rand McNally, 1965c.

——. "Negotiation by Proxy," *Journal of Conflict Resolution*, 9/4 (Dec. 1965d), pp. 538–41.

——. Introduction to J. David Singer, ed., *Quantitative International Politics.* New York: Free Press, 1968a.

——. "Man and World Politics: The Psycho-Cultural Interface," *Journal of Social Issues*, 24/3 (July 1968b), pp. 127–56.

——, ed. *Quantitative International Politics: Insights and Evidence.* New York: Free Press, 1968c.

——. "The Global System and Its Sub-Systems: A Developmental View," in James N. Rosenau, ed., *Linkage Politics.* New York: Free Press, 1969a, pp. 21–43.

——. "The Incompleat Theorist: Insights without Evidence," in Klaus Knorr and James N. Rosenau, eds., *Contending Approaches to International Politics.* Princeton: Princeton University Press, 1969b.

——. "Knowledge, Practice, and the Social Sciences in International Politics," in Norman A. Palmer, ed., *A Design for International Relations Research: Scope, Theory, Methods, and Relevance.* Monograph 10, American Academy of Political and Social Science (Oct. 1970), pp. 137–49.

——. "Modern International War: From Conjecture to Explanation," in Albert Lepawsky et al., eds., *The Search for World Order.* New York: Appleton, 1971a, pp. 47–71.

——. "Individual Values, National Interests, and Political Development in the International System," in Irving Louis Horowitz, ed., *Studies in Comparative International Development*, 6/9 (1971b), pp. 197–210.

——. "The Correlates of War Project: Interim Report and Rationale," *World Politics*, 24/2 (Jan. 1972a), pp. 243–70.

------. *The Scientific Study of Politics: An Approach to Foreign Policy Analysis.* Morristown, N..J.: General Learning Press, 1972b.

------. "Theorists and Empiricists: The Two-Culture Problem in International Politics," in James N. Rosenau, Vincent Davis, and Maurice A. East, eds., *The Analysis of International Politics.* New York: Free Press, 1972c, pp. 80-95.

------, and Hirohide Hinomoto. "Inspecting for Weapons Production: A Modest Computer Simulation," *Journal of Peace Research*, 1 (1965), pp. 18-38.

Singer, J. David, and Paul Ray. "Decision-Making in Conflict: From Interpersonal to International Relations," *Bulletin of the Menninger Clinic*, 30/5 (Sept. 1966), pp. 300-12.

Singer, J. David, and Melvin Small. "The composition and Status Ordering of the International System, 1815-1940," *World Politics*, 18/2 (Jan. 1966a), pp. 236-82.

------. "Formal Alliances, 1815-1939: A Quantitative Description," *Journal of Peace Research*, 3 (1966b), pp. 1-32.

------. "National Alliance Commitments and War Involvement, 1815-1945," *Peace Research Society Papers*, 5 (1966c), pp. 109-40.

------. "Alliance Aggregation and the Onset of War, 1815-1945," in J. David Singer, ed., *Quantitative International Politics.* New York: Free Press, 1968, pp. 247-86.

------. *The Wages of War, 1816-1965: A Statistical Handbook.* New York: Wiley, 1972.

Singer, J. David, and Michael D. Wallace. "Inter-Governmental Organization and the Preservation of Peace, 1816-1965: Some Bivariate Relationships," *International Organization*, 24/3 (Summer 1970), pp. 520-47.

Singer, J. David, Stuart A. Bremer, and John Stuckey. "Capability Distribution, Uncertainty, and Major Power War, 1816-1965," in Bruce M. Russett, ed., *Peace, War, and Numbers.* Beverly Hills: Sage, 1972, pp. 19-48.

Skjelsbaek, Kjell. "Shared Memberships in Intergovernmental Organizations and Dyadic War, 1865-1964," in Edward H. Fedder, ed., *The United Nations: Problems and Prospects.* St. Louis: Center for International Studies, University of Missouri, 1971, pp. 31-61.

Small, Melvin, and J. David Singer. "Formal Alliances, 1816-1965: An Extension of the Basic Data," *Journal of Peace Research*, 3

(1969), pp. 257- 82.

———. "Patterns in International Warfare, 1816- 1965," in James F. Short, Jr., and Marvin E. Wolfgang, eds., "Collective Violence," Academy of Political and Social Science, *Annals*, 391 (Sept. 1970), pp. 145- 55.

———. "Diplomatic Importance of States, 1816- 1970: An Extension and Refinement of the Indicator," *World Politics*, 25/4 (July 1973), pp. 577- 99.

Small, Melvin, et al. *The Strength of Nations: Comparative Capabilities Since Waterloo.* Forthcoming.

Smelser, Neil J. *Essays in Sociological Explanation.* Englewood Cliffs, N.J.: Prentice-Hall, 1968.

Smock, Charles D. "The Relationship between Test Anxiety, Threat-Expectancy, and Recognition Thresholds for Words," *Journal of Personality*, 25 (1956), pp. 191- 201.

Smoker, Paul. "Fear in the Arms Race," *Journal of Peace Research*, 1 (1964), pp. 55- 64.

———. "Trade, Defense, and the Richardson Theory of Arms Races: A Seven Nation Study," *Journal of Peace Research*, 2 (1965), pp. 161- 76.

———. "The Arms Race as an Open and Closed System," *Peace Research Society Papers*, 8 (1967), pp. 41- 62.

Snow, C. P. *Science and Government.* Cambridge, Mass.: Harvard University Press, 1961.

Snyder, Glenn. *Deterrence by Denial and Punishment.* Princeton: Center of International Studies, Princeton University, 1959.

———. *Deterrence and Defense.* Princeton: Princeton University Press, 1961.

Snyder, Richard C. "Some Perspectives on the Use of Experimental Techniques in the Study of International Relations," in Harold Guetzkow et al., eds., *Simulation in International Relations.* Englewood Cliffs, N.J.: Prentice-Hall, 1963, pp. 1- 23.

———, and Edgar Furniss. *American Foreign Policy: Formulation, Principles, and Programs.* New York: Rinehart, 1954.

Snyder, Richard C., and James Robinson. *National and International Decision-Making.* New York: Institute for International Order, 1961.

Snyder, Richard C., H. W. Bruck, and Burton Sapin. *Decision-Making as an Approach to the Study of International Politics.* Princeton: Organizational Behavior Section, Princeton University, 1954.

Sohn, Louis B., and David H. Frisch. "Arms Reduction in the 1960's," in David H. Frisch, ed., *Arms Reduction: Program and*

*Issues*. New York: Twentieth Century Fund, 1961, pp. 21- 37.

Sorokin, Pitirim A. *Social and Cultural Dynamics*, vol. III, *War and Revolution*. New York: American Book, 1937.

Stone, Philip, et al. *The General Inquirer: A Computer Approach to Content Analysis*. Cambridge, Mass.: M.I.T. Press, 1966.

Stouffer, Samuel A. *Social Research to Test Ideas*. New York: Free Press, 1962.

Summer Study on Arms Control. *Collected Papers*. Boston: American Academy of Arts and Sciences, 1961.

Tanter, Raymond. "Dimensions of Conflict Behavior within and between Nations, 1958- 60," *Journal of Conflict Resolution*, 10/1 (March 1966), pp. 41- 64.

Taylor, Charles, and Michael C. Hudson. *World Handbook of Political and Social Indicators*. 2d ed. New Haven: Yale University Press, 1972.

Taylor, Maxwell. *The Uncertain Trumpet*. New York: Harper, 1959.

Thibaut, John, and Harold Kelley. *The Social Psychology of Groups*. New York: Wiley, 1959.

Thomas, William, and Florian Znaniecki. "The Definition of the Situation," in Theodore M. Newcomb and Eugene L. Hartley, eds., *Readings in Social Psychology*. New York: Holt, 1947, pp. 76- 77.

Thrall, Robert M., et al., eds. *Decision Processes*. New York: Wiley, 1954.

Tiryakian, Edward A. "Aftermath of a Thermonuclear Attack on the U.S.: Some Sociological Considerations," *Social Forces*, 6 (1959), pp. 291- 303.

United Nations. Department of Economic and Social Affairs. *Report on the World Social Situation*. 1957.

——. Security Council, Commission for Conventional Armaments. *Summary Records*, March 26, 1947.

United States. Department of State. *The Defense of Peace: Documents Relating to UNESCO*. Washington: Government Printing Office, 1946.

——. Congress. Senate. Committee on Foreign Relations. *Hearings* before the Subcommittee on Disarmament, 1956.

——. Congress. Joint Committee on Atomic Energy. *Biological and Environmental Effects of Nuclear War. Hearings* before the Subcommittee on Radiation, June 1959.

——. Department of State. *Documents on Disarmament, 1945- 1959*, vol. II. Washington: Government Printing Office, 1960.

——. Congress. Joint Committee on Atomic Energy. *Technical Aspects of Detection and Inspection Controls of a Nuclear Weapons Test Ban.* Washington: Government Printing Office, 1960.

——. Department of State Publication 7277. Washington: Government Printing Office, 1961.

——. Arms Control and Disarmament Agency. *Blueprint for the Peace Race.* Washington: Government Printing Office, 1962.

——. Department of Health, Education, and Welfare. *Toward a Social Report.* Washington: Government Printing Office, 1969.

——. *U.S. Foreign Policy for the 1970's: A New Strategy for Peace.* Washington, DC: Government Printing Office, 18 February 1970, 25 February 1971, 9 February 1972, and 3 May 1973.

*Social Report.* Washington: Government Printing Office, 1969.

Urlanis, Boris T. *Wars and Population.* Moscow: Progress Publishers, 1971.

Van Dyke, Vernon. *International Politics.* New York: Appleton, 1957.

Vayrynen, Raimo. "On the Definition and Measurement of Small Power Status," *Cooperation and Conflict,* 6/2 (1971), pp. 91–102.

Veblen, Thorstein. *The Nature of Peace.* New York: Huebsch, 1919.

Vladimirov, S. "Disarmament and Plans for Establishment of an International Police Force," *International Affairs* (Moscow), 4 (1960), pp. 44–49.

Vogel, Arthur. "Toward a Foreign Policy Reporting System," *World Affairs,* 133/2 (Sept. 1970), pp. 106–14.

Von Neumann, John, and Oskar Morgenstern. *Theory of Games and Economic Behavior.* Princeton: Princeton University Press, 1947.

Wallace, Anthony F.C. *The Modal Personality of the Tuscarora Indians.* Washington: Government Printing Office, 1952.

——. *Culture and Personality.* New York: Random House, 1961.

Wallace, Michael D. "Power, Status, and International War," *Journal of Peace Research,* 1 (1971), pp. 23–35.

——. "Status, Formal Organization, and Arms Levels as Factors Leading to the Onset of War, 1820–1964," in Russett, ed., *Peace, War, and Numbers.* Beverly Hills: Sage, 1972.

——. *War and Rank among Nations.* Lexington, Mass.: D. C. Heath, 1973.

——, and J. David Singer. "Inter-Governmental Organization in the International System, 1815–1964: A Quantitative Description," *International Organization,* 24/2 (Spring 1970), pp. 239–87.

Walton, J. T. *How Europe Armed for War, 1871–1914.* London:

n.p., 1916.

Waltz, Kenneth. "Electoral Punishment and Foreign Policy Crises," in James N. Rosenau, ed., *Domestic Sources of Foreign Policy.* New York: Free Press, 1967, pp. 263-94.

———. *Man, The State, and War.* New York: Columbia University Press, 1959.

———. "The Stability of a Bipolar World," *Daedalus* (Summer 1964), pp. 881-909.

Warriner, Charles K. "Groups are Real: A Reaffirmation," *American Sociological Review*, 21/5 (Oct. 1956), pp. 549-54.

Webb, Eugene, et al. *Unobtrusive Measures: Nonreactive Research in the Social Sciences.* Chicago: Rand McNally, 1966.

Weiss, Herbert K. "Stochastic Models for the Duration and Magnitude of a 'Deadly Quarrel,' " *Operations Research*, 11 (Jan.-Feb. 1963), pp. 101-21.

White House Disarmament Staff. *Pathway to Peace.* Washington, D.C., 1957.

Wiesner, Jerome B. "Inspection for Disarmament," in Louis Henkin, ed., *Arms Control: Issues for the Public.* Englewood Cliffs, N.J.: Prentice-Hall, 1961.

Wilcox, Leslie, et al. *Social Indicators and Societal Monitoring: An Annotated Bibliography.* Amsterdam: Elsevier, 1972.

Wolfers, Arnold. "The Actors in International Politics," in William T. R. Fox, ed., *Theoretical Aspects of International Relations.* Notre Dame: University of Notre Dame Press, 1959, pp. 83-106.

Wolfson, Murray. "A Mathematical Model of the Cold War," *Peace Research Society Papers*, 9 (1968), pp. 107-24.

World Diplomatic Directory and World Diplomatic Biography. London: World Diplomatic Directory Service, 1951.

Wright, Quincy. *A Study of War.* Chicago: University of Chicago Press, 1942, 1965.

———. "Proposal for an International Criminal Court," *American Journal of International Law*, 46 (1952), pp. 60-72.

———. "Project for a World Intelligence Center," *Journal of Conflict Resolution*, 1/1 (March 1957), pp. 93-97.

Young, H. D. *Statistical Treatment of Experimental Data.* New York: McGraw-Hill, 1962.

Zimmern, Alfred. *The American Road to World Peace.* New York: Dutton, 1953.

Zinnes, Dina A. "An Analytical Study of the Balance of Power Theories," *Journal of Peace Research*, 3 (1967), pp. 270-88.

# Correlates of War
# Project Bibliography

## I. Theoretical Orientation and Research Strategy

"Inter-Nation Influence: A Formal Model," *American Political Science Review*, 57/2 (June 1963) 420-30 [Singer].

"Multipolar Power Systems and International Stability," *World Politics*, 16/3 (April 1964) 390-406 [Karl W. Deutsch and Singer].

"The Political Matrix of International Conflict," in McNeill, ed., *The Nature of Human Conflict*, 1965, 139-54 [Singer].

"Escalation and Control in International Conflict: A Simple Feedback Model," *General Systems*, 15 (1970) 163-73 [Singer].

"From *A Study of War* to Peace Research: Some Criteria and Strategies," in Whiting, ed., *Journal of Conflict Resolution*, Quincy Wright Memorial Issue, 14/4 (December 1970) 527-42 [Singer].

"The Outcome of Arms Races: A Policy Problem and a Research Approach," IPRA Third General Conference, *Proceedings*, Oslo, (1970) 137-46 [Singer].

"Modern International War: From Conjecture to Explanation," in Lepawsky et al., eds., *The Search for World Order: Essays in Honor of Quincy Wright*, 1971, 47-71 [Singer].

"The Correlates of War Project: Interim Report and Rationale," *World Politics*, 24/2 (January 1972) [Singer].

"Historiche Tatsachen u. Wissenschaftliche Daten am Beispiel der Erforschung von Kriegen," ("Historical Facts and Scientific Data in the Study of War") in Ludz, ed., *Soziologie und Sozialgeschichte: Aspekte und Probleme* (1973) 221- 41 [Melvin Small and Singer].

"The Historical Experiment as a Research Strategy in the Study of World Politics," *Political Inquiry*, 2/1 (1974) 23- 42 [Singer].

"Aggregation and Confusion: The Levels Problem Revisited," forthcoming [James L. Ray].

"The Future of Events Data Marriages: A Question of Compatibility," *International Interactions*, 2 (1975) 45- 62 [Russell J. Leng].

"The Correlates of War Project: Continuity, Diversity, and Convergence," in Hoole and Zinnes, eds., *Quantitative International Politics: An Appraisal*, New York: Praeger (1976) 21- 66 [Singer].

"The Applicability of Quantitative International Politics to Diplomatic History," *Historian*, 38 (February 1976) 281- 304 [Melvin Small].

## II.  Constructing the Indicators and Generating the Data

"The Composition and Status Ordering of the International System: 1815- 1940," *World Politics*, 18/2 (January 1966) 236- 82 [Singer and Melvin Small].

"Formal Alliances, 1815- 1939: A Quantitative Description," *Journal of Peace Research*, 1 (1966) 1- 32 [Singer and Melvin Small].

"National Political Units in the Twentieth Century: A Standardized List," *American Political Science Review*, 62/3 (September 1968) 932- 51 [Bruce M. Russett, Singer, and Melvin Small].

"Formal Alliances, 1816- 1965: An Extension of the Basic Data," *Journal of Peace Research*, 3 (1969) 257- 82 [Melvin Small and Singer].

"Inter-Governmental Organization in the Global System, 1816- 1964: A Quantitative Description," *International Organization*, 24 (Spring 1970) 239- 87 [Michael D. Wallace and Singer].

"Patterns in International Warfare, 1816- 1965," *Annals of American Academy of Political and Social Science*, 391 (September 1970) 145- 55 [Singer and Melvin Small].

"A Sociometric Analysis of Diplomatic Bonds, 1817-1940," East Lansing, Mich.: Events Data Conference, 1971 [Stuart A. Bremer].

"Formal Alliance Clusters in the Interstate System, 1816-1965," Washington: APSA Meetings, 1972 [Stuart A. Bremer].

*The Wages of War, 1816-1965: A Statistical Handbook*, New York: Wiley, 1972 [Singer and Melvin Small].

"Measuring the Concentration of Power in the International System," *Sociological Methods and Research*, 1/4 (May 1973) 403-37 [James L. Ray and Singer].

"Diplomatic Importance of States, 1816-1970: An Extension and Refinement of the Indicator," *World Politics*, 25/4 (July 1973) 577-99 [Melvin Small and Singer].

"Measuring Systemic Polarity," *Journal of Conflict Resolution*, 19/2 (June 1975) 187-216 [Bruce Bueno de Mesquita].

"Toward a Multi-Theoretical Typology of International Behavior," in Malitza, ed., *Mathematics and International Relations*, forthcoming [Russell J. Leng and Singer].

"Composition of the Global/International System, 1816-1970: Inclusion Criteria and a Revised Population," Ann Arbor, Mich.: MHRI Mimeo [Robert Bennett].

"Civil Wars, 1816-1970: A Typology and Tentative Population," Ann Arbor, Mich.: MHRI mimeo [Susan Jones and Robert Bennett].

## III. Testing Some Preliminary Models

"National Alliance Commitments and War Involvement, 1815-1945," *Peace Research Society (International) Papers*, 5 (1966) 109-40 [Singer and Melvin Small].

"Alliance Aggregation and the Onset of War, 1815-1945," in Singer, ed., *Quantitative International Politics: Insights and Evidence*, 1968, 247-86 [Singer and Melvin Small].

"Inter-Governmental Organization and the Preservation of Peace, 1816-1965: Some Bivariate Relationships," *International Organization*, 24 (Summer 1970) 520-47 [Singer and Michael D. Wallace].

"Power, Status, and International War," *Journal of Peace Research*, 1 (1971) 23-35 [Michael D. Wallace].

"Capability Distribution, Uncertainty, and Major Power War, 1820-1965," in Russett, ed., *Peace, War, and Numbers*, 1972, 19-48 [Singer, Stuart A. Bremer, and John Stuckey].

"Status, Formal Organization, and Arms Levels as Factors Leading to the Onset of War, 1820-1964," in Russett, ed., *Peace, War, and Numbers*, 1972, 49-69 [Michael D. Wallace].

"Shared Memberships in Intergovernmental Organizations and Dyadic War, 1865-1964," in Fedder, ed., *The United Nations: Problems and Prospects*, 1972, 31-61 [Kjell Skjelsbaek].

*Dimensions Historiques de Modeles Dynamiques de Conflict: Application aux Processus de Course aux Armements, 1900-1965*, Geneva: Graduate Institute of International Studies, Doctoral thesis, 1972 [Urs Luterbacher].

"The Impact of Alliances on Industrial Development," East Lansing, Mich.: Michigan State University mimeo, March 1973 [Bruce Bueno de Mesquita].

"The Population Density and War Proneness of European Nations, 1816-1965," *Comparative Political Studies*, 6/3 (October 1973) 329-48 [Stuart A. Bremer, Singer, and Urs Luterbacher].

"Alliances, Capabilities, and War: A Review and Synthesis," in Cotter, ed., *Political Science Annual*, 4 (1973) 237-80 [Bruce Bueno de Mesquita and Singer].

"Status Inconsistency and the War Behavior of Major Powers, 1815-1965," Toronto: Conference on International Relations Theory, December 1973 [Harald von Riekhoff].

*War and Rank Among Nations*, Lexington, Mass.: Lexington Books, 1973 [Michael D. Wallace].

"Alliance Polarization, Cross-Cutting, and International War, 1815-1964: A Measurement Procedure and Some Preliminary Evidence," *Journal of Conflict Resolution*, 17/4 (December 1973) 575-604 [Michael D. Wallace].

*Status Inconsistency and War Involvement among European States, 1816-1970*, Ann Arbor, Mich.: University of Michigan, Doctoral thesis, 1974 [James L. Ray].

"Status Inconsistency and War Involvement in Europe, 1816-1970," *Peace Science Society (International) Papers*, 23 (1974) 69-80 [James L. Ray].

"Behavioral Indicators of War Proneness in Bilateral Conflicts," in McGowan, ed., *Sage International Yearbook of Foreign Policy Studies* II, 1974, 191-226 [Russell J. Leng and Robert Goodsell].

"The Realist Prescription and Its Critics: An Exploratory Empirical Study of Inter-Nation Influence," Middlebury, Vt.: Middlebury College mimeo, 1975 [Russell J. Leng].

*Probability Models of War Expansion and Peacetime Alliance Forma-*

*tion*, Ann Arbor, Mich.: University of Michigan, Doctoral thesis, 1974 [Yoshinobu Yamamoto].

"Major Power Intervention in Ongoing War: A Probability Model, 1816-1965," Ann Arbor, Mich.: University of Michigan mimeo, forthcoming [Yoshinobu Yamamoto and Stuart A. Bremer].

"Structural Clarity and International War: Some Tentative Findings," in Murray, ed., *Interdisciplinary Aspects of General Systems Theory*, 1975, 126-35 [Singer and Sandra Bouxsein].

"Distance and International War 1816-1965." IPRA Fifth General Conference, Oslo, *Proceedings* (1975) 481-506 [Nils Petter Gleditsch and Singer].

"Systemic Polarization and the Occurrence and Duration of War, 1816-1965," Washington: ISA Meetings, 1975 [Bruce Bueno de Mesquita].

"The Trials of Nations: An Improbable Application of Probability Theory," Ann Arbor, Mich.: University of Michigan mimeo, 1975 [Stuart A. Bremer].

"The Powerful and the War-Prone: Relative National Capability and War Involvement, 1820-1964," forthcoming [Stuart A. Bremer].

"The Costs of Combat: Predicting Deaths, Duration, and Defeat in Two-Nation Interstate War, 1816-1965," Washington: ISA Meetings, 1975 [Cynthia A. Cannizzo].

"The Incidence of Intervention in Interstate War, 1816-1965," Cambridge, Mass.: Peace Science Society (International) Meetings, 1975 [Cynthia A. Cannizzo].

*Costs of Combat: A Statistical Model for Predicting the Cost and Outcome of Interstate War, 1816-1965*, Ann Arbor, Mich.: University of Michigan, Doctoral thesis, 1976 [Cynthia A. Cannizzo].

"Status, Power, and Interstate Conflict: The Major Powers, 1820-1970 (A Research Note and Some Preliminary Findings)," Washington: ISA Meetings, 1975 [Charles S. Gochman].

"Military Confrontation and the Likelihood of War: The Major Powers 1820-1970," Cambridge, Mass.: Peace Science Society (International) Meetings, 1975 [Charles S. Gochman].

*Status, Conflict, and War: The Major Powers, 1820-1970*, Ann Arbor, Mich.: University of Michigan, Doctoral thesis, 1975 [Charles S. Gochman].

"Hostilities in the European State System, 1816-1970," Cambridge, Mass.: Peace Science Society (International) Meetings, 1975 [Michael D. Mihalka].

"From Military Hostilities to War: Escalation of Dyadic Conflict,

1816-1965," Austin: University of Texas mimeo, 1975 [Michael D. Mihalka].

*Interstate Conflict in the European State System, 1816-1970,* Ann Arbor, Mich.: University of Michigan, Doctoral thesis, 1976 [Michael D. Mihalka].

"From Bosnia to Sarajevo: A Comparative Discussion of Interstate Crises," *Journal of Conflict Resolution,* 19/1 (March 1975) 3-24 [Alan N. Sabrosky].

"The War-Time Reliability of Interstate Alliances, 1816-1965," Washington: ISA Meetings, 1975 [Alan N. Sabrosky].

*Capabilities, Commitments, and the Expansion of Interstate War, 1816-1965,* Ann Arbor, Mich.: University of Michigan, Doctoral thesis, 1976 [Alan N. Sabrosky].

"The War Proneness of Democratic Regimes," *Jerusalem Journal of International Relations,* 1/4 (Summer 1976) 50-69 [Melvin Small and Singer].

"The Effects of War on National Power, 1860-1965: Postwar Changes in Energy Consumption," Washington: ISA Meetings, 1975 [Hugh G. Wheeler].

*The Effects of War on Industrial Growth, 1816-1965,* Ann Arbor, Mich.: University of Michigan, Doctoral thesis, 1975 [Hugh G. Wheeler].

"Effects of War on Industrial Growth," *Society,* 12/4 (May/June 1975) 48-52 [Hugh G. Wheeler].

## IV. Practical Implications: Policy and Teaching

"Knowledge, Practice, and the Social Sciences in International Politics," in Palmer, ed., *A Design for International Relations Research,* Monograph 10, Philadelphia: American Academy of Political and Social Science (October 1970) 137-49 [Singer].

"Foreign Policy Indicators: Predictors of War in History and in the State of the World Message," *Policy Sciences,* 5/3 (September 1974) 271-96 [Singer and Melvin Small].

"The Peace Researcher and Foreign Policy Prediction," Philadelphia: Peach Research Society Presidential Address, 1972, in *Peace Science Society (International) Papers,* 21 (1974) 1-13 [Singer].

"The Scientific Study of War," Learning Package Series, Number 14, New York: Consortium for International Studies Education of the ISA, 1975 [Stuart A. Bremer, Cynthia A. Cannizzo, Charles W. Kegley, James L. Ray].

# Index